BOOKS AND THE BRITISH ARMY

IN THE AGE OF THE AMERICAN REVOLUTION

BOOKS
AND THE BRITISH ARMY
IN THE AGE OF
THE AMERICAN REVOLUTION

Ira D. Gruber

Copublished
with
The Society of the Cincinnati
by
The University of North Carolina Press
Chapel Hill

© 2010 The University of North Carolina Press
All rights reserved

Set in Matthew Carter's Miller typefaces
by Tseng Information Systems, Inc.
Manufactured in the United States of America

♾ The paper in this book meets the guidelines for permanence
and durability of the Committee on Production Guidelines
for Book Longevity of the Council on Library Resources.

The University of North Carolina Press has been a member of the
Green Press Initiative since 2003.

Library of Congress Cataloging-in-Publication Data
Gruber, Ira D.
Books and the British Army in the age
of the American Revolution / Ira D. Gruber.
p.   cm.
Includes bibliographical references and index.
ISBN 978-0-8078-3378-0 (cloth : alk. paper)
1. Great Britain. Army—Officers—Books and reading.
2. Great Britain. Army—Officers—History—18th century.
3. Books and reading—Great Britain—History—18th century.
4. United States—History—Revolution, 1775-1783—British forces.
5. Military art and science—Great Britain—History—18th century.
I. Title.
DA67.G83 2010
355.00941′09033—dc22
2010014221

14 13 12 11 10   5 4 3 2 1

For Pat

and our grandchildren

Anna Beth, Audrey, Caroline, Emma, Olivia, and Will

CONTENTS

MAP AND ILLUSTRATIONS

MAP

ILLUSTRATIONS

Preface

his is a book about books—the books that shaped the British army in the age of the American Revolution. Although historians have understood that books were important to the eighteenth-century British army and its officer corps, they have never studied comprehensively the books on war that mattered most to the army and its officers in the age of the American Revolution. This book attempts to do just that. It is based on the careers and preferences of some forty-two officers who served Britain between the wars of Louis XIV and the French Revolution and who left records of the books that they owned, bought, read, recommended, and wrote. These officers had literally hundreds of books on war to choose among: histories, biographies, and memoirs; treatises on artillery and military engineering; classics of the ancient world; and essays on the art of war—to say nothing of regulations for drill, lists of officers, compilations of maps and plans, and books on such disparate topics as the laws of war and military medicine. What then were our officers' preferences? How did their preferences change across time? And what can their changing preferences tell us about the lives they led and the wars they waged?

The books on war that our officers valued most can tell us about the eighteenth-century British army, its officer corps, and the history of warfare. Those books can help us understand not only how successive generations of British officers remembered the wars they had fought and prepared for wars to come but also how they shaped their careers in the army and adapted to shifting currents in warfare. How, for example, did they explain their failures in the War of the Austrian Succession? How did that explanation affect their preferences for books? And how, in turn, did books shape their attitudes toward themselves and their conduct in the ensuing Seven Years' War and War for American Independence? In short, knowing what books British officers preferred from one era to another allows us to get a better understanding of the army, its officer corps, and the history of warfare—especially, the Military Revolution, the eighteenth-century military

Enlightenment, the beginnings of a profession of arms, and the development of the art of war in the age of the American Revolution.

In studying these forty-two officers and identifying the books they preferred and neglected, I have had the help of many booksellers, cataloguers, soldiers, and scholars. The eighteenth-century booksellers who inventoried libraries often provided remarkably complete and accurate records of the books that officers owned: the author and title, the place and date of publication, and sometimes even the editor or translator. Such complete entries have helped not just in assembling a composite list of books that officers preferred but especially in deciphering fragmented references to books in other sources: in officers' reading notes and manuscript lists, in their orders to booksellers, and in the footnotes and marginalia of books they wrote. Even so, many abbreviated references to books would have defied decryption without the help of such online databases as WorldCat and the British Library Public Catalogue, databases that have been developed over the past thirty years but have only recently become rich enough to sustain searches for the most obscure titles or fragments of titles. Beyond that, it would not have been possible to get an understanding of the books that our forty-two officers neglected—to explore systematically eighteenth-century advertisements for books on war—without the help of an exceptionally strong collection of early modern books on war, the kind of collection that exists in the United States only at the Anderson House Library of the Society of the Cincinnati in Washington, D.C.

Indeed, the Society of the Cincinnati has been indispensable to the preparation of this book. Scholars such as Alan C. Aimone, Mark Danley, Alan Guy, J. A. Houlding, Peter Paret, Clifford J. Rogers, Arlene and John Shy, John Tottenham, Samuel J. Watson, and the late Don Higginbotham and William L. Willcox have contributed to my understanding not only of the Military Revolution, military professionalism, and the eighteenth-century art of war but also of British officers and their libraries. So too have archivists and librarians—particularly, John Dann of the William L. Clements Library at the University of Michigan; Norman Higson of the Hull University Library; Melinda Flannery and Lee Pecht of the Fondren Library, Rice University; and Glenise Mathieson of the John Rylands University Library of Manchester. But no one has been more intimately involved with this book than the members and staff of the Society of the Cincinnati. The Society has brought together and opened for scholarly research the finest collection of eighteenth-century books on war in the United States. It has further encouraged historical research through grants to scholars, the annual George Rogers Clark Lecture, and support of occasional publications. Dr. David F. Musto, chair of the Society's History Committee, and William Greer, the

Society's most passionate bibliophile, have been particularly generous to me. Musto invited me to give the Clark Lecture in 2002 and agreed subsequently to support, in part, the publication of this book; and Greer encouraged my research and expanded my understanding during each of my visits to Washington. Ellen McCallister Clark, currently director of the Anderson House Library, and Julia Blakely, collections development librarian from 2001 to 2005, worked assiduously to acquire the titles that my officers preferred and to open the Society's collections for my research—to allow me to compare editions of the most important books and to search, altogether, nearly four hundred eighteenth-century books on war. Finally, Sandra Powers, director emerita of Anderson House Library, supported this project from its inception: identifying some of the most obscure titles in the officers' records, checking all of the entries in Parts II (Books Preferred) and III (Books Not Taken), and reading critically the remainder of the text. I am especially grateful to her and to William Greer—wonderfully well-informed and enthusiastic supporters of this foray into eighteenth-century books on war.

In preparing my typescript for publication, I have had the additional good fortune to work with the University of North Carolina Press. Charles Grench, Senior Editor, has been thorough, judicious, and patient in evaluating and improving my manuscript. He persuaded three excellent scholars to serve as readers. The late Professor Don Higginbotham of the University of North Carolina and Professor Fred Anderson of the University of Colorado each provided generous and learned appraisals; and Professor Holly Mayer of Duquesne University, remarkably meticulous and thoughtful analyses of the initial and revised manuscripts. I am grateful to all of them, but especially to Charles Grench for his persistent and tactful support of what must have seemed an unusual scholarly undertaking and collaboration between the Press and the Society of the Cincinnati. I also wish to thank Ron Maner, Managing Editor of the Press, for helping prepare my manuscript for production, as well as the director and board of the Press for their continued support of historical scholarship. Brian R. MacDonald was a meticulous and learned copyeditor.

All illustrations in this book have been taken from books and manuscripts that belong to the Robert Charles Lawrence Fergusson Collection of the Society of the Cincinnati and that are preserved in the Society's library at Anderson House, 2118 Massachusetts Avenue NW, Washington, D.C. Those illustrations are based on photographs made for and reproduced by permission of the Society of the Cincinnati, Washington, D.C.

BOOKS AND THE BRITISH ARMY

IN THE AGE OF THE AMERICAN REVOLUTION

Places of Publication

A French Connection

ooks were essential to the eighteenth-century British army and its officer corps. Successive governments relied on books to set standards for the army: to define the obligations of officers in serving their king and country; to prepare officers to lead the combat arms, particularly the artillery and engineers; and to provide uniform tactics for an army that was widely scattered in peacetime—to teach companies and troops how to march, maneuver, and fire so as to blend together effectively in war. Beyond that, officers turned to privately printed books to expand their knowledge of wars and warfare: to understand military history, to keep abreast of developments in the art of war, to share specialized knowledge and encourage fellow officers to become students of warfare, and to prepare for assignments around the world. Indeed, eighteenth-century British officers bought, read, and recommended hundreds of books on war, books ancient and modern in a variety of European languages. They were particularly attracted to histories, biographies, and memoirs; texts on artillery and engineering; the classics of Greece and Rome; and Continental treatises on the art of war.[1]

Officers who aspired to high command were most likely to appreciate books on war and become students of warfare. James Wolfe, who commanded the British forces that captured Quebec in 1759, found inspiration in the writings of fellow officers like Richard Viscount Molesworth and Richard Kane, kept up with the latest works from France and Prussia, and shared his knowledge of books with men entering the service. John Lord Ligonier, commander in chief during the Seven Years' War, and Sir Henry Clinton, commander in chief in America during the War for Independence, shared Wolfe's enthusiasm for books and study. Ligonier read broadly throughout his career and assembled an impressive collection of books on war. Clinton, who had served as aide to Ligonier, did much the same, reflecting on his reading in more than a dozen notebooks and developing a remarkably consistent understanding of war based on a synthesis of theory and practice.[2]

Historians have recognized the importance of books on war for the eighteenth-century British army and its officer corps, and they have drawn on those books while studying nearly every aspect of warfare. Yet, for all of their reliance on books on war, historians have rarely tried to establish which books mattered most in the eighteenth century. It is by no means easy to know what officers preferred in an era when there were few standard reading lists and when few officers recorded their preferences. And it is understandable that historians, recognizing that books were important but finding it difficult to connect officers to particular titles, have tended to rely on books that were frequently reprinted or translated into English, that attracted officers as subscribers, and that were coherently and persuasively written. Such an approach to choosing among the hundreds of books on war available in the eighteenth century is understandable if not entirely satisfying. It does not establish, comprehensively, which books on war eighteenth-century British officers preferred, how their preferences changed over time, or what books were considered authoritative from one era to another.

By far the most thorough and thoughtful analysis of books in the eighteenth-century British army is in J. A. Houlding's *Fit for Service*. In explaining the changes that the British government made in its drill regulations between the War of the Spanish Succession and the wars of the French Revolution and Napoleon, Houlding went well beyond official publications. He examined another 120 books written by individual soldiers and scholars, books that complemented the official regulations and dealt with such varied topics as drill, tactics and strategy, engineering, artillery, amphibious operations, history, and the classics. But Houlding did little to judge, explicitly, the importance of particular books. He did emphasize works that influenced the development of drill regulations as well as works that were reprinted frequently or translated into English and works that he found unusually thoughtful and persuasive. This approach did not necessarily reveal the preferences of eighteenth-century British officers. By emphasizing books that complemented drill regulations and that were written in English, Houlding omitted many books that were popular with eighteenth-century British officers and included many more that were not.[3] I did try to allow for the preferences of those officers in analyzing the origins of British strategy in the War for American Independence and the education of Sir Henry Clinton. But my approach was more narrowly focused than Houlding's and dealt with relatively small numbers of officers and books — fewer than twenty officers and sixty books.[4]

This book attempts, then, to provide the basis for a much more comprehensive understanding of the importance of books on war for British army officers in the age of the American Revolution, an understanding that includes more officers and many more books than previously considered. It is based on the preferences of forty-two officers, the books on war that those officers owned, bought, recommended, cited, or discussed between the War of the Spanish Succession and the wars of the French Revolution—altogether some 650 titles. It also extends to books on war that those officers neglected—another 243 titles. Because many among the forty-two officers were students of war—men with the means and inclination to acquire books—and because many had long and diverse careers, their preferences provide substantial evidence of the relative importance of nearly 900 books on war available in eighteenth-century Britain.

Moreover, the lists of the books that our forty-two officers preferred and neglected, together with the appendixes drawn from the lists, provide a basis for explaining how successive generations of officers understood themselves, their service, and warfare: how the interests and preferences of officers changed from one period to another, and what shaped their understandings within each period. The lists and appendixes suggest not merely the shifting importance of particular kinds of books—of, say, histories or treatises on the art of war or Continental works—but also the relative importance of specific titles from one period to another. Which specific books did our officers most admire in the first half of the eighteenth century? What books shaped their views on war during the Seven Years' War and the War for American Independence? What books did they consistently neglect? These lists and appendixes provide a basis for approaching those questions—for gaining an appreciation of the ever-changing books on war that were important for the eighteenth-century British army officer.

In short, knowing the preferences of our officers—knowing the books on war that they preferred and neglected from one era to another—should substantially improve our understanding of the eighteenth-century British army and its officer corps. We should be able to see not just how successive generations of officers interpreted the past and prepared for the future but also how successive generations fit into the larger history of warfare. How were British officers affected by what historians have called the English Military Revolution and the eighteenth-century military Enlightenment? Above all, what can our officers and their choice of books tell us about the development of military professionalism and the art of war in the eighteenth-century British army?

The Officers

But who were our forty-two officers? They were men of long, active, and varied service—service that for most of them centered in Britain's wars of the mid-eighteenth century. Although three were killed in action and twelve died while still on duty, these officers served on average twenty-seven years (thirty-five years if the service of partially retired general officers is included).[5] Seven completed their careers during the War of the Spanish Succession or the ensuing Jacobite rebellions; and six continued on the army lists into the wars of the French Revolution and Napoleon.[6] But, including the six who continued after 1792, thirty-five saw most of their active service during Britain's wars of midcentury and the War for American Independence. And at least thirty-four of the forty-two officers experienced combat during their careers, sixteen in two or more wars. These officers fought in nearly every theater of every war from 1701 until 1783: on the Danube, in Flanders, and in Spain during the War of the Spanish Succession; in Scotland during the Jacobite rebellions of 1715, 1719, and 1745; in Germany, on the coast of France, in Flanders, and in North America during the War of the Austrian Succession; in North America, on the coasts of France, in Germany and Portugal, and in the West Indies during the Seven Years' War; and in North America and the West Indies during the War for American Independence.[7] Several among them were on active service for more than a half century: Henry Hawley, John Earl Ligonier, and Humphrey Bland from the War of the Spanish Succession to the Seven Years' War and Sir Thomas Blomefield from the Seven Years' War through the Napoleonic Wars.

However long and varied their careers, these forty-two officers cannot be considered representative of eighteenth-century British army officers. Our officers were clearly a privileged lot—wealthier, better educated, more influential, and far more successful—than the majority of their fellow officers. Nowhere is their status more apparent than in their branches of service, regimental assignments, and rank. At a time when two-thirds of all commissions were purchased and when the price of commissions was carefully regulated to reflect rank and the desirability of particular units, established prices for commissions provide a clear indication of hierarchy within the army. Guards regiments—especially the three regiments of foot guards—were the most prestigious units within the army: in 1767 a lieutenant colonelcy in a regiment of foot cost £3,500, but in the foot guards, £6,700. Cavalry regiments were at the same time more desirable than infantry: whereas a first commission in infantry sold for £400, a first commission in horse or dragoons cost between £1,000 and £1,600. And rank everywhere had its

sharply escalating costs: from £400 for an ensigncy to £3,500 for a lieutenant colonelcy of foot and from £1,000 for a cornetcy to £4,700 for a lieutenant colonelcy of dragoons.[8] By all of these measures our forty-two officers
were very privileged. They were about 50 percent more likely than other
officers to be in cavalry regiments; five times more likely to be in guards
regiments; and nearly five times more likely to achieve at least the rank
of major.[9] Promotion to major and lieutenant colonel required more than
money, but money was usually a part of those promotions. Indeed, when a
general officer could rent a house for £50 per year, £3,500 for a lieutenant
colonelcy was no small sum: it was more than many officers could hope to
raise in a lifetime.[10]

Rank and regiment were not the only indications of the superior wealth
of most of our officers. Not all were well off: Thomas Cuthbert and Thomas
Harrison were chronically short of money; Samuel Bagshawe and Robert
Donkin lived in straitened circumstances for years before inheriting or finding another source of income to supplement their pay and allowances; and
John Montresor died in debtors' prison after failing to clear his public accounts. Others too might have lived precariously, the beneficiaries of promotion for merit that pushed them beyond their private means (perhaps
William Howe, William Wade, and James Wolfe).[11] But a very clear majority
of our officers would rank as far wealthier than most officers of their era. It
was not just that more than half of our officers served in guards regiments
(when fewer than 10 percent of all officers did) or that 80 percent were able
to pay the price at least of a majority (when about 18 percent of all officers
could). It was also that many of the forty-two had large estates and seats in
Parliament. Well over half of our officers had substantial property in London and in the country, the kind of wealth that permitted them both to
advance rapidly in the army and to become prominent in society and politics.[12] An officer did not have to have a fortune to enter Parliament, but he
certainly had to have friends who did. Contested elections cost hundreds or
thousands of pounds. Candidates were expected to pay for the transporta-
tion, food, drink, and lodgings—if not the votes—of their supporters; and
even when seats were not contested, members were expected to patronize
their constituents.[13] That 36 percent of our forty-two officers were members
of Parliament (when only 2 percent of all officers were) and that our officers
served on average nearly fifteen years in the Commons suggest how unusually wealthy those officer members were.[14] Indeed, most of our officers were
men of uncommon means.

So too were they better educated than most of their fellow officers. At a
time when a young man could be commissioned with only a grammar school

education and promoted without examination, our officers seem to have been remarkably well educated. At least eight had studied in prestigious schools (Eton and Westminster), universities (Oxford, Cambridge, or Leiden), or Inns of Court; two were graduates of the Royal Military Academy at Woolwich; and another five had gone to the Continent for periods of independent study.[15] Others—officers like John Ligonier, John Montresor, and James Wolfe—had little formal schooling, but they became impressive scholars and students of warfare. Indeed, all save a few of our forty-two officers (possibly Thomas Cuthbert or William Howe) developed lifelong interests in books and learning. More than half of our officers accumulated substantial libraries and became fluent in at least one foreign language.[16] Of the six who wrote books on war, five (Samuel Bever, Campbell Dalrymple, Robert Donkin, Thomas More Molyneux, and George Smith) sought to synthesize their reading and their experience so as to demonstrate the advantages of a sustained, reflective approach to the art of war.

Men of such wealth and learning also had more than their share of "interest"—more ties to men with social, political, and military power than most officers in the eighteenth-century British army. At least eight of our forty-two officers were born into noble families: two (Hugh Lord Percy and George Viscount Townshend) were the eldest sons of peers and six, the younger sons or grandsons.[17] Another three were baronets, one a knight, and two, the sons of knights.[18] Others, like James Stanhope and John Ligonier, were raised to the peerage for their services or, like Samuel Bagshawe and Henry Clinton, had the patronage of peers. Still others benefited from the favor of the royal family. Henry Hawley received commissions, cash, and appointments from four British monarchs. John Earl Ligonier was successively a Privy Counsellor to George I and aide-de-camp, chief of staff, and Privy Counsellor to George II. Humphrey Bland and Lord John Murray also served as aides-de-camp to George II; and Sir Charles Hotham, Thomas Paget, and Sir Charles Hotham Thompson were grooms of the bedchamber to George II or George III. A few officers (William Wade, James Wolfe, and Henry Clinton) had the advantage of being sons of generals or admirals.[19] And at least fifteen of our officers—or 36 percent of the forty-two—had the wealth and connections to become members of Parliament. Our officers had, in short, far more than their share of "interest."

No wonder that young men with such advantages should also have had unusual opportunities within the army. At least a dozen served at one time or another as aides-de-camp to important senior officers; and nearly all were able to draw upon the experience to advance their careers. Henry Hawley, who began as an aide to his uncle during the War of the Spanish

Succession, progressed rapidly to the staff of King George I and to cavalry commands in the War of the Austrian Succession. James Wolfe was chief of staff to Sir John Mordaunt in the expedition to Rochefort of 1757, an expedition that gave Wolfe a chance to win the favorable notice of the king's principal ministers and, eventually, an independent command in North America. George Lord Townshend was too tactless to take advantage of his service as aide-de-camp to William Augustus, Duke of Cumberland, commander of British forces in Flanders during the War of the Austrian Succession. But when Cumberland fell from power, Townshend used his political connections to become third in command to Wolfe in 1759 and to gain a share of the credit for the conquest of Canada—credit that led to more important commands. So too did John Montresor draw upon his service with Wolfe at Louisbourg and Quebec to become chief engineer during the War for American Independence. John Earl Ligonier had been an aide-de-camp to King George II before commanding various allied forces during the War of the Austrian Succession and becoming commander in chief of the British army during the Seven Years' War. Ligonier, in turn, helped his aides-de-camp, Henry Clinton and Charles Hotham Thompson, gain important staff positions with allied forces in Germany during the Seven Years' War and, Campbell Dalrymple, become governor of Guadeloupe later in the same war. Finally, when Lord Townshend became master general of ordnance, he appointed his aide, Thomas Blomefield, inspector of artillery—a post that Blomefield held with distinction for more than forty years.[20]

Wealth, education, influence, and military connections were clear advantages to men entering the eighteenth-century British army. But such advantages did not ensure successful careers: officers had eventually to prove themselves worthy of rank and responsibility. Our forty-two officers proved exceptionally worthy. They not only advanced to the highest ranks in the army (64 percent became colonels or generals when only 5 percent of all officers did). They also exerted an influence on the army quite out of proportion to their numbers. Humphrey Bland and John Ligonier, who had first served under Marlborough in the War of the Spanish Succession, provided strong leadership for the army into the wars of midcentury: Bland wrote the standard drill book for the 1730s and 1740s; he and Ligonier proved among the most effective of allied combat commanders during the War of the Austrian Succession; and as commander in chief, Ligonier provided clear central direction of all British forces in the Seven Years' War. He had a hand in selecting officers like James Wolfe and George Lord Townshend to command in North America, officers who shared his interest in the art of war and his talent for leading men in combat. Wolfe and Townshend worked together well enough to defeat the French and capture Quebec in 1759; and Townshend survived to lead British forces in Germany and Portugal and to shape the army as master general of ordnance during the War for American Independence—to define the curriculum at the Royal Military Academy and to control through his protégé, Thomas Blomefield, the development of artillery through the wars of the French Revolution and Napoleon. Although neither Samuel Bever, Campbell Dalrymple, nor George Smith achieved high rank, all contributed substantially to the education of their fellow officers. Bever's *Cadet* (1756) and Dalrymple's *Military Essay* (1761) were among the most important books on war written by Englishmen during the eighteenth century. Both books encouraged a more disciplined and thoughtful approach to the art of war, and both sought to introduce British officers to the latest Continental authorities. So too did Smith as inspector of the Royal Military Academy and as author of *An Universal Military Dictionary*. Henry Clinton needed no introduction: he had already studied in France and become a meticulous reader of Continental books on war. He would eventually rise to command the British army in North America during the War for Independence.[21]

Our forty-two officers were, then, an exceptional group of men. They entered the army with more wealth, education, and interest than most of their fellow officers; and they came to have far more than their share of high rank and responsibility. Although neither they nor their preferences can be considered as statistically representative of the eighteenth-century British army officer corps, their preferences for books on war are probably as meaningful as any that we are likely to get. There are, no doubt, other records of the books on war that eighteenth-century British officers owned, read, recommended, and cited. But there are certainly not enough—beyond the forty-two considered in this study—to provide for a representative sampling of eighteenth-century British officers' preferences. Without such a sampling, we are not likely to do better than the preferences of our forty-two. Our officers were men of long and diverse service that stretched from the War of the Spanish Succession through the War for American Independence. They saw combat in nearly every theater of every war; they had among them officers of all the combat arms; and they had the incentive as well as the means to become students of the art of war—to buy, read, write, and recommend the most authoritative books on war. Thus, if not representative of their fellow officers, they were at least the officers who were most likely to shape opinion within the officer corps; and we do know the books on war that they preferred.[22] What were their preferences and how did those preferences change from one era to another?

Books Preferred

First, consider the books that our officers preferred and did not prefer. All told, the forty-two officers owned, cited, noted, or recommended 650 books on war; they neglected another 243 on war that were available in Britain during the eighteenth century. A comparison of the two lists shows that our officers tended to take their time acquiring or noticing books on war. Of the books they preferred, 37 percent were published before 1700, another 46 percent between 1700 and 1760, and only 17 percent after 1760. Just the opposite was true of the books they neglected: only 46 percent were published before 1760 and the remaining 54 percent after 1760. They were most likely to prefer books published in the 1740s and 1750s and to neglect those published in the 1760s, 1770s, and 1780s.[23] And, reflecting, it seems, their high rank and aspirations for command, our officers had much stronger interests in military and naval history, engineering, the art of war, and the classics than in drill, discipline, and medicine. At least, books on military and naval history, engineering, and the art of war together with the classics made up more than 84 percent of the books they preferred and only 62 percent of the books they neglected, while the reverse was true of books on drill, discipline, and medicine—only 8 percent of those preferred and 18 percent of those neglected.[24]

A further comparison of books preferred and neglected suggests that our officers were very discriminating in the books that they bought, read, and recommended—that they clearly preferred some authors to others and that they further distinguished among the works of particular authors. For all of their interest in the Duke of Marlborough, Marshal Turenne, Prince Eugene of Savoy, Frederick the Great, and Charles XII of Sweden, our officers did not subscribe to every book dealing with these celebrated commanders— at least, not to Bancks's Marlborough or Eugene; Beaurain's Turenne; Laveaux's or Stille's Frederick; or Alderfield's, Grimarest's, or Nordberg's Charles XII. Many of our officers admired Guibert's *Essai Géneral de Tactique* but not his subsequent *Défénse du Systême de Guerre Moderne* or his *Observations sur la Constitution Militaire et Politique des Armées de S. M. Prussienne.* They thought Mésnil-Durand's *Projet d'un Ordre Francois en Tactique* an important book while ignoring his *Fragments de Tactique, Réflexions sur l'Ordre et les Manoeuvres de l'Infanterie,* and *Réponse a la Brochure Intitulée: l'Ordre Profond et l'Ordre Mince*; and they owned only seven of Le Blond's fourteen or more treatises on engineering and artillery.[25]

Moreover, a comparison of books they did and did not prefer shows that our officers had a remarkably strong interest in books on war published on the Continent. Just over half of the 650 books that occupied their shelves and thoughts were published on the Continent and in languages other than English; by contrast, more than 60 percent of the 243 books that they neglected were published in the British Isles and in English.[26] Their taste for Continental authorities was particularly pronounced in books published between 1710 and 1760 when 59 percent of books they preferred were Continental and 68 percent of the books they neglected were British.[27] This Continental enthusiasm extended even to books that were available in English. More than a quarter of our officers expressed a preference for Guibert's *Essai Géneral de Tactique*, but none owned or recommended the English translation. So too did three of twenty-three officers have Lloyd's *Essai sur la Grande Guerre de Main de Maitre, ou Instruction Militaire du Roi de Prusse pour Ses Generaux* (1761), but none acquired the English version that appeared the next year. The same was true of Jeney's *Le Partisan*, which appealed to Ligonier in the original French and to Smith in German but to none of our other officers in English.[28]

These trends—these interests in particular books and kinds of books—are even more pronounced in our officers' choices among the 650 books on war that they preferred. If we take into account the popularity of individual titles—if we consider the 1,265 choices that our forty-two officers made among the 650 books—we see a shifting emphasis from history to the art of war. All other types of books on war—from treatises on engineering and artillery, drill and discipline, and the laws of war to the classics and tracts on defense—were nearly the same percentage of the 650 books on war as of the choices that our forty-two officers made among those books. But military histories, which were 35 percent of the 650 books on war, were only 27 percent of the officers' choices; and books on the art of war, which were 16 percent of the books were more than 20 percent of the choices.[29]

This preference for the art of war is even more apparent among the 92 books or clusters of books that the officers preferred above all others, the books that attracted at least 10 percent—and three or more—of the officers who had an opportunity to own, cite, note, or recommend them. If we analyze the officers' 630 choices among these 92 most popular books (rather, among the 268 editions of the most popular books), we find not just a further increase of interest in the art of war but a particularly sharp increase beginning in the middle of the eighteenth century. The 92 most popular books on war were quite evenly divided among military history (24 percent), engineering and artillery (24 percent), the art of war (24 percent), and the classics (21 percent). But in choosing among these kinds of books, officers showed a preference for the art of war (30 percent) at the expense of engineering and artillery (21 percent), the classics (19 percent), and, especially, military history (17 percent).[30] These proportions, which represent the choices forty-two officers made among 92 titles from 1721 until 1799, mask the marked shift in interests that occurred in the middle of the century. Until then, from 1721 to 1754, fourteen of our officers had chosen the classics more often than any other kind of book on war (30 percent of the time); thereafter, the remaining twenty-eight of our officers preferred the art of war over engineering and artillery, the classics, and military history (32 percent to 21, 16, and 17 percent, respectively).[31]

To appreciate that shift—to understand that it was based on a sharp increase of interest in Continental books on the art of war—we must look more closely at the choices officers made before and after 1756. First, consider the choices that fourteen of our officers made from 1721 to 1754. Those officers repeatedly preferred forty-four of what would be the ninety-two most popular books on war with our forty-two officers. The fourteen who made their choices before 1754 were most interested in the classics (Caesar, Polybius, Vegetius, Thucydides, Xenophon, Arrian, and Frontinus) and in military history (Kane's and Campbell's accounts of the Duke of Marlborough and Prince Eugene in the War of the Spanish Succession, Espagnac's histories of the War of the Austrian Succession, and Biggs's *Military History of Europe*). They turned only slightly less often to treatises on engineering and artillery and on the art of war: to Vauban, Coehoorn, Le Blond, Saint-Rémy, and Bisset for siegecraft and artillery; and to Folard, Feuquières, Turenne, and Machiavelli for the art of war. Although our fourteen officers were clearly dependent on the classics and on Continental treatises on fortifications and the art of war, and although only ten of their forty-four favorite books had been written by an Englishman, our officers were able to read all save eleven of those forty-four books in English. Moreover, their preferences for the classics and histories of Marlborough's campaigns as well as their reliance on Humphrey Bland's *Treatise* for drill gave them some insulation from contemporary Continental influences from roughly 1715 until 1745. Our fourteen officers preferred—in descending order—the classics, British military history, and Continental treatises on engineering and the art of war, nearly three-quarters of which were available in English.[32]

By contrast, the twenty-eight officers who would express their preferences for books on war between 1756 and 1799 chose Continental books on the art of war above treatises on engineering and artillery, the classics, and military history. This reversal was inspired in large part by a growing appreciation for Continental soldiers and Continental books.[33] Until the War of the Austrian Succession, the British had been satisfied with their army and its tactics. Their forces, under the Duke of Marlborough, had enjoyed considerable success against the French in the War of the Spanish Succession. They had won a series of memorable battles; taken many towns and fortresses by siege; and codified their tactics in postwar regulations for infantry and cavalry. But when their forces returned to the Continent for the War of the Austrian Succession, they were far less successful. They lost a procession of battles and sieges in the Low Countries—from Fontenoy to Rocoux to Lauffeldt and Maastricht—and had to offset those defeats with victories overseas. By the 1750s the British were reforming their tactics, traveling abroad to study the art of war, and reading Continental authorities. They were also beginning to write their own books on the art of war, books like Samuel Bever's *Cadet* of 1756 and Campbell Dalrymple's *Military Essay* of 1761 that encouraged officers to study books and methods originating in France.[34] So it was that by 1756 the British had acquired a fresh appreciation for Continental books on the art of war, an appreciation reflected in the choices that officers made when buying, citing, recommending, and reading books on war.

The officers who expressed their preferences after 1756 continued to value the books on war that their predecessors had most admired, but they put a much greater emphasis on books dealing with the art of war—particularly books written by French and other Continental authorities. They continued to admire the classics; histories of Marlborough's and Eugene's campaigns; Vauban, Coehoorn, and Le Blond on siegecraft; and Folard, Feuquières, Turenne, and Machiavelli on the art of war. But, remembering French victories in the War of the Austrian Succession, they not only acquired the latest French treatises and campaign histories but also discovered a number of earlier Continental books on the art of war and military engineering. Altogether, they added some forty-eight titles to the list of ninety-two books on war that our officers liked best. They chose most often Continental books on the art of war, embracing the new works of Saxe, Guibert, Frederick, Guischardt, and Turpin de Crissé; and discovering, somewhat belatedly, the works of Puységur, Montecuccoli, and Santa Cruz de Marcenado. They acquired recent histories of Luxembourg, Charles XII, and campaigns during the War of the League of Augsburg and the War of the Austrian Succession; and they revisited earlier studies of Saxe and the War of the Austrian Succession. They did much the same for fortifications and siegecraft: adding recent books by Clairac to earlier works of Le Blond, Bisset, Belidor, Goulon, and Maigret. They did, of course, include some books by British authors among their favorites: Bever on the art of war; Muller and Pleydell on engineering and artillery; and Lloyd and Cambridge on the history of their wars. Yet of the forty-eight books that they added to the list, thirty-three were by Continental authors; and twenty-three of those works were available only in French.[35]

The pervasive influence of French and other Continental authorities extended well beyond the 92 most popular books on war. Our officers were men of wealth and learning who bought, read, and recommended books from throughout Europe and the British Isles. The 650 books on war that they preferred had been published in fifty-six cities or towns and twelve nations, from the British Isles to the Low Countries, France, Switzerland, Italy, Austria, Germany, and Sweden.[36] Although our officers were more likely to own a book on war that had been published in London (45 percent) than in Paris (16 percent), The Hague (8 percent), Amsterdam (7 percent), or Vienna (2 percent), and although 48 percent of their books were in English, the remainder were in French (39 percent) and six other European languages (14 percent).[37] Moreover, their books varied considerably in origin and language from one era to another. Most of their earliest books on war—some 107 published between 1500 and 1650—were in French, Italian, or Latin, the work of Continental authors and publishers. The next generation of their books, 166 that appeared from 1650 to 1710, was predominately English. But the books they acquired in the middle of the eighteenth century—the books they turned to after their defeats in the War of the Austrian Succession—were far more French and Continental than English. Nearly 60 percent of their 266 books published between 1710 and 1760 were in languages other than English, the work of men like Vauban, Saxe, Folard, and Feuquières. This enthusiasm for French and Continental theorists shaped our officers well beyond the Seven Years' War and into the era of the American Revolution. By then, their books were becoming increasingly English— and would remain so through the rest of the century.[38]

These shifts of interest in books on war proved a boon to printers, publishers, and booksellers in Britain and on the Continent. It is difficult to distinguish among the various businesses involved in the production of eighteenth-century books. It is clear that during the century some 250 firms benefited from the growing and changing interests of British army officers in books on war. Few of these firms specialized in the editing, printing, and sale of military titles. Only 19 firms published four or more of the books that our officers preferred. Even so, the military book trade flourished in London, Paris, The Hague, and Amsterdam where more than three-quarters of the preferred books on war were published and where changing tastes were most apparent.[39] London printers, publishers, and booksellers had the largest share of the British officers' market at both the beginning and the end of the eighteenth century, and that market was strong enough to encourage a few publishers to develop a substantial list of books on war. John Millan was the most prominent during the Seven Years' War and the War for American Independence, offering a wide assortment of military books from Kane's history of Marlborough's campaigns to treatises on artillery and engineering to annual lists of officers in the army. Millan's strongest domestic competition came from J. Nourse (whose offerings included Le Blond's and Muller's works on artillery and engineering and Saxe's *Reveries*), from R. & J. Dodsley (who published a new translation of Polybius's history as well as books and manuals on the art of war), and from T. & J. Egerton (who had an extensive and varied list by the 1790s).[40]

But even with the advantages of proximity and language, London publishers were no match for Continental rivals during the middle of the eighteenth century. In this period, when French authorities were in vogue, our British officers clearly preferred the military books of France and the Netherlands to those of the British Isles. Our officers owned, read, and recommended more books published by Claude and Charles-Antoine Jombert of Paris than by any other publisher, British or Continental. They were particularly attracted to the Jomberts's offerings in engineering and mathematics (Belidor, Clairac, Deidier, and Le Blond) and in the history and art of war (Deschamps, Puységur, and Ray de Saint-Geniès). Our officers also turned repeatedly to the books of a few Dutch publishers: Pierre Gosse, P. A. De Hondt, and Henry Scheurleer, all of whom flourished at The Hague in the middle of the century. Gosse's books on the history and theory of war (Dumont's *Eugene* and La Maire d'Olainville's *Turenne*) as well as his memoirs and treatises on fortification (Villars and Goulon) gained places on British shelves and reading lists. So too did De Hondt's and Scheurleer's military histories and engineering texts—especially De Hondt's 1737–42 edition of Vauban's *Attaque et Defense* and Scheurleer's campaign histories of the War of the Austrian Succession and his edition of Coehoorn's *Nouvelle Fortification*.[41] In short, our British officers were more likely to patronize the publishers of mid-eighteenth-century Paris, The Hague, and Amsterdam than those of London.[42]

This mid-eighteenth-century surge of interest in French and Continental books on war was most clearly reflected in the thirty books that our officers preferred above all others. Twenty of those books were contemporary Continental works; five, classics of the ancient world; and five, English histories, treatises on war, and lists of army officers. The classics, in a variety of languages and editions, continued to appeal to officers even at the height of their enthusiasm for contemporary French and Continental books. Our forty-two officers clearly preferred Caesar's *Commentaries* to all other books on war; and they were only slightly less enthusiastic about Polybius, Vegetius, Thucydides, and Xenophon. So too did they value a few English books: histories of Marlborough's campaigns in the War of the Spanish Succession, Humphrey Bland's *Treatise of Military Discipline*, Muller's works on fortification and siegecraft, and Dalrymple's *Military Essay*. But, for our officers, classical and English works could not rival contemporary Continental treatises, particularly on the art of war and siegecraft. Our officers were particularly attracted to Saxe, Folard, Feuquières, Turenne, Puységur, Guibert, Montecuccoli, Frederick, Guischardt, Turpin de Crissé, and Machiavelli—all of whom eclipsed every British writer on the art of war. When it came to military engineering and artillery, our officers did place Muller among their foremost authorities; but they clearly preferred Vauban and Clairac, and after Muller, they thought mainly of the Dutch and French (Coehoorn, Le Blond, and Saint-Rémy). Even in choosing histories and systems of drill, our officers turned as often to the Continental as to their own authorities. After studying Marlborough's campaigns, they sought the histories and commentaries of Eugene and Espagnac; and after Bland's drill, *Regulations for the Prussian Cavalry* and *Regulations for the Prussian Infantry*. Indeed, eight of the thirty books that they valued above all others were available in only French or German during this period.[43]

This preference for Continental books—particularly for books by French authorities—was not confined to our officers. Young men aspiring to a commission in the mid-eighteenth-century British army, cadets studying at the Royal Military Academy at Woolwich, junior officers hoping to advance in their "profession," and senior officers dispensing advice all knew the importance of learning French and reading Continental books. When in 1760 Lieutenant Colonel John Doyne recommended a friend's son for a commission, he described the young man as having a "Genteel Education particularly in the modern languages, Mathematics, drawing & Fortification with every other Branch of learning that may . . . render him worthy of a Commission."[44] George Lord Townshend, the master general of the ordnance, certainly agreed with Doyne's priorities. In prescribing the curriculum for the Royal Military Academy at Woolwich in 1776, Townshend required that cadets in the Upper Academy devote more time to French than to any other subject—twelve hours per week, eleven months per year. No wonder that fourth-class cadets were reading Thucydides, Polybius, Santa Cruz, and Guischardt in French.[45] Those who did not have the benefit of a Woolwich education but who did have money and ambition often went to

France to study—either before or after receiving a commission. A number of prominent young men prepared for a career in the army by studying at the Academy in Caen—by studying fencing, riding, drawing, mathematics, and French.[46] Others, including such future generals as Henry Clinton, William Keppel, William Augustus Pitt, and John Hale, went to France for periods of independent study after being commissioned.[47] And senior officers like John Huske, Samuel Bever, and John Burgoyne routinely advised subordinates to become fluent in French. As Burgoyne told the officers of his regiment about 1760, "To those who do not understand French, I would recommend a serious and assiduous application till they attain it. The best modern books upon our profession are written in that language."[48]

The Military Enlightenment and the Military Revolution

If, then, many eighteenth-century British soldiers shared our officers' preference for French books on war, and if the books that they preferred were products of an eighteenth-century military Enlightenment, we might ask whether British officers were, in turn, inspired by their reading to contribute to that Enlightenment. According to Azar Gat, French military writings of the mid-eighteenth century were influenced more by contemporary intellectual trends than by European wars. Taking their lead from studies of natural science, the arts, government, and society—from the works of Newton, Voltaire, Montesquieu, and Rousseau—veteran French commanders scoured the past for the "rules and principles" that shaped warfare. Guillaume Le Blond, the French mathematician and military engineer whose books attracted a quarter of our officers, said quite explicitly that war was based on "rules and principles derived from the experience of various generations" and that the best guides to those rules and principles were the writings of such experienced commanders as Montecuccoli, Feuquières, and Folard.[49] Our officers clearly agreed with Le Blond: they included among their favorite books on war all of the treatises that are now most closely identified with the French military Enlightenment: the works of Vauban, Saxe, Folard, Feuquières, Puységur, Guibert, Turpin de Crissé, Maizeroy, and Mesnil-Durand. But their preference for these works did not inspire a British military Enlightenment. Fewer than fifty British soldiers of the eighteenth century wrote books about war; and fewer still were interested in establishing "rules and principles" for warfare. Thomas More Molyneux's analysis of amphibious operations (*Conjunct Expeditions*, 1759) was quite exceptional; and no British soldier contributed as much to the military Enlightenment as Henry Lloyd, the Welsh soldier of fortune who served in the French, Prussian, Austrian, Brunswickian, and Russian armies and who sought principles of war in his *History of the Late War in Germany* (1766).[50]

Why was Molyneux so exceptional? And why was the foremost British contributor to the military Enlightenment a Welsh soldier of fortune who served in Continental armies? To judge primarily by our officers, it was as much a matter of timing as of taste or habit of mind. In the years between the War of the Spanish Succession and War of the Austrian Succession when most of Europe was at peace and when French soldiers were beginning to search for "rules and principles" for warfare, British officers were satisfied with what they had achieved under Marlborough, secure from all except an occasional rebellion in Scotland, and content to sink into the routines of garrison life in an army scattered in small units throughout the British Isles and an overseas empire. Few of our officers were inspired by the intellectual currents of the Enlightenment to study warfare systematically. Most were willing to follow Humphrey Bland's *Treatise*, shaping their tactics to what had succeeded at the turn of the century and eschewing theoretical debates. Even after returning to the Continent during the War of the Austrian Succession—after finding that their forces were not as formidable as they had been under Marlborough—our officers were more inclined to study French authorities than to undertake their own independent analysis of warfare. In the 1750s and 1760s, they clearly preferred to take their "rules and principles" from Vauban, Saxe, Feuquières, and Folard—from the luminaries of the French military Enlightenment.

In much the same way, our officers were more often the beneficiaries of than contributors to what historians now call the Military Revolution of early modern Europe. As early as 1761, Campbell Dalrymple observed that a "military revolution" had occurred with the invention of gunpowder and asked whether another might be in the offing, whether Europeans might choose to return to the arms in use before gunpowder. Dalrymple's contemporaries did debate the relative merits of shock and fire—of pike and musket—but they did not give up the advantages of gunpowder.[51] And it would take another two centuries for historians to return to what Dalrymple had called a "military revolution." When they did, they would invest the phrase with far more meaning than it had had for eighteenth-century soldiers. In its twentieth-century guise, in the guise given to it by Michael Roberts in 1955, the Military Revolution has been concerned with the relationships between warfare and the development of the modern state. Roberts began with sixteenth-century changes in weapons and tactics that led, in turn, to larger armies and more powerful states by the late seventeenth century. Geoffrey Parker and other scholars have gradually expanded the Military Revolution in time and space: from the fourteenth to the eighteenth centuries; from Europe to the Americas, Africa, and Asia; and from the land to the sea.[52] Indeed, scholars have so stretched the Military Revolution as to raise doubts about its being revolutionary; and although it retains its name and importance, the Military Revolution has become, as Clifford J. Rogers would have it, a "punctuated equilibrium evolution"—short bursts of rapid development in warfare and statecraft within long periods of incremental change.[53]

Such a military revolution took place in Europe from roughly 1300 to 1800. During those five centuries, successive changes in tactics and technology encouraged states to raise progressively larger armies, which required, in turn, ever more powerful central governments. The process began in the fourteenth century when infantry forces equipped with improved bows and pike were able to defeat cavalry for the first time in centuries, impelling states to invest in more infantry and give greater power to commoners. In the next century, men developed artillery capable of destroying medieval castles and inspiring architects to design new, massive, angled-bastion fortresses from Italy to France, Spain, and the Low Countries, fortresses that could hold out against improved guns but that required larger forces to build and garrison.[54] Further improvements in artillery—in artillery that could be mounted broadside on oceangoing warships—persuaded Europeans of the later sixteenth century to begin maintaining navies of specialized warships to protect their overseas trade and colonies.[55] By then, better handguns and field artillery together with improved tactics had also led states to increase the size of their armies and to think of conquering one another. During the Thirty Years' War, 1618–48, a few European states maintained up to 150,000 men in garrisons, armies, and fleets; and in the ensuing wars of Louis XIV of France, between 1659 and 1714, at least one national standing army of more than 300,000 men. So it was that discrete improvements in technology and tactics had in the course of nearly five centuries brought steady and then spectacular growth in the size of armies (to a total 1.3 million Europeans under arms by 1709).[56]

Larger armies required more powerful national governments, and these governments eventually assembled the resources to complete the Military Revolution. Beginning in the 1630s in Sweden and France and in the 1640s in England, Europeans created central administrations to support and control ever-larger armed forces. These administrations gathered revenues or, at least, gained the credit needed to provide weapons, supplies, clothes, and pay for tens of thousands of soldiers and sailors. They also employed thousands of civilian workmen to build and maintain fortresses and warships; regulated industries and raw materials essential to producing weapons; and touched the lives of ordinary people in collecting taxes and filling the ranks of their forces. Beyond that, they suppressed private armies and imposed tighter discipline on their standing forces: taming the nobility, protecting civilians from the army, and providing security at home and abroad. Such measures sometimes enhanced the power of kings and sometimes forced kings to share power with representative bodies. But, in most cases, such measures increased the power of the state and gave Europeans the means to extend their empires overseas. By the late eighteenth century, Europeans controlled about a third of the land on earth, having used their military superiority to establish colonies in the Americas, Africa, India, Southeast Asia, and the East Indies and to turn back Turkish offensives in Eastern Europe and the Mediterranean.[57]

The Military Revolution took different forms in different places, depending on the resources, politics, military practices, and vulnerability of individual states. Historians do not agree on the timing or sequence of events in England. They do agree that, because the English enjoyed considerable natural security and were able to remain aloof from Continental wars from roughly 1453 to 1652, England was slow to invest in the massive new fortifications, specialized warships, and improved artillery that brought larger forces and the Military Revolution to other European states in the late sixteenth or early seventeenth century. They also agree that the Military Revolution had come to England by the eighteenth century.[58] What remains in dispute is when and how that revolution began in the British Isles. Did the revolution take place during the Civil Wars of the mid-seventeenth century or during the wars against France at the turn of the eighteenth century? And did changes in warfare drive Englishmen to increase the powers of their state (as during the Civil Wars) or did the development of a more powerful state lead to changes in English ways of making war (as after the Glorious Revolution)?[59]

The evidence seems to favor those who believe the Military Revolution came to England during the Civil Wars, was diluted during the Restoration, and reached fruition after the Glorious Revolution. To combat the royalist forces of King Charles I, Parliament mobilized on "an entirely unprecedented scale," adopting weapons and tactics that had been developed on the Continent, creating England's first standing army and navy, and extending the power of the state—particularly its power to tax—so as to control and support its forces. These measures gave Parliament victory over the royal-

ists, domestic security, and the navy it needed to defeat the Dutch and Spanish at sea.[60] But these measures did not ensure political stability; and when
the Stuarts returned to England in 1660, they and their followers modified
many of the military policies adopted during the Civil Wars. The Restoration Parliament cut spending for the armed forces so severely that the army
was smaller in 1675 than it had been in 1475, the navy was unable to defend
English trade and colonies against the Dutch, and unemployed officers of
the army and navy were unpaid and unable to keep up their military skills.
The officers who remained on active service were permitted to resume buying and selling their commissions, a measure that promised to bind aristo-
crats to the crown and shift some of the costs of raising men to the officers,
but a measure that placed wealth before merit in the selection and promotion of nearly all officers. Although Parliament eventually spent enough on
the navy to prepare it for wars against France, the English did not restore
their army until they had undergone another political revolution.[61]

The Glorious Revolution gave England the religious and political unity
needed to bring its Military Revolution to fruition. To defend their constitution and Protestant faith—to counter threats of French hegemony in
Europe and of a Catholic king in Britain—Parliament and the new monarchs, William and Mary, took the most comprehensive measures. They
imposed taxes to secure the government's credit and raise standing forces
of unprecedented size, created a permanent and responsible bureaucracy
to manage those forces, appointed men trained in the tactics of Continental warfare to lead their fleets and armies, and ensured that soldiers were
subordinate to the king in Parliament. Because their public debt and taxes
were comparatively light and their rights and religion protected, Englishmen supported these measures not just at the beginning of the War of the
League of Augsburg but also through the ensuing century of wars with
France and other European states. From 1689 to 1783, England was able,
by steadily increasing its tax receipts and public debt, to build the kind of
standing armed forces and permanent administration that were common to
the European Military Revolution—to draw upon the unique political heri-
tage of the Glorious Revolution to become a great power and to succeed in
all of its wars save that for American Independence.[62]

How then did the Military Revolution affect the men who would lead
British forces in the age of the American Revolution? Most important, the
English Military Revolution provided the foundation for a British profession of arms: constitutional stability, secure financing, expanding knowledge of warfare, and increasingly attractive careers for men of wealth and
talent in a standing army. Although the Military Revolution included the

buying and selling of commissions—a practice that worked against merit and the development of a profession of arms—the Military Revolution in England did coincide with an era of limited war in Europe, comprising three-quarters of a century of relatively stable international life before the cataclysmic wars of the French Revolution and Napoleon. During that relatively stable era, the British government was secure and powerful enough to impose standards on its army and officer corps. The officers, for their part, had the opportunity and incentive to become students of warfare and to think of themselves as members both of an emerging British profession and of an international community of soldiers. They were increasingly drawn to travel and study abroad, learn foreign languages, and immerse themselves in Continental books on war. The Military Revolution together with an era of limited war provided a remarkably fortuitous foundation for a British profession of arms.[63]

The Beginnings of a British Profession of Arms

But even with this foundation, it would take kings, politicians, and soldiers more than half a century after the War of the Spanish Succession to begin to turn the men who led the British army into professional officers. From the start, the Hanoverian kings could offer secure careers within a well-established hierarchy. Although they could not end the buying or selling of commissions or profiteering from regimental funds, they found ways of raising, training, and promoting officers that emphasized merit as well as wealth and influence; they encouraged officers to place service to the state before private ambition and to adopt collective rather than individual values; and they insisted that officers be attentive to their duty if not uniformly expert in the art of war. They worked primarily within the British government and army, using combinations of civil, military, and judicial powers to shape the officer corps. They also used the power of the press—the books and pamphlets that our officers preferred—to promote change. Hanoverian kings were not able to do all that they wished to improve their officers. Yet, by the War for American Independence and with the help of ministers and senior officers as well as a variety of publications, they made considerable progress toward a British profession of arms.[64]

Consider specifically what they achieved and how their achievements affected the men who would lead the army in the era of the American Revolution. They began by creating careers for officers. At the end of the War of the Spanish Succession, King George I and Parliament established a standing army that offered long-term employment for nearly 2,000 officers and half pay for others whose units had been disbanded at the peace. Over the ensuing half century, kings and parliaments gradually increased the size of the army from roughly 35,000 to 45,000 men in peacetime to more than 100,000 during the wars of midcentury. Such forces required an officer corps of not less than 2,000 men in peace and nearly 5,000 in wartime and made it possible for thousands of men to become career officers, part of a well-defined hierarchy under kings and ministers.[65] Two-thirds of these officers made their careers in the infantry; most of the remainder served in the cavalry, and a few, in the artillery and engineers. Each branch had it own peculiar requirements and peacetime assignments; and each, its path to preferment that combined wealth and influence with merit. But all officers were expected to become skilled in combined-arms warfare and ready for service ranging from general engagements and formal sieges on the Continent, to amphibious operations along the coasts of Europe, to battles and skirmishes with imperial rivals and native peoples overseas. British victories in the wars of midcentury together with the accession of the young King George III in 1760 increased the popularity of the army and of careers in the officer corps. Those officers who made their lives in the service—as most now did—had the time and incentive to develop professional skills and habits of mind; and many did just that in the years before and during the War for American Independence.[66]

By then, British officers were becoming increasingly aware of their place within an emerging profession. Beginning in 1754 the War Office published an annual *List of the General and Field-Officers as They Rank in the Army. Of the Officers in the Several Regiments . . . on the British and Irish Establishments*. This hierarchical listing let every general, colonel, lieutenant colonel, and major know where he ranked within the army and where every other officer ranked within his regiment. Officers could judge their prospects for advancement, keep up with the progress of friends, and see at a glance where units were posted from one year to the next throughout the world. So clearly useful and popular were the lists that when a portion of the army was deployed overseas for an extended period, as during the Seven Years' War or the War for American Independence, publishers offered supplemental lists for the officers in particular theaters. No wonder that a quarter of our forty-two officers owned at least one copy of the lists (some, like Maxwell, had long runs) or that the lists were among the thirty titles that our officers valued most.[67] The lists reminded officers of their careers within a profession of arms.

So too did other books written by and for officers during the wars of the mid-eighteenth century.[68] In *The Cadet* of 1756, Samuel Bever cautioned young officers to make sure that they were well suited to the "Profession of Arms" and aging generals to remain active during peacetime lest they "insensibly lose all taste for their Profession."[69] Above all, he urged officers to become students of warfare. Next to martial exercise, there was nothing better for a soldier than studying mathematics and history, "the two sources whence a thorough knowledge of his own Profession is to be drawn"; and it was, Bever thought, the "Duty of every Military man who wishes to succeed in his Profession, to study, not only the Post he *at present* occupies, but also those which a laudable Ambition prompts him to aspire to *hereafter*."[70] Like Bever, Humphrey Bland advised officers to take the trouble to learn "what relates to our profession." But he went further, reminding officers of the special burden of their calling. "The military profession has," Bland wrote, "in all ages, been esteemed the most honourable, from the danger that attends it. The motives that lead mankind to it, must proceed from a noble and generous inclination, since they sacrifice their ease, and their lives, in the defense of their country."[71] Thomas Simes also compared his with other professions—arguing that young men entering the army ought to be at least as well prepared as those beginning divinity, medicine, and law.[72]

Such lists and books together with service in the wars of the mid-eighteenth century gave British officers a heightened sense of professional identity. By the 1770s, kings, ministers, and officers regularly used the word "profession" to describe careers within the army. As King George III wrote to his secretary at war in 1773, Lieutenant Colonel Isaac Barré's resignation was no loss to the army because Barré had forgotten "the subordination to which [his] profession subjects [him]." Conversely, in the following year Secretary at War Lord Barrington was pleased to be able to allow Lieutenant Colonel Hervey to retire temporarily on half pay in recognition of "the merit of your past services and your Zeal and Attachment to your profession."[73] Officers and young men aspiring to be officers frequently spoke of preparing for their profession. In 1770 Lieutenant Stanton of the 14th Foot asked to be put on half pay so that he might serve in another army in "the hope of acquiring a greater knowledge of my Profession"; and General Richard Pierson sought a commission for his "nearest kinsman," Francis Pierson, who was studying in Brunswick "to qualify him for the profession."[74] By the middle of the eighteenth century, British army officers were identifying themselves ever more explicitly with the profession of arms and coming to appreciate the value that clergymen, lawyers, and doctors of medicine had long found in their professional communities.

Even so, the buying and selling of commissions remained an obstacle to the development of a professional officer corps throughout the eighteenth century: the cost of commissions not only kept some men from advancing as far as merit might have taken them but also encouraged others to think of a return on their investment rather than service to the state. The Hanoverian kings, having tried and failed to abolish the purchase system established by the Stuarts, concentrated on controlling its effects. They worked with boards of general officers to regulate the price of commissions and the terms of purchase; they reserved some commissions for worthy officers who could not afford to pay; and they considered merit in approving sales. Gradually, they developed requirements for buying a first commission and for promoting officers that emphasized accomplishments as well as wealth and influence. By the 1760s, a young man aspiring to be an officer had to be sixteen years of age, suitably educated (in such subjects as foreign languages, mathematics, drawing, and fortifications), and well recommended for his health and character. An experienced officer seeking promotion had to have more than money: he had to have the length of service for the rank that he sought. In making appointments, kings regularly sought advice from ministers and senior officers, but they jealously guarded their right to decide and took particular care in selecting men to command regiments or armies.[75] In short, while the Hanoverians could not eliminate the effects of wealth, they could and did reward service to the state.

They also worked with Parliament and senior officers to damp another effect of the purchase system—the opportunities that captains and colonels had to enrich themselves at the expense of the public and the army. Until the War of the Austrian Succession, captains expected more than pay and allowances in return for their commissions; they expected an annual share of excess regimental subsistence funds, of funds that were created in part by fraudulent musters. In 1747 George II improved the accuracy of musters and began requiring captains to reimburse the government for excess subsistence payments. He eventually converted the captain's share of excess payments into a modest, fixed annual fee. He and George III were not so successful in depriving colonels of perquisites. Like captains, colonels expected more than pay and allowances. They believed that they were entitled to benefit not just from lucrative military appointments but also from funds paid annually to their regiments for food, clothes, weapons, equipment, and other expenses. Although kings and Parliament had few successes in trimming the perquisites of colonels (in 1780 they stopped them from buying muskets), their efforts forced senior officers to consider that a commission required service to the state as well as an opportunity to profit from that service.[76]

The Hanoverians were not able to end the purchase system or reduce substantially the perquisites for colonels—to eliminate the effects of wealth on the officer corps. They were able, with the help of senior officers, to define what was expected of an eighteenth-century officer and, in so doing, to provide standards for an emerging British profession of arms. Consider first what kings and officers meant by responsible service to the state. In issuing commissions and publishing the Articles of War, kings said explicitly that an officer was required to be loyal to the British crown and church, obedient to his superiors, and courageous and competent in leading men to war. But it remained for officers commanding companies, regiments, and armies as well as for kings, ministers, boards of general officers, reviewing officers, and courts-martial to explain the meaning of a commission and the Articles of War—to teach an officer his duty. By the middle of the eighteenth century, that duty was becoming increasingly well defined. A responsible officer was to consider that he was ever subordinate to the civilian authorities of the state: in 1756 a major general was rebuked by the secretary at war for sending a patrol through the streets of Plymouth without first consulting the local magistrates.[77] A responsible officer knew that he could be dismissed from the service, losing the value of his commission, for dishonorable or scandalous behavior: offering a disloyal toast, failing to pay or seeking bankruptcy to avoid debts, taking unfair advantage of a fellow officer in a duel or fight, cheating a fellow officer in a game of cards, or seeking homosexual favors from subordinates.[78]

Above all, officers learned that they were expected to serve with their regiments, behave courageously, and obey orders, particularly in the face of the enemy. In peacetime, an officer could, with the approval of his commanding officer and the adjutant general, enjoy leaves of up to six months or even longer; but an officer who overstayed a leave or quit his regiment could be cashiered. In wartime, all officers, including those on half pay, were to be ready to serve; and those who refused to join their regiments faced almost certain dismissal as the Earl of Effingham discovered in June 1775 when he declined to fight against the British colonists of North America. There were occasional exceptions: a respected officer who needed more than a few months leave to deal with private affairs was permitted to go temporarily onto half pay; another officer who had lost an arm in the service was allowed to decide whether to accompany his regiment to America in 1775; and Lord Kirkcudbright somehow managed to be on leave from the 30th Foot from 1766 until 1775. Yet by the middle of the eighteenth century, officers understood that being with their regiments was an essential part of responsible service to the state.[79]

Serving courageously and obediently was an even more important part of an officer's emerging sense of responsibility. Especially during the reign of George II, any officer who behaved as a coward or failed to do his utmost in battle was in danger of being shot. A captain of marines was executed in 1745 for cowardice during an engagement between a British warship and a French privateer; and that same year, a lieutenant of infantry was sentenced to death for deserting the garrison under siege at Ostend (he was later pardoned, ostensibly for having been delirious when he deserted, and dismissed from the army). In August 1756 Lieutenant General Thomas Fowke was tried, convicted, and sentenced to a year's suspension for failing to relieve Minorca in the spring of that year. George II, thinking the sentence too lenient, cashiered Fowke. (Considering that Admiral John Byng was executed for his part in the expedition to Minorca, Fowke was fortunate.)[80] Later in the Seven Years' War, Lord George Sackville was dismissed from the army for having failed to respond promptly to orders during the Battle of Minden. The king, again wishing to convey his impatience with the court as well as with Sackville, had the sentence read to every British regiment as a punishment "much worse than death." Although the British repelled a French raid on Jersey in 1781, George III superseded the lieutenant governor for having surrendered prematurely.[81] Because the trials of men like Byng and Sackville were widely publicized, by the end of the Seven Years' War no officer could mistake his responsibility to serve the state.

Books and pamphlets played an important part in defining that responsibility. Once Byng had been executed for failing to relieve Minorca, every officer who took part in an unsuccessful expedition or who was suspected of being slow to do his duty in the face of the enemy was sure to produce a pamphlet explaining himself; and courts-martial or courts of inquiry inspired literally dozens of pamphlets, particularly when the accused was an officer of wealth and standing. The trial of Lord George Sackville for disobedience during the Battle of Minden in 1759 brought more than twenty books and pamphlets; the parliamentary inquiry into the conduct of Sir William Howe in the War for American Independence, some twenty-five; and the controversy between Sir Henry Clinton and Charles Earl Cornwallis at the end of the American War, another half dozen.[82] Our forty-two officers had vestiges of each of these and other controversies in their libraries, including Fearne's *Trial of Admiral Byng*, Sackville's *Trial of Sackville*, Galloway's *Reply to Sir William Howe*, Clinton's *Narrative of His Conduct*, and Cornwallis's *Reply to Clinton's Narrative*.[83] When an officer's life was in the balance, such pamphlets made dramatic reading; but even when the stakes were lower, these pamphlets were very instructive. A responsible officer obeyed orders, behaved courageously, and did his best to engage and defeat the enemy.

Just as the wars of midcentury heightened an officer's sense of responsibility, so too did they increase his esprit de corps, his awareness of being part of a British profession of arms. The army had been widely scattered in the three decades after the War of the Spanish Succession. It was not just that regiments were posted in different parts of the British Isles and overseas but that companies and troops were further dispersed, keeping the peace and supporting the government. In those decades, while regiments were assembled for reviews and training less than two months a year, an officer had little chance to know anyone outside his company or troop.[84] But the wars of the mid-eighteenth century and the ensuing War for American Independence brought the army and regiments together for years on end. Officers now lived together in far larger numbers, developing increasingly strong social and professional ties. Such ties were reinforced by a growing tendency of families to make careers in the army and of inspectors and courts-martial to stress the importance of camaraderie.[85] Officers regularly recommended sons and nephews for commissioning. A reviewing officer noted in 1777 that a regiment was not fit for service in part because the officers were divided by some "misunderstanding."[86] At roughly the same time, courts cashiered two ensigns for fighting and a lieutenant for challenging his major to a duel. Officers sometimes acted informally to sustain the morale and effectiveness of a regiment, forcing one fellow officer to resign and recommending against the promotion of another.[87]

Less obvious but even more important in binding officers together—in reminding them of their special and separate calling—were the rituals and routines of army life. Lord John Murray's 42nd or Highland Regiment of Foot served for more than six years in the War for American Independence. Although not all the officers of the regiment liked one another, they did develop an esprit de corps that sustained them through an increasingly discouraging war. That esprit was nourished by formal celebrations: of the monarchy (the king's and queen's birthdays, the accession and coronation of George III, and the restoration of 1660); of the united kingdoms of England, Ireland, Scotland, and Wales (the patron saint's day of each); of the Anglican Church (Christmas, New Year's Day, and Easter among them); and of the British army (anniversaries of battles and regimental exploits as well as changes in command). More often, officers of the 42nd came together in informal pursuits of pleasure: regular drinking and dining; casual entertainments (music, dancing, games); subscription and charitable concerts, balls, and plays; and such outdoor recreations as walking, hunting, bathing, sleighing, riding, golf, and horse racing. Such rituals and recreations, together with the shared dangers and drudgery of war, produced camaraderie among the officers that strengthened the regiment and led to lifelong friendships. The officers of the 42nd remained in touch with their families and civilian friends throughout the American War, but their primary attachments in those years were to their fellow officers, to attachments that were increasingly professional.[88]

Similarly, prolonged service in the Seven Years' War and the War for American Independence encouraged British officers to become students of warfare, to go beyond their regimental duties to study the art of war. Beginning in the 1750s, kings and senior officers, remembering defeats in the War of the Austrian Succession, placed an increasing emphasis on the education of young men entering the officer corps. They did not establish requirements for a commission in the infantry or cavalry, but their expectations were reflected in the credentials that candidates offered and that usually included a genteel education and systematic preparation for a career in the army (enrollment in an academy to study foreign languages, mathematics, drawing, and fortifications).[89] The Hanoverians did establish standards for the education of cadets at the Royal Military Academy at Woolwich, which had been created in 1741 as a school for artillery officers. Beyond that, kings George II and George III sought to ensure that officers serving in infantry and cavalry regiments knew their duty and could work together effectively in wartime. They published regulation drill books in 1757 and 1764 and required annual inspections of regiments to evaluate the skill of officers and to see that they followed established ways of marching, maneuvering, and delivering fire—to see that they could respond predictably and effectively to the demands of battle.[90] With such official encouragement, British officers became increasingly interested in studying warfare not just during the Seven Years' War and the War for American Independence but in the years between those wars when there was time for reading, traveling, and observing foreign armies.

Perhaps most impressive was the energy and intelligence that they now devoted to writing about war, to codifying what they knew about the theory and practice of warfare. Until the middle of the century, it had not been "very fashionable" for a junior officer to read or write about his duty.[91] Fewer than ten British officers had written, compiled, or translated books on war in the forty years before the Seven Years' War. All of those books were focused on history and discipline, and only three were among the ninety-two books on war that our forty-two officers valued most: Kane's account of Marlborough's campaigns, Williamson's translation of Turenne's *Memoirs*, and Bland's *Treatise*.[92] No wonder that well into the 1750s officers complained about the ignorance of their colleagues. Henry Hawley, a lieutenant general of cavalry, believed that all officers needed to read military history and theory to prepare for the "myriad accidents of war" and that Britain had neglected their education.[93] General James Wolfe was even more critical of his colleagues than Hawley. He attributed General Edward Braddock's defeat near Fort Duquesne in 1755 and the slow pace of the siege of Louisbourg in 1758 to ignorance. Wolfe was particularly exasperated to find fellow officers at Louisbourg unaware that he had borrowed his light infantry tactics from Xenophon: "Our friends here are astonished at what I have done because they have read nothing."[94]

Even before Wolfe complained, other British officers had begun creating books to educate their colleagues. They did so to understand what had made the French and Prussians successful in the War of the Austrian Succession and to prepare for the renewal of war with France.[95] Although consistently deferential to Continental authorities, British officers gradually began to incorporate their own ideas and experiences in the books that they wrote. In the thirty years following the outbreak of the Seven Years' War, at least thirty-six British officers produced books on war.[96] Those thirty-six represented a significantly higher proportion of all officers than the eight who had written in the four decades before the Seven Years' War; and the thirty-six also produced more important books than their predecessors.[97] Because British officers were now preoccupied with Continental books and methods, they departed from the topics that had interested their colleagues in the first half of the century: before 1753, British officers' books had dealt with history and drill while almost completely neglecting the art of war; after 1753—after the renewal of war with France—their books focused far more on the art of war and drill than on military history. Kane's *Campaigns* and Bland's *Treatise* remained in print and in vogue into the Seven Years' War. But they were soon eclipsed by British officers' translations of such Continental authorities as Saxe's *Reveries* (1757), Clairac's *Field Engineer* (1758), *Regulations for the Prussian Cavalry* (1757), *Regulations for the Prussian Infantry* (1754), and Turpin de Crissé's *Essay on the Art of War* (1761). Campbell Dalrymple, J. C. Pleydell, and Samuel Bever went well beyond translations in their treatises on raising and training men, constructing field fortifications, and educating officers; yet they too remained dependent on Continental ideas.

The books that British officers created represented only a small fraction of all the books on war that British officers preferred in the age of the American Revolution. Even so, the books that British officers translated and wrote in the three decades after the start of the Seven Years' War were important for the development of a professional officer corps and a distinctive approach to the art of war. Altogether, British officers produced some 60 books on war between 1753 and 1783. Although their fellow officers neglected half of these books, the remaining 30 had an influence out of proportion to their number.[98] Of these 30 books, 14 were among the most authoritative of the 650 books on war that our forty-two officers preferred; that is, 14 appealed to at least 10 percent and to no less than three of our officers.[99] And 5 among those 14 fell within the 10 that our officers valued most: a history of Marlborough's campaigns; translations of works by Saxe, Clairac, and Vegetius; and a treatise by Bland. Those 5 books not only reflected and shaped British officers' thinking about warfare—not only embodied the prudential way of war that would encumber British operations in the War for American Independence—but also marked British officers' growing appreciation for a reflective approach to their service—an appreciation for a history and theory of war that would sustain a profession of arms.

British officers who translated or wrote books on war made one other important contribution to the development of a profession of arms: they encouraged their colleagues to become students of Continental warfare. A small number of officers like Charles Earl Cornwallis and Sir Henry Clinton took this advice quite literally, going abroad to study at an academy, visit battlefields and fortifications, or serve with a foreign army. Many British officers, like James Wolfe, who lacked the means and influence of a Cornwallis or a Clinton, had to be content with reading and reflecting on what were thought to be the best books on war, the books by the foremost French, Dutch, and Prussian soldiers of the first half of the eighteenth century.[100] Our forty-two officers clearly preferred Continental authorities. Three-quarters of the ninety-two books on war that our officers held in the highest esteem were written and published on the Continent (five-sixths of the thirty they liked best). Our officers looked to the Continent for all kinds of books on war, from maps and plans to international laws of war, from regulations for cavalry and infantry to histories of recent campaigns, and from commentaries on the classics of Greece and Rome to contemporary treatises on engineering and artillery. Above all, and especially in the three decades after 1750, our officers became students of the Continental art of war. They placed Saxe, Folard, Feuquières, Puységur, Turenne, and Guibert above any British authority—except perhaps the Duke of Marlborough.[101] Paradoxical as it might have seemed, Continental books and ideas became an important foundation for a British profession of arms.

Those British officers who produced books on war—who urged their colleagues to become students of the Continental art of war—were remarkably well supported by kings, ministers, and fellow officers. King George II, the Duke of Cumberland, and King George III all allowed officers to dedicate books to them, thereby encouraging the efforts of Adam Williamson, Samuel Bever, Humphrey Bland, Campbell Dalrymple, and George Smith.[102] Fellow officers also helped by subscribing to books translated or written by their colleagues. More than nine hundred, including all who would command British forces during the War for American Independence, supported the publication of Bennett Cuthbertson's *System* in 1768 as did five hundred Robert Donkin's *Military Collection* in 1777 and another four hundred George Smith's *Universal Military Dictionary* in 1779.[103] These hundreds of subscribers represented very significant portions of an officer corps that did not reach five thousand in any of these years. Beyond that, kings rewarded officers who became authors with promotions and sinecures. The Hanoverians were particularly generous to Humphrey Bland whose *Treatise* provided a uniform drill for British forces for nearly forty years and to Sir William Fawcett whose translations brought Saxe's *Reveries*, *Regulations for the Prussian Infantry*, and *Regulations for the Prussian Cavalry* to more than a generation of British officers. Like Bland and Fawcett, Samuel Bever, Campbell Dalrymple, and Robert Donkin all received promotions or appointments for their publications.[104]

Indeed, in the middle decades of the eighteenth century, the British began to develop a professional officer corps. By then, young men could anticipate a career in the army that entailed long unbroken service with the time and the incentives to become thoroughly immersed in their duty. Although the Hanoverian kings had not been able to end the buying and selling of commissions, they had insisted that merit as well as wealth be considered in making appointments; and they had reduced the opportunities that captains and colonels had to profit by their commissions, emphasizing service to the state above return on private investment. But Hanoverians were not content just to emphasize merit and service; they were determined to do considerably more to develop a responsive and skilled officer corps. Gradually, and with the support of senior officers, they encouraged responsibility, esprit, and learning among all officers. They used their powers of command and court-martial to define responsibility as loyalty to the crown, subordination to civilian officials, and respect for fellow officers as well as attention to duty, obedience to superiors, and courage before the enemy. They worked in much the same ways to develop esprit and learning: esprit, by favoring army families, supporting rituals and routines that bound men together, and punishing selfish behavior; learning, by raising standards for young men entering the service, reviewing regiments annually, supporting publications designed to educate officers, and rewarding officers for their scholarship. These efforts—the efforts of kings George II and George III and some of their most senior officers—to identify and reward merit, to encourage responsible service to the state, and to promote esprit and learning were not uniformly successful; yet taken together, they marked the beginning of a British profession of arms.

In all of their efforts to develop a professional officer corps, the British depended on books—especially the books on war that our officers considered to be most authoritative. Kings and ministers had long used the Articles of War to define an officer's obligations in serving the state. Beginning in the 1750s, they began supporting the publication of annual *Lists* (reminding officers of their professional ties) and drill books (bringing uniform tactics to the army). They also encouraged individual officers to become students of war and to write books for their colleagues. The officers, impressed by the success of French and Prussian commanders during the War of the Austrian Succession, responded by producing an unprecedented number of books— usually synthesizing or translating Continental authorities. British officers also began to write in extenuation of their own unsuccessful operations, to explain that they had behaved responsibly and, therefore, professionally— following orders, acting courageously, and doing all that was possible to engage and defeat the enemy. Perhaps most important, officers acquired, read, and reflected on the Continental works that were most admired in the middle of the eighteenth century: military histories, treatises on engineering and artillery, and, above all, studies of the art of war.

A Prudential Art of War

But what did the books that our officers preferred contribute to an understanding of the art of war in the British army? We cannot, of course, be sure. It is difficult enough to judge the impact of a book or cluster of books on an officer corps, on men who had much in common; it is nearly impossible to link ideas to actions in a complex and interactive undertaking such as war. We can say what books our officers admired most; we can trace the shifting popularity of particular books across time; and we can identify and synthesize the arguments of a relatively limited number of books—that is, we can begin to see how books and clusters of books might have contributed to an approach to war. We can also demonstrate how at least one of our officers, Sir Henry Clinton, understood the books that he preferred and how that understanding was reflected in the war he waged as commander in chief during the War for American Independence. Beyond that, we can speculate on how books on war affected other British commanders in the Seven Years' War and the War for American Independence. How did the books that our officers thought most authoritative—the Continental books that they came to prefer in the middle of the eighteenth century—affect British officers as they made their plans and conducted their operations in the age of the American Revolution?

To approach that question we should begin by considering the ten books that our officers preferred above all others: the classics of Caesar, Polybius, and Vegetius; the English accounts of Marlborough's campaigns and Bland's *Military Discipline*; and the French treatises of Vauban, Saxe, Feuquières, Folard, and Clairac.[105] Those ten books provide us with a reasonably balanced sample of the ninety-two books that our officers considered authoritative. History is underrepresented and the classics overrepresented among the ten; but books on the art of war, engineering and artillery, and drill are present in almost exactly the right proportions. So too are Continental books almost the same proportion of the ten as of the ninety-two most authoritative books.[106] It is true that the ten books do not fully reflect the mid-eighteenth-century surge of interest in Continental books on war, the surge that is apparent in the thirty books that our officers preferred above all others. Yet if we make allowance for the changing popularity of each of the most valued books, if we put slightly more emphasis on books that were increasing in popularity, we will be able to give Continental texts their due.[107] In short, the ten books that our officers valued most—Caesar to Bland in Appendix B—offer not only a reasonably accurate representation of the ninety-two books on war that our officers considered authoritative but also a reasonably succinct expression of the art of war that those officers preferred in the age of the American Revolution.

That art of war was far from settled. British officers of the mid-eighteenth century did agree on the broad outlines of tactics. While the French were debating the relative importance of firepower and of shock—of muskets and cannon on the one hand and of bayonets and sabers on the other—the British had clearly decided to rely primarily on firepower to defeat their enemies. Their manual of arms and drill included exercises for the bayonet, and bayonets were considered to be important in defending infantry against cavalry and in assaulting fortifications; but the British manual of arms and drill were devoted mainly to developing and controlling musketry, and British officers expected to win battles with firepower rather than with shock.[108] The British did not, however, agree that battles were desirable, that campaigns should be planned to bring the enemy to a decisive action. Some clearly thought it better to win with the fewest risks, employing—as had Marshall Saxe in the Low Countries during the War of the Austrian Succession—sieges, skirmishes, maneuvers, and an occasional defensive battle to exhaust the enemy and gain a favorable peace. Others, thinking of Frederick the Great's successful defense of Prussia during the Seven Years' War, believed it best to risk battle, to overcome the enemy by engaging and destroying his forces. This was a debate, as King George II put it tendentiously, between generals who proposed "Little Attempts that had small Danger & small utility" and generals "who went to the grand object."[109]

But what do the books that our officers preferred have to say about the desirability of going to "the grand object," of risking battle, to decide a campaign or war? What was the prevailing tendency in the mid-eighteenth-century British art of war? Our officers' favorites among the classics (Caesar, Polybius, and Vegetius) do not provide clear answers to those questions. Caius Julius Caesar's *Commentaries*, by far the most popular book among our officers, was written to demonstrate Caesar's aggressiveness and success in all kinds of war—from counterinsurgency operations in Gaul to all-out civil war within the Roman Republic of the first century B.C. Because Caesar was usually independent of governmental control—because he had far more authority than most eighteenth-century commanders—he was able to begin campaigns with offers to negotiate with his enemies, to make peace without loss of life. When his enemies—whether the rebellious tribes of Switzerland, Germany, and Gaul or his rivals in Rome—rejected his overtures, he was free to use force in a variety of ways. He built field works to contain the Swiss, he asked the Germans to withdraw east of the Rhine, and he avoided battle with the Belgae, all before engaging and defeating each in turn. When his enemies raised large armies, sometimes larger than his own, he employed sieges and blockades as well as general actions to gain victories. Thus, he broke Vercingetorix's rebellion in Gaul with a successful battle interspersed between equally successful sieges of Bourges and Alise; and thus he defeated Pompey in Greece with an abortive siege of Durrazo that led to the climactic Battle of Pharsalia. In all of his campaigns, Caesar exhibited a broad grasp of strategy to complement his tactical versatility, a clear sense not just that the security of Gaul was related to control of Germany and Britain but also that victory in his civil war with Pompey depended upon success in Spain, Egypt, Syria, and Africa as well as in Greece. Caesar's *Commentaries* offered examples of a bold, aggressive commander who was never afraid to risk battle but who used a variety of measures to conquer his enemies.[110] No wonder that Sir Henry Clinton could read the

Commentaries in contradictory ways, finding support for both an aggressive use of battle and a prudential resort to siegecraft.[111]

Polybius provided similarly contradictory evidence for eighteenth-century readers. His *History* of the rise of Rome during the Punic, Social, and Asian wars of the late third century B.C. was primarily a celebration of the Roman system of government—a system that relied on its citizens for security and military power. His history was also a celebration of gifted generals and their success in great battles. The Roman state was able, during its wars with Carthage, to overcome recurring disasters: the loss of fleets and armies, the rash actions of its generals, and the superior conduct of its enemies. It drew upon the support of a loyal and hardy people to rebuild its fleets, raise new armies, and find generals who were able eventually to secure Rome and carry the war successfully overseas—to conquer in some fifty-three years their known world. When the Carthaginian general Hannibal invaded Italy, he employed veteran troops and skillful tactics to defeat all save the most prudent Roman generals. Fabius avoided battle and concentrated on depriving Hannibal of his supplies and allies; but the Romans allowed other, more aggressive generals to engage Hannibal, who, as at Cannae, used superior tactics to destroy larger Roman forces. Eventually, the Roman system prevailed. Rome was able to raise new armies, liberate Italy, and find a general who was more than a match for Hannibal. Scipio challenged Hannibal in Carthage and destroyed his army at the climactic battle of Zama. Similarly, in the Social War in Greece, the democratic Achaean League joined with Macedonia to overcome the treacherous tyrants of Aetolia and Sparta; popular governments had prevailed over tyrannies. In Asia it was merely one unsavory monarch against another for the control of Coele-Syria, a contest decided by battle. Polybius clearly wanted to emphasize the importance of systems of government in securing a state, but he also acknowledged the impact of great battles in deciding a war.[112]

Unlike Caesar and Polybius, Flavius Vegetius Renatus preferred a thoroughly cautious approach to war, one in which logistics were as important as engagements in defeating an enemy. Vegetius, a fourth-century A.D. Roman, admired the military methods of the republic and early empire, the methods that he thought had provided the foundation of Roman power and security. His ideal Roman army would be recruited carefully, trained thoroughly, and employed prudently. He believed that rustic lads of good character were ever the best soldiers, young men accustomed to hard physical labor who would accept the stern discipline and incessant training required to make effective soldiers—to learn to march, fight, and fortify a camp. Such young men would be organized into relatively small armies (12,000 to 24,000) that would be better fed and disciplined and, therefore, superior to larger enemy forces. A good general made sure that his men were ready for battle. He trained them in all seasons; he built their confidence by skirmishing successfully against the enemy; he took care that they were not surprised when on the march or in camp; and he prepared them for a general engagement—showed them how to form a line of battle and how to turn an enemy's flank. But he also did all that he could to avoid a battle. Because battles were usually fatal to "the worsted enemy," a general considered "every plan," tried "every expedient," and took "every method" before resorting "to this last extremity." A skilled commander would exhaust his enemy by depriving him of supplies, attacking his detachments, and denying him any opportunity for a successful battle—would, with minimal risk and loss of life, induce his enemy to abandon a campaign or war.[113]

John Churchill, Duke of Marlborough, was much more aggressive than Vegetius, but like Caesar he had to use a variety of methods to defeat his enemies. Marlborough, who commanded allied forces in the Low Countries during the War of the Spanish Succession, went to the Continent in 1702 determined to seek battle, "to strike some great blow and establish his Reputation."[114] He soon found himself mired in a war of sieges and maneuvers, constrained as much by his allies as by his enemies. Only four times during ten campaigns was he able to bring on a general engagement, and only one of those directly affected the outcome of the war. His most famous victories had limited consequences: at Blenheim in 1704, he saved Vienna and drove the French west of the Rhine; at Ramillies in 1706, he opened the way for the gradual conquest of the Spanish Netherlands; and at Oudenarde in 1708, he began an offensive that took by siege Ghent, Bruges, and Lille. But his narrow and costly victory over the French at Malplaquet in 1709 had the most decisive results. At Malplaquet, according to Richard Kane, Marlborough should not have attacked: he could have completed his siege of Mons without risking battle. But "wanton with success . . . we attacked" and threw away "many men's lives when there was no Occasion." Sickened by the losses, the British government decided to reduce its commitment to the war and make a separate peace with France. While they negotiated, Marlborough continued in his command, without the forces to risk battle but with the skill to outmaneuver the French and capture important posts on their frontier—to wage a campaign of siege and maneuver that Kane thought "amongst the greatest he ever made."[115] Because Marlborough did not write his memoirs, he was dependent on subordinates like Kane and John Millner and historians like John Campbell to tell his story.[116] Each of these biographers was sympathetic with Marlborough; and together they appealed to an ever-growing proportion of our officers, making Marlborough after Caesar and Vauban the most admired of their authorities on war. But Kane and Campbell celebrated Marlborough as much for his virtuosity in sieges and maneuvers as in general engagements.

Humphrey Bland, who had served as a junior officer under Marlborough and a cavalry commander during the War of the Austrian Succession, wrote his *Treatise of Military Discipline* to provide uniform ways of preparing the British army for war—but not for conducting a war. He first published his *Treatise* in 1727 when the army was scattered throughout the British Isles and empire (often in units no larger than companies of forty-five or fifty men) and when the methods that had made the army formidable under Marlborough were being forgotten. Bland assumed that he was preparing men for a Continental war, for engagements between armies that contained infantry, cavalry, artillery, and engineers. He also assumed that those men would take part in various forms of combat from general engagements and formal sieges to skirmishes. He then explained how to organize companies of infantry in battalions of roughly five hundred men and train those battalions for active service in an army. To be effective as part of an army, a battalion had to be able to respond to standard orders: it had to be able to march at various rates; change rapidly from one formation to another; and deliver its fire in controlled ways, depending on circumstances. It had to be able to form and maintain a line of battle whether attacking or retreating, to shift rapidly from line to square to meet cavalry, and to deliver fire by volley or subdivision. Bland also included instructions for preserving an army in camp or on the march—instructions for providing shelter, posting guards, and keeping records that had proved their worth in Flanders.[117] Although he had little to say to cavalry and almost nothing to engineers or artillerists, his *Treatise* appealed strongly to our officers until the middle of the eighteenth century. By then, the British government was issuing manuals that replaced Bland and diminished his popularity. The last of his nine editions appeared in 1762.

Except for Vegetius, the classical and British books on war that our officers admired most provided a comprehensive approach to the art of war: they considered general engagements as well as sieges and maneuvers as ways to achieve victory. By contrast, the leading Continental authorities were more cautious: they were far less willing to risk battle than Caesar, Marlborough, or Scipio. Sébastien Le Prestre de Vauban, the great French military engineer of the late seventeenth century who was more esteemed by our officers than any author except Caesar, devoted a lifetime to building, defending, and capturing fortresses—to securing the frontiers and waterways of Western Europe. But Vauban went beyond what might have been expected of someone who sought security in fortifications; he took a prudential approach to the attack of a fortified place. He prepared thoroughly, assembling not only forces that were large enough to conduct the siege and to keep relief from reaching the garrison but also supplies to support the attackers for at least a month. He then proceeded patiently, using time, industry, and explosives—rather than lives—to break the will of the defenders. He began digging toward the fortress well beyond the range of the defenders' artillery; and he took time to prepare trenches that were dry, spacious, and secure against fire and sorties from the garrison. Once his trenches were within forty yards of the main line of defense, the outward edge of the massive ditch guarding the fortress, he relied on artillery to dismount the defenders' guns and on mortars and mines to ruin their works, to fill the ditch and breach the bastions and curtain walls. It was always better, he thought, to capture a fortress by bombardment than by assault. Only when it came to the defense of a fortress was he willing, of necessity, to expend lives. His garrison would prepare carefully to withstand a siege, laying in supplies and ammunition, removing all houses and trees around the defensive works to gain an unobstructed view of the attackers, and taking care that no one deserted to the enemy. Beyond that, the garrison would do more than defend its works. The troops would contest every advance toward their lines, sallying forth repeatedly to attack the enemy's trenches and batteries. Such attacks would slow the pace of the siege, exhaust the attackers' will and supplies, and gain time for a relieving force to arrive. If no relief came and if the main defensive works were in ruin, the garrison might surrender with honor.[118]

Louis-André de La Mamie Clairac was even more defensive minded than Vauban. Vauban built fortifications and explained how to defend them; but he also devoted much time and effort to waging war offensively, especially to capturing fortresses with minimal risks and losses. Clairac, a French engineer who had seen active service during the War of the Austrian Succession, was concerned primarily with defensive warfare, with using field fortifications to defend a country or to make smaller forces equal to larger. His *L'Ingenieur de Campagne*, which was first published in 1749, was popular not just with our officers but also with others who would serve in the Seven Years' War and the War for American Independence. Its increasing stature was reflected in a second French edition of 1757 and in separate English translations of 1758, 1760, and 1776. Although Clairac knew that field works required improvisation—the application of materials at hand to terrain and tactical considerations—he sought to construct his works, whenever possible, according to the principles for permanent fortifications. He built spaciously, providing protection and maneuvering room for all of his forces within parapets that were from six to seven and a half feet high (up to twelve feet thick) and that were protected by ditches that were from six to seven and a half feet deep. He made sure that his works were complementary, that the defensive fire of each provided cover for and was covered by the fire of other works. And he took particular care that when the defenders fired straight before them, their fire swept every part of the ditch guarding his parapet as well as the faces of each salient angle, the most vulnerable part of any work. All of his works were sustained by redoubts, buildings, elevations in the terrain, and waterways so as to provide protection for the army and for important towns, roads, and river crossings. No wonder that, at the beginning of the War for American Independence, the rebellious colonists promptly translated Clairac for themselves, hoping that his works would give them a chance against British regulars.[119]

Because they were engineers, Clairac and Vauban might well have been expected to think defensively or, at least, to approach war cautiously. But what of other French authorities of that era? What of Maurice Comte de Saxe, the celebrated commander of the War of the Austrian Succession who was more influential with our officers than any Continental author except Vauban? Saxe was, as commander and author, the personification of prudence. In his *Reveries*, which appeared in many editions during the 1750s, Saxe offered detailed advice on leading men to war. His troops, raised by universal obligation, would be trained to march in step and to use a variety of weapons; they would be organized in relatively small, nimble armies (no larger than 46,000 men); and they would rely on either fire or shock according to tactical circumstances. Saxe prepared for general engagements; but he was "far from approving of them. . . ." He did not attack another army unless he could do so "with advantage"—unless his flanks were well covered and he could place a large part of his army against a small part of the enemy's. He preferred to lure the enemy into attacking him in a well-prepared position or, better still, to exhaust the enemy with maneuvers, sieges, and small encounters. Saxe thought it possible "to make war without trusting anything to accident; which is the highest point of skill and perfection, within the province of a General."[120]

Jean Charles de Folard, a French soldier and theorist of the early eighteenth century, was more offensive minded than Saxe—except when it came to general engagements. Folard drew upon his experience in the War of the Spanish Succession and his extensive reading of history to create a theory of tactics and to provide a lengthy commentary on Polybius. He is best known for his endorsement of the column as the way to tactical success. Although he had never seen a column in action, he believed that soldiers in column equipped with pikes or bayonets would always defeat soldiers in line with muskets and artillery, that shock would ever be superior to fire. He conceded that columns would sometimes be vulnerable to artillery fire; but he thought they were particularly well suited to French soldiers who preferred offensive to defensive action. He based his tactics primarily on his understanding of the Greek phalanx and a few famous battles: Epaminondas's victory at Leuctra, Scipio's at Zama, and Gustavus Adolphus's at Lutzen. Reflecting on those battles, Folard concluded that cavalry and infantry could be mixed successfully in a column and that together they would prevail not just offensively but also defensively.[121]

When Folard began to comment on Polybius's history—on warfare in general—he became noticeably more cautious. He did criticize his contemporaries for squandering superior forces by remaining inactive, giving up territory, and avoiding battle; and he advocated taking the offensive, even seeking a decisive battle, to set a positive tone at the beginning of a war. Yet he also asserted that a commander should never seek a general engagement without very substantial reasons and careful preparations. In the Second Punic War, Roman generals should have refused to engage the whole of Hannibal's army. They should have secured their supplies, developed strong defensive positions, and struck at the Carthaginians whenever their forces were dispersed. Had they done so, Folard thought, the Romans could have destroyed the Carthaginians without risk. So too should Aratus in the Social War have been careful to have assembled his army before attacking the Aetolians' rear guard at Caphyes. He was not, and the Aetolians were able to turn about and defeat his army piecemeal. Folard admired aggressive commanders who were able to win and exploit great battles. He was highly critical of generals who offered battle or pursued an enemy rashly, who failed to take ordinary precautions (to assemble adequate supplies before a siege or to protect their forces when in camp or on the march), and who refused to expand their experience with systematic study of warfare and their enemies. Folard was much closer to Saxe as a commentator than as a tactician.[122]

Antoine de Pas, Marquis de Feuquières, was similar to Folard in his preference for offensive action and in his wariness of battle. Feuquières, a French officer whose *Memoirs* reflected on the wars of Louis XIV from 1672 until 1709, was clear that "the principal View of a General in every Species of War [offensive, defensive, or between equals] . . . , should always be to act on the Offensive, because this is a Form of War most easy to be sustained, at the same time that it produces the greatest advantage to the Prince."

Even so, Feuquières was wary of general engagements—of battles in which both armies attacked to the front and in which both might suffer the loss of their artillery and baggage as well as substantial numbers of men. Because such battles could be won and lost (the French had won at Fleurus in 1690 with brilliant tactics and lost at Blenheim in 1704 with faulty assumptions and lack of action), Feuquières recommended both careful preparations for and prudent conduct of campaigns. A prince, anticipating war, should plan carefully to avoid unwanted general engagements. A general, entrusted with the conduct of the war, should always choose when and how to engage the enemy; he should never be forced to fight. Indeed, he "should never be disposed either to offer or receive Battle, except in those Conjunctures, wherein the Benefits that will redound to his Prince, from a prosperous Event, will be much greater than any Disadvantages he can possibly sustain by a Defeat." French commanders had risked battle at Blenheim with no good reason and at Ramillies with no adequate prospect of success. Feuquières took a similar approach to sieges: aggressive conduct combined with care for men. When besieging a place, he would impose a tight blockade, march out to engage any relieving force, and advance his trenches where easiest to support the work of the sappers (possibly where the defenses were strongest); he would also rely on bombardment rather than on mining or storming to save lives. When defending a fortress or town, he would prepare carefully, exploit blunders of the attackers, and add trenches within his walls to seal breaches and prolong the siege.[123]

Saxe, Folard, and Feuquières as well as Vauban and Clairac—the French authorities that our officers admired most—were more cautious collectively than any of their favorite classical and British authors except Vegetius. Caesar, Polybius, and Marlborough offered examples of aggressive commanders who were accomplished in all aspects of war—of men who preferred the offensive and who were as ready to risk battle as to employ sieges, maneuvers, and skirmishes to defeat their enemies. Vegetius was, of course, the exception among the most popular classical authors: he admired generals who sought to defeat their enemies with minimal risks and losses, generals who avoided general engagements and exhausted the enemy with small attacks on magazines, supply trains, and detachments. Contemporary French authorities were on the whole closer to Vegetius than to Caesar, Polybius, or Marlborough. Saxe, Folard, and Feuquières thought offensively. But if each understood the advantages of acting against—rather than reacting to—the enemy, each was wary of general engagements and assaults on lines or fortifications. Each preferred maneuvers, skirmishes, and sieges to a general action; and each was more aggressive than either Vauban or Clairac. Vauban, best known for designing the fortresses that guarded French frontiers, also developed techniques for conducting sieges with a minimum of risks. He ever preferred to expend time, labor, and munitions rather than lives in capturing a fortress or town. Clairac was even more defensive minded than Vauban. He designed field works primarily to protect a country or an army against superior enemy forces. In short, the French authorities on war that our officers valued most—those which became especially popular in the mid-eighteenth century—offered a more cautious approach to the art of war than the most popular of the classical and British authors.

But how did our officers read their favorite books? Did they accept the more cautious approach to war then fashionable on the Continent—the war of sieges, maneuvers, and defensive battles? Or, did they, like King George II, prefer a war of general engagements, a war waged by commanders "who went to the grand object"? We can only suggest answers to those questions. We have reading notes for five of our forty-two officers; but only one of those sets of notes is comprehensive—only one reflects an officer's understanding of a variety of books over a significant portion of his career. That one set allows us to see how Sir Henry Clinton read many of the books that our officers thought most authoritative and to judge the relative importance that he attached to classical, British, and Continental authorities. Clinton was an intelligent, experienced, and unusually well-informed officer. He had entered the army in the 1740s, studied independently in France, served as aide-de-camp to two of the most celebrated soldiers of the mid-eighteenth century (Sir John Ligonier, the British commander in chief, and Prince Charles of Brunswick, commander of allied forces in Germany), revisited European battlefields of the Seven Years' War with the historian and soldier Major General Henry Lloyd, and risen steadily in the army to become by 1778 commander in chief of British forces in the War for American Independence. Those experiences gave Clinton a very broad knowledge of books about war; and from the 1760s until his death in 1795, he regularly made notes on his reading in the history and theory of war. His notes, contained in a dozen commonplace books and additional loose sheets, include reflections on thirteen of the twenty books that our officers valued most—indeed, on nearly all of the best-known books of his era except those dealing with military engineering and discipline.[124]

Clinton's reflections were remarkably consistent with his own cautious nature and with the prudential theories of warfare that were emerging on the Continent. He clearly preferred those commanders who were wary of general engagements. In Caesar's *Commentaries*, he admired the barbarians who took strong posts and refused battle. In Marlborough's campaigns he not only disparaged the French and Bavarian generals who risked battle at Blenheim (Marlborough was in an untenable position and would soon have been forced to withdraw "for want of a secure line of supply") but also praised Marlborough for skillful maneuvers, which in 1711 turned the French out of a line of fortifications without a battle ("this affair places the Duke of Marlborough's character higher than any achievement during the whole campaign as it was effected without any action").[125] So too did Clinton prefer the more thoughtful and cautious theories of war that he found in Folard's commentaries and Feuquières's *Memoirs*. A commander needed to prepare carefully for a campaign or war; he had to know what motivated his enemy and what resources might be found in the theater of operations. A commander also needed to know that in defending a country it was best to rely on a mobile army supported by militia acting with "the caution of Fabius at first" and "the execution of Caesar at last." Not that Clinton shared Caesar's willingness to engage the enemy. Even on the offensive, Clinton would avoid a general action "except in certain situations for be it remembered, one victory obtained by the assailing army does not decide the contest; one battle lost by him does too often."[126] If a general action became unavoidable or even desirable, he would protect his flanks and attempt to turn one of the enemy's, employing—as Folard recommended—columns of infantry to turn and roll up the enemy's line. Clinton's enthusiasm for columns was, in this instance and in general, inspired by his passion for security. To a greater extent than most of his contemporaries, he was willing to mix columns and lines of infantry—shock and fire—to get the most effective disposition against infantry, artillery, or cavalry, or combinations thereof. Clinton was a remarkably consistent and cautious reader.

A French Art of War and the Winning of American Independence

Clinton was also a most unusual reader, the only one of our forty-two officers—indeed, the only prominent British officer of his era—to leave a detailed record of military reading. How then are we to assess the connections between the books that British officers preferred and the wars that they waged—specifically, the War for American Independence? Even when the evidence is as abundant as with Clinton—even when there are reading notes to complement papers and memoirs—it is extremely difficult to establish causal connections between ideas and actions in war. Each commander has preconceptions about warfare that have been shaped by experience, study, and reflection; and those preconceptions affect each decision he makes in developing strategy for a war, conducting operations throughout a campaign, and deciding on tactics for a particular maneuver or engagement. Each of his decisions requires considerably more than an application of theory to practice. Each requires a balancing of his government's war aims with the shifting circumstances of the war—with the size and strength of opposing forces, the interaction of those forces, and the behavior of the contending populations. Each decision also reflects the commander's willingness to accept responsibility, take risks, and work with other commanders. The more a decision is considered in isolation, the more difficult it is to explain the relationships between theory and practice in that decision. Conversely, the more that decisions are considered together, the easier it is to see patterns in those decisions and to judge the relationships between theory and practice. We can, for example, compare the overall conduct of each British commander in the War for American Independence with prevailing ideas about war. We can judge the extent to which the cumulative actions of each conformed to the prevailing Continental preference for an offensive war waged by sieges, maneuvers, and defensive battles—for an offensive strategy coupled with defensive operations and tactics. We can also ask how each commander's approach to warfare affected the progress of the war. Were prudential measures well suited to putting down a rebellion? Would a uniformly more aggressive approach have been better?

Thomas Gage, commander in chief at the beginning of the American War, might have been expected to be a cautious commander, one who sought to minimize risks and casualties. If not a student of Continental warfare, his whole experience seemed to emphasize the value of prudential measures. In Flanders during the War of the Austrian Succession, he had seen Marshal Saxe wage war successfully with maneuvers, sieges, and an occasional defensive battle. In North America during the French and Indian War, Gage had been present when less cautious actions brought disaster: when General Edward Braddock was surprised on a wilderness road near Fort Duquesne and when General James Abercromby was repulsed in assaulting the French lines at Fort Ticonderoga. Gage had also been with Jeffrey Lord Amherst while he persistently and carefully conquered Canada. But when in 1773 Bostonians destroyed a shipment of tea to forestall parliamentary taxation, Gage offered to carry out "coercive measures"; and he did so all too aggressively. He did not develop a strategy or even a plan of operations. He merely sought to help the British government use force to intimidate the colonists and support royal government. Yet, in ordering an expedition to destroy colonial stores at Concord, he neglected ordinary security for a detachment that would be marching through a hostile countryside;

and in deciding on a frontal attack to drive the colonists from their works at Bunker Hill, he rejected a proposal to turn the rebel flanks. It is not clear why he was suddenly so aggressive: perhaps he was stung by criticisms of his moderate treatment of the colonists; perhaps he sought to live up to his optimistic estimates of what he could do; most likely he underestimated the colonists' ability to stand against regular troops.[127] In any case, his aggressive tactics brought costly British defeats and the War for American Independence.

Gage's successor, Sir William Howe, was more cautious but less consistent in prosecuting the American War. Like Gage, Howe had been exposed to the best practitioners of siege and maneuver warfare, serving against Saxe in Flanders and with Amherst in North America. But unlike Gage, Howe had also served with the most aggressive and celebrated British commander of the French and Indian War, James Wolfe, who had risked a general engagement to capture Quebec in 1759. Howe's enthusiasm for battle was clearly tempered by his first experience in the American War—by his having led the disastrous British attack at Bunker Hill. Even so, he succeeded Gage as commander in chief and went to New York in the spring of 1776 intending to use force decisively to end the rebellion: to destroy the Continental army in a general engagement and then, with the support of the British navy and troops from Canada, to isolate and conquer New England. He soon changed his mind and deviated from plans that the British government had approved. When his brother, Admiral Richard Lord Howe, arrived with a peace commission, General Howe agreed to shape his strategy to promote a negotiated settlement. He rejected proposals for trapping and destroying the Continental army at New York City and devoted the remainder of the campaign to turning movements that drove the Americans successively from Long Island, Manhattan, West Chester, and New Jersey. However successful, those maneuvers did not bring peace; and when at the end of 1776 the rebels surprised his detachments at Trenton and Princeton, Howe was forced to modify his strategy once again.

Discouraged by the failure of conciliation, Howe oscillated between two very different strategies to end the rebellion in 1777: the one, to destroy the Continental army in a climactic battle; and the other, to encourage a negotiated settlement by recovering territory and restoring Loyalists to power in the middle colonies. He opened the campaign in June by trying to lure the Continental army into battle in New Jersey. That failing, he embarked his army for Pennsylvania, going by way of the Chesapeake Bay so as to avoid an opposed landing in the Delaware River and to attract Loyalists in Maryland, Delaware, and Pennsylvania. On reaching the head of Chesapeake Bay and finding the colonists far less loyal than he had hoped, he sought another general engagement. On September 11 he attacked and defeated the Continental army at Brandywine Creek on the road to Philadelphia. But he did not destroy that army, and he devoted the ensuing two months to taking and securing Philadelphia. Not until the beginning of December did he try again to engage the Continental army. Howe's halting efforts to end the rebellion in 1777 exasperated the British government not just because those efforts were conciliatory and unsuccessful but also because they came at the expense of another British army under General John Burgoyne that had been ordered south from Canada to cooperate with Howe along the Hudson River. Learning that Burgoyne had surrendered at Saratoga, the government recalled Howe.[128]

John Burgoyne lost his army at Saratoga in part because he was not supported by Howe and in part because he undertook a European campaign in a sparsely populated wilderness. He intended to lead his army across rivers and lakes some 350 miles from Quebec to Albany to join Sir William Howe in isolating and conquering New England—in subduing what the British thought the most rebellious of the colonies. Burgoyne was a cavalry officer who had studied the art of war on the Continent and admired French books above all. On assuming command at Quebec in the spring of 1777, he assembled 138 artillery pieces to accompany an army of about eight thousand men. He would use this disproportionately large siege train to overcome rebel fortifications along the way and thus force his way to Albany without risking an offensive battle—much as Saxe had advanced along the Meuse in the War of the Austrian Succession. But assembling and moving such a large number of guns seriously impeded Burgoyne's progress. He did not embark on Lake Champlain until the third week of June or capture Fort Ticonderoga and Skeensboro until July 6 and 9; and it took him another three weeks to advance twenty-three miles overland from Skeensboro to Fort Edward on the Hudson. Although he was then fewer than fifty miles from Albany, he had to delay another six weeks assembling horses, wagons, and forage before crossing to the west bank of the Hudson and giving up his supply line to Canada. Not until mid-September was he at last across the river and on the road to Albany. He soon found that he had given the rebels all too much time to gather their forces and build fortifications blocking his way at Bemis Heights about twenty-five miles north of Albany. Twice he tried to turn their position at Bemis Heights; twice he failed. By then it was the second week in October. Burgoyne's provisions were running short, and he had little prospect of being relieved by British forces from New York City. He turned back to Saratoga where on October 17 he surrendered. He was the victim not just of Howe's neglect but also of his own insistence on mounting a prudential European campaign in a wilderness. His surrender brought France into the war and an abrupt change in British plans.[129]

To end the rebellion with smaller regular forces and against more formidable enemies, the British government adopted a new strategy and appointed Sir Henry Clinton commander in chief. Until Burgoyne surrendered, the government had given Sir William Howe considerable latitude in shaping British strategy. But thoroughly disenchanted with Howe's efforts to promote a negotiated peace, the government now sought greater control over both its strategy and its commander in chief. The government still hoped that Clinton might end the rebellion by destroying the Continental army in a decisive battle, but because he was to detach some of his troops for an attack on the French West Indies, he was to join increasingly with the Royal Navy and Loyalists in carrying on the war against the rebellious colonists, by combining amphibious raids from Maine to Virginia with a gradual reconquest of the South and a blockade of New England. The government expected that Clinton would not only adhere to the new strategy but also prosecute the war more aggressively than Howe.

Clinton did follow the new strategy, but he was not as aggressive or successful as the government had hoped. It was relatively easy for him to support the new strategy that required a greater reliance on Loyalists and the navy in combating the rebellion: he had long advocated establishing Loyalist enclaves as bases for the British and employing the navy against rebel lines of supply and trade. It was more difficult for him to support the government's preference for a decisive battle. He was predisposed to wage war offensively by sieges, maneuvers, and defensive battles rather than by attacks on the enemy's army. Beyond that, he had become commander in chief when British forces were being diverted from North America and when French forces were arriving unpredictably to assist the rebels. No wonder that Clinton seemed lethargic in carrying out the government's strategy: he found many reasons to make war according to the most prudent and fashionable French methods; theory and practice seemed for him to go well together.[130] He did try repeatedly to lure the Continental army into attacking him, by marching from Philadelphia to New York City in June 1778, by foraging in New Jersey later that summer, by taking posts on the Hudson that obstructed rebel communications across the river in 1779, and by returning unexpectedly to New York in the late spring of 1780. But with the exception of an inconclusive rearguard action at Monmouth in 1778, he did not succeed in precipitating the defensive battle he sought; and he was never able to cooperate effectively with the British navy in attacking the

French squadrons that came to Rhode Island in 1778, 1780, and 1781. He fared far better in raiding rebel ports from New England to the Chesapeake, in taking Charleston and its garrison by siege in May 1780, and in initiating what he hoped would be the gradual reconquest of the South—the gradual restoration of Loyalists to power in South Carolina or, perhaps, the Eastern Shore of Virginia and Maryland. As late as the spring of 1781, Clinton continued to believe that he could end the rebellion by avoiding defeat, by outlasting the Americans and their French allies.[131]

Yet to carry out his plans for recovering the South, Clinton had to rely on Charles Earl Cornwallis, the "most active and aggressive general that the British had sent to America." Like Clinton, Cornwallis had learned the art of war primarily in Europe: as a cadet at the military academy in Turin and as an aide-de-camp with allied forces in Germany during the Seven Years' War. But Cornwallis never came to share Clinton's preference for a war of sieges, maneuvers, and defensive battles. Quite the contrary, Cornwallis went to America in 1776 ready to risk almost any offensive action to end the rebellion. Although he allowed the Continental army to slip away from him at Trenton in late 1776, he served otherwise creditably and contentedly under Howe in the middle colonies. He was far less content as second in command to Clinton. Cornwallis chafed under Clinton's conduct of the indecisive Battle of Monmouth in 1778 and quarreled openly with him during the siege of Charleston in 1780. When subsequently left to carry out Clinton's plans for a gradual reconquest of the South, and when unable to raise adequate Loyalist forces to secure Georgia and South Carolina, Cornwallis decided that a decisive victory was indispensable to recovering the South. He destroyed a Continental army at Camden in August 1780 but still could not enlist Loyalists enough to control rebel partisans in South Carolina. He sought a second victory over the remnants of Continental forces in North Carolina but succeeded mainly in allowing his detachments to be defeated at King's Mountain in October 1780 and Cowpens in January 1781. Nor did he fare better when he again pursued rebel forces into North Carolina and fought them inconclusively at Guilford Court House in March 1781. He abandoned the interior of the Carolinas to the rebels and took his army to Virginia, still seeking a decisive victory. Instead, he won only small engagements before being ordered to fortify a naval base on the Chesapeake; he then proceeded to Yorktown, where he was besieged and captured by the combined forces of France and the United States.[132]

How then had French ideas about war contributed to the winning of American independence? Paradoxical as it might seem, those ideas influenced both sides in the war in ways that decidedly favored the rebellious

American colonists. George Washington and other American commanders had come to understand warfare through British eyes. Serving with British officers during the French and Indian War, reading the books that the British thought most authoritative (Saxe, Vauban, and Clairac, as well as histories of Marlborough and Frederick the Great), and employing British soldiers to prepare them for war, Washington and his generals had learned to appreciate the prudential French way of war that British officers then preferred—the war of sieges, maneuvers, skirmishes, and defensive battles that had brought Marshal Saxe victories in Flanders with a minimum of risks. Although some Americans preferred the more aggressive warfare of Frederick the Great, Washington saw from the beginning of the Revolutionary War that his inexperienced forces would fare better with the methods of Saxe than with those of Frederick the Great. Washington knew that the Continental Congress and the American people expected him to defend places of strategic importance—New York City, the Hudson River, Philadelphia. He also knew that he would sometimes be forced to attack the British to sustain the morale of his own forces. Yet, to carry on the war without jeopardizing the Continental army and the rebellion, Washington and his generals fought mainly on the strategic and tactical defensive. They were driven from New York City and much of New Jersey in 1776; they lost Philadelphia in 1777; and they came under intense pressure from Congress to attack the British, to bring the war to a short and bloody conclusion. They sometimes did attack—at Trenton, Germantown, and Monmouth. More often, they persisted in carrying on the war by maneuvers, skirmishes, defensive battles, and sieges; and those measures, which suited their circumstances and which were consistent with prevailing French theories, eventually brought some of the most important American victories of the war: Saratoga, Cowpens, Guilford Court House, and Yorktown.[133]

French ideas also contributed to British defeat—if less conspicuously than to American victory. The British government sought from the beginning of the war to use force decisively to end the rebellion: at first, by intimidating the people of New England; then, by destroying the Continental army in a climactic battle in the middle colonies; and finally, either by destroying the Continental army in battle or by joining with Loyalists and the Royal Navy to recover the colonies piecemeal. The government's plans had little to do with prudential French warfare. Assuming that its regular forces were superior to the rebels, the government was willing to risk offensive measures to end the rebellion as quickly as possible. But British generals were far from cooperative or consistent in carrying out their government's plans. Howe, Burgoyne, and Clinton waged war much more cautiously than the government intended. Howe did so to favor his hopes for a negotiated peace; Burgoyne and Clinton, to end the rebellion with a minimum of risks and costs. None of them shaped his operations exclusively to suit French theories—to wage an offensive war with maneuvers, skirmishes, defensive battles, and sieges. Yet each did so to such an extent as to jeopardize the government's plans for ending the rebellion. Ironically, the two British commanders—Gage and Cornwallis—who sought to attack and destroy American forces, suffered defeats because they were all too aggressive.

The most important effect of French theories was, perhaps, the least obvious. It was the latitude that those theories gave Howe, Burgoyne, and Clinton to deviate from the British government's plans. Because many British officers subscribed to the prudential methods of Saxe and Vauban, the British government had to be more tolerant than it wished of generals who made war patiently and carefully; and such patience and care were neither consistent with the government's plans nor well suited to ending a rebellion. A minister who had served in the British army and who railed against the Howes' conciliatory efforts acknowledged that General Howe had been skillful in turning the rebels out of New York without suffering heavy casualties: "Sir Wm Howe has shewn great knowledge in his profession. . . . It is very clear that the Rebels will never face the Kings troops, but as they understand the taking of strong posts and entrenching themselves so expeditiously it requires more than common abilities to carry an offensive operation without considerable loss, and Sir Wm Howe has infinite merit in that particular."[134] Such prudential methods were best suited to wars in which neither side sought to destroy the other and in which both were willing to take time to limit casualties and avoid defeats. Such methods had eventually brought victory for the British in the French and Indian War. In the American War, the British had to destroy the United States, and they had to do so before the new nation became well established and won the support of European states. The British government was more than willing to take risks to end the American rebellion—quickly. But it was obstructed for more than six years by prevailing French ideas that not only encouraged its commanders in chief to pursue cautious operations but also shielded those commanders from criticism and recall.

Britain was unlucky that so many of its commanders preferred French books and ideas during the War for American Independence. Yet that preference was a part of a more beneficial and durable development within the army, the emergence of a professional officer corps. Since the middle of the century, British officers had become increasingly aware of the advantages and expectations of a career in the army. They knew that the British government and people were willing to support a standing army under civilian control. They knew that they could expect a satisfying return on the time and money required to gain a commission and learn the duties of an officer. They soon came to understand how they fit into the army's hierarchy and what it would take to get ahead. Although most bought and sold their commissions, and although colonels still expected to profit from regimental funds, officers knew that kings opposed profiteering and supported knowledgeable, responsible service to the state. They learned that a commissioning oath and the Articles of War meant serving with their regiments, mastering tactics, respecting fellow officers, obeying commands, and behaving courageously in combat. They also learned that books shaped nearly every aspect of their service and that studying the art of war was becoming increasingly fashionable among those with the ambition and means for higher command. In short, the men who led the British army in the age of the American Revolution were—and knew that they were—part of an emerging profession of arms: a profession supported and controlled by the state, defined by regulations and customs, aware of its special calling, and sustained by a shared commitment to responsible and knowledgeable service to the state.

Notes

ABBREVIATIONS

Add MSS	Additions to the Manuscripts, British Library, London, England
BJL	Brynmore Jones Library, Hull University, Hull, Yorkshire, England
BL	British Library, London, England
ESRO	East Suffolk Record Office, Ipswich, Suffolk, England
GB	Great Britain
JRULM	John Rylands University Library of Manchester, Manchester, England
KCAO	Kent County Archives Office, Maidstone, Kent, England
NAM	National Army Museum, Chelsea, London, England
PRO	Public Record Office, Kew, London, England
WO	War Office Papers, Public Record Office, Kew, London, England

1. Gruber, "For King and Country," pp. 27–28; Houlding, *Fit for Service*, chap. 3; Gruber, "British Strategy," pp. 17–22; and C. Duffy, *Military Experience*, pp. 50–57.

2. Willson, *Life of Wolfe*, pp. 165–66, 276, 295–98; Whitworth, *Ligonier*, pp. 171, 179; Gruber, "Education of Clinton," pp. 131–53.

3. Consider the differences between the 120 books that Houlding discussed (*Fit for Service*, pp. 153–256, 426–34, 441–59) and the 650 that forty-two eighteenth-

century British army officers preferred (Part II and Appendixes A and B of this book). Houlding did discuss a high proportion of the books that the officers valued above all others—17 of the 20 books on war that the officers thought most authoritative, books that at least a quarter of the officers owned, read, or recommended. But beyond those 17 titles, his choices diverged sharply from theirs. Of the 120 privately published books on war that he considered, fewer than 75 were among the 650 that the officers preferred; and only 33 were among the 92 books that attracted the attention of 10 percent or more of the officers. It is likely that the officers read and benefited from more than 75 of Houlding's privately published books, but no more than 75 of those books appear in their inventories, catalogues, and lists.

That Houlding's and the officers' preferences should diverge so sharply is primarily a reflection of his and their very different interests. Concerned primarily with analyzing the training of the rank and file of the British army, Houlding emphasized books on drill and discipline (35 percent) followed, in descending order, by treatises on the art of war (21 percent), engineering and artillery (20 percent), military history (9 percent), and the classics of ancient Greece and Rome (7 percent). The forty-two officers, who were far more interested in war in general than in drill or discipline in particular, turned first to military history (35 percent) and then to engineering and artillery (20 percent), the art of war (16 percent), the classics (10 percent), and, sparingly, to drill and discipline (8 percent).

It is clear that Houlding's list of books—the most extensive and authoritative that we have had—is strikingly different from the comprehensive list of books that some forty-two eighteenth-century British officers preferred, that his list includes some books that our officers neglected and excludes many more that they admired, particularly Continental works that they were reading in French. Houlding mentions Puységur's *Art de la Guerre* and Santa Cruz de Marcenado's *Reflexions Militaires et Politiques* exclusively as sources for Samuel Bever's *Cadet*. In fact, French editions of Puységur and Santa Cruz made their way into the libraries of a third and a fifth of our officers, respectively. So too did Montecuccoli's *Memoires*, Guischardt's *Mémoires Militaires*, and Espagnac's histories of the War of the Austrian Succession each reach a quarter of the officers who might have sought them; and Machiavelli's *L'Art de la Guerre*, Maizeroy's *Mémoire*, and Beaurain's *Luxembourg* each attracted a fifth or more of our forty-two officers, usually in French editions. By the middle of the eighteenth century, British officers had far more extensive and cosmopolitan tastes in books on war than Houlding or any other scholar has recognized.

4. Gruber, "Classical Influences," pp. 175–90; Gruber, "British Strategy," pp. 14–31; Gruber, "Anglo-American Military Tradition," pp. 21–47; Gruber, "Education of Clinton," pp. 131–53.

5. See Appendix E for summaries of our officers' service. The officers killed in action were Bever, Dury, and Wolfe; those who died while on duty, Bagshawe, Blomefield, Dormer, Dundas, Harrison, Hawley, Hesse, Howe, Robert Murray, Paget, Stewart, and Wade. Another fourteen remained in the list of officers—although in partial retirement—at the time of their deaths. See Part I for biographical sketches.

6. Dormer, Howe, Robert Murray, Paget, Seton, Stanhope, and Winde completed

their active service by, roughly, 1720; Blomefield, Clinton, Debbieg, Donkin, Percy, and Townshend remained on the lists into the wars of the French Revolution and Napoleon. See Appendix E and Part I.

7. It seems unlikely that Calderwood, Hotham, Maxwell, and Stewart experienced combat; we do not know about the services of General Officer, Gentleman in the Army, Smith, and Winde. See Appendix E for summaries and Part I for details of the other officers' active service.

8. Recommendations of a Board of General Officers to William Wildman Barrington, Jan. 31, 1766, and Barrington's reply to Charles Gould, Feb. 8, 1766, WO, 71/10, PRO. In his reply Barrington said that the king approved the recommendations for the prices of commissions and would order that they "be invariably observed for the future."

9. The number of officers serving in the British army grew steadily through the eighteenth century with peacetime levels from 1,950 (1718–39) to 2,900 (1783–93) and wartime crests of 4,600 (Seven Years' War) and 4,100 (War for American Independence); see Houlding, *Fit for Service*, p. 19. The proportions of cavalry and guards officers fluctuated slightly from one era to another and from peace to war. In 1774, when the army was still on a peacetime footing and when the proportion of cavalry and guards officers was probably slightly higher than in wartime, about 15 percent of all officers were mounted, about 10 percent were serving in the guards, and about 18 percent were majors, colonels, or general officers. By comparison, 21 percent of our officers (of the thirty-nine whose service is known) served in the cavalry at one time or another; 52 percent were in the guards; and 80 percent advanced at least to the rank of major. Compare GB, WO, *List of the Army* with Appendix E, which shows the branch of service, guards affiliation, and highest rank for each of the thirty-nine officers whose service has been established.

10. Houlding, *Fit for Service*, pp. 99–116 (esp., pp. 105–6).

11. See sketches of these officers in Part I.

12. The officers of substantial means were Calderwood, Clinton, Dormer, Dundas, Dury, Hotham, Hotham Thompson, Ligonier, Maxwell, Molyneux, Lord John Murray, Robert Murray, Oglethorpe, Paget, Parker, Percy, Seton, Stanhope, Townshend, Tryon, Wade, Winde, and Wortley Montagu (see Part I).

13. Namier and Brooke, *House of Commons*, 1:4–5, 13–16, 21, 23, 32, 47–48.

14. The fifteen officers who were members of Parliament were (with years of service): Clinton (1772–84, 1790–94), Dundas (1770–74), Hotham (1723–27, 1729–38), Hotham Thompson (1761–68), Ligonier (1748–63), Molyneux (1759–76), Lord John Murray (1734–61), Robert Murray (1722–27, 1734–35, 1738), Oglethorpe (1722–54), Paget (1722–27), Parker (1769–80), Percy (1763–76), Stanhope (1702–17), Townshend (1747–64), and Wortley Montagu (1747–68). See biographical sketches in Part I. The percentage of all officers who were members has been calculated for 1774 when there were 75 officer-members and, roughly, 3,500 officers. Compare Namier and Brooke, *House of Commons*, vols. 2 and 3, with GB, WO, *List of the Army*, 1774.

15. Those who studied at Eton were Oglethorpe, Percy, Stanhope, and Townshend; those at Westminster, Hotham Thompson and Wortley Montagu; those at

Oxford, Molyneux, Oglethorpe, Parker, and Stanhope; those at Cambridge, Percy and Townshend; those at Leiden, Wortley Montagu; those at the Inns of Court, Hotham Thompson; those at the Royal Military Academy, Blomefield and Debbieg; and those on the Continent, Clinton, Donkin, Ligonier, Townshend, and Wolfe. See biographical sketches in Part I.

16. Those who became fluent(F) and had substantial libraries(L) were: Bagshawe(F), Bever(F), Blomefield(F), Calderwood(F,L), Clinton(F,L), Dalrymple(F), Debbieg(F), Donkin(F), Dormer(F,L), Dundas(F), Dury(F,L), General Officer(L), Gentleman in Army(L), Harrison(F), Hawley(F), Hesse(F), Hotham(F), Hotham Thompson(L), Ligonier(F,L), Maxwell(L), Molyneux(F), Montresor(F,L), Lord John Murray(L), Oglethorpe(L), Parker(F), Percy(F,L), Seton(L), Smith (F,L), Stanhope(F,L), Stewart(F,L), Townshend(F,L), Tryon(F,L), Wade(F,L), Winde(F,L), Wolfe(F,L), and Wortley Montagu(F,L). See Part I.

17. The younger sons or grandsons of peers: Lord John Murray, Robert Murray, Paget, Parker, Tryon, and Wortley Montagu. See Part I.

18. The baronets were Hotham, Hotham Thompson, and Maxwell; the knight, Clinton; and the sons of knights, Molyneux and Oglethorpe. See Part I.

19. For each of these officers, see sketches in Part I.

20. See Part I. Others served as aides-de-camp as well: Bland and Lord John Murray to George II during the War of the Austrian Succession and Donkin to the military governor of Martinique during the Seven Years' War.

21. For sketches of the careers of these and all except two of our forty-two officers, see Part I (we cannot be sure of the identity of General Officer and Gentleman in the Army).

22. Nearly two-thirds of our forty-two officers—some twenty-seven—left inventories or catalogues of their libraries: Bagshawe, Harrison, Hesse, Howe, Maxwell, Robert Murray, Paget, and Tryon (inventories) and Calderwood, Cuthbert, Dormer, Dury, General Officer, Gentleman in the Army, Hotham, Hotham Thompson, Ligonier, Montresor, Moyle, Lord John Murray, Oglethorpe, Seton, Stanhope, Stewart, Wade, Winde, and Wortley Montagu (catalogues).

The remainder of our officers expressed their preferences much more directly, if not so comprehensively: six (Bever, Bland, Dalrymple, Donkin, Molyneux, and Smith) included references, notes, or bibliographies in the books that they wrote; five (Blomefield, Debbieg, Parker, Percy, and Smith) ordered or purchased books; four (Clinton, Hawley, Percy, and Townshend) kept notes on their reading; three (Dundas, Townshend, and Wolfe) assembled lists of books for fellow officers; and one (Percy) discussed books in his correspondence.

23. Compare Appendixes A and C.

24. Ibid.

25. Compare these authors in Parts II and III.

26. Compare Appendixes A1 and A3 with Appendixes C1 and C2.

27. Compare Appendixes A3 and C2.

28. Compare Guibert, Lloyd, and Jeney in Parts II and III.

29. Compare Appendixes A and A4; and see Appendix D.

30. Appendix B4.

31. Appendixes B4 and D.

32. Appendixes B and B4.

33. Ibid.

34. See Appendix B and Bever and Dalrymple in Part I.

35. Appendixes B and B4.

36. Appendixes A2 and A3.

37. Appendixes A2, A1.

38. Appendix A1.

39. Appendix A2.

40. This discussion of publishers is based on an analysis of the 650 books that our forty-two officers preferred (Part II) and of advertisements in some of those books. See especially Millan's and Egerton's advertisements in the Society of the Cincinnati's copies of GB, WO, *List of the Army*, 1759, 1767, 1769, 1773 and Dalrymple, *Military Essay*.

41. Part II and advertisements in the Society of the Cincinnati's copies of Le Blond, *Essai sur la Castrametation*; Le Blond, *Traité de l'Artillerie*; and *État Militaire de France 1780*. For the Dutch publishers, see as well the Society of the Cincinnati's copies of Jeney, *Le Partisan*, and Estrades, *Lettres*.

42. Appendix A2 and A3.

43. See Appendix B, Caesar through Saint-Rémy. In establishing the thirty books on war that our officers valued above all others, I have considered Kane only once, under Marlborough.

44. Doyne to Lord Barrington, Dec. 11, 1760, Barrington Papers, HA 174/1026/3b, ESRO.

45. Townshend, *Rules and Orders*.

46. Jeffrey Amherst to Sir Jeffrey Amherst, May 10, 1771, Amherst Papers, U1350 C6/4, KCAO. See as well Namier and Brooke, *House of Commons*, 2:433; 3:102–8, 257.

47. Warrant for leave of absence to Henry Clinton, Oct. 23, 1748, extended, June 23, 1749; similar warrants at this time to Keppel, Pitt, and Hale, WO, 25/3191, PRO.

48. [Beaumont Hotham] to Charles Hotham, Sept. 8, 1747, Hotham Papers, DDHO 4/1, BJL; Bever, *Cadet*, 125; and quoting Burgoyne's advice, c. 1760, in De Fonblanque, *Political and Military Episodes*, pp. 19–20.

49. Gat, *History of Military Thought*, pp. 27–54 (quoting p. 30).

50. Speelman, *Lloyd*, especially chaps. 3, 6.

51. Dalrymple, *Military Essay*, p. 56.

52. Rogers, *Military Revolution*, chaps. 1–4, 12–13; Parker, *Military Revolution*; Black, *Military Revolution?*.

53. Rogers, *Military Revolution*, pp. 76–77. Rogers has borrowed "punctuated equilibrium" from evolutionary biologists Stephen Jay Gould and Niles Eldridge and shaped their idea, most insightfully, to the Military Revolution.

54. Ibid., chaps. 3, 7, 8; Parker, *Military Revolution*, chap. 1.

55. Parker, *Military Revolution*, chap. 3; Guilmartin, *Gunpowder and Galleys*, chap. 6.

56. Parker, *Military Revolution*, chaps. 1, 2, 5; Rogers, *Military Revolution*, chaps. 1, 2, 5–7, 9–10; Roberts, *Gustavus Adolphus*, 2: chaps. 3–11; Parker, *Thirty Years' War*, chap. 6; M. Duffy, *Military Revolution*, intro.

57. Rogers, *Military Revolution*, chaps. 1, 2, 4, 11, 12; Parker, *Military Revolution*, chaps. 2, 4; Wheeler, *Making of a World Power*, chaps. 1–4.

58. Parker, *Military Revolution*, pp. 25–38; Brewer, *Sinews of Power*, chap. 1; Wheeler, *Making of a World Power*, chap. 1; Braddick, "English Military Revolution," pp. 965–75.

59. Those who believe the Civil Wars brought the Military Revolution to England include Wheeler, *Making of a World Power*, chap. 1, and Braddick, "English Military Revolution," pp. 965–75; those who think the Military Revolution came after the Glorious Revolution—if at all—include Brewer, *Sinews of Power*, chap. 1, and Black, *Military Revolution?*.

60. Quoting Braddick, "English Military Revolution," p. 965; relying primarily upon Wheeler, *Making of a World Power*, chaps. 2–9, and Kennedy, *Rise and Fall of British Naval Mastery*, chap. 2.

61. Brewer, *Sinews of Power*, chaps. 1–2 (esp. 57–59); Kennedy, *Rise and Fall of British Naval Mastery*, chap. 2; Braddick, "English Military Revolution," pp. 965–69; Wheeler, *Making of a World Power*, chaps. 4, 9; and Bruce, *Purchase System*, pp. 2–3, 11–17.

62. Brewer, *Sinews of Power*, chaps. 2–6; Kennedy, *Rise and Fall of British Naval Mastery*, chaps. 3–4.

63. Teitler, *Genesis*, chap. 2, argues that an era of limited war provides the best environment for the development of a professional officer corps. Bruce, *Purchase System*, pp. 17–38, describes the efforts of successive kings from William III through George III to abolish or regulate the buying and selling of commissions; but the system survived and worked against the development of a British profession of arms.

64. In judging the progress that the British made in creating a profession of arms in this era, I have used criteria that historians have found applicable to the development of professions before the Industrial Revolution. I have been particularly attracted to the criteria employed by Rosemary O'Day in studying the clergy of the Church of England who, as emerging professionals, had much in common with officers of the British army (advancement determined by wealth as well as merit, autonomy impaired by an aggressive crown, expertise measured by service as well as learning, and corporate identity diminished by isolation yet reinforced by clothing as well as by rituals and special responsibilities in matters of life and death). O'Day believes that there are seven features that need to be present—in combination—in a pre–Industrial Revolution profession: hierarchical organization; emphasis on service; internal control of recruitment, training, and placement; internal enforcement of standards and discipline; possession of specific expertise (practical and theoretical); a well-developed career structure; and a strong esprit de corps. I have drawn upon those criteria, which can be understood to encompass the criteria of other

thoughtful historians of this era (such as John Brewer, Wilfrid Prest, and D. J. B. Trim), to measure the progress of the eighteenth-century British army officer corps toward a profession of arms. See O'Day, "Anatomy of a Profession," p. 28; Trim, *Chivalric Ethos*, pp. 6–13, 23–30; Brewer, *Sinews of Power*, pp. 55–57; Houlding, *Fit for Service*, p. 113; Hayes, "Social and Professional Background," chap. 3.

I have not adopted the criteria or accepted the conclusions of Samuel Huntington. I think his criteria too brittle—at once too comprehensive and too rigorous—to be useful in judging an emerging profession. But I have found his insistence on standards valuable in reminding us of the differences between an emerging and a more developed profession. He and other social scientists are right to say that a powerful state can deprive an occupation of the autonomy it needs to become a profession; that an emphasis on financial remuneration can be destructive of the merit and responsibility needed in a profession; and that if the expertise and efficiency of an organization are to rise to a professional level, they must depend on more than the voluntary efforts of its members. Yet such criticisms would have been more valuable had they been accompanied with some understanding of the progress that the British had made in this era toward the development of a profession of arms. Huntington, *Soldier and State*, pp. 7–30.

65. See especially Brewer, *Sinews of Power*, pp. 55–59, for the importance of long, continuous service as a foundation for a British profession of arms (including the prospect of half pay for officers whose regiments were disbanded at the end of a war). Strength report of the British army and militia, [1752–62], Barrington Papers, HA 174/1026/3b 283, ESRO; Curtis, *Organization of British Army*, pp. 1, 50, for strength of the army in 1775, 1781 and pp. 34–47, 120, for bureaucratic support. Houlding, *Fit for Service*, pp. 9–11, 99, and Gruber, "For King and Country," pp. 26–31, for numbers of officers.

66. Curtis, *Organization of British Army*, p. 1; Strength report, [1752–62], Barrington Papers, HA 174/1026/3b 283, ESRO; Houlding, *Fit for Service*, preface, chaps. 1, 3, 5, 6, makes clear that although the British army had a uniform drill, the army was usually too dispersed in peacetime for more than the most elementary training in infantry tactics.

67. *List of the General and Field-Officers* . . . in Part II and Appendix B. See as well *List of His Majesty's Land-Forces in North America*, 1761 and *List of the General and Field Officers in North America*, 1778.

68. See prefaces to Kane, *System of Camp-Discipline*; Cuthbertson, *System*; and Donkin, *Military Collections*.

69. Quoting Bever, *Cadet*, pp. 143, 169.

70. Ibid., pp. 130, 152.

71. Bland, *Treatise*, p. 133.

72. See advertisement in Simes, *Military Guide*.

73. Quoting George III to Barrington, Feb. 9, 1773, Barrington Papers, HA 174/1026/111, ESRO; Barrington to Hervey, July 5, 1774, WO 4/92, PRO.

74. Stanton to Barrington, Mar. 9, 1770, and Pierson to Barrington, Nov. 9, 1770, Barrington Papers, HA 174/1026/6a/1, ESRO.

75. Hayes, "Social and Professional Background," chaps. 2, 3, 4; Hayes, "Royal House of Hanover," pp. 328–57; Guy, *Oeconomy and Discipline*, chaps. 4, 6; Brewer, *Sinews of Power*, p. 57; Gruber, "George III Chooses a Commander in Chief," pp. 166–90. Barrington to Gould, Feb. 8, 1766, WO 71/10, PRO; Dury to Barrington, Nov. 8, 1757, and Doyne to Barrington, Dec. 11, 1760, Barrington Papers, HA 174/1026/3b, ESRO; R. Pierson to Barrington, Nov. 9, 1770, Barrington Papers, HA 174/1026/6a/1 and Home to Barrington, n.d., Barrington Papers, HA 174/1026/6a/2, ESRO.

76. Guy, *Oeconomy and Discipline*, pp. 78–80 and chap. 6.

77. Gruber, "For King and Country," pp. 27–29; Barrington to Home, Sept. 28, 1756, WO 4/52, PRO.

78. Barrington to Lord Adam Gordon, July 26, 1774, WO 4/92; verdicts of general courts-martial for Edward Johnson, May 5–8, 1746, WO 71/19, for William Beaumont, Aug. 7–9, 1749, WO 71/21, for Sir William Kerr, Feb. 24, 1752, WO 71/21, and for Henry Heron, May 28–29, 1754, WO 71/22, PRO.

79. Hayes, "Social and Professional Background," chap. 5; Barrington to Robert Hill, June 15, 1756, WO 4/52, Barrington to Sorrell, May 12, 1774, and to Hervey, July 5, 1774, WO 4/92, Barrington to Wilson, Feb. 3, 1775, and to Effingham, June 1, 1775, WO 4/93, Barrington to officers on half pay, Aug. 16, 1775, WO 4/94, PRO; Captains, 30th Foot to Gould, Apr. 16, 1775, Barrington Papers, HA 174/1026/6a/3, ESRO.

80. Charteris, *Cumberland*, 1:207, 2:204; Barrington to Fowke, June 5, Aug. 14, 1756, WO 4/52, verdict general court-martial for Edward Strudwick, WO 71/18, and for Thomas Fowke, Aug. 10, 1756, WO 71/22, PRO.

81. Mackesy, *Coward of Minden*, chaps. 7–9, quoting, p. 226; verdict general court-martial, Moses Corbet, May 1, 1781, WO 71/28, PRO.

82. Mackesy, *Coward of Minden*, pp. 267, 269–70; Gruber, *Howe Brothers*, pp. 366–70; and Willcox, *Portrait*, pp. 475–76, 533.

83. See each in Part II, Books Preferred.

84. Houlding, *Fit for Service*, chap. 1.

85. Brewer, *Sinews of Power*, pp. 55–57; Reviews of 3rd Foot, May 30, 1774, WO 27/30, and 18th Foot, May 15, 1777, WO 27/36, PRO.

86. Doyne to Barrington, Dec. 11, 1760, Barrington Papers, HA 174/1026/3b; Pierson to Barrington, Nov. 9, 1770, Barrington Papers, HA 174/1026/6a/1, Hadington to Barrington, Jan. 12, 1773, and Home to Barrington, n.d., Barrington Papers, HA 174/1026/6a/2, ESRO; quoting Review of 18th Foot, May 15, 1777, WO 27/36, PRO.

87. Verdicts of general courts-martial for two ensigns, Oct. 1777, and two captains of the 50th Foot, [1781–82], WO 71/54, 58, PRO; Sackville to Barrington, June 17, 1759, and Doyne to Barrington, Dec. 11, 1760, Barrington Papers, HA 174/1026/3b, ESRO.

88. Gruber, *John Peebles*, pp. 2–15.

89. Doyne to Barrington, Dec. 11, 1760, and Dury to Barrington, Nov. 8, 1757, Barrington Papers, HA 174/1026/3b, ESRO.

90. Houlding, *Fit for Service*, pp. 198–201, 208–15; see W. Howe's review 4th Foot, Apr. 7, 1774, WO 27/30, PRO, for a particularly detailed explanation of what

was expected of a regiment and its officers on the eve of the War for American Independence. Charteris, *Cumberland*, 2:204–10; Roy, "Profession of Arms," pp. 192, 212–19.

91. Quoting Hayes, "Social and Professional Background," pp. 212–13. See also Robson, "Armed Forces," pp. 171, 176, 186–87, and Childs, *Armies and Warfare*, pp. 89–90.

92. The eight who wrote or translated books before 1754: Bland, General Officers (*Report of the Board of General Officers into the Conduct of Cope, Lascelles, and Fowke*), Ingoldsby (*Case of Ingoldsby at Fontenoy*), Kane, Molesworth, Parker, Sackville, and Williamson. See Part II, Books Preferred, and Part III, Books Not Taken.

93. Bever, *Cadet*, pp. 94, 115–17, 125, 131; Hawley, "Some Thoughts . . . Touchant le Millitaire," May 1725 (quoted here), and "Remarks on the Posthumous Treaty of Marechal Saxe of the Legions," [post 1753], Hawley Papers, 7411-24-16-4, and 7411-24, NAM.

94. Willson, *Life of Wolfe*, pp. 130–31, 144, 274–75, 380(quoted), 384–85.

95. Houlding, *Fit for Service*, pp. 195, 216.

96. Bever, Bland, Clairac (Vallancey, translator), Clinton, Cornwallis, Cuthbertson, C. Dalrymple, Donkin, Douglas, *Essay on Field Fortification* (Pleydell, translator and author), Hinde, Justinus (Clarke, translator), Kane, Le Cointe (an officer, translator), Molyneux, Moody, *New Regulations for Prussian Infantry*, *Regulations for Prussian Cavalry*, and *Regulations of Prussian Infantry* (Fawcett, translator), Rogers, Sackville, Saxe (Fawcett, translator), Simes, Stevenson, Turpin de Crissé (Otway, translator), and Vegetius (Clarke, translator)—all in Part II, Books Preferred. Bligh, Bonneville (Vallancey, translator), Burgoyne, W. Dalrymple, *Essay on Command Detachments* (Young), Frederick (an officer, translator), *Genuine and Particular Account* (an officer), Guibert (Douglas, translator), Howe, La Faussille, Ligonier, Mac Intire, Maizeroy (Mante, translator), *Memoirs of Blakeney*, Pembroke, Williamson, Wolfe, and Young—all in Part III, Books Not Taken.

97. While the number of commissioned officers increased from roughly two thousand in 1713–52 to four thousand in 1753–83 (doubled), the number of officers producing books on war increased from eight in 1713–52 to thirty-six in 1753–83 (quadrupled). The number of important books (Appendix B, The Authorities) also increased from three in 1713–52 to fourteen in 1753–83.

98. The thirty books preferred (in Part II): Bever, Bland, *Cautions and Advices*, Clairac, Clinton (two titles), Cornwallis, Cuthbertson, C. Dalrymple, Donkin, Douglas, *Essay on Field Fortification*, Hinde, *History of Justin*, Kane, Le Cointe, Molyneux [two titles], Moody, *New Regulations Prussian Infantry*, *Regulations for Prussian Cavalry*, *Regulations for Prussian Infantry*, Rogers, Sackville, Saxe, Simes [two titles], Stevenson, Turpin de Crissé, and Vegetius.

99. The fourteen (see Appendix B): Bever, Bland, Clairac, C. Dalrymple, *Essay on Field Fortification*, Kane, Le Cointe, *Regulations for Prussian Cavalry*, *Regulations for Prussian Infantry*, Saxe, Simes (two titles), Turpin de Crissé, and Vegetius.

100. See Bever, Dalrymple, Clinton, and Wolfe in Part I and Wickwire, *Cornwallis*, pp. 24–29.

101. Appendix B.

102. See dedications to Turenne, *Military Memoirs*; Bever, *Cadet*; Bland, *Treatise*; Dalrymple, *Military Essay*; Smith, *Universal Military Dictionary*—all in Part II.

103. See lists of subscribers in Cuthbertson, *System*; Donkin, *Military Collections*; and Smith, *Universal Military Dictionary*—all in Part II.

104. Houlding, *Fit for Service*, pp. 170–71.

105. See Appendix B, Caesar through Bland.

106. Appendixes B3 and B2.

107. See Appendix B5.

108. Houlding, *Fit for Service*, pp. 166–67.

109. H. S. Conway to the Duke of Devonshire, Dec. 14, 1757, Chatsworth Manuscripts 416.51, Chatsworth House.

110. Caesar, *Commentaries*, trans. Bladen.

111. Clinton's notebooks, nos. 3, 10, Clinton Papers, JRULM.

112. This understanding of Polybius's history is a synthesis of Polybius, *History*, trans. Hampton; Polybius, *History*, trans. Grimeston; and Polybius, *Histoire de Polybe*, trans. Thuillier, commentary Folard.

113. Vegetius, *Military Institutions*, trans. Clark, quoting 85.

114. Kane, *System of Camp-Discipline*, pp. 39–40.

115. Quoting ibid., pp. 80, 90.

116. Ibid.; Millner, *Compendious Journal*; and Campbell, *Military History*.

117. Bland, *Treatise*.

118. Vauban, *De l'Attaque*.

119. Clairac, *Field Engineer*, trans. Muller; and Clairac, *L'Ingenieur de Campagne*, trans. Nicola.

120. Saxe, *Reveries*, trans. Fawcett, quoting pp. 163, 132, and 164 (in reprint).

121. See Folard's "Traité de la Colonne" in Polybius, *Histoire*, trans. Thuillier, commentary Folard, 1:xxii–c, and 7.

122. Polybius, *Histoire*, trans. Thuillier, commentary Folard, 1–6.

123. Feuquières, *Memoirs*, quoting 1:152 and 2:163 (in reprint).

124. Gruber, "Education of Clinton," pp. 131–53; and Gruber, "Clinton," in *Oxford Dictionary of National Biography*, 12:140–43.

125. Quoted in Gruber, "Education of Clinton," p. 141.

126. Ibid.

127. Alden, *Gage in America*; Shy, "Thomas Gage," pp. 3–38. Gage clearly underestimated the colonists: "These People show a spirit and Conduct against us they never shewed against the French and every body has judged of them from their former Appearance and behaviour when joined with the kings Forces in the last war; which has led many into great mistakes." Gage to Lord Barrington, June 26, 1775, Barrington Papers, HA 174/1026/6a/2, ESRO. It is even possible that Gage thought his troops would make an oblique attack at Bunker Hill and that the ensuing frontal assault was the result of a breakdown of British discipline.

128. Gruber, *Howe Brothers*.

129. Nickerson, *Turning Point*; De Fonblanque, *Political and Military Episodes*; and Ward, *War of the Revolution*, 1:398–431, 2:477–542.

130. Indeed, Clinton regularly criticized his colleagues for being too aggressive. According to Clinton, General Thomas Gage had twice exposed his troops to demoralizing defeats at the beginning of the war—in sending a detachment to Lexington and Concord and in attacking the colonists at Bunker Hill. Clinton doubted the destruction of stores at Concord worth the risk; and he was sure that the British should have found an alternative to a linear frontal assault at Bunker Hill—a turning movement or an attack in columns covered by artillery. Clinton was also critical of Generals William Howe and John Burgoyne for allowing detachments to be surprised: Howe, by overextending his posts in New Jersey at the close of the campaign of 1776; and Burgoyne, by foraging too far from his line of march from Canada in the summer of 1777. In both instances—at Trenton and at Bennington—the rebels had won small, inspiring victories. But Clinton was most critical of his unruly subordinate, Charles Earl Cornwallis. After capturing Charleston in May 1780, Clinton left Cornwallis to recover the rest of South Carolina and, eventually, restore royal government throughout the South. He expected Cornwallis to proceed deliberately from south to north, securing one place before proceeding to another. He was, therefore, exasperated to find Cornwallis careening about the Carolinas: allowing detachments to be surprised at King's Mountain and Cowpens, pursuing rebel forces to Virginia, returning to North Carolina to fight inconclusively at Guilford Courthouse, and then abandoning the interior of the Carolinas to the rebels so that he might campaign in Virginia. Clinton thoroughly disapproved of the strategic and tactical risks that Cornwallis had taken and that contributed so conspicuously to British defeat. Gruber, "Education of Clinton," pp. 145–46.

131. Gruber, "Education of Clinton"; Willcox, *Portrait*; and Willcox, *American Rebellion*.

132. Wickwire, *Cornwallis*, quoting p. 2.

133. Gruber, "Anglo-American Military Tradition," pp. 21–47.

134. Lord George Germain to William Eden, Jan. 1, 1777, Auckland Papers, Add MSS, 34,413, BL.

PART I

Officers and Their Books

he following sketches analyze the careers and libraries of forty-two eighteenth-century British army officers whose preferences for books on war have formed the basis for this study. These officers have not been chosen at random and cannot be considered representative of eighteenth-century British officers. Rather they have been included in this study exclusively because they were among the few British officers of their era who left records of preferences for books on war. It is, therefore, important to know who these officers were, what experiences they had, and how influential they might have been. It is also important to know as much as possible about their preferences for books: how they were expressed and what they were.

Our officers might not have been representative of eighteenth-century British officers: they were wealthier, more successful, and far more influential than most. But because they were exceptional, their preferences for books are especially important. Nearly all of our officers had the inclination and means to acquire books; they believed that books were essential to mastering the art of war; and they knew which books were considered to be authoritative. Beyond that, by the middle of the century, they had risen to important commands and were determined to reform the army after its defeats in the War of the Austrian Succession. They sought, above all, to encourage fellow officers to become students of the art of war and thoroughly professional in their duties. Their efforts not only shaped their fellow officers but also created valuable evidence of the books that mattered most to British officers in the age of the American Revolution.

As the sketches of the officers and their books make clear, every record of an officer's preferences is important, but not all of the records are of equal value. Most rare and valuable are reflections on and recommendations for military reading, the kind of reflections that Sir Henry Clinton and Hugh Lord Percy preserved in small leather-bound notebooks and the recommendations that James Wolfe and George Viscount Townshend prepared for aspiring officers. Less rare but no less valuable are the bibliographies that Samuel Bever, Campbell Dalrymple, and Robert Donkin included in the books they wrote for their fellow officers, suggestions for further reading on the art of war, ancient and modern. More usual are records of books bought, sold, and owned: books that Thomas Blomefield, Hugh Debbieg, and George Lane Parker bought at the sale of another officer's library in June 1773; books that William Tryon listed while seeking reimbursement for household goods destroyed by fire; and books that wealthy men like Sir William Maxwell, Lord John Murray, and Sir Charles Hotham Thompson had when they commissioned inventories of their libraries. Most often we learn of the books that an officer owned when he died. Inventories prepared by executors were common for small libraries like those of Thomas Cuthbert, Thomas Harrison, and Robert Murray; catalogues, for libraries large enough to warrant a sale—such as those of James Dormer and John Earl Ligonier. However varied in quality, all of the records of our officers' preferences are important to an understanding of the books that mattered to eighteenth-century British army officers.

The sketches of the officers and their books should be read in conjunction with Appendix E, a comprehensive list of our forty-two officers arranged by the date on which each entered the army, earliest to latest. Appendix E includes a summary of each officer's service and his books—including the number of books on war that he preferred and the dates on which his preferences were recorded. Taken together, and adjusted to suit peculiarities in each officer's service, these summaries reveal that our officers had on average 725 books in their libraries, that they preferred (again on average) some 35 books on war, and that the median date of the records for their preferences was 1766. The sketches do contain three entries that might well seem anomalous: General Officer, Captain George Smith, and Gentleman in the Army. The "General Officer, Lately Deceas'd" has not been identified. Yet as the annotated catalogue for the sale of his books makes clear, his fellow officers appreciated his remarkably fine collection. Captain George Smith probably never held a commission in the British army, but he and his preferences for books were unusually influential. He served the British for more than a decade as inspector at the Royal Military Academy and as the author of an authoritative military dictionary. Gentleman in the Army was, according to the annotated catalogue of the sale of his books, "C Hatfield." Although he cannot be identified with certainty, he was most likely Captain Alexander Hatfield, a learned man and officer, who served in the 15th Light Dragoons from 1778 until 1791. Finally, as in most biographical dictionaries, each of the sketches for our officers contains a list of scholarly sources, including in each case the specific records that establish his preferences for books on war.

Source Abbreviations Used in Part I

Add MSS	Additions to the Manuscripts, British Library, London, England
ANB	*American National Biography*
BJL	Brynmore Jones Library, Hull University, Hull, Yorkshire, England
BL	British Library, London, England
DAB	*Dictionary of American Biography*
DNB	*Dictionary of National Biography*
GB	Great Britain
HRHC	Harry Ransom Humanities Center Research Library, University of Texas, Austin, Texas
JRULM	John Rylands University Library of Manchester, Manchester, England
KCAO	Kent County Archives Office, Maidstone, Kent, England
NAM	National Army Museum, Chelsea, London, England
NLS	National Library of Scotland, Edinburgh, Scotland
ODNB	*Oxford Dictionary of National Biography*
PRO	Public Record Office, Kew, London, England
PROB	Probate Records, Public Record Office, Kew, London, England
SAHR	Society for Army Historical Research
SRO	Scottish Record Office, Edinburgh, Scotland
WLC	William L. Clements Library, University of Michigan, Ann Arbor, Michigan
WO	War Office Papers, Public Record Office, Kew, London, England

Bagshawe, Colonel Samuel (1713–62).

Samuel Bagshawe's commissioned service in the British army coincided with the European and colonial wars of the mid-eighteenth century; and throughout his career, he had the patronage of his Derbyshire neighbors, the powerful Dukes of Devonshire. Yet debt, poor health, and limited experience of combat blighted his career. His father having died before he was born, Bagshawe was raised by his uncle, William Bagshawe of Ford Hall, Derbyshire. At eighteen, young Samuel ran away from school to enlist as a private in the British army and to spend seven years serving in the garrison at Gibraltar. Only then was his uncle able to extricate him from enlisted service and to get him a commission in the army. With the help of the Duke of Devonshire, Samuel rose rapidly to become by 1743 a captain in the 39th Foot on the Irish establishment. Three years later, while experiencing combat for the first time in a raid on the French coast at L'Orient, he lost a leg. He survived the wound, rejoined his regiment, and, with a loan from his uncle, purchased the lieutenant colonelcy of the 39th. He also married happily into a well-connected Irish family.

But, encumbered by debt, poor health, and a succession of administrative assignments, Bagshawe went little farther in the army. In 1754 he accompanied his regiment to India hoping to make his fortune and reputation. His health broke before he could do either, and he went home in 1756—to save his life and, with the death of his uncle, to gain a measure of solvency as the heir to Ford Hall. Failing to get an active command in the Seven Years' War, he kept busy managing his Derbyshire estate and looking after administrative details for his regiment. When the 39th returned from India in 1759, Bagshawe went to Ireland to rebuild the regiment and take a seat in the Irish Parliament. In January 1760 he gained the colonelcy of a new regiment to be raised in Ireland, the 93rd Foot. The 93rd proved expensive and frustrating: as fast as Bagshawe could recruit men for his regiment, the government diverted those men to older, better-established regiments. His health broke once again, and he died on the way to London in August 1762.

Bagshawe's books on war—the books in the library at Ford Hall in 1751—were few but well chosen. There was a popular translation of Polybius, a history of Marlborough's campaigns, two books on fortification based on Vauban, two editions of Humphrey Bland's *Treatise of Military Discipline* (the standard English drill book of the mid-eighteenth century), and two books dealing with Chevalier Folard's widely discussed ideas on the art of war. Most of these books on war were in French and were only a small part of a diverse library that contained an assortment of works on divinity, geography, mathematics, and poetry as well as popular novels and books on gardening and medicine. Bagshawe's books on war, which included six of the ten most popular of that era, suggested aspirations for a career in the army that were never to be fulfilled.

[This sketch of Bagshawe and his books has been drawn from Alan J. Guy's letter to Ira Gruber of Sept. 3, 1987; Guy, *Colonel Samuel Bagshawe*; and Bagshawe's correspondence, c. 1752–60, in the Bagshawe Papers, 2/2/1-59, JRULM.]

Bever, Lieutenant Colonel Samuel (fl. 1742–58).

Little is known about the life and service of Samuel Bever. He was commissioned in the British army in the early 1740s—too late for the list of 1740 but probably well before July 1746 when he became a captain in the 46th Foot. He remained in the 46th for the rest of his career in the army, rising to major in December 1755 and to lieutenant colonel in February 1757. His promotion from captain to lieutenant colonel in little more than a year was probably the result of the army's expansion for the Seven Years' War and the publication of *The Cadet*, his book for young officers in 1756. But Bever did not serve long as a lieutenant colonel. In 1757 he sailed with his regiment from Ireland for North America to take part in that summer's abortive campaign against the French fortress at Louisbourg on Cape Breton. The next year he and his regiment were reassigned to the British forces advancing north along Lake Champlain toward Canada. On July 8 he was killed while leading an assault on the French works at Fort Carillon. A second edition of his *Cadet* appeared in 1762.

Although his life and service were relatively brief and obscure, Bever's attitudes toward his profession and professional reading are clear. Believing that all too many of his fellow officers were idle and ignorant, he sought to encourage those officers to become students of war, to learn more than the rudiments of their duty. His *Cadet* offered a distillation of ancient and modern ideas about waging war—a celebration of discipline, realistic training, simplified tactics, and habitual coordination of infantry, cavalry, and artillery. It also offered suggestions for improving the performance of officers at every rank—suggestions for turning the idle and ignorant into learned, disciplined, and reasonable leaders. His officers would study mathematics, fortification, and geography as well as the history and theory of war. They would also learn Latin and French so as to have access to what he considered the best books.

Although Bever had an almost slavish preference for books in French, his taste was otherwise quite conventional. Of the eighteen books on war that he cited most frequently and recommended most enthusiastically, all except one were in French. Bever even cited French editions of books that were widely available in English, presumably because he thought the French translations and commentaries superior; and he ignored books written in English that were widely admired by other officers, books like Humphrey Bland's *Treatise of Military Discipline* and John Muller's works on siegecraft and fortification. Notwithstanding this bias, his favorite books on war were among the most popular in mid-eighteenth-century England. Among the ancients, he preferred Caesar, Polybius, and Vegetius; among the engi-

neers, Vauban, Clairac, and Le Blond; and among the theorists, Folard, Puységur, and Saxe. Only Feuquières's *Memoires* and Turpin de Crissé's *Essai*
escaped Bever's preference for the most fashionable of contemporary Continental books on war.

[SAHR, *Army List of 1740*; GB, WO, *List of the Army*; William Eyre to Robert Napier,
Lake George, 10 July 1758, in Pargellis, *Military Affairs in North America*, p. 421,
recorded Bever's death; Houlding, *Fit for Service*, pp. 169, 345, 364; Bever, *Cadet*.]

Bland, Lieutenant General Humphrey (1686?–1763).

Humphrey Bland seemed ill-mannered to subordinates; but he built a long,
successful career in the British army on forceful leadership in battle, loyalty
to Protestant monarchs, and talent for codifying tactics and administration. Born into an Anglo-Irish family about 1686, he entered the army as
an ensign in a cavalry regiment on the Irish establishment in 1704, served
under the Duke of Marlborough in the War of the Spanish Succession, and
distinguished himself in helping to put down the Jacobite rebellion in Scotland in 1715. During the ensuing decades of peace, he wrote his *Treatise of
Military Discipline* (1727) and won colonelcies of regiments on the Irish
establishment. When the War of the Austrian Succession began, he went
to the Continent to serve as quartermaster general of British forces, aide-
de-camp to King George II, and commander of cavalry in several important engagements. He was with George II at Dettingen (1743), commanded
the first line of cavalry at Fontenoy (1745), returned home with the Duke of
Cumberland to lead the British cavalry in defeating the Jacobites at Culloden (1746), and went back to the Continent to serve under Cumberland in
defending the United Provinces against the French (Bland was wounded at
Lauffeldt in the summer of 1747). By the end of the War of the Austrian Succession, Bland was a lieutenant general and governor of Gibraltar where,
once again, he sought to codify routine procedures—in this case, regulations for the garrison and its relations with civilians. He devoted the last decade of his life, 1753–63, to serving as commander in chief in Scotland and
colonel of the 1st Dragoon Guards.

Although Bland clearly valued books that could teach inexperienced officers how to make war successfully, he recommended few books beyond his
own. His *Treatise of Military Discipline*, which went through nine editions
between 1727 and 1763 and which was then more esteemed than any other
work of its kind in English, provided comprehensive advice for training and
leading men. He explained how to march, how to deliver controlled fire in a

variety of tactical circumstances, how to change from columns to lines, how to defend infantry against cavalry (to form and preserve a square), and how to protect an army against surprise whether in camp or on the march. He emphasized the importance of discipline and training as well as sound administration in making an army effective. Yet, for all the reliance he placed on his own book, he had little to say about other books on war—beyond, that is, recommending Vauban and Coehoorn for the details of siegecraft and giving examples of sound practice from the War of the Spanish Succession. He expressed little interest in broad discussions of the art of war.

[DNB; Skrine, Fontenoy; SAHR, Army List of 1740; GB, WO, List of the Army, 1755; and Bland, Treatise.]

Blomefield, General Sir Thomas (1744–1822).

Sir Thomas Blomefield had an unusually long, diverse, and successful career as an officer of artillery—a career that included active service from the Seven Years' War through the Wars of Napoleon and that was as fruitful on proving grounds as on battlefields. After a false start as a midshipman in the Royal Navy, Blomefield entered the Royal Military Academy at Woolwich to study artillery and engineering. He was then fourteen and soon became a protégé of the distinguished scholar and teacher, John Muller. He left Woolwich in 1759 to serve in the Seven Years' War on the coasts of France, in the West Indies (including the siege of Havana in 1762), and in West Florida. During the War for American Independence, he was brigade major of artillery with British forces advancing south from Canada in the campaigns of 1776 and 1777. Wounded and then captured at Saratoga, he returned home to become aide-de-camp to the master general of ordnance and then inspector of artillery and superintendent of the Royal Brass Foundry. In an unobtrusive, scholarly way he drew on his knowledge of chemistry, mathematics, and warfare to make dramatic improvements in guns and powder. The guns he tested and approved were considered exceptionally durable and safe, exceptionally well suited to the prolonged, rapid fire needed in the siege of a fortress or town. Blomefield continued as inspector of artillery for more than forty years, from 1780 until his death in 1822. During that time, he also commanded artillery successfully (at Copenhagen in 1807) and rose steadily to the rank of general and colonel-commandant of artillery.

Notwithstanding his scholarly instincts, Blomefield left only a glimpse of his taste in books on war in the era of the American Revolution. In June 1773 he attended the auction of a General Officer's library at Covent Garden. His purchases on that occasion were, it seems, shaped not just by the books that were offered for sale and the bidding but also by the books that he wanted for his own collection. Thus, he bought none of the books on artillery or mathematics that were offered and only two of the better-known books on fortification and the art of war (Clairac's *Field Engineer* and Feuquières's *Memoirs*). He concentrated that day on buying the kind of books that would round out rather than begin a collection of military books: one on fortification, three or four on the history of war, and one on perspective in drawing. He also bought books on diverse subjects ranging from law and diplomacy to grammar, plays, poetry, novels, and philosophy.

[*DNB*; GB, WO, *List of the Army*, 1759, 1768, 1772, 1779; and annotated copy of *Catalogue of the Library of a General Officer*, BL.]

Calderwood, Lieutenant Colonel William (d. 1787).

Calderwood had wealth, learning, and powerful friends. All of his service was in the elite and expensive 1st Horse Guards: he entered the regiment in April 1761; rose gradually to captain (1770), major (1778), and lieutenant colonel (1781); and died while still on the regimental rolls at Lausanne, Switzerland, in July 1787. Because he was commissioned late in the Seven Years' War, and because his regiment did not fight in the American War, he probably never saw active service or found his military duties especially onerous.

Books on war were only a small part of Calderwood's fine library, a library that reflected far more of his wealth, learning, and cosmopolitan interests than his devotion to the profession of arms. In 1786 he owned more than four hundred books dealing with mathematics, physics, chemistry, astronomy, geography, philosophy, and metallurgy, as well as history, biography, law, philology, economics, theology, architecture, and music. At the same time, he had only eleven books on war. Those eleven books were, however, what might have been expected of a learned, wealthy cavalry officer. There were two military histories (one in Italian, one in French), Caesar's *Commentaries* in Latin, and Vauban in French. But the heart of the military collection—some seven books on cavalry tactics and the art of war—included the latest and most admired books available in the decade before the American Revolution, just the books that a fashionable young officer in the 1st Horse Guards should own: Bland's *Treatise*, Saxe's *Reveries*, *Regulations for the Prussian Cavalry*, and Guibert's *Essai General de Tactique*.

[GB, WO, *List of the Army*, 1759, 1761, 1766, 1768, 1771, 1772, 1779, 1786, 1789. Calderwood's library was sold by Sotheby and Company on April 10, 1788. The catalogue for that sale, less its title page, is in the British Library, London; and a microfilm copy of the catalogue is in the Harry Ransom Humanities Center Research Library at the University of Texas, Austin, Texas. *Gentleman's Magazine*, July 1787, p. 642, contains a notice of Calderwood's death; and Board of General Officers to William Wildman Barrington, Jan. 31, 1766, and Barrington to Charles Gould, Feb. 8, 1766, establish the purchase prices of commissions — prices that show 1st Horse Guards to have been one of the most expensive regiments in the army. In 1766 a lieutenant's commission in the 1st Horse Guards cost about three times more than a lieutenancy in an ordinary regiment of foot. See the board's correspondence with Barrington in WO, 71/10, PRO.]

Clinton, General Sir Henry (1730–95).

Sir Henry Clinton served in the British army for fifty years, from the War of the Austrian Succession to the Wars of the French Revolution. He had the intelligence, courage, and family connections to rise to high command, but he never gained the self-confidence to make the most of his talents and opportunities. The son of an admiral who was also the royal governor of New York (1741–53), Clinton matured under the influence of a strong-willed mother and in the presence of resentful colonists, neither of whom helped him overcome what his father called a family tendency toward diffidence. He entered the army at fifteen as a lieutenant in an independent company of foot in New York and advanced rapidly with the help of paternal relatives, the powerful 1st and 2nd Dukes of Newcastle under Lyme. During the War of the Austrian Succession, he served with Anglo-American forces that occupied the French fortress of Louisbourg on Cape Breton, was promoted to captain lieutenant, and, at the Peace of Aix-la-Chapell, obtained leave to go to France to study the art of war. Returning to England, he became a lieutenant and captain in the elite 2nd Foot Guards (1751) and aide-de-camp to the commander in chief of the British army (1756). After the Seven Years' War began, he transferred to the 1st Foot Guards and in 1760 went with his new regiment to Germany where he became aide-de-camp to the celebrated allied commander Prince Charles of Brunswick. He soon established himself as a brave, knowledgeable officer and a student of the art of war. By war's end he was one of the youngest and most respected colonels in the army.

His career continued to flourish in the ensuing years of peace, the dozen years between the Peace of Paris (1763) and the beginning of the War for American Independence (1775). He gained command of the 12th Foot in 1766, took part in the following summer's maneuvers, and in 1769 accompanied his regiment to Gibraltar, where he became second in command of the garrison. In 1772 he was promoted to major general and elected to Parliament for a seat controlled by his cousin, the 2nd Duke of Newcastle. Severely depressed by the death of his wife in August 1772, Clinton eventually sought solace in his career. Leaving his young children with his sisters-in-law, he traveled to the Continent to study the battlefields of the Seven Years' War and to observe the Russo-Turkish War in progress. In early 1775, when rebellion threatened the British Empire in North America and the government sought to sustain its authority with force, he agreed to become third in command of the army at Boston. Clinton doubted the wisdom of using force to settle the Anglo-American crisis, but he accepted appointment out of a sense of duty and a desire to exorcise his grief. He reached Boston in May 1775, just after fighting had begun.

For the next three years, Clinton served as third and then second in command of the army in the rebellious colonies. He demonstrated an excellent understanding of the strategy and tactics of the war, but lacking confidence in himself, he could not impose his understanding on successive commanders in chief. At Boston in June 1775, he failed to dissuade General Thomas Gage from a costly frontal attack on the rebels entrenched on Bunker Hill. The following summer, he failed to convince Gage's successor, General William Howe, that he should trap the Continental army at New York City. And in the summer of 1777, he also failed to persuade Howe that he was expected to cooperate with another British army ordered south from Canada across Lake Champlain: Howe went by sea to Philadelphia, leaving the Canadian army, unsupported along the upper Hudson River, to surrender at Saratoga. Frustrated with his inability to shape events and with the conduct of the war, Clinton tried to resign. The government, equally frustrated with Howe and the war, insisted that Clinton become commander in chief. He succeeded Howe at Philadelphia in May 1778.

Clinton was no more successful as commander in chief than he had been as a third or second in command. He could never muster the confidence to wage war aggressively or to take firm control of his subordinates. Soon after the Canadian army surrendered, France entered the war on the side of the rebels. The British government ordered Clinton both to attack St. Lucia in the French West Indies and to carry on the war against the rebels with diminished forces. If unsuccessful in destroying the Continental army in a climactic battle, he was to cooperate with the Royal Navy and loyal colonists in ending the rebellion—in recovering the colonies gradually from south to north. Clinton did succeed in evacuating Philadelphia, in fighting his way to New York City, and in defending his posts against a French fleet that arrived in the summer of 1778. He also managed to send troops to the West Indies and to begin a successful reconquest of the South. But Clinton was too unsure of himself to risk a general engagement with the Continental army or to exercise firm control over his forces in the South. After capturing Charleston by siege in the spring of 1780, he left his aggressive second, Charles Lord Cornwallis, to complete a gradual reconquest of the southern colonies. When he subsequently learned that Cornwallis had suffered defeats and advanced abruptly into Virginia—leaving the Carolinas vulnerable to attack—Clinton lacked the will to insist that Cornwallis return to North Carolina and adhere to the strategy of gradual reconquest. Instead, he allowed Cornwallis to establish himself at Yorktown, Virginia, where in the fall of 1781 he was trapped by Franco-American forces. Cornwallis's surrender ended the American War and Clinton's active military service.

Clinton returned home in the spring of 1782 to find that he was blamed for Cornwallis's surrender, if not the loss of the colonies. He devoted the remainder of his life to answering his critics and restoring his reputation. He engaged in a pamphlet war with Cornwallis, wrote an extended manuscript history of the American War, and insisted that the government honor him properly for his service (he rejected an Irish barony). Only gradually were his friends able to get him some of the recognition and respect that he believed he deserved. They brought him back into Parliament (1790) and saw that he was promoted to general (1793) and made governor of Gibraltar (1794). But he never fully recovered from the humiliations of the American War. He died in London in December 1795.

Although there is no comprehensive list of Clinton's books, he was one of the most assiduous and thoughtful readers in the eighteenth-century British army. From at least 1760 until the end of his life, Clinton regularly made notes on his reading and service, regularly recorded his thoughts in leather-bound notebooks. Only occasionally did Clinton include the titles of the books that he was reading, but he did so often enough to make clear that he was reading many of the books most admired by his contemporaries in the British army. With the exception of treatises on fortifications and siegecraft, he read broadly and discriminatingly on war, ancient and modern. He knew intimately the works of Caesar, Vegetius, and Polybius; the campaigns of Turenne, Eugene, Marlborough, Frederick the Great, and Ferdinand of Brunswick; and the commentaries of Folard, Feuquières, Puységur, and Montecuccoli. He also kept up with the latest tactical treatises from

CHAP. XVIII.

Expedition up the North River under Sir Henry Clinton—Reduction
of the Forts Montgomery and Clinton.—Burning of Æsopus.

C H A P.
XVIII.

1777.
Expedition
up the North
River under
fir Henry
Clinton.

A BODY of recruits arrived from Europe at New York about the close of September 1777. This reinforcement enabled fir Henry Clinton to undertake an expedition which he could not before have attempted, without leaving the defences of New York too feebly guarded. It may here be obferved, that the fituation of New York, commanded in a variety of points, which were thence of neceffity to be occupied by the Britifh, had a very unfavourable influence on the conduct of the war; for the protection of that great depofitary of our ftores required fo confiderable a number of men as moft materially cramped exertion in the field. The object of fir Henry Clinton's expedition was to take poffeffion of the forts which forbad the paffage of our veffels up to Albany; and the ulterior view in the meafure was not fo much to create a diverfion in favour of general Burgoyne (the neceffity of which was not fufpected), as to open a communication which might have been important when that commander fhould have fixed himfelf at Albany. The enterprife was entirely fpontaneous on the part of fir Henry Clinton, and was conducted with more energy than moft of the military operations that took place in America. A force amounting nearly to three thoufand men was embarked on board craft of different kinds, convoyed by fome fhips of war under the command of commodore Hotham. This armament proceeded up the Hudfon

to

Sir Henry Clinton's marginalia in his copy of Charles Stedman's *History of the American War* (1794), 1:358, show how carefully Sir Henry read his history and how jealously he guarded his reputation nearly two decades after the American War. Clinton's own account of the war was not published until the twentieth century (see Willcox, *American Rebellion*).

Mésnil-Durand and Guibert to Dundas, Hinde, and Mirabeau. He retained, perhaps from his studies in France and his service in Germany and Eastern Europe, a slight preference for Continental authorities and for books written in French; but his preferences were very similar to those of British contemporaries. Of the thirty books on war that he specified in his notes, fourteen were among those most popular with his contemporaries in the British army.

However conventional his selection of books, Clinton's reading of those books was unusually idiosyncratic—unusually consistent with his thoughtful and cautious nature. Throughout his career he admired commanders who saw war in the broadest possible context, who made their plans consistent with the underlying political, economic, and geographic conditions that shaped war. So too did he admire commanders who made war with the fewest possible risks, who defeated their enemies with skillful combinations of skirmishes, maneuvers, and sieges. Clinton was particularly uneasy with commanders who sought to destroy their enemies in battle, noting "there is nothing I dread so much as these brave generals." If battle became unavoidable, he preferred turning the enemy's flank to attacking the center of his position, an attack that promised to disorder the enemy's army without incurring heavy casualties. Similarly, he favored tactical formations that offered the most security: columns of infantry for assaults on fortifications and for encounters with cavalry; three ranks of infantry—rather than two—for engagements with opposing infantry. He found support for his preferences throughout his reading, not just in books that shared his prudential approach to war. Most eighteenth-century British officers celebrated Julius Caesar as the personification of an aggressive commander. Clinton was less impressed with Caesar than he was with his enemies who were too shrewd to be drawn into battle with him. Clinton's was an unusually consistent and cautious understanding of war.

[*ODNB*; Namier and Brooke, *House of Commons*, 2:222–23; Gruber, "Education of Clinton," pp. 131–53; GB, WO, *List of the Army*, 1775; Gruber, "George III Chooses a Commander in Chief"; Willcox, *Portrait*. Clinton's reading notes are in "from Guicharde" and "Extracts from Projet de Tactique" in letter book in box entitled "Memoranda" [c. 1762–75], three untitled sheets in box marked "Arnold, Gibraltar, Intelligence, . . . Tactics" (n.d.), "Extract from Polien" in unmarked box at the end of the collection [post-1758], Clinton Papers, WLC; and in Clinton's notebooks, nos. 1–22, Clinton Papers, JRULM. His annotated copy of Stedman, *History of the American War*, is in the library of the Society of the Cincinnati in Washington, D.C.]

Cuthbert, Captain Thomas (fl. 1737–70).

Thomas Cuthbert entered the British army as an ensign in the 19th Regiment of Foot in 1737—on the eve of the great wars of the mid-eighteenth century. He remained with his regiment for more than thirty years, serving throughout the War of the Austrian Succession and the Seven Years' War and into the decade of peace before the War for American Independence; but he never rose above the rank of captain. That he should have advanced so slowly at a time of war when officers could win promotion by distinguishing themselves in combat or by moving from one regiment to another suggests that Cuthbert was a man of modest means and ambitions and had to be—or was—content to make a career as a company-grade officer in an established regiment. But if he lacked the money, patronage, and ambition for more rapid advancement, he was also unlucky. He was promoted to lieutenant in 1744 and to captain in 1756 just as wars were beginning; and his regiment did not see enough active service to accelerate his rise. The 19th went to the Continent during the War of the Austrian Succession and fought at Fontenoy (1745), Rocoux (1746, where Cuthbert was wounded), and Lauffeldt (1747). But the regiment remained at home throughout the Seven Years' War, seeing action only briefly in the attack on Belleisle off the coast of Brittany in the spring of 1761 (Cuthbert was there in May, just before the French surrendered). And Cuthbert retired from the army—after further service in England (1761–63) and at Gibraltar (1763–70)—well before the War for American Independence began. He died in Scotland about 1784.

Cuthbert's library, catalogued in February 1785, reflected both his modest means and limited military ambitions. Only three of his seventy-seven books were on war, and of those three, only *Regulations for the Prussian Infantry* was popular with his fellow officers. The others—a book illustrating the campaign of 1745 in the Low Countries and a book of advice for officers—appealed almost exclusively to Cuthbert.

[SAHR, *Army List of 1740*; Ferrar, *A History of the 19th Regiment*, pp. 69, 74, 76–77, 82–83, 87, 92, 94, 97; GB, WO, *List of the Army*, 1755–61, 1765–72, 1776, 1779; Skrine, *Fontenoy*, 367; and "Catalogue of Books which Belonged to . . . Captn Thomas Cuthbert," [c. Feb. 17, 1785], CC 8/12/13, SRO. Although Ferrar's *History*, p. 92, says that Cuthbert retired from the army "19th July 1778," it seems more likely that he retired in 1770; at least, he does not appear in any *List of the Army* after 1770.]

Dalrymple, Colonel Campbell (fl. 1740–63).

Dalrymple had a relatively brief and prominent career in the British army. He was commissioned in 1740 or 1741, probably in the 3rd Dragoons, a regiment that served on the Continent during the War of the Austrian Succession and was present at the battles of Dettingen and Fontenoy. By 1755 Dalrymple had become lieutenant colonel of the 3rd Dragoons. During the ensuing Seven Years' War, his regiment remained at home, and he undertook a study of war to provide suggestions for improving the army. Just before the results of that study were published in *A Military Essay* of 1761—and on the strength of a recommendation from his mentor, Field Marshal Lord Ligonier—Dalrymple became governor of Guadeloupe, a West Indian island recently captured from the French. He was also promoted to the rank of brigadier general in America and colonel in the British army. But in early 1763, as the end of the war and his governorship approached, he asked to be given a respite from further regular service with his regiment. He left the army in 1767.

His *Military Essay* became one of the three or four best-known books on war in English during the era of the American Revolution. He had written that book to improve the raising and training of the army. Inspired by the examples of ancient Greece and Rome and by the ideas of the celebrated French commander of the War of the Austrian Succession, Marshal Saxe, he began by recommending that the British army be recruited from hardy citizen soldiers, from the militia, rather than from the dregs of society who were lured or forced into service. He went on to emphasize discipline and systematic training in preparing soldiers for war—bringing regiments together for days of marching, firing, and maneuvering. His regiments would practice deploying from column to line and then advancing, retreating, and charging in line, all the while giving controlled fire. He would create relatively small, skilled armies in which infantry, cavalry, and artillery were closely coordinated. He would also require British commanders to write about their experiences of war—to provide the basis for a British art of war that would free his countrymen from dependence on contemporary French theorists.

The books that he recommended to support his ideas for renovating the army showed just how dependent he and his countrymen were on Continental authorities—ancient and modern. Dalrymple was not so exclusively devoted to foreign works as Samuel Bever; he did cite Orrery's *Treatise of the Art of War* and recommended English translations of the classics. But, except for Orrery, he referred almost exclusively to foreign authorities on the art of war; and those authorities were invariably among the authors preferred by his fellow officers. He cited Caesar, Polybius, Vegetius, and Thucydides among the ancients and Saxe, Feuquières, Folard, and Puységur among contemporary authors. How better to persuade his countrymen to improve their methods of raising and training soldiers than by referring to the most admired books on war? He, of course, did just that.

[SAHR, *Army List of 1740*; GB, WO, *List of the Army*, 1755, 1763, 1768; Skrine, *Fontenoy*, p. 367; Bolitho, *Galloping Third*, chap. IX; Dalrymple to Lord Bute, Feb. 27, 1763, Fortescue, *Correspondence of George the Third*, 3:44–50; Whitworth, *Ligonier*, p. 341; Dalrymple, *Military Essay*.]

Debbieg, General Hugh (1731–1810).

Debbieg was educated at the Royal Military Academy at Woolwich and served throughout his career as an engineer. Although he remained in the army for more than half a century, his active service began during the War of the Austrian Succession and ended soon after the War for American Independence. He left Woolwich in 1746 to take part in a raid on the French coast at L'Orient. He then joined British forces defending the Austrian Netherlands and distinguished himself at the Battle of Lauffeldt and the siege of Bergen-op-Zoom. After the Peace of Aix-la-Chapelle, he made military surveys both in the Low Countries and in Scotland. But in the Seven Years' War he served primarily in North America where as second-ranking engineer he helped conduct the successful siege of Louisbourg (1758) and went with General James Wolfe to capture Quebec the following summer. During the War for American Independence, he remained at home, building fortifications, conducting surveys, and giving the ministry advice on America and its people. He retired from active service soon after the war but continued to design fortifications and to advance in rank. He died in London in May 1810.

Debbieg's preferences in books on war—at least, those expressed in the purchases he made in June 1773—ran decidedly toward his specialty, engineering. He was then a well-educated and experienced officer who probably had his share of military books. But the auction of a General Officer's library that included more than two hundred books on war gave Debbieg a chance to fill out his collection. He did buy some very standard works: three books on engineering (Sturm's *Veritable Vauban*, Clairac's *L'Ingenieur de Campagne*, and Bisset's *Theory of Fortification*), two on artillery (Le Blond's *Traite de l'Artillerie* and Saint-Rémy's *Memoires d'Artillerie*), and one on the art of war (Feuquières's *Memoires*). But most of Debbieg's purchases—

a dozen books on fortification, military history, and the art of war—were peripheral rather than central works, books for an officer who had already assembled his basic library. Indeed, all of Debbieg's purchases tended to be somewhat older books (sixteen of eighteen had been published before 1750) and, in keeping with his emphasis on engineering—a field still dominated by the French—books that had been written in French or Dutch rather than in English (only one of eighteen was in English).

[GB, WO, *List of the Army*, 1759, 1775, 1779, 1786, 1789, 1798; Debbieg obituary, June 2, 1810, *The Times*, London, England; annotated copy, *Catalogue of the Library of a General Officer . . . 1773*, BL.]

Donkin, General Robert (1727–1821).

Donkin had a long and precarious career in the British army, a career that was retarded by a lack of money and family connections but advanced by talent, nerve, and good fortune. As he ruefully observed in 1777, he was one of those officers who, "without interest," could scarcely expect to rise above the rank of lieutenant colonel. Yet by taking advantage of opportunities created by the Seven Years' War, the War for American Independence, and the Wars of the French Revolution—and by outliving most of his generation— he rose well beyond his expectations.

Donkin entered the army late in the War of the Austrian Succession— probably about 1746 as an ensign in the 2nd Foot on the Irish establishment. By 1750 he was third in seniority among the ensigns of the 2nd and serving in Dublin under Lieutenant Colonel George Lord Forbes. He remained with the 2nd Foot in Ireland for nearly ten years, learning his regimental duties, imbibing Forbes's enthusiasm for Roman military virtues, and advancing to lieutenant (1754). But he was unable to go farther until the Seven Years' War brought an expansion in the army. In 1759 he followed Lord Forbes into the newly created 76th Foot, giving up the security of the established 2nd for the chance to purchase a captaincy in the 76th and, possibly, accelerate his career. Although Forbes moved on to command another regiment, Donkin stayed with the 76th to serve in expeditions that captured Belleisle off the coast of France in the spring of 1761 and Martinique in the West Indies in early 1762. When his colonel, William Rufane, was appointed governor of occupied Martinique, Donkin became a member of the governor's staff.

The Peace of Paris nearly ended Donkin's military career. The British government returned Martinique to France, disbanded the 76th Foot, and retired Donkin on half pay. Donkin had lost his gamble for preferment through the 76th. He had not abandoned his hopes for a career in the army. In 1764 he joined other ambitious British officers in Paris—to improve his knowledge of French and to study the art of war. But he was not able to return to active service until December 1770. Then, perhaps with the help of Rufane who had become a major general, Donkin managed to buy a captaincy in the 23rd Foot, an established regiment that would be secure against retrenchment but that would soon be sent to North America to sustain royal government against increasingly rebellious colonists. Although some British officers refused, under the circumstances, to serve in America, to use force against civilians, Donkin was not among them. In the spring of 1773 he sailed with the 23rd for New York. Within two years he would take part in the opening engagements of the War for American Independence.

The American War brought Donkin a variety of opportunities. During the campaigns at Boston and New York—from the spring of 1775 through the autumn of 1776—he served as a company commander in a regiment that was almost constantly in action. Donkin not only survived the fighting from Lexington and Concord to Fort Washington but also published his *Military Collections and Remarks* during the winter of 1776-77 at New York. His book, designed to raise money for the widows and orphans of British soldiers and to celebrate the military virtues of republican Rome, called attention to Donkin's learning and long service. The following summer, while he continued as a captain in the 23rd with the army en route to Philadelphia, he was promoted to lieutenant colonel and permitted to buy a majority in the 44th Foot. Donkin remained as major of the 44th for the ensuing two years while the regiment was with the army that occupied Philadelphia, withdrew through New Jersey, fought at Monmouth, and garrisoned New York City. In September 1779, when the 44th embarked for Quebec, Donkin sold his majority and became lieutenant colonel commanding the Royal Garrison Battalion, a provincial regiment that spent the remainder of the war defending Bermuda. Although the Royal Garrison Battalion would be disbanded in 1783, Donkin had by then gained a secure place among the senior officers of the army.

It seems unlikely that Donkin saw active service after the American War. But benefiting from a long life and from successive promotions of senior officers during the wars of the French Revolution and Napoleon, he gradually rose from colonel (1790) to major general (1794), lieutenant general (1801), and general (1809). He died at ninety-four in 1821, one of the last veterans of the Seven Years' War to remain in the list of general officers.

Donkin's career clearly affected his ideas about war. From his mentor, Lieutenant General George Lord Forbes, Earl of Granard, and from his own precarious service, he came to admire the military traditions of ancient Rome. He believed that republican Rome had conquered the world because it had an excellent military constitution—because its soldiers were citizens, because those citizens were obedient, hardy, and disciplined soldiers, and because every soldier could aspire to high command. Romans often chose men of talent to command their forces. Donkin particularly admired Julius Caesar, whom he thought the greatest general of antiquity, a general skilled in all aspects of war—from recruiting men to supplying forces, winning battles, and exploiting victories. Donkin also admired some of his contemporaries—commanders like the Duke of Marlborough and Frederick the Great—and he acknowledged that Britain had been successful in war. But he thought the basic military constitution of eighteenth-century Britain defective: civilians were too soft and selfish to be good soldiers; officers required too much influence and too little talent to gain promotion; and senior officers were too closely controlled by ministers to become great generals. To correct these defects and increase the power and security of Great Britain, the British need only embrace the military constitution of republican Rome.

In making these arguments in his *Military Collections and Remarks* of 1777, Donkin drew upon his experience in the British army, his knowledge of European military history and treatises on the art of war, and, above all, his and Lord Forbes's reading of the classics. With the exceptions of Frontinus and Polyaenus, he cited nearly all of the classical works on war that his contemporaries most admired: Caesar, Vegetius, Polybius, Thucydides, Xenophon, Arrian, Plutarch, and Aelianus—usually in the original Latin or Greek or, at least, in what he thought sound French translations. Beyond that, he referred regularly to the Duke of Marlborough's campaigns and to French and Continental authorities on the art of war: Saxe, Feuquières, Turenne, Puységur, and Montecuccoli. Donkin did not cite books on fortifications, siegecraft, and drill; and he completely ignored recent British books on war. But his references and quotations to the classics and to Continental books on the art of war (altogether, some twenty-five titles) included nearly all of the works most admired by his fellow officers.

[Donkin, *Military Collections*, esp. preface and pp. 58, 132, 134–35, 172, 207 for autobiographical details; Houlding, *Fit for Service*, pp. 109, 309, 414; GB, WO, *List of the Army*, 1755–60, 1763, 1768, 1772, 1775, 1777 (NY), 1778 (NY & Phila), 1779, 1779 (NY), 1786, 1798, 1804, 1811, 1822; Whitworth, *Ligonier*, pp. 348, 364–65; Nicolas, *Martinique*, 1:216; Stewart, *Service of British Regiments*, pp. 145–47, 208–10, 414; Gruber, "For King and Country," pp. 25–40; Peebles's diary, Sept. 10, 1779, Gruber, *John Peebles*, p. 292.]

Dormer, Lieutenant General James (1679–1741).

Dormer's career in the British army spanned the first four decades of the eighteenth century, but his principal service was confined to little more than a decade during the War of the Spanish Succession and the Jacobite rebellion of 1715. With a fine education, considerable wealth, and strong family connections, he was able to enter the army in 1700 as a lieutenant in the elite 1st Foot Guards. He soon proved that he was a loyal and effective officer. Wounded at Blenheim on the Danube in 1704, he recovered to raise a regiment in Ireland, to distinguish himself at Saragossa in Spain (1709), and to be captured at Brihuega (1710). He was then exchanged and commanded another regiment at the close of the war. In 1715, when Jacobites invaded England, he again raised a regiment and served as a brigade commander under his former commander from the war in Spain, Earl Stanhope. Although he saw no more combat, he continued to advance in the army—to colonel of the 6th Foot in 1720, to lieutenant general and colonel of the 1st Horse Grenadier Guards in 1738, and to governor of Hull in 1740. He died in Buckinghamshire in December 1741.

Notwithstanding his long career in the army, Dormer created a library better suited to a bibliophile than to a soldier. All except thirty of the more than three thousand books in his "elegant" collection were of a nonmilitary character: histories, memoirs, travel accounts, novels, poetry, religious tracts, and architectural studies. And of his thirty books on war, twenty-seven were either classical works or military histories. He owned no fewer than twelve different editions of Caesar's *Commentaries* and works by another eight classical authors including Vegetius, Thucydides, and Xenophon. His military histories were written mainly in the seventeenth century and dealt with Continental campaigns. Indeed, only four of his books on war were published after 1700, and of them only one reflected on the art of war—Feuquières's *Memoires*.

[*DNB*; SAHR, *Army List of 1740*; *Catalogue of the Library Collected by Lieutenant General Dormer* (London, 1764).]

Dundas, Colonel James (1721–80).

James Dundas of Dundas, Linlithgow, Scotland, saw only brief and fragmented service in the British army. The grandson of a soldier and eldest surviving son of an old Scottish family, Dundas had served as a company commander in the Scots brigade before entering the British army as a captain in the 25th Foot in the midst of the War of the Austrian Succession (1747). When that war ended and his regiment was reduced, Dundas abandoned a military career. In the ensuing twenty years, he settled into married life, succeeded his father as head of the Dundas family, won a seat in Parliament for Linlithgowshire, and became a burgess of Edinburgh. Not until 1779 when France, having intervened in the War for American Independence, threatened to invade Britain, did Dundas reenter the British army. To assist the government and to gain a colonelcy for himself, he volunteered to raise, train, and lead an infantry regiment, the 94th Foot. He did not serve long: he embarked with his new regiment for the West Indies but became ill and died at sea en route from St. Lucia to Jamaica in July 1780.

In the course of raising and training the 94th, Dundas acquired a "List of Some of the best Books upon Military Discipline to be study'd by a young officer." This list did not include books dealing with the details of drilling a company "as practice in Service brings a young man Insensibly to that." Instead the list was devoted, in about equal measure, to technical works on engineering and artillery and to works on the art of war. Among some twenty-four titles were the best-known books of that era: Vauban, Clairac, and Muller on engineering; and Folard, Feuquières, Saxe, and Turpin de Crissé on the art of war. The list was clearly up-to-date, including important new books like Guibert's *Essai Général de Tactique* of 1772 and a dozen other books published since 1750. Yet because the list emphasized engineering and the art of war, and because the French continued to dominate those specialties, two-thirds of the twenty-four books were in French.

["A List of Some of the best Books upon Military Discipline to be study'd by a young officer," 1779, Dundas of Dundas, Adv. MS, 80.7.2, NLS (quoted here); Namier and Brooke, *House of Commons*, 2:357; and GB, WO, *List of the Army*, 1780.]

Dury, Major General Alexander (d. 1758).

Alexander Dury served throughout his career in the British army in the elite 1st or Grenadier Foot Guards. He clearly had the wealth, competence, and commitment to rise steadily in his regiment and in the army. Commissioned an ensign in June 1721, he became a company commander in December 1738. Because his regiment did not go to the Continent for the opening campaigns of the War of the Austrian Succession, he remained in England, using his fluency in French to help the government arrest leading Jacobites and secure high-ranking prisoners of war. Early in 1747 he went with his regiment to join the allied army opposing the French in the Austrian Netherlands. He fought at Lauffeldt and was subsequently promoted to colonel and made commissary of forage and bread for the left wing of the army. He was promoted again—to major general—at the beginning of the Seven Years' War and given command of a brigade of the guards in expeditions against the French coast. During the abortive raid on St. Malo in September 1758, he was killed while covering the British withdrawal from St. Cas Bay.

Dury's library, which was sold soon after his death, reflected both his wealth and his strong, continuing enthusiasm for books on war. It was not unusual that a man of his means should have owned more than 500 books or that most of those books (the classics, histories, and memoirs, as well as poetry, plays, novels, and travel accounts) should have dealt with nonmilitary subjects. What was unusual about Dury's library was the size and strength of his military collection. More than a fifth of all of his books (some 120 titles) were on war; and his books on war included nearly all of the most recent and popular works (from Caesar and Vauban to Saxe, Muller, and Turpin de Crissé—11 of the 12 books that were most popular with his fellow officers). And because he died while still on active service, his military collection was unusually current (more than three-fifths of his books on war were published within twenty-five years of his death). Like other officers of his era, Dury owned more books on war in French than in English. Yet because he was especially interested in military history and in instructional manuals—in books that were more likely to be in English than books on the art of war or on fortifications and artillery—nearly two-fifths of his military titles were in English. Dury's was an unusually strong collection of recent books on war, including books on war in English.

[Dalton, *George the First's Army*, 2:264; Skrine, *Fontenoy*, pp. 367–69; SAHR, *Army List of 1740*; GB, WO, *List of the Army*, 1755; Whitworth, "Dury," pp. 146–53; Whitworth, *Ligonier*, pp. 260–64; *Catalogue of the Library of Gen. Alexander Dury*.]

General Officer (d. before June 1773).

Whatever the nature of his service in the British army, the "General Officer, Lately Deceas'd" whose books were auctioned by S. Baker and G. Leigh, booksellers, in June 1773, had an exceptionally fine collection of books on war. His whole library was not unusually large—about 550 titles—and there was nothing unusual about his nonmilitary books. He had the kind of mixture of scientific and humanistic works that often filled the shelves of English gentlemen: chemistry, astronomy, mathematics, and natural history, as well as history, philosophy, poetry, law, drama, religion, and architecture. But his military collection was truly exceptional for both its size and its quality. It was not just that the proportion of his library devoted to books on war, about 40 percent, was well beyond that for his contemporaries. It was also that he owned more books on war—some 220—than any of his fellow officers with even the most bookish instincts, more than twice as many as Dury or Ligonier or Oglethorpe or the "learned" Captain Winde.

So too was the quality of his collection exceptional. He owned thirty-five of the fifty military books that his contemporaries preferred to all others; and he frequently owned multiple copies of those most popular titles. Moreover, his collection was well balanced and up-to-date, divided roughly in quarters among the art of war, engineering and artillery, history and the classics, and drill and duty. Because he bought most of his books after 1740 (most were published after 1740), and because he bought books in a variety of European languages (more than two-thirds in French), he had clearly sought to keep abreast of the latest and best books on war and, to a remarkable extent, he had succeeded. It is difficult to think of more than a few books popular with his contemporaries—such as Thucydides, Grotius, and Arrian—that were not in his library in 1773.

[Annotated copy, *Catalogue of the Library of a General Officer*, BL.]

Gentleman in the Army.

This anonymous gentleman in the army, who sold his library when going abroad in 1799, was a man of wealth, learning, and—above all—eclectic interests. The 235 titles in his library dealt with an unusually wide range of topics. Like many of his fellow officers, he built his nonmilitary collection (224 titles) around his interests in history, biography, and the classics. And, like many other officers, he had a smattering of sermons, poetry, drama, philosophy, and travels. But his interests went well beyond these conventional topics to include the law, mathematics, natural history, and economics, as well as painting, music, and language.

Although his eclectic tastes did not extend to his books on war, those books did reflect a far stronger interest in the classics and in history than in the art of war: this gentleman was more a reader than a soldier. He had no book on engineering or artillery and no French treatise on fighting a battle or conducting a campaign. Instead, his books on war ran to the classics (Xenophon, Thucydides, Arrian, and Polybius—if not Caesar) and to modern military history (Voltaire's *Charles XII* and *Eugene and Marlbor-*

ough's Military History)—all save one in an English translation. His only current books on war were David Dundas's *Principles of Military Movements Chiefly Applied to Infantry* and a *List of the Army* for 1797. Whoever this gentleman was, his books were not those of a man preoccupied with soldiering.

[*A Catalogue of Books of a Gentleman in the Army*, HRHC.

A note with the microfilm edition of "Sotheby & Co Catalogues of Sales, 1734–1850" says that the "Gentleman in the Army" was C Hatfield; and GB, WO, *List of the Army*, 1759, 1768, 1772, 1779, 1786, 1789, and 1798 and Venn, *Alumni Cantabrigienses*, Part II, 3:286, show that there were three officers who had served in the British army and who might have been the C Hatfield who sold his library in 1799. But the evidence is not conclusive for any of the three. The most likely, to judge by the library (which included a history of the University of Cambridge and a number of books on the law), was Alexander Hatfield who was educated at Cambridge, admitted to the Inner Temple, and served in the 15th Light Dragoons from 1778 until he retired as a captain in 1791. By education, taste, and rank, Alexander Hatfield could easily have been the C (for Captain) Hatfield who sold his books in 1799. But Alexander was not then "in the Army" as the catalogue says, and he does not seem to have been a likely prospect for "going abroad" (he was a married man of forty-three with a prominent wife and children). Lieutenant Colonel John Hatfield might also have been the C Hatfield who sold his books. Hatfield had entered the army in 1757, served throughout the Seven Years' War and the War for American Independence in the 43rd Foot, gained a captaincy in a company of invalids in 1787, and remained in the army list in 1798 as a lieutenant colonel and captain of invalids. He might well have been the C (for Colonel) Hatfield who sold his books, perhaps in preparation for retiring abroad at the age of fifty-nine or sixty. But there is nothing in John Hatfield's service to connect him to the library that was being sold. A third prospect is another John Hatfield, who was in 1798 a captain on half pay—that is, a captain in a regiment that had been raised for the War for American Independence and disbanded at the peace. This, third Hatfield could have been a C (for Captain) Hatfield and could have been going abroad in 1799; but he was not exactly "in the Army" and there is no way to connect him with the contents of the library. Among the three Hatfields, the best candidate would be Alexander Hatfield, retired captain of light dragoons. There is not, however, a sure connection between Alexander and C Hatfield.]

Harrison, Captain Thomas (fl. 1755–63).

Thomas Harrison's service in the British army was relatively brief and obscure. He seems to have entered the army in 1751 or 1752, well before the Seven Years' War began in Europe. When the government subsequently mobilized for war, Harrison became a lieutenant in the newly created 56th Foot (December 1755). He remained in that regiment for the rest of his career and life, in a regiment that served in the British Isles until 1761 and, then briefly, in the West Indies. He died a captain and company commander of the 56th in 1763.

Harrison's library, reflecting the length of his service, taste, and means, was small and fragmented. Altogether, and counting magazines bound as books, he owned fewer than fifty books—many only vaguely described in the appraisal of his "goods" that followed his death. His nonmilitary books included a history of England, a small Bible, a book of advice for a family, and a practical guide to arithmetic. He did, it seems, appreciate poetry, owning fashionable translations of Horace and Ovid as well as the works of James Thomson, the Scottish poet, and four dictionaries.

His six military books were somewhat better focused than the rest of his library. In addition to a list of the army, his books dealt mainly with the history and the art of war, ancient and modern: two untitled treatises on the art of war in English, Guischardt's *Mémoires Militaires sur les Grecs et les Romains*, Sallust's works, and Frontinus's *Stratagemes*. Harrison was just getting started with his career and his library when he died.

[GB, WO, *List of the Army*, 1758–61, 1763, 1764; Houlding, *Fit for Service*, pp. 112, 130, 344; "A Declaration instead of an Inventory of all and singular the goods Chattels and Credits of Thomas Harrison Esquire late of the Parish of St. Margaret Westminster . . . and a Captain in the fifty sixth Regiment of foot . . . valued and appraised on the twenty second day of October in the year of Our Lord one thousand seven hundred and sixty three . . . ," PROB 3 60/32, PRO.]

Hawley, Lieutenant General Henry (c. 1684– or 1685–1759).

Hawley served in the British army for more than sixty-five years—rising from a cornet in the War of the Spanish Succession to a lieutenant general in the Seven Years' War. His career was built upon personal courage, royal patronage, and loyalty to the Protestant succession; but it was also marred by his shortcomings as a leader. Hawley liked to say that he "began the world with nothing," to create the impression that he had made his way in the army on talent alone. In fact, when his father, Colonel Francis Hawley, was killed in action during the War of the League of Augsburg, young Henry received considerable help from royal patrons and his own family. King William III promptly commissioned Henry, then a child of six or seven, an ensign in the army; Henry's uncle, Major General Erle, appointed him an aide-de-camp at age thirteen; and Queen Anne's consort, Prince George of Denmark, not only made him a cornet in an elite regiment at twenty but also arranged for him to sell his cornetcy at such a profit that he could afford a captaincy in the 4th Dragoons (1706). Hawley entered the War of the Spanish Succession as a captain and, once again, aide to his uncle—seeing action in Spain and gaining brevet promotion to major. By 1711, and with a gift of £1,000 from Queen Anne, he had bought the lieutenant colonelcy of his regiment. Hawley won another brevet promotion in 1712, became aide-de-camp to the new king (George I) in 1714, and was wounded leading his regiment against Jacobite rebels at Dunblane, Scotland, in 1715. Kings George I and II repaid his loyalty by giving him command successively of the 33rd Foot (1717), the 13th Dragoons (1730), and, over the objections of the ministry, the 1st Royal Dragoons (1740); George II also promoted him to brigadier general in 1735 and major general in 1739.

When the War of the Austrian Succession began, Hawley went to the Continent with his regiment and led the second line of British cavalry in George II's impressive victory at Dettingen in 1743. But Dettingen would mark the apex of Hawley's career. Thereafter, he would often be connected with or responsible for British failures. He commanded the cavalry in the allied defeat at Fontenoy in 1745. Early the following year—and while serving as commander in chief in Scotland—he led royalist forces to defeat at the hands of the Jacobite rebels at Falkirk Muir. He was given a chance to redeem himself, to command the left wing of the British army in the climactic battle of the rebellion, the Hanoverian victory at Culloden Moor in April of 1746. But on returning to the Continent, he once again commanded cavalry in a conspicuous allied defeat, the Battle of Lauffeldt in July 1747. That was his last important service. He went home, convinced that he had not been properly recognized. He was appointed to the staff in Ireland and, in 1752, to the lucrative governorship of Portsmouth. Yet when at the outset of the Seven Years' War, he was ordered to organize the defenses of Kent, his detractors pronounced him unfit for the task. James Wolfe, who had served under Hawley, observed that "they could not make choice of a more unsuitable person, for the troops dread his severity . . . and hold his military knowledge in contempt."

Wolfe was not alone in criticizing Hawley for being an excessively harsh disciplinarian. (Hawley acknowledged killing an officer who refused to obey orders.) But it is ironic that Wolfe should also have criticized Hawley for being ignorant of his duty. Hawley himself was highly critical of his fellow officers, saying that all too few of them became students of war and that not one in six colonels knew how to manage a regiment on campaign. Indeed, Hawley thought that all officers should be required to study the art of war— to read books, attend regimental courses in fortifications and tactics, take part in summer maneuvers, and pass examinations before each promotion. He would even have abolished the sale of commissions and provided retirement benefits to help refresh the officer corps.

Hawley did, moreover, read and reflect on some of the best books on war. He claimed that he had begun studying war as early as 1707, when he became a major; and he clearly continued to do so into the 1750s. He particularly admired Caesar's *Commentaries* and Saxe's *Traité des Legions* because both emphasized discipline and the value of close cooperation between infantry and cavalry. In the course of taking extensive notes on these books, he not only drew comparisons between them and the works of other authorities like Humphrey Bland and the Marquis Feuquières but also reflected on the campaigns of such famous commanders as Turenne, Eugene, and Marlborough. But Hawley does not seem to have read much beyond these basic books or to have shared his reading and reflections with other officers. He expected that others would have been surprised to know that he was a student of war. Wolfe certainly would have been.

[*DNB* (quoting Wolfe); Hawley's "Remarks on the Posthumous Treaty of Marechal Saxe of the Legions" [post-1753], "Some Remarks on the Discipline and Conduct of Regimental Officers, etc.," 1725, MS autobiography, n.d., and "Some Thoughts . . . Touchant le Millitaire," May 1725, Hawley Papers, 7411-24 ("Remarks" and "Some Remarks"), 7411-24-15 (Autobiography), and 7411-24-16 ("Thoughts"), NAM; GB, WO, *List of the Army*, 1755; Skrine, *Fontenoy*, pp. 73, 131.]

Hesse, Lieutenant Emanuel (d. 1759).

Emanuel Hesse served in the 60th or Royal American regiment of infantry from February 1756 until February 1759. He was a native of Hesse Cassel and one of several German officers in the first battalion of the 60th Foot. That battalion, which had been raised in North America, served primarily in New York and Pennsylvania from 1756 to 1758. In the fall of 1758 the first battalion was with Major General John Forbes when he captured Fort Duquesne (Pittsburgh) from the French. It is not clear whether Hesse took part in the Duquesne campaign; but he was with his battalion at Lancaster, Pennsylvania, during the following winter, and he died there on February 22, 1759, after a long illness.

Hesse owned a small number of fine books, some twenty-nine titles dealing mainly with military engineering. He did have two Bibles, two books of grammar, one of geography, and four of music. But the rest of his library was clearly and discriminatingly focused: no classics, no drill books, and no French treatises on the art of war but nearly all of the most widely admired books on engineering and siegecraft. He had Vauban's *De l'Attaque et de la Défense des Places*, Du Fay's *Maniere de Fortifier . . . de Vauban*, Clairac's *L'Ingenieur de Campagne*, Muller's treatises on the *Elementary Part of Fortification* and on the *Practical Part of Fortification*; and another seven books on engineering, including those of Goulon and Belidor. To complement these basic texts, he had histories of sieges as well as primers in mathematics, construction, and the proportional compass. His was a small but finely specialized collection.

[See Bulacher, Schlegel, and Klamp to Bouquet, Cassel, Jan. 18, 1760, "Inventory of the Effects of Hesse," (Philadelphia, Feb. 25, 1760), and "Unidentified List: Perhaps Continuation of Hesse's Effects," (Feb. 25, 1760?) in Waddell, *The Papers of Henry Bouquet*, 4:426–28, 469–71. It seems very likely that the "Unidentified List" is an inventory of Hesse's library. The list was drawn up by the same two men—Captain J. Schlösser of the 60th Foot and Johann Conrad Schweighauser, a Philadelphia merchant representing Hesse's family—who did the "Inventory of the Effects of Hesse"; the list includes printed music that might have been used by Hesse in playing the flute included in his "Inventory"; and the list contains an unusual number of books in German—Bibles, grammar, arithmetic, and other books—that could easily have belonged to Hesse but to few other British officers of that era. See GB, WO, *List of the Army*, 1759, for an identification of Schlösser and *Papers of Bouquet*, 4:426–28, 469–71, for notes on Hesse, Schweighauser, and Schweighauser's tie to Hesse's family.]

Hotham, Colonel Sir Charles (1693–1738).

Although Sir Charles Hotham served in the British army for thirty-two years, he was more a courtier than a soldier. He entered the army at age thirteen as a captain in his father's regiment, the 27th Foot; and he rose rapidly to lieutenant colonel of the 7th Dragoon Guards by 1720. But much of his youth was devoted to study and travel. He was an intelligent, athletic, and engaging young man who during a stay in Hanover became fluent in several languages and began a lifelong friendship with the future King George II of Britain. When Hotham was thirty in 1723, he succeeded his father as 5th baronet and was elected to the British House of Commons for Beverley in Yorkshire, a seat his father had held and that he would hold for all save two years during the remainder of his life. He subsequently married the sister of his good friend, Philip Dormer, the future 4th Earl of Chesterfield who was already a member of Parliament and who would become a celebrated diplomat, minister, and writer. With the accession of King George II in 1727, Hotham became a groom of the bedchamber and three years later, the king's special envoy to King Frederick William of Prussia. Although Hotham failed to negotiate a double wedding of the heirs apparent and princesses royal of Britain and Prussia, he won his king's approval by upholding the dignity of Great Britain in the face of the drunken, brutal, and inconsistent behavior of the Prussian king. He returned home to become successively colonel of the 18th Foot (1732) and of the 1st Troop of Horse Grenadier Guards (1735). He died in 1738 of a persistent illness.

There is no comprehensive list of Hotham's library. But his papers contain a collection of twenty-two pamphlets, published between 1676 and 1715, that deal with the military history of Europe and America at the turn of the eighteenth century. These pamphlets are all in English and are cast in the form of journals, memoirs, or brief histories. Most describe the sieges, battles, and campaigns of the wars of Louis XIV—beginning with his contests with the Dutch Republic and Spain in the 1670s but concentrating on events in the Low Countries during the War of the League of Augsburg and the War of the Spanish Succession when most of Europe was aligned against the French. The pamphlets also touch upon European struggles with the Ottomans along the Danube and upon Anglo-French campaigns in North America as well as English conquests of Ireland and Scotland. Hotham preserved what is a fine, small collection of English pamphlets on the wars of Louis XIV.

[Stirling, *The Hothams*, 1:115–238; Sedgwick, *House of Commons*, 2:152; and Pamphlets of Sir Charles Hotham (1693–1738), Hotham Papers, DDHO 20/154, 155, BJL.]

Hotham Thompson, Major General Sir Charles (1729–94).

Sir Charles Hotham Thompson served primarily as a staff officer during Britain's wars of the mid-eighteenth century. The son of the 7th Baronet Hotham and nephew of the 5th baronet, Sir Charles Hotham (1693–1738, q.v.), he was educated at Westminster School and the Middle Temple and commissioned an ensign in the 1st Foot Guards in 1746. In January 1747 he went with his regiment to Flanders where he took part in the Battle of Lauffeldt and became aide-de-camp to the Earl of Albemarle, commander of British forces in the Low Countries. Hotham had the education, intellect, and temperament to be a most effective aide; and he continued to serve Albemarle through the remainder of the War of the Austrian Succession. When the Seven Years' War began, Hotham was appointed aide-de-camp to Lord Ligonier, the British commander in chief, and then adjutant, successively, to the British forces that attacked St. Malo in 1758 and to the much larger British contingent that served in Germany under Prince Ferdinand of Brunswick during the remainder of the war. By 1763 Hotham was a colonel, a member of Parliament for St. Ives, and a favorite of the new king George III.

Although he remained in the army another twelve years and continued to take his military duties seriously, Hotham had neither the health nor the experience for high command. Unsuccessful in his attempt to become adjutant general of the army in 1763, he accepted appointments as groom of the bedchamber (1763) and colonel of the 63rd Foot (1765); and for three years, from 1765 to 1768, he was usually with his regiment in Ireland when Parliament was not in session. But by 1768, he had taken possession of his family estates in Yorkshire and seemed more interested in rebuilding his country house, Dalton Hall, than in pursuing a career in the army or politics. He left Parliament in 1768, gained the colonelcy of a regiment on the English establishment (the 17th Foot), and spent his time increasingly at Dalton. In 1771 he succeeded his father as 8th baronet and, the following year, took the name Thompson as part of an inheritance from his mother's family. When the War for American Independence began in 1775, Sir Charles was a major general and among those officers considered for a command in the colonies. The king soon chose other men to lead his forces; and Sir Charles, knowing that he was too senior to serve with his regiment in America, retired from the army. He died at Dalton in January 1794.

Sir Charles's library reflected not only his wealth, education, and cosmopolitan tastes but also his close associations with some of the most respected soldiers of his day. Most of the eight hundred titles on his shelves at Dalton Hall in 1784 touched on war only tangentially. Like other eighteenth-century English country gentlemen, Sir Charles had a great variety of books: from Bibles, sermons, and works of theology to memoirs, natural histories, and travel books to monthly magazines and current pamphlets. His collection was especially strong in drama, political history, and the classics—subjects that had diverted him since his years at Westminster School—and in furniture and architecture, which had become the preoccupation of his years at Dalton.

His books on war, roughly sixty in all, were just the books that were most admired by British army officers in the middle of the eighteenth century. Sir Charles had bought books on war in the twenty years since the Seven Years' War: memoirs, a biography, and a book on the art of war. But his most active collecting had ended with his most active service in the army. Even so, the books on war that he owned in 1784 were a remarkably fine collection. He had eleven of the fifteen works that were most admired by his fellow officers—from Caesar and Vauban to Folard and Feuquières to Turenne and Thucydides. And his collection included books on every aspect of war— from the classics to the modern art of war, from engineering and artillery to infantry tactics, from history and biography to the laws of war and peace, and from memoirs to lists of the British army. Most of his books were in English or French; a few, in Latin, Italian, and Spanish. The only conspicuous omissions from his library were the most recent French books on the art of war—Saxe, Turpin de Crissé, and Guibert—and several standard works on engineering, including those of Clairac and Muller. His library did show a slight Prussian bias, but it was, on the whole, a wonderfully balanced approach to the books on war that British officers found most authoritative in the mid-eighteenth century.

[Namier and Brooke, *House of Commons*, 2:641–43; Stirling, *The Hothams*, 2:1–261; Sir Charles Hotham's MS Autobiography, n.d., reading notes, n.d., Catalogue of the Books at Dalton, 1784, and books now with his letters and papers, Hotham Papers, DDHO 4/293 (autobiography), DDHO 4/283, 284 (reading notes), DDHO 20/159 (catalogue), and DDHO 4/287 and 20/120 (books), BJL; and Gruber, "George III Chooses a Commander in Chief," pp. 175, 178, 180.]

Howe, Major William (fl. 1715–32).

Scarcely anything is known of the life and service of Major William Howe whose books were inventoried in January 1734. It does seem likely that he was the William Howe who entered the British army as a minor and captain in the Earl of Hertford's or 15th Regiment of Foot in 1711 and who became a company commander in the same regiment (by then called Harrison's) in August 1715. It also seems likely that he remained a captain for many years (in 1740 an officer had served on average twenty-six years before reaching the rank of major in an infantry regiment). Promotion was slow in the three decades following the War of the Spanish Succession because Britain was more often at peace in those years than at any other time between 1688 and 1815. The army had come home from the War of the Spanish Succession to do little more than put down an occasional minor rebellion in Scotland, keep order elsewhere in the British Isles, and garrison outposts in the overseas empire. In 1719 Howe's regiment helped disperse Jacobites and several hundred Spanish troops at Glenshiel in the Scottish Highlands. But the 15th had not gone north to meet an earlier rebellion in 1715; and it did not engage in the retaliatory raid on the Spanish port of Vigo in 1719 or join in the defense of Gibraltar in 1727. In those years, the 15th moved about England, occasionally gathering for training, reviews, or peacekeeping. Perhaps around 1730 Howe was promoted to major; at least, it was about that time that he bought a copy of Humphrey Bland's *Military Discipline*, a book that was first published in 1727 and that would have been especially useful to a new major in training his regiment to maneuver and fire. But it seems unlikely that Howe served long as a major. He was dead before 1734, before his fortieth birthday.

The inventory of his library, taken in January 1734, suggests that Howe had little interest in books on war. Only two of his forty-nine books were on military topics, and those two—Bland's *Military Discipline* and *Rules and Articles for the Government of His Majesty's Horse and Foot Guards*—were virtually required reading for field-grade officers in the army of George II. The new king, who had reviewed the 15th at Blackheath in 1728, was trying to bring some uniformity to his regiments, some standardized ways of training and fighting. Howe's military reading seems to have begun and ended with those books.

[Dalton, *English Army Lists*, 6:389; Dalton, *George the First's Army*, 1:154, 189; Houlding, *Fit for Service*, pp. 35, 42, 67, 95, 178–79, 300, 399; Inventory of Books of Major Wm Howe, Jan. 29, 1734, CC 8/12/8/1, SRO.

Musgrave, *Obituary*, 3:265, lists an obituary for William Howe, colonel in the army, citing the *London Magazine*, for 1732, p. 97, and saying that Howe died May 22, 1732. But Howe's obituary does not appear in the *London Magazine* for 1732, and the reference may not be to Major William Howe of the 15th Foot.]

Ligonier, Field Marshal John Earl (1680–1770).

Ligonier had an unusually long and successful career in the British army— from a volunteer at the outset of the War of the Spanish Succession to a field marshal and commander in chief at the close of the Seven Years' War, nearly sixty-five years of active service that placed him among the most accomplished and important of all eighteenth-century British soldiers. He made his reputation at first on personal courage, persistent concern for his men, and tactical skill. Born in France, he became a Protestant refugee in 1697 and then a volunteer in Queen Anne's army at the beginning of the War of the Spanish Succession. He was soon able, with the help of an uncle, to purchase a captaincy in the 10th Foot (1702) and to show his aptitude for leading men in combat. He took part in Marlborough's principal battles and sieges from Blenheim to Malplaquet—winning brevet promotion to major for leading the assault at the siege of Menin, escaping more than twenty bullets that pierced his clothing at Malplaquet, and emerging from nine years of campaigning on the Danube and in the Low Countries as a colonel (1711). Following an interlude as commander of the garrison on Minorca, from 1713 to 1716, and a brief assignment as adjutant to the British commander during the attack on the Spanish port of Vigo in 1719, he settled in Ireland with his new regiment, the 8th Horse. For two decades, while he lived in Dublin and served as a Privy Counsellor to George I and as an aide-de-camp to George II, he concentrated on making his regiment a model for discipline and morale.

During the War for the Austrian Succession, Ligonier showed that he was more than a fine regimental commander, that he had the administrative and tactical skills to lead far larger bodies of men. In 1740 he accompanied George II to Hanover to command troops and to serve as the king's chief of staff. He was a lieutenant general and division commander during the allied victory at Dettingen in 1743. Subsequently, he served well in a succession of allied defeats. He led the sixteen thousand allied infantry at Fontenoy in 1745 (shattering the center of the French army and covering the subsequent allied withdrawal), the British contingent of thirty thousand at the Battle of Rocoux in 1746 (inflicting disproportionate casualties on the French and withdrawing coherently in the face of a more numerous enemy), and the allied cavalry at Lauffeldt in 1747 (using the cavalry to keep the French from destroying the allied army). At war's end he was greatly honored for his service. He had already been promoted to general (1746). He was now elected to Parliament (1748); made a member of the Privy Council (1749); and appointed successively lieutenant general of ordnance (1749), colonel of the 2nd Dragoon Guards (1749), governor of Plymouth (1752), and colonel of the Royal Horse Guards (1753).

Although he would not again command an army in the field, Ligonier was to prove as commander in chief during the Seven Years' War that he was a fine strategist as well as an able administrator. From 1756 to 1763, he worked with various ministries—but especially with that of the Duke of Newcastle and William Pitt—to raise and train ever-larger forces, to choose able commanders, and to coordinate strategies for a war that spread from North America to Western Europe, the West Indies, Africa, India, and the Philippines. He recommended younger officers like Jeffrey Amherst and James Wolfe for important commands. He organized raids on the French coast and sent troops to Germany to save Hanover and support Prussia. He helped Pitt develop the plans and provide the forces that eventually conquered Canada in 1760. And he organized the defenses of Britain when the French threatened invasions. Even after George III came to the throne and both Pitt and Newcastle resigned, Ligonier continued to organize the forces needed to combat the French in Germany and India and the Spanish in Portugal, Cuba, and the Philippines—to help Britain gain a favorable peace. His influence waned under the new king, and he lost some of his appointments; but he emerged from the Seven Years' War a field marshal, a colonel of the 1st Foot Guards, and an earl in the English peerage. He died in April 1770.

Ligonier's library reflected not just his long service and increasing wealth but also his conviction that a soldier needed to be a student of war. He did not have an unusually large proportion of military books in his library; only about one hundred of his fourteen hundred books dealt with war. But Ligonier's hundred books represented one of the largest, most comprehensive, and most discriminating collections of military books owned by any eighteenth-century British officer. Only three of our forty-two officers owned more books on war than Ligonier; and none of the forty-two had a better-balanced collection than he. About a third of his books were devoted to military history; about a third, to the art of war; and about a third, to engineering, the classics, and drill. His collection included, moreover, an unusually high proportion of the most widely admired books on war—all of the ten most popular with his contemporaries in the British army and two-thirds of the top thirty. His was just the collection that might have been expected of a man who had served a long time and in a variety of positions and who had kept up with his reading (two-thirds of his books had been published in the last one-third of his life). He clearly remained a student of war to the end of his career.

[Whitworth, *Ligonier*; *DNB*; GB, WO, *List of the Army*, 1763; Namier and Brooke, *House of Commons*, 2:43; and *Catalogue of the Library of Ligonier*, pp. 147–63.]

Sir John Ligonier, whose likeness appeared in John Entick's *General History of the Late War* (1763–64), 2:308, was British commander in chief during the Seven Years' War and one of the army's most influential students of warfare. His protégés included Sir Henry Clinton, Campbell Dalrymple, and James Wolfe.

Maxwell, Sir William (c. 1715–71).

Remarkably little is known about Maxwell's service in the British army. He was born about 1715, the eldest son of the 2nd baronet. He succeeded his father in 1730 and entered the army as an ensign in the 6th Foot in 1734. Promotion was slow in that decade of peace, and Maxwell remained an ensign when his regiment returned from Ireland to England at the beginning of the war with Spain in 1739, the War of Jenkins' Ear. Perhaps because a substantial number of the men in his regiment were drafted into the marines in 1739, the 6th Foot did not serve on the Continent in the War of the Austrian Succession. Nor, except for two of its companies that were among the British troops routed at Prestonpans in October 1745, did the 6th fight in Scotland during the Jacobite rebellion of 1745–46. And the 6th seems to have missed much of the action in the Seven Years' War while serving as part of the garrison at Gibraltar from 1753 until at least 1761. It is not clear how long Maxwell remained with his regiment: he was in the army list of 1740 and out of the list by 1755. He seems to have retired to his seat, Merton Hall, near Monreith, Wigtownshire, in southwest Scotland. He died in Edinburgh in August 1771.

To judge by his library, Maxwell never developed a strong interest in his military service. Fewer than twenty of the thirteen hundred titles in his library at Merton Hall in 1769 dealt with war. He did have nine volumes of the army lists (published between 1755 and 1768) which suggest that he kept up with fellow officers even after he left the army; and he did own Saxe's *Reveries*, showing that as late as 1757 he was interested in the larger issues of raising, training, and leading men to war. But he had no books that would have helped him understand his duty as a company or field-grade officer, nothing to teach him how to control the fire and movement of men in battle or to manage them in camp. His interests were primarily in the art, law, and history of war; and in those fields he had some very fine books: Caesar's *Commentaries*, Grotius's *De Jure Belli ac Pacis*, and Montecuccoli's *Memoires*, as well as standard works on Cromwell, Marlborough, and the military and naval history of Scotland and Britain. His interests in war were more those of a prominent and well-educated country gentleman than of a soldier.

[*Burke's Peerage*; Cokayne, *Complete Baronetage*, 4:311; SAHR, *Army List of 1740*; GB, WO, *List of the Army*, 1755, 1759, 1768; Houlding, *Fit for Service*, pp. 45, 109–10, 122, 353; Skrine, *Fontenoy*, pp. 367–70; Prebble, *Culloden*, pp. 317–18; "Inventory of the books at present in Sir William Maxwell Baronet of Monreith his library at Merton, 1 March 1769," CC 8/12/12, SRO.]

Molyneux, Colonel Thomas More (c. 1725–76).

Molyneux was an officer in the elite Scots Guards during Britain's wars of the mid-eighteenth century. Because his regiment saw limited active service and because he was of a reflective nature, Molyneux was better known as a writer than as a soldier. The second son of a prominent Surrey landowner, he was educated at Wadham College, Oxford (B.A., 1745), and commissioned an ensign in the Scots Guards in 1747. It is possible that he served with his regiment both in an expeditionary force that raided the French coast in 1757 and in the allied army that fought in Germany under Prince Ferdinand of Brunswick later in the war. It is certain that he had the time and inclination during those war years—presumably while the guards were posted in London—to write extensively on British tactics and operations. In 1756 he published *The Target*, a study of defensive tactics for infantry. Three years later, he completed a more detailed history and analysis of British amphibious operations, *Conjunct Expeditions*. By then, Molyneux had also succeeded his older brother as a member of Parliament for Haslemere, the Sussex borough where his family owned "considerable property" and had a strong electoral interest. He would retain that seat for the rest of his life, voting often with the government (to support British laws in North America during the Stamp Act crisis of 1766) but retaining his independence and a reputation for eccentricity. By the end of the Seven Years' War, Molyneux was both a member of Parliament and a captain and lieutenant colonel in the Scots Guards. Although he was promoted to colonel in 1773 and remained in the guards when the War for American Independence began, he did not accompany his regiment to New York in 1776; and he does not seem to have been considered seriously for a command in America. He died in October 1776.

Whatever his reputation as a regimental officer, Molyneux was known for his military writings, particularly his study of Britain's amphibious operations, *Conjunct Expeditions*, which was published in London in 1759 at the height of the Seven Years' War and at a time when raiding warfare was essential to British strategy. He began his study with a history of joint expeditions since the first century B.C., a history designed to show that most of those expeditions had failed—primarily because generals and admirals neither prepared carefully nor cooperated effectively. For every successful raid on a foreign port, there were numerous conspicuous failures. The larger the expedition the more likely it was to fail. When there were more than four thousand men in the landing party, commanders had found it difficult to disembark rapidly enough to achieve the tactical surprise essential in raiding warfare; and larger forces were usually employed against better prepared enemy defenses. But with depressing consistency expeditions had failed for want of basic planning and cooperation. Forces sailing without adequate artillery, cavalry, and entrenching tools were not likely to succeed, particularly when their generals and admirals could not agree. The most recent raid on the French port of St. Malo had ended with the loss of seven hundred men killed, wounded, and captured—a heavy price, Molyneux said, for a diversionary attack.

Molyneux did think the British could do much better. With systematic preparations, expeditionary forces could strike quickly, forcefully, and securely. He would employ new flat-bottomed boats to land three regiments of infantry in order of battle, fully organized to engage the enemy. He would build other shallow-draft boats that could bring artillery close to the shore—boats mounting twenty-four-, nine-, and six-pound guns to support the infantry as it disembarked and was most vulnerable to enemy forces. These artillery boats would also be able to maneuver close to fortifications guarding harbors and rivers, bringing heavy fire on works that might otherwise have been impervious to the guns of the fleet and army. And by including horses to draw artillery and provide mounts for dragoons, Molyneux's forces would have the mobility and firepower to be secure almost anywhere ashore. Indeed, forces so organized and equipped would be able to disembark and reembark with such freedom as to enjoy the surprise that would make amphibious warfare consistently effective.

In writing *Conjunct Expeditions,* Molyneux drew upon a remarkably wide range of books, ancient and modern. It was not just that he had the education, time, and motivation to assemble an impressive bibliography; he also had the scholarly instincts to compare and evaluate conflicting interpretations that reflected national and personal biases. He made particularly effective use of some twenty-five general histories, books that treated warfare as a part of larger political histories. His guides to the ancient world were Temple Stanyan's *Grecian History* and Lawrence Echard's *Roman History,* as well as classical texts. For early Britain he relied on a synthesis of such sixteenth-century English chroniclers as Raphael Holinshed, John Stowe, William Camden, and John Speed and the seventeenth-century biographer John Spelman, whose *Life of Alfred the Great* showed how innovative Britons could be in repelling raiders from the sea. For an understanding of Anglo-French conflicts in the seventeenth and eighteenth centuries, Molyneux regularly compared the British histories of Abel Boyer and John Oldmixon with the French of Gabriel Daniel, Isaac de Larrey, and Voltaire. He read Samuel F. Pufendorf for a wider, European perspective.

Molyneux relied even more heavily on books about war, citing in the marginalia of *Conjunct Expeditions* more than fifty titles in military history and theory. His selections included many of the best-known books on war of his era. He took illustrations and principles from the standard classical works of Caesar, Vegetius, Polybius, Thucydides, Frontinus, and Polyaenus. He referred repeatedly to such contemporary, Continental authorities on the art of war as Folard, Feuquières, Puységur, Montecuccoli, and Santa Cruz de Marcenado. Although he did not cite Saxe's or Turpin de Crissé's treatises or do more than mention Vauban, Eugene, and Frederick the Great, he made comprehensive use of authoritative naval and military histories. Campbell and Lediard were his primary guides to the British navy; Ramsay and Turenne, to Turenne; Voltaire to Charles XII; and Quincy and Voltaire, to the military history of Louis XIV. For more recent amphibious operations, he gathered pamphlets and other firsthand accounts from opposing sides. Molyneux wrote history to instruct his fellow soldiers, and he wanted that history to be persuasive and reliable, based on the most authoritative books that he could find.

[Namier and Brooke, *House of Commons*, 1:386, 2:148; Foster, *Alumni Oxonienses 1715-1886*, 3:967; Houlding, *Fit for Service*, pp. 19, 32, 202 n.97; GB, WO, *List of the Army*, 1759, 1768, 1775; Molyneux, *Conjunct Expeditions*; *Gentleman's Magazine*, Oct. 1776.]

Montresor, Captain John (1736–99).

John Montresor served as an engineer in the British army for nearly twenty-five years—exclusively in North America from the Seven Years' War to the War for American Independence. Born at Gibraltar and educated as an engineer, Montresor followed his father into the army. In 1754 he became an ensign in the 48th Foot and an additional engineer under Major General Edward Braddock, commander of British forces in America. He was wounded when Braddock's army was destroyed near Fort Duquesne in July 1755. But Montresor recovered to prove a valuable and versatile subordinate to a succession of British commanders as they sought first to protect the frontiers of the British colonies and then to conquer Canada. He led detachments along the upper Hudson River in the summer of 1756, accompanied the British commanders in chief to Halifax in 1757 and Louisbourg in 1758, cleared enemy forces from Cape Breton in the winter of 1758, and went with James Wolfe to Quebec in 1759 (commanding the light infantry company of the 48th Foot during the ensuing siege and battle). He endured harsh winter weather as well as enemy attacks to convey dispatches between British commanders in Canada and New York in 1760; and as the war in North America came to an end, he was busy surveying the Kennebec and St. Lawrence Rivers.

Montresor remained with the British army in America after the Peace of Paris, serving in a variety of roles and establishing himself as a prominent military engineer. When in 1763 Indian tribes attacked the northwest frontiers of the colonies, he led an expedition to relieve the British garrison at Detroit. The next year he returned to improve the defenses of Detroit and to seek peace with the western tribes at Sandusky. He was now married, and after he settled his family on an island near New York City, he devoted himself increasingly to traditional engineering duties. He had emerged from the Seven Years' War with the rank of practitioner engineer. He went to Britain in the winter of 1765–66 to seek preferment and returned as engineer extraordinary and barrackmaster in North America. British leaders were by then shifting their army from the frontiers to the cities of North America—

in part, at least, to intimidate the colonists who were growing increasingly violent in their resistance to British rule. Montresor built barracks and fortifications from Boston to Albany to New York City and Philadelphia. He also surveyed the boundary between New York and New Jersey. By the time the colonists and regulars fought at Lexington and Concord in the spring of 1775, Montresor was with the army at Boston.

That autumn he became chief engineer in America and aide-de-camp to the new British commander in chief, General William Howe. Montresor would serve in those posts for more than two and a half years while Howe shifted his forces from Boston to the middle colonies and tried to use a combination of force and persuasion to end the rebellion. Montresor was with Howe at the evacuation of Boston and the capture of New York City in 1776; he accompanied him into New Jersey during the spring of 1777; and later that summer he assisted him in the Pennsylvania campaign, directing British artillery during the Battle of Brandywine, building defensive works about Philadelphia, and helping open the Delaware River to British shipping in the fall. When Howe resigned his command in May 1778, Montresor remained briefly as chief engineer to the new commander in chief, Sir Henry Clinton. Montresor was with the army as it evacuated Philadelphia and marched and fought its way through New Jersey to New York City in 1778; but failing to keep Clinton's confidence, he resigned his posts and sailed for England.

Montresor's career in the army had ended. He sold his commission in March 1779, bought an estate in Kent, and devoted the remainder of his life to raising his family and clearing the complicated accounts from his service in America. He did testify during the Parliamentary inquiry into General Howe's conduct of the American War in May 1779—giving tepid support to his former commander in chief. He put far more energy into clearing his own accounts. He succeeded at first in winning reimbursement for many of the expenses he claimed to have incurred in America, and he used the funds he received not just to buy additional properties in Kent and in London but also to travel with his family for extended periods on the Continent. But the government eventually disallowed many of his claims; and in 1798 he lost much of his property and his liberty. Montresor died in debtors' prison June 26, 1799.

His library, which contained more than eight hundred books and two thousand maps, drawings, and plans, reflected both his career as a military engineer and his life as a country gentleman. His tastes in books that did not deal directly with war were unusually varied, ranging from history and biography to travel, poetry, drama, music, theology, law, art, religion, medicine, and astronomy—with a preference for history, travel, music, and theology. Much the same was true of his sixty-seven books on war: they covered a wide range of topics but showed a decided preference for history, engineering, and the art of war and for books that were admired by his contemporaries. He had histories and biographies dealing with great events and personalities in Western warfare from ancient Greece and Rome to the eighteenth century—from Alexander the Great and Hannibal to Vauban, Marlborough, Eugene, and Saxe. There was some emphasis on sieges in the Low Countries, but there were also accounts of campaigns overseas from North America to the West Indies and India. So too were his books on engineering and the art of war carefully chosen. They included half of the twenty titles most often preferred by British officers of his day, titles such as Clairac's *Field Engineer* and Coehoorn's *Nouvelle Fortification*; Bland's *Treatise of Military Discipline* and *Regulations for the Prussian Infantry*; and Saxe's *Reveries* and Guibert's *Essai Général de Tactique*. Although Montresor retired from the army in 1779, he continued to buy books on war—in both French and English—through the 1780s and 1790s. His remarkable collection of drawings, plans, and maps included the work of other engineers and cartographers, but most were his own careful creations, plans of fortifications and barracks as well as maps of rivers, bays, and roads in North America, the West Indies, Europe, and Africa.

[*DAB*; *ANB*; *DNB*; GB, WO, *List of the Army*, 1759, 1768, 1772; Gruber, *Howe Brothers*, p. 343; *First Part of W. Collins's Catalogue for 1800. Part of the Library of John Montresor*; *W. Lowe's Catalogue for 1800. Containing Books of John Montressor*.]

Moyle, Lieutenant Colonel Thomas Coppinger (fl. 1766–87).

Thomas Coppinger Moyle had a relatively brief but successful career as an officer with the 28th Foot in Ireland, North America, and the West Indies during the American Revolution. It is possible that he had been in America at the end of the Seven Years' War—as a junior officer in a regiment that was disbanded in 1763. He entered the 28th as an ensign in March 1766 when the regiment was struggling to preserve its discipline and to sustain royal government in the British colonies of North America. The next year his regiment rotated to Ireland where it continued to struggle to maintain its discipline and to uphold the law while Moyle rose from ensign to captain (by July 1770). When the War for American Independence began, Moyle and the 28th returned to America to serve at New York and Philadelphia in the campaigns of 1776 and 1777 and to go on to the West Indies in the fall of

1778. By 1779 Moyle was the senior captain in his regiment and during the next year became a major in the army. At the end of the war, he returned to England and served as the lieutenant colonel of the 13th Foot (August 1783). He retired from the army in 1787.

Moyle was—to judge by the books that he took to America—a determined and discriminating reader. Not daunted by the difficulty of keeping up with books while on campaign, Moyle had at New York in June 1777 some thirty-eight titles or, allowing for multivolume sets, a total of eighty-four books. His preferences were clearly those of a cultivated man and a practical soldier, a man interested primarily in English literature and military engineering. He had a small, strong collection of poetry and drama: Shakespeare's and Pope's works, Milton's *Paradise Lost*, and selections from Thompson, Cotton, and Sommerville. He also had a half-dozen contemporary novels by Sterne, Fielding, Mackenzie, and Cleland; satires by Churchill, Rousseau, and Goldsmith; two runs of English periodicals; and four books dealing with horses and racing. Presumably because he was by 1777 well acquainted with his duty as a company commander, he had only five books on war—four of which were practical treatises on military engineering and one a book of advice for a junior officer. Moyle clearly preferred to take his engineering—and his literature—from works in English: from John Muller's books or Pleydell's translation of *An Essay on Field Fortification . . . for the Use of an Officer of Infantry*. His traveling library was large and unusually well focused.

[Ford, *British Officers in American Revolution*, pp. 11, 132; GB, WO, *List of the Army*, 1765, 1768, 1772, 1775, 1776, 1779, 1782, 1786, 1789; Houlding, *Fit for Service*, pp. 98, 131, 315; Shy, *Toward Lexington*, p. 383; Stewart, *Service of British Regiments*, pp. 160–62; Everett, *Somerset Light Infantry*, pp. 106, 396; "Catalogue of Books Capt. Moyle" after entry in John Peebles's diary, June 13, 1777, Cunninghame of Thorntoun Papers, GD 21/492, 3, SRO.]

Murray, General Lord John (1711–87).

Lord John Murray served in the British army for nearly sixty years, becoming eventually the most senior general in the army. Yet he gained remarkably little satisfaction from his long service and high rank. He began his career in 1727 when King George II brought him into the elite 3rd Foot Guards—presumably to benefit from his talents and to ensure the allegiance of his half brother, the 2nd Duke of Atholl, a prominent Anglo-Scottish politician. Lord John proved loyal to the Hanoverians and advanced rapidly in the army. When the War of the Austrian Succession began, he went to Flanders as aide-de-camp to the king, became colonel of the quintessentially Scottish regiment (the 42nd Foot or Black Watch) in 1745, and commanded British detachments in the campaign of 1747 (performing well against superior French forces). But the campaign of 1747 marked the end of his active service. He was a major general when the Seven Years' War began and too senior to accompany his regiment to America without a separate command—a command that he was never able to get. He quarreled with two of the most powerful men in Scotland—the Dukes of Argyll and Atholl—over the control of his regiment; he neglected the interests of his constituents in Perthshire and lost his seat in Parliament; and when he appealed to the ministry for a command, he was rejected. Nor did he fare better during the War for American Independence. He had been a dutiful colonel of his regiment—keeping up its strength, providing books for the officers, securing pensions for disabled veterans, and allowing veterans to live rent free on his lands. But by 1775 he was an aging and comparatively inexperienced general—too inexperienced to compete successfully for a command in North America. He did raise a second battalion for his 42nd, completely at his own expense, but never got the command that he sought. He died in Paris in 1787.

Lord John Murray commissioned inventories of his books in 1762. Those inventories revealed a library that was sound and comprehensive but also dated, a library that a well-educated and successful general might have owned in the 1740s. Altogether, Murray had about 450 books in 1762, including some 48 on war. Those on war, like the rest of his collection, dealt primarily with history and the classics: Caesar's *Commentaries*, Marlborough's campaigns, and narratives of the War of the Austrian Succession. Murray also had small collections of treatises on engineering (including Vauban's), on the duty of junior officers (multiple copies of Bland's *Treatise of Military Discipline*), on the art of war, and on the laws of war. But, with the exception of books like Turpin de Crissé's *Essai sur l'Art de la Guerre* of 1754 and Cambridge's *Account of the War in India* of 1761, there was little in his library that had been published after 1750. His military collection, like his career, seemed to have flourished in the 1740s. He owned no more than about a third of the books that other officers most admired in the era of the Seven Years' War and the War for American Independence.

[*DNB*; Namier and Brooke, *House of Commons*, 2:186–87; Townshend, *Life of Townshend*, p. 114; Forbes, *Black Watch*, p. 92; "Memr of Lord John Murrays Service in the Army," n.d., "Catalogue of my books at Perth," Mar. 29, 1762, "Catalogue of my books that were sent to London April 7, 1762," Mar. 29, 1762, and "Catalogue of my books at London," June 23, 1762, Lord John Murray Papers, 17/1/7 (service) and 5/3/7 (catalogues), JRULM. See as well "Lord John Murray's miscellaneous military papers," n.d., for his reading notes on John O'Rourke's *Treatise on the Art of War* (1778) and Lord John Murray to Revrd. Mr. Fagan, Nov. 5, 1767, for his having given military books to the officers of the 42nd, Murray Papers, 5/2/16 and 5/1/1-110, JRULM.]

Murray, Brigadier General Robert (1689–1738).

Murray's career in the British army never quite fulfilled its promise. Born into a prominent Scottish family—the son and brother of successive Earls of Dunmore—he entered the elite 3rd Foot Guards in 1705 during the War of the Spanish Succession. Whatever his wartime service, he gained only steady promotion; and once the fighting was over, he had little opportunity for active service during the rest of his career. His regiment did not take part in putting down the Jacobite rebellions of 1715 and 1719, and only one battalion of the regiment embarked for the attack on the Spanish port of Vigo in 1719. During the ensuing decades of peace, Murray sat as a member of Parliament for nearly fifteen years and continued to advance in the army. He became colonel of the 37th Foot in 1722 and of the 38th in 1735. He was also promoted to brigadier general in 1735 and had an apartment at Windsor Castle. But his regiments required little of him in those years of peace, and he died in 1738 before the War of the Austrian Succession provided more demanding opportunities to exercise command.

Murray's library, like his career, was devoted more to peace than to war. He owned fewer than a hundred books at the end of his life. Most of those were general histories: of the ancient world, of China, of the European conquest of Mexico, of Turkey and Algiers, and, above all, of the British Isles. He had his share of plays and poetry to complement the histories, from Virgil's works to Milton's *Paradise Lost*; and books of travel, volumes of periodicals, and pamphlets. Characteristically, he owned more books of statutes and proceedings of Parliament than books on war; and only one of his three books on war was not a history, Martin Bladen's translation of Caesar's *Commentaries*. There were no modern treatises on the art of war or military engineering, no books of drill, and no laws of war or lists of the army. Murray had clearly settled into the rhythms of a peacetime army.

[Sedgwick, *House of Commons*, 2:285; Dalton, *George the First's Army*, 1:130, 216 and 2:416–17; GB, WO, *List of the Army*, 1759; Houlding, *Fit for Service*, pp. 179,

414; "Inventory of the Honble Brigadier General Robert Murray . . . ," May 6–15, 1738, and "Inventory of goods etc at Murray's apartment in Windsor Castle," May 20, 1738, PROB 3 37/69, PRO.]

Oglethorpe, General James Edward (1696–1785).

Oglethorpe, best known for founding Georgia, was a talented soldier whose career in the British army was blighted by Jacobite inclinations. His parents had gone into exile with James II and continued their connections with the Stuarts well into the reign of Queen Anne. His father also retained friends enough in England to buy his youngest son a commission in the elite 1st Foot Guards (before 1709) and to see that he was well educated at Eton and Corpus Christi College, Oxford. But young Oglethorpe spent little time in the army. When in 1715 the Jacobites rebelled, he resigned his commission and went abroad—to serve as a volunteer with the celebrated Prince Eugene of Savoy against the Turks and to complete his education on the Grand Tour, which included an audience with the Stuart Pretender. Oglethorpe eventually went home to inherit his family's estate at Westbrook and to enter Parliament for Haslemere (Surrey) in 1722, a seat that he would hold for thirty-two years.

He might then have settled in the life of a country gentleman and independent member of Parliament—might never again have served as a soldier—had not a friend died in debtors' prison. Oglethorpe became passionately interested in penal reform, shifted his allegiance to the government of Sir Robert Walpole, and won the support of the king and Parliament for a new colony in North America. In June 1732 he got a charter to settle this colony, Georgia, as a refuge for debtors and as an outpost against the Spanish in Florida, a shield for British colonies farther to the north. Reaching Georgia in early 1733, Oglethorpe spent the next decade defending the infant colony against internal dissension (the colonists chafed under prohibitions against slavery and rum) and external aggression (the Spanish tried repeatedly to destroy the new colony). In 1737 he went home to get the authority and forces he needed to secure his colony—to become commander in chief in South Carolina and Georgia and to raise a regiment of six hundred volunteers. Returning with his new regiment just in time for the outbreak of war with Spain, he used force and diplomacy to defend Georgia. He gained the support of native tribes, launched preemptive attacks on St. Augustine, and blocked Spanish offensives against his colony. When his resources ran thin, he went home once again to raise money and men and to answer, successfully, charges that he was not using his forces effectively against the Spanish. He never returned.

While he was recruiting men to serve in Georgia, the Jacobites rose in Scotland, and the government ordered him to use his recruits against the rebels who had defeated the king's forces near Edinburgh and invaded England. By mid-December 1745, the rebels, finding Englishmen all too loyal to the Hanoverians, had turned back toward Scotland with the British army close behind. It was then that Oglethorpe joined in the pursuit and that his military career came to an end. When the British commander, the Duke of Cumberland, ordered Oglethorpe to attack the rear guard of the rebels near Penrith, Oglethorpe delayed, allowing the rebels to withdraw without a fight. Cumberland eventually overtook and defeated the rebels; and he eventually brought charges against Oglethorpe for failing to attack. Although acquitted "most honorably," and although continued in the army, Oglethorpe saw no further military service. His regiment was disbanded at the end of the War of the Austrian Succession; Georgia became a royal colony in 1752; and he lost his seat in Parliament in 1754. He was promoted once more, to general in 1765; but he remained in retirement until his death in 1785.

Oglethorpe had a library to match his wealth, learning, and varied interests. Most of his several thousand books had little to do with war. He had unusually strong collections in history and the classics. He also had broadly representative works in English and French literature (plays, poetry, satire, and novels), in natural history and geography, and in English law. His books on war—some 120 titles—were much the same: best for history and the classics and nicely representative for military engineering, if not for the art of war. There were standard histories, biographies, and memoirs dealing with English or British forces from the English Civil War to the War of the Spanish Succession and the Seven Years' War. There was an even more comprehensive collection of the classics from Caesar to Vegetius, Polybius, Thucydides, Xenophon, Arrian, Frontinus, and Aelianus. Oglethorpe had the books from antiquity that were most admired by his fellow officers, often in more than one edition. His military engineering selection was only slightly less impressive. Except for Clairac and Muller, he had the usual eighteenth-century authorities from Vauban to Le Blond, Coehoorn, and Bisset. What was not so impressive was his selection of books on the art of war. He did own some of the most admired works of the late seventeenth and early eighteenth centuries (Folard, Feuquières, and Montecuccoli). But he had not kept up with mid-eighteenth-century trends. He had nothing by Saxe, Turpin de Crissé, Guibert, or Dalrymple and none of the Prussian *Regu-*

lations that became popular with the Seven Years' War. His collection of books on war was relatively large, but it was stronger in history, the classics, and engineering than in the art of war; and it, like his career, had crested in the 1740s.

[*DNB*; *ANB*; Sedgwick, *House of Commons*, 2:305–6; SAHR, *Army List of 1740*; Minutes of a General Court Martial, Sept. 29 to Oct. 10, 1746, for MG James Oglethorpe, Add MSS, 51,378, BL; Charteris, *Cumberland*, 1:222–40; *Catalogue of the Library of General Oglethorpe* (The title of this catalogue was supplied by Leonard L. Macdall in 1935.), HRHC.]

Paget, Brigadier General Thomas (c. 1685–1741).

Paget's service in the British army, which began during the War of the Spanish Succession and ended on the eve of the War of the Austrian Succession, was favored by wealth and close ties to the royal family. He was born about 1685, the grandson of the sixth Lord Paget, and commissioned in 1707. Although there is no record of his service during the War of the Spanish Succession, he was by March 1711 a captain and lieutenant colonel in the 1st Foot Guards and, three years later, a groom of the bedchamber to the Prince of Wales, the future King George II. In 1715 he was promoted to lieutenant colonel of the first troop of the Horse Grenadier Guards. Neither he nor his troop seems to have served against the Jacobites in 1715 or 1719 or in defense of Gibraltar in 1727. Paget was returned to Parliament for Ilchester (1722–27); remained in favor with the new King George II; and advanced steadily in the army: to colonel of the 32nd Foot in 1732, colonel of the 22nd in 1738, and brigadier general in 1739. He died while serving with his regiment and as deputy governor of Minorca in May 1741.

Paget's library was relatively small for a man of his means and social standing. Most of his two hundred books were devoted to theology, English literature, and rural estate management. He owned commentaries and sermons by John Tillotson, William Wake, and Robert South; the poetry and plays of William Shakespeare, Ben Johnson, Alexander Pope, and John Dryden; and assorted works on architecture, law, carpentry, animal husbandry, and gardening. There were also romances, novels, and travel books but few histories and only five books on war. Although Paget's career in the army spanned nearly thirty-five years, he had in 1741 only one book on the art of war, a single drill book (Humphrey Bland's *Treatise*), and three military histories. Paget might well have been a loyal and attentive officer, but he was not an avid student of warfare.

[Sedgwick, *House of Commons*, 2:320; SAHR, *Army List of 1740*; Dalton, *English Army Lists* ... , 6:50; Dalton, *George the First's Army*, 1:96, 186; Houlding, *Fit for Service*, p. 18; *Gentleman's Magazine*, June 1741, p. 332; "An Inventory of All and Singular the Goods Chattells and Credits of the Honble Brigadier Thomas Pagett ... 1 June 1741," PROB 3 41/22, PRO.]

Parker, Lieutenant General George Lane (1724–91).

George Lane Parker served in the British army for more than forty years during the mid-eighteenth century, establishing himself as a knowledgeable and responsible—if not distinguished—officer. He was the second son in a family of wealth and learning: his father, the 2nd Earl of Macclesfield, was a well-known astronomer who built an observatory, library, and laboratory at Shirburn Castle, Oxfordshire. Young Parker was educated at Hertford College, Oxford (B.A., 1743), and entered the elite 1st Foot Guards as a lieutenant in May 1749. It is not clear whether he saw active service during the Seven Years' War, whether he was with those companies of the 1st Foot Guards that took part in raids on the coast of France in 1758 or joined the British contingent in Germany in 1760. But he emerged from the war a captain in the guards and a colonel in the army; and during the decade of peace that followed, he entered Parliament for Yarmouth (1769), was promoted to major general (1770), and became colonel of the 20th Foot (1773).

Although Parker took his military duties seriously and supported the government in Parliament (as a member for Tregony, 1774–80), he did not command British forces in the War for American Independence. On the eve of the American War, his regiment was repeatedly judged "Fit for immediate Service," and he was clearly esteemed for his knowledge of raising and training men. Yet, when in the winter of 1774–75 King George III considered officers to command his forces in America, he did not include Parker among the leading candidates; and Parker was subsequently too senior to accompany his regiment to the colonies (he would have been serving under a commander in chief who was his junior in the army). Parker remained at home helping the government prepare the army for an ever-larger war. He was one of a few general officers who regularly inspected infantry regiments, and in 1779 he proved an innovative commander of the forces assembled for training at Warley (he "sought to introduce more realism by marching his troops through rough country"). By war's end he was a lieutenant general and, since March 1782, colonel of the 12th Dragoons. He died in September 1791.

General Parker's bookplate, created after his promotion to lieutenant general in 1777 and included in his copy of Guillaume Le Blond, *The Military Engineer* (1759), shows the importance that one prominent officer attached to his collection of books on war.

Although Parker clearly valued books, only the eight purchases he made at the sale of a General Officer's library in June 1773 indicate his preferences. Parker was then near the apex of his career, a major general of three years' standing who was a responsible regimental commander aspiring to serve as a general officer. His purchases, which depended in part on contested bidding, reflected a broad and well-informed interest in the art of war. He did acquire fashionable editions of the most admired of the classics: Caesar's *Commentaries* and Vegetius's *Institutions Militaires*. But the remainder of his purchases were books that would fill out rather than start a collection. He chose among the titles on military engineering Dazin's *Nouveau*

Sisteme . . . de Défendre les Places (not Vauban, Clairac, or Muller); among those on the art of war, Santa Cruz de Marcenado's *Reflexions Militaires et Politiques* and Henry Lloyd's *Essai sur la Grande Guerre de Main de Maitre* (not Saxe, Folard, or Feuquières); and among those on duties and discipline, *Extract of Orders and Regulations for Garrison and Camp Duties* and Dupré d'Aulnay's *Traite Général des Subsistances Militaire* (rather than Bland's *Treatise* or *Regulations for the Prussian Infantry*). On that June day, Parker bought only books on war, books of the kind needed by a discriminating officer who was fluent in French and who was rounding out his library. He did not return the next day when most of the General Officer's nonmilitary titles were offered for sale.

[Namier and Brooke, *House of Commons*, 3:249; *DNB*; Foster, *Alumni Oxonienses 1715-1886*, 3:1066; GB, WO, *List of the Army*, 1755-62, 1775, 1789; Houlding, *Fit for Service*, pp. 314, 340, 361; reviews, 20th Foot, Apr. 2, 1774, and June 7, 1775, WO 27/30 and 27/35, PRO; Parker's reviews, 1st Foot, May 13, 1777, 18th Foot, May 15, 1777, and 50th Foot, June 2, 1777, WO 27/36, PRO; Gruber, "George III Chooses a Commander in Chief," pp. 184-85; and annotated copy, *Catalogue of the Library of a General Officer*, BL.]

Additional evidence of Parker's preferences has recently begun to appear. On October 30, 2007, Sotheby's auctioned some nine hundred books from the library of the Earls of Macclesfield. According to the catalogue (*The Library of the Earls of Macclesfield removed from Shirburn Castle*), many of the eighteenth-century military books auctioned in 2007 were Parker's as were some "vellum-bound military notebooks," which remained with the current Earl of Macclesfield. Since the Sotheby's auction, the Society of the Cincinnati has acquired nineteen of Parker's books (identified by his book plates); but many more remain in other hands, and neither the books sold in 2007 nor the military notebooks have been considered for this study.]

Percy, General Hugh, Lord Percy, Duke of Northumberland (1742–1817).

Although Percy (as he was known from 1766 to 1786) was an officer in the British army for fifty-nine years, his active service was confined to two relatively brief periods during the Seven Years' War and the War for American Independence. The eldest son of the 1st Duke of Northumberland, he was born in 1742, educated at Eton College (1753–58), and, possibly, saw his first military service as a volunteer in Germany under the distinguished allied commander Prince Ferdinand of Brunswick. He was said to have been present at the Battles of Bergen in April 1759 and Minden in August 1759.

If so, he was not with his regiment. He received his first commission in the British army as an ensign in the 24th Foot on May 1, 1759, and his second, as a captain in the 85th Foot on August 6, 1759; and neither regiment was in Germany in 1759. Moreover, he matriculated at St. John's College, Cambridge, on January 11, 1760; and his regiment, then the 85th, remained at home during 1760 and 1761. Whatever his service, he was by the end of the Seven Years' War a captain and lieutenant colonel in the 1st Foot Guards and a member of Parliament for Westminster.

During the ensuing decade of peace, Percy married, became colonel of the 5th Foot (1768), and sat regularly in Parliament. Like many in the House of Commons, he seemed unsure how best to deal with the growing quarrel between Britain and its North American colonies. In voting against repeal of the Stamp Act in 1766, he supported the right of Parliament to tax the colonists. But he did not consistently support the king's government in Parliament, and he persuaded his constituents in Westminster that he was against the coercive measures that Parliament took in early 1774 to sustain its authority in Massachusetts. Later that spring, he insisted on accompanying his regiment to Massachusetts—on doing his duty as colonel of the 5th Foot and enforcing the very measures that he had opposed. After reaching Boston, he also said repeatedly that only force could sustain British authority in North America.

However tangled his feelings about the colonies, Percy served with distinction in America. At the opening engagement of the war in April 1775, he led a detachment from Boston to relieve British troops that had come under fire while destroying military stores at Lexington and Concord. Promoted to major general for that service, he became a principal lieutenant to the new British commander in chief, General William Howe. When Howe invaded the middle colonies in 1776, Percy had a leading part in capturing New York City. He commanded a battalion of the guards during the British victory on Long Island and a division of the army in the successful assault on Fort Washington. At the close of the campaign, he was second in command of troops that captured Rhode Island; and he aspired to even greater responsibilities in the next campaign. But when Americans surprised British detachments in New Jersey at Christmas 1776, Percy found himself under unexpected—and undeserved—criticism. Howe, peevish over the reverses in New Jersey that spoiled his hopes for peace, not only blamed Percy for failing to capture Providence and delaying the collection of forage at Rhode Island but also rejected his administrative decisions. Percy, feeling he had become the butt of Howe's frustrations, asked for and received permission to go home.

King George III was not pleased that Percy had quit the army, but he continued to favor him with military appointments—in part because of his success in leading men and administering his regiments and in part because of his political power, especially after he succeeded his father as Duke of Northumberland in 1786. He became a lieutenant general in 1777 and a general in 1793; and he served successively as colonel of the 2nd Horse Grenadier Guards (1784–88), of the 2nd Life Guards (1788–1817), and of the Horse Guards (1806–12). But he did not again command British forces in wartime. He died in July 1817.

Percy was clearly a student of war: he made careful notes on military texts, drew upon the history and theory of war when planning operations, and bought books while on campaign. Even so, there is no comprehensive list or inventory of his library, nothing more than fugitive clues to the books he preferred. Those clues suggest a wide and discriminating understanding of the books on war that were available on the eve of the War for American Independence. In notes, references, and purchases made between 1772 and 1775 he specified eight books and authors that included some of the most admired of that era: Guibert, Feuquières, Frederick the Great, and Saxe on the art of war; Marshal Broglie's *Campagnes . . . en Allemagne 1759–1761. Avec . . . Instruction pour l'Infanterie . . .* ; Mante's *History of the Late War in North-America*; Manstein's *Memoirs of Russia*; and Pleydell's translation of an *Essay on Field Fortification . . . for the Use of Officers of Infantry*. At the zenith of his career, Percy was—and intended to be—current in his military reading.

[Namier and Brooke, *House of Commons*, 3:269; *DNB*; Venn, *Alumni Cantabrigienses*, part II, 5:92; Bolton, *Letters of Percy*, pp. 35–43; Percy to his father, Jan. 11, 1777, Percy Papers, LI, Alnwick Castle; Gruber, *Howe Brothers*, p. 192.

For the specific books and authors that Percy preferred, see Percy's military notebook, n.d., Syon Miscellany, F 3/5, and Percy to General Harvey, July 28, 1775, Percy Papers, L, Alnwick Castle; and Percy to Thomas Percy, Nov. 25, 1774, Bolton, *Letters of Percy*, p. 44.]

Seton, Captain Robert (fl. 1702–15).

Little is known of the life and service of Robert Seton. It seems likely—to judge by his regiment, residence, and library—that he was born into a Scottish family of wealth and prominence about 1685. He was commissioned an ensign in the Third or Scots Foot Guards in August 1702, promoted to lieutenant in October 1703, and remained in the Scots Guards as a lieutenant and captain in 1715. It is probable that he spent much of his time with the regiment in or near London (the Scots Guards did not enter the War of the Spanish Succession until 1710 or take an active part in putting down the Jacobite rebellions of 1715 or 1719). He might have been among the 3rd Guards who went to Spain in 1710 or who joined the expedition against the Spanish port of Vigo in 1719. But there is no clear record of his service in the army after 1715. A Robert Seaton was appointed clerk of "Courts Martial in Scotland" in 1722, and Robert Seton was quartermaster to the 41st Foot in 1724 (renewed in 1727)—suggesting that Captain Robert Seton of the guards might have chosen or been forced by wounds or illness to quit his regiment. All that is known for sure is that Captain Robert Seton died sometime before March 1732.

To judge by the books that he owned, Seton did not read extensively about war or warfare. Of more than sixteen hundred books in his library in 1732, only twenty-nine dealt with war; and of those twenty-nine, only four, including Hexham's *Principles of the Art Militarie* and Freitag's *L'Architecture Militaire*, provided explicit instruction in the art of war. The remaining volumes were devoted mainly to the military history of Europe and the British Isles—especially to wars between Scotland and England—and to the classics. Seton did own the most widely admired books on war from the ancient world—Caesar's *Commentaries*, Thucydides' *Peloponnesian War*, and Vegetius's *De re Militari*—as well as a copy of Machiavelli's *Art of War*. And Seton had books on war in French, Latin, and other European languages. But his books were clearly dated. Only six of his military titles were published after 1700; and all save one of those six, a military dictionary, were histories. There was no Vauban or Bland in Seton's library—indeed, no evidence that he had more than a passing interest in the art of war.

[Dalton, *English Army Lists . . .* , 5:219; Dalton, *George the First's Army*, 1:130 and 2:326, 347; Fortescue, *History of the British Army*, 2:10, 530; and Catalogue of books belonging to "deceased" Captain Robt Seton, Mar. 14, 1732, CC 8/12/8(2), SRO. Seton does not appear in such standard sources as Musgrave, *Obituary*, Paul, *Scots Peerage*, and Sedgwick, *House of Commons*.]

Smith, Captain George (fl. 1772–83).

Captain George Smith served Great Britain as inspector of the Royal Military Academy at Woolwich from 1772 to 1783. Although he was responsible for the education of cadets at Woolwich, and although he was expected to be an accomplished officer, Smith probably never held a commission in the

British army. He was an Englishman; he had been an officer in the Prussian army (most likely a captain of artillery); and he remained "Captain" Smith after returning home to become "Inspector" at Woolwich and to write *An Universal Military Dictionary* (1779). But Inspector Smith does not seem to have been one of the three Captains George Smith in the British army before or during the War for American Independence. Nor does his name appear elsewhere in the lists of the army for the period in which he might have served (1740–89)—not even among the officers of the Royal Regiment of Artillery who shared his military specialty or among the British officers assigned to the staff of the Royal Military Academy while he was "inspector."

If, then, Inspector Smith did not serve in the British army, why should he be included in this study of officers who did? Why should his preferences for books on war be given any more consideration than those of other British subjects who served in foreign armies and became authorities on the art of war, officers like the well-known Major General Henry Lloyd? Primarily, because unlike others with foreign pedigrees, Smith did serve the British army for more than a decade and because he was officially responsible for the education of aspiring British officers. As inspector of the Royal Military Academy from 1772 to 1783, Smith was far more than a disciplinarian. He was charged with enforcing the rules of the academy: with being present throughout the instructional year to maintain discipline and to encourage cadets to respect their officers and civilian instructors (the masters). Even more important, he was required to supervise all instruction—specifically, to accompany the cadets when they left the academy for field exercises, to maintain a "Military Library," and to recommend "such Books . . . as he may think best adapted to the several Capacities and a due Course of Military Knowledge."

Smith was given these duties—was appointed inspector—to bring rigor to the Royal Military Academy. The academy had been established in 1741 to prepare young men for careers as officers of artillery and engineering. By the 1760s the academy had grown lax: neither the cadets nor their masters were attentive to their duties. The lieutenant governor, James Pattison, made improvements; but he needed someone to supervise the education of cadets. He found that person in Captain George Smith, an "honourable and upright" man, an experienced artillery officer, and a careful student of warfare. Soon after being appointed "inspector of studies" in 1772, Smith proposed—and Pattison agreed—to establish four distinct classes for the cadets in both the lower and the upper school of the academy and to require that the cadets pass examinations "in the presence of the inspector" before advancing to the upper school. Beyond that, Smith required the masters to report monthly on the progress of cadets and to provide increased, individual instruction. He probably also had a part in instituting entrance examinations for the academy in 1774. But only gradually was Smith, with the support of Pattison and the Board of Ordnance, able to overcome the resistance of the masters.

Smith remained at Woolwich for more than a decade, devoting much of his time at first to reforming the academy and writing his *Universal Military Dictionary*. During his last years at Woolwich, he turned increasingly to Freemasonry. He had become a Mason while in Germany, and after returning to England, he took an active part in the lodges near the academy. He served as master of the Royal Military Lodge of Woolwich for four years, as provincial grand master of Kent after 1778, and as junior grand warden of the Grand Lodge, briefly in 1780. His work as master of the Royal Military Lodge and as author of *The Use and Abuse of Free-Masonry* (London, 1783) brought him into conflict with other Freemasons who objected to his having recruited Masons among the inmates of the King's Bench prison and having advocated the admission of women into the society. In 1784 he was expelled from the society, allegedly for forging a certificate of recommendation for distressed brethren. By then he had ended his tenure as inspector at Woolwich (1783) and had published *Bibliotheca Militaris* (1783). He is said to have died at the turn of the nineteenth century.

Although Smith's *Bibliotheca Militaris* has not been found, he left ample evidence of his preferences for books on war. While at Woolwich, he worked steadily on a book that he thought essential to the study of war, a comprehensive dictionary of the terms that officers—particularly artillerists and engineers—needed to understand in performing their duties. As early as 1773 he was attending the posthumous sale of a General Officer's library, buying the kinds of books that he could use in creating his dictionary. He was patient and thorough in this work, which engaged, he said, "my utmost application for some years." He sifted through scores of books and drew upon his own experience to provide clear, authoritative entries on an extensive list of topics dealing with warfare from antiquity to the middle of the eighteenth century, from drill and discipline (EXERCISE, WORDS of COMMAND) to military laws and regulations (COURTS MARTIAL, MUTINY), to the art of war (TACTICS, WAR) and military engineering (FORTIFICATION, MINING, and SIEGE). But the most extensive entries, those that included the most sophisticated tables and equations, dealt with artillery. He wrote learned essays on topics great (ARTILLERY, CANNON, GUNNERY, and PROJECTILE) and small (CARRIAGES, LABORATORY, and PROOF). Finally, he added not just a list of the books that he had consulted in writing his dictionary but also, under "BOOKS, *military*," some ninety titles of works that he thought would best explain artillery, fortification, and the art of war to the general public and ensuing generations of soldiers. His *Universal Military Dictionary*, published in 1779, was—and remains—a tribute to his learning and clarity of mind.

Altogether, in his *Dictionary* and purchases Smith expressed preferences for 176 books on war. Excluding duplicates (23) and books that have not been identified (another 26), we have 127 titles that Smith cited, recommended, or purchased. Of those, the 95 cited or recommended in his *Dictionary* provide the clearest indication of the books he valued most—at least, the books that he thought most useful in creating a dictionary and providing for the education of the "public" and "posterity." His choices reflected not only his emphasis on artillery, engineering, and the art of war (about 90 percent of the 95 titles) but also his determination to include the latest, "best military books in the English, German, Dutch, and French languages" (more than two-thirds were in a language other than English; and just under two-thirds had been published after 1750). The few books that did not fit tightly into his criteria—the few general histories of European wars that he recommended—were, he thought, relevant to the art of war. Although Smith excluded the classics as well as modern works on drill, discipline, and the laws of war, and although he put greater emphasis than his British colleagues on Dutch and German works, his lists included nearly all of the works that contemporary British officers admired most on artillery and engineering (Vauban, Clairac, Muller, Coehoorn, Le Blond, Saint-Rémy, Pleydell, and Belidor) and on the art of war (Marlborough, Folard, Puységur, Guibert, Montecuccoli, Frederick, Guischardt, Turpin de Crissé, and Eugene). Smith did omit Saxe and Turenne, both of whom he praised in the preface to his *Dictionary*, and Feuquières, who was required reading at the academy.

Smith's purchases at the sale of a General Officer's books in June 1773 were less focused than the recommendations in his *Dictionary*. He bought books primarily on war but also on philosophy, drama, drawing, geography, and music. His selections on war, some thirty-six titles, were further shaped by those which were offered and by the competitive bidding. Yet his preferences were clear. He bought most often books that dealt with military engineering and artillery, a comprehensive assortment of titles from the seventeenth and eighteenth centuries that were often in French and that included the most widely preferred books of that era, Vauban's *De l'Attaque et de la Défense des Places* of 1737 and Muller's *Treatise of Artillery* of 1757. Smith also bought a number of authoritative books on tactics and the art of war, books ranging from first editions of Bland's *Treatise of Military Discipline* (1727) and *Regulations for the Prussian Infantry* (1754) to Turenne's *Military Memoirs and Maxims* (1744) and the classical works of Aelianus and Polyaenus. He complemented these purchases with memoirs and campaign histories, including Espagnac's well-known accounts of the campaigns of 1746 and 1747 and Voltaire's *Histoire de la Guerre de Mil Sept Cent Quarante & Un* (1756). In short, Smith's purchases in June of 1773 were well suited to his work as inspector at Woolwich and as author of the dictionary he would publish six years later.

The books that Smith bought, together with those that he subsequently cited and recommended, included 46 of the 92 books that his contemporaries valued above all others, the books that appealed to at least 10 percent and three of our officers (Appendix B). But because Smith concentrated on works dealing with artillery, engineering, and the art of war, the 127 books that he preferred did not contain as high a proportion of the most admired books on war as did the libraries of many of our officers. Conversely, his preferences did include an unusually high proportion of books on war that other officers ignored. Smith's preferences were authoritative and sharply focused.

[See "Smith, George," in Mackey et al., *Encyclopaedia of Freemasonry*; Guggisberg, *"The Shop,"* pp. 1, 9, 24–30, 261, 269. Neither Mackey nor Guggisberg says that Smith was an "artillery" officer in the Prussian army; but Smith suggests that he was in his *Universal Military Dictionary*—first, by the description he provided of the inspector at Woolwich (an officer of "great abilities and experience" who could supervise instruction in artillery or engineering; see ACADEMY); second, by the overwhelming emphasis he placed on artillery in his "universal" dictionary; third, by the depth of technical learning that he exhibited on topics such as CARRIAGE, GUNNERY, and PROJECTILE (but not on similar topics in engineering or the art of war); fourth, by the preponderance of artillery officers in the list of subscribers to his dictionary; and fifth, by the definition of CAPTAIN in his dictionary, which included a seemingly eccentric and autobiographical reference to Prussian practices ("The captains of artillery in the Prussian service rank as majors in the army and have an extraordinary pay on account of the great qualifications that monarch demands of them").

The three Captains George Smith who served in the British army before and during the War for American Independence were: George Smith who joined the 34th Foot in 1757, became a captain in the 68th in 1762, and left the army in 1765; George Smith who served exclusively in the 67th Foot, rising from lieutenant in 1757 to captain lieutenant in 1761 and remaining a captain lieutenant until he left the army in 1767; and George Amos Smith who advanced from lieutenant (1762) to captain

(1772) in the 52nd Foot and served in America from 1774 to 1778. Captain George Amos Smith was clearly not Inspector Smith; and it is very unlikely that either of the other Captains George Smith was the inspector—that either quit the British infantry to become a Prussian officer and to develop an expertise in artillery before joining the staff at Woolwich in 1772. See SAHR, *Army List of 1740*; GB, WO, *List of the Army*, 1759, 1765–72, 1779, 1786, 1789; Kane, *List of Royal Regiment of Artillery*; and Ford, *British Officers in America, 1754-1774*; and Ford, *British Officers in American Revolution*.

For the duties of the "inspector" at Woolwich, see Townshend, *Rules and Orders* (quoted here).

For lists of the books that Smith purchased, cited, and recommended, see the annotated copy of *Catalogue of the Library of a General Officer*, BL, and Smith, *Universal Military Dictionary*, vii (quoted here). I have concluded that Inspector Smith was the "Captain Smith" who bought books at the sale of a General Officer's Library in London, in June 1773. The records of the sale show that "Captain Smith" bought more books than any other British officer who attended the sale—more, in fact, than Thomas Blomefield, Hugh Debbieg, and George Lane Parker combined. The records also show that "Captain Smith" bought just the kinds of books on war that an officer would have needed to serve as inspector at Woolwich and to create a military dictionary with a strong emphasis on artillery, engineering, and the art of war—including four of the exact titles that Captain George Smith of Woolwich would cite and recommend in his *Universal Military Dictionary* of 1779. Beyond that, there was no Captain Smith in the Royal Regiment of Artillery or in the Corps of Engineers in 1773—no one who shared Inspector Smith's specific interests in books on artillery or engineering. The ten Captains Smith in the *List of the Army* for 1773 were about evenly divided between the infantry and the cavalry; and as many as six of the ten, attached to regiments in Ireland or North America, might well have been out of the country at the time of the sale.]

Stanhope, Lieutenant General James Earl (1673–1721).

Stanhope's service in the British army, which began during the War of the League of Augsburg and ended in the War of the Spanish Succession, was mixed increasingly with politics and diplomacy. The son of a British diplomat, he was born in Paris and educated at Eton and Trinity College, Oxford. He left Oxford at sixteen to accompany his father to Madrid, where he learned the language and culture that would shape the rest of his life. He began his military career in 1691 as a volunteer with the Duke of Savoy against France in the War of the League of Augsburg. The next year he entered the British army as an officer in the 28th Foot, served briefly in Flanders, and became captain and lieutenant colonel in the 1st Foot Guards in 1695. By the time he was twenty-nine, he was the colonel of the 11th Foot and a member of Parliament. Stanhope clearly had the talent as well as the education, wealth, and ambition for an exceptional career in war or politics.

During the ensuing War of the Spanish Succession, he enjoyed enough success as a soldier and diplomat to become a principal figure in the British government. Beginning in 1702, Stanhope served almost exclusively with British forces in Spain. He distinguished himself storming the defenses of Vigo in 1702; took part in the siege and capture of Barcelona in 1705; and, as minister to Spain from 1706, advocated more aggressive measures than the allied commanders were willing to take. Resigning in disgust, he managed to win appointment as both minister and commander of British forces in Spain (eventually as a lieutenant general). He captured Minorca in the Balearic Islands in 1708 and pressed the allies into an offensive that led to victories over the Bourbons at Almenara and Saragossa and the capture of Madrid in 1710. But the Bourbons, reinforced, drove the allies from Madrid and overtook Stanhope's wing of the army at Brihuega in December 1710. Surprised and defeated, Stanhope found himself a prisoner of war, his military career at an end. He returned home in 1712 to become a leader of the House of Commons and from 1714 a principal minister under the new King George I. He was not considered a trustworthy colleague or an effective manager in domestic affairs. As a secretary of state, he suppressed the Jacobite rising of 1715; negotiated an alliance that contained Spanish aggression in Italy; and defended Sweden against Russia and Denmark. He suffered a stroke while speaking in Parliament and died in February 1721.

Stanhope's library was, like his career, devoted more to politics and diplomacy than to war. Greek and Latin classics, histories of the ancient world and modern Europe, philosophy, poetry, drama, and music dominated the nine hundred titles on his shelves in 1721. He owned fewer than twenty-five books on war; and most of those were the classics: Caesar, Vegetius, Polybius, Thucydides, Xenophon, Arrian, and Polyaenus—the most widely admired books on war from the ancient world and the books that a wealthy, Oxford-educated soldier would have been most likely to have owned at the turn of the eighteenth century. Indeed, there were only two books on war in Stanhope's library that reflected his own active service—an *Abridgment of Military Discipline* of 1686 and a *Code Militaire de Louis XIV* of 1708. He did not have the most popular contemporary works in military history and theory, the memoirs of Turenne and Montecuccoli and the treatises of Vauban and Feuquières; and his career in the army ended before many of the famous eighteenth-century books about war were published. His was the library of a politician and diplomat who had been a soldier.

[*DNB*; Sedgwick, *House of Commons*, 2:435–36; Catalogue of the books of James Stanhope, Earl Stanhope, July 14, 1721, Stanhope MSS, U1590 C11, KCAO.]

Stewart, Lieutenant Colonel John (d. 1750).

When John Stewart died in February 1750, he was serving in Ireland as lieutenant colonel of the 17th Foot. Beyond that there is little that is sure about his career in the British army. It is possible that he was the "John Steuart" who was appointed Captain Lieutenant of Lowther's Marines when that regiment was raised in 1739. There is no other officer in the Army List of 1740 or, for that matter, in the lists for the years from 1707 to 1727 who could have been the Lieutenant Colonel John Stewart of the 17th Foot in 1750. But there is no indication of how or when the captain lieutenant of marines made his way to lieutenant colonel of foot. The War of the Austrian Succession clearly accelerated promotions within the British army, and Stewart might well have taken advantage of vacancies in the 17th Foot, which served on Minorca throughout the war, to rise rapidly to captain, major, and then lieutenant colonel. He was with the regiment after it went home to Ireland in 1749; and he died there the following February. It is also remotely possible that Stewart had entered the army during the War of the Spanish Succession (there was a second lieutenant John Stewart in Row's Fusiliers at Blenheim in 1704), that he had gone onto half pay before the end of that war, and that he reentered the army at the beginning of the War of the Austrian Succession, either directly into the 17th or through some other regiment.

Although there is no clear record of his service, Lieutenant Colonel John Stewart was a man of wealth and social standing in his native Scotland; and his library at Stewartfield displayed the conventional tastes of a gentleman and an officer. He had many political histories and memoirs, English and French belles lettres, a number of the classics in translation, numerous religious tracts, and a few books on politics. Only about a dozen of his 350 books dealt primarily with war, but that dozen was carefully chosen. There were two copies of Caesar's *Commentaries*, Machiavelli and Folard on the art of war, Bentivoglio's and Boyer's histories of recent wars on the Continent, and Burchett's naval history. Like many of his fellow officers, he valued books written by French authorities. But his passion for military reading had clearly cooled during the quarter century of peace that followed the War of the Spanish Succession. He had no books on war published after 1730 — no books published during the last years of his service in the army.

[Catalogue of Books (of "Collonel John Stewart") in the House of Stewartfield, Sept. 22, 1752, and petition of Robert Dalrymple, Sept. 14, 1752, CC8/12/10, SRO. In his petition asking that the catalogue be made, Dalrymple asserted that he was a creditor of Stewart, who had died in Ireland "upwards of two years ago." Stewart's obituary in the *Gentleman's Magazine*, Feb. 1750, p. 91, corroborates Dalrymple's assertion and adds that Stewart was lieutenant colonel in Wynyard's Foot (17th Foot). See as well Dalton's *English Army Lists* and *George the First's Army*; SAHR, *Army List of 1740*; Leslie, *Succession of Colonels*; and Houlding, *Fit for Service*, pp. 18, 20, 108–9. LTC John Stewart should not be confused with BG John Stewart of Sorbie (c. 1673–1748) whose career is sketched in Sedgwick, *House of Commons*, 2:448.]

Townshend, Field Marshal George, 1st Marquis (1724–1807).

Townshend's service in the British army was long and diverse — extending from the War of the Austrian Succession to the War for American Independence, from Western Europe to North America, and from the command of armies to the management of military and imperial administrations. The eldest son of a viscount, he entered the army with the advantages of wealth, political connections, and an excellent education (Eton College and Cambridge University). He also began with the energy and determination to become a student of war and a distinguished soldier. But Townshend proved a difficult subordinate and an uneasy superior; and for all his advantages — including many opportunities to command in wartime — he never quite realized his military ambitions.

During the wars of midcentury, he tarnished his own performances with unseemly criticism of his superiors. He entered the army as a volunteer at the beginning of the War of the Austrian Succession, took part in the allied victory over the French at the Battle of Dettingen (1743), and won commissions as captain, successively, of the 7th Dragoons and the 20th Foot. For his service in the campaigns of 1745 and 1746 — in fighting the French in the Low Countries and the Jacobites in Scotland — he was appointed aide-de-camp to the young British commander in chief, the Duke of Cumberland. But when Cumberland returned to the Continent and suffered reverses in the final campaigns of the war, Townshend could not contain his criticisms. He went home, took a seat in Parliament, and continued to criticize Cumberland until he made his own position in the army untenable. He resigned his commission in 1750 and devoted his energies to his family and politics, sponsoring parliamentary legislation in 1755 to create a militia that would, he thought, add to the security of the British Isles by diminishing the power of the regular army and the Duke of Cumberland.

Such politics kept Townshend out of the army for nearly eight years and jeopardized his military career even longer. He returned to active service only after the Seven Years' War had begun, Cumberland had resigned from the command of the army, and William Pitt had risen to power in the British government. In 1758 Pitt offered Townshend a chance to serve as a brigadier general in North America, to go as third in command of an expeditionary force that was to attack Quebec the following summer. Townshend accepted the offer and served with impatience under the celebrated James Wolfe, leading a wing of the army in the climactic battle on the Plains of Abraham and assuming command after Wolfe was killed. Townshend consummated the victory by taking Quebec, but he promptly returned home to criticize his former commander and to claim more than his share of the credit. Even so, Townshend was honored with the colonelcy of the 28th Foot and command of a brigade in the British forces serving in Germany. He used that opportunity to get greater responsibilities during the last year of the war— promotion to lieutenant general and command of a division of the Anglo-Portuguese army that was fighting the French and Spanish in Portugal.

By war's end, Townshend had completed his active military service and begun to concentrate on politics as well as military and imperial administration. In 1763 he supported the ministry of George Grenville and was appointed lieutenant general of ordnance. The following year, he succeeded his father in the House of Lords and began to work more closely with his brother, Charles, who was to become chancellor of the exchequer in 1766 and author of taxes that would disrupt the British Empire in America. Through Charles, Townshend gained appointment as lord lieutenant of Ireland in 1767. He tried to use that post to control Irish politics; he succeeded mainly in raising storms of opposition and abuse that led to his recall in 1772. He returned home to support the North ministry and become master general of ordnance throughout the War for American Independence. He also continued to receive promotions from a succession of governments— to colonel of the 2nd Dragoon Guards in 1773, general in 1782, marquis in 1786, and field marshal in 1796. He died in September 1807.

Throughout his career in the army, Townshend had been an avid student of war. He regularly drew on the history and theory of warfare to reflect on the progress of a particular campaign or to criticize a superior; and when he became master general of ordnance, he prescribed very specific readings for the cadets who were attending the Royal Academy at Woolwich.

Because he sought the latest and best books on war, his own readings and his requirements for cadets included some twenty-five of the most widely admired books of his era. He returned repeatedly to the classical works of Caesar, Vegetius, Polybius, and Thucydides; to the engineering texts of Vauban, Clairac, Muller, and Coehoorn; to the theoretical works of Saxe, Feuquières, Puységur, and Turpin de Crissé; and to the memoirs and histories of Turenne, Santa Cruz de Marcenado, Luxembourg, and Frederick the Great. With the exception of drill books—such as *Regulations for the Prussian Infantry*—Townshend was wonderfully comprehensive and discriminating in his selections of books on war.

[*DNB*; Townshend, *Life of Townshend*; Namier and Brooke, *House of Commons*, 3:548–52; George Townshend's notebook, [post-1747], and "Observations on ye defence of ye Kingdom," [c. 1780], Add MSS 50,012.A and 50,012.B, BL; Townshend's journal, Quebec, summer 1759, including a list of books inside the front cover, and another journal, summer 1759, Townshend Papers, 6806-41-4-2-3, and 6806-41-4-2-4, NAM; and Townshend, *Rules and Orders*, WO 30/120, PRO.]

Tryon, Lieutenant General William (1729–88).

William Tryon's career in the army began inauspiciously. The son of a wealthy English landowner and grandson of a peer, he entered the army through the elite 1st Foot Guards in 1751. He was a lieutenant and captain in the guards when the Seven Years' War began. But the only active service he saw during that war was in the disastrous raid on Cherbourg and St. Malo in the late summer of 1758. Among the last of the British landing party to withdraw from the beach at St. Cas, he was fortunate to receive only slight wounds and to escape drowning en route to his transport. He remained in England for rest of the war, presumably because his company was not included in the detachments of the guards that served with allied forces in Germany. By 1763 he was a lieutenant colonel with twelve years' service, a minimum of combat experience, and relatively poor prospects of promotion in a peacetime army. To revive his flagging career, Tryon sought appointment as a royal governor in the British colonies of North America.

This unorthodox approach to preferment in the army succeeded far better than he might have hoped. With the help of his wife's relation, the Earl of Hillsborough, who was then president of the Board of Trade, Tryon was able to become lieutenant governor (1764–65) and governor of North Carolina (1765–71). And he made the most of those opportunities. Using a combination of firmness and openness, he won support for the Angli-

can Church and royal government among many prominent North Carolini-
ans. Although he failed to persuade the colonists to accept parliamentary
taxation, he did mobilize them to put down a local rebellion against taxes,
leading their militia in a decisive battle at the Alamance River in May 1771.
Tryon's success in North Carolina helped him win the governorship of New
York (1771–80). He once again sought to strengthen royal authority. When
the British government persisted in taxing the colonists and the colonists
resisted with force, Tryon became an advocate of coercive measures. He welcomed the arrival of the British army, offered advice to successive British
commanders, organized Loyalist militia, and led a series of raids on the
coasts of Connecticut and New York—raids that became so indiscriminately
destructive of property and lives as to offend even his friends. But Tryon's
success as a governor and his zeal in resisting rebellion clearly impressed
the British government. He gradually won the military promotions and appointments that he had sought when first setting out for North Carolina. By
the end of the War for American Independence, he was a lieutenant general
in the army and colonel of the 29th Foot. He also had the wealth and social standing to enjoy his relatively brief retirement—to take a constructive
interest in the plight of American Loyalists, to support his regiment, and to
create an active social life in London and various English resorts. He died
in January 1788.

Tryon's library, when destroyed by fire in 1773, reflected both his broad
education and his specialized interest in war. He had more than two hundred nonmilitary books including some of the most widely admired works
by modern English and French authors—by Locke, Milton, Shakespeare,
and Pope as well as by Molière and Voltaire. He was particularly interested in the political history and law of Great Britain, Western Europe, and
North America; but he also had a number of books dealing with philosophy, poetry, and religion and a few, with mathematics, geography, and agri-
culture. His books on war, about forty in all, were as carefully chosen as
his nonmilitary works. He had more than three-quarters of the books on
war that were most popular with British officers of his era: from the classics of Caesar, Polybius, and Thucydides to the modern engineering texts
of Vauban, Clairac, and Muller; and from the treatises on the art of war of
Saxe, Puységur, and Montecuccoli to the drill books of Bland and the Prussians and the histories of Marlborough and Turenne. His was an unusually
well-balanced collection: about equal numbers of history, drill, engineering, and the art of war—the whole complemented with a few representative
volumes on the laws of war. In short, Tryon was a man and soldier with discriminating tastes in books.

[*ANB*; Nelson, *William Tryon*; GB, WO, *List of the Army*, 1759, 1779, 1786; "An Inventory of the Furniture [and books] which was destroy'd in His Excellency Governor Tryon's House . . . the 29 December 1773," in Bargar, "Governor Tryon's House."]

Wade, Lieutenant Colonel William (fl. 1715–58).

Wade's career in the British army was shaped by accidents of birth, politics, and regimental assignments. He was born sometime before 1700, likely the illegitimate son of Field Marshal George Wade (1673–1748). He entered the army in 1715 as an ensign in George Wade's 33rd Regiment of Foot, moved with the elder Wade to the 3rd Dragoon Guards in 1717, and remained in the 3rd Dragoon Guards for the rest of his career. But if serving under a near relation, he did not enjoy rapid promotion. Britain was at peace and promotions were slow for nearly twenty-five years after William received his first commission; and when war did come again, the 3rd Dragoon Guards saw little active service. During the War of the Austrian Succession, the 3rd was one of the few cavalry regiments that went neither to the Continent nor to Scotland. William was said to have been present at the Battle of Culloden that marked the end of the Jacobite rebellion in 1746. If so, he was apart from his regiment. It is possible that he was with the 3rd Dragoon Guards in the first British contingent to go to Germany at the outset of the Seven Years' War—in the summer of 1758. Again, if so, he served for only a few months: he was out of the regiment by the beginning of 1759, perhaps dead. Whatever the circumstances, William Wade, who had become a captain in early 1719, was not promoted to major until 1733 or to lieutenant colonel until 1751; and he remained a lieutenant colonel for the rest of his career.

Wade might not have had the pedigree or the wealth—to say nothing of the opportunity—to become a colonel in the mid-eighteenth-century British army. He did have, by the end of his career, a fine library of some 350 books, a library that reflected the tastes of an educated Englishman and a student of warfare. About 300 of his books were of a general nature: novels, poetry, philosophy, the classics, and political history as well as a few works devoted to anatomy, architecture, and travel. His 45 books on war included many of the titles considered most authoritative by his contemporaries—from Caesar and Vauban to Folard, Bland, Turenne, Polybius, and Kane—an up-to-date balance of ancient and modern, English and French titles. His military collection was particularly strong in history (the French civil wars of the seventeenth century, the War of the Spanish Succession, and the opening campaigns of the Seven Years' War), the classics (in addition to Caesar and Polybius, Arrian, Plutarch, and Josephus), and discipline (from Bland to Bever). And, what was unusual, he had a few books dealing with military law, British and French.

[Dalton, *George the First's Army*, 1:264, 361 and 2:204; SAHR, *Army List of 1740*; Skrine, *Fontenoy*, pp. 367–70; Prebble, *Culloden*, pp. 317–318; *DNB* for Field Marshal Wade and his illegitimate children; GB, WO, *List of the Army*, 1755, 1758, 1759 (the lists of 1755 and 1758 refer to Lieutenant Colonel Wade of the 3rd Dragoon Guards as George Wade; perhaps William had assumed the given name of his father after his father's death; perhaps a compiler confused the given names of son and father; but there was only one Wade who was a colonel or lieutenant colonel in the British army in 1755, and that was the William Wade who had been in the 3rd Dragoon Guards since 1717); Savory, *Army in Germany during the Seven Years' War*, p. 461; Catalogue of Colonel Wade's Books, 1758, Amherst MSS, U1350 F26, KCAO.]

Winde, Captain William (fl. 1675–1715).

The "Learned Capt. Winde" is an intriguingly obscure figure—someone who entered the English army under Charles II, served as an officer of both cavalry and engineering, developed an exceptional collection of books on war, and died in the reign of George II. His service record suggests that he was born about 1650. At least, he received his first commission, as cornet in the King's Troop of Horse Guards in 1667, and advanced steadily thereafter. He became a lieutenant in the Horse Guards in 1676 and, two years later, captain of a troop of horse that he was commissioned to raise for service in Jersey. By 1679 he had also been appointed engineer to the Office of Ordnance—all the while retaining his lieutenancy in the Horse Guards until 1687. But he did not remain in the English army after William and Mary came to the throne in the Glorious Revolution of 1688. Captain Winde did have the interest and the means to continue to build an impressive collection of military books; and he eventually managed to live comfortably in London, establishing a reputation for his learning and perhaps his longevity. He died sometime before the end of 1740, when he would have been about ninety.

By the time that his library was sold in the autumn of 1740, Winde had accumulated about seventy-five books on war in a library of more than fifteen hundred titles. Most of his military collection had been assembled during and immediately after his years of active service—during the Dutch Wars, the War of the League of Augsburg, and the War of the Spanish Succession. He had an especially strong collection of French, Dutch, and Italian books on military engineering and artillery, a collection of some thirty-seven books that reflected the late-seventeenth-century preeminence of Continental writers in those specialties. Indeed, many of his engineering and artillery texts—such as those of Vauban, Coehoorn, Landsberg, and Saint-Rémy—would remain authoritative throughout the eighteenth century, among the books most prized by British officers who fought in the Seven Years' War and the War for American Independence as they had been by their predecessors in the War of the Spanish Succession. (Only five of those thirty-seven books were in English.) Winde's other military books were of a much more diverse nature, ranging from the classics to the history, law, and art of war to the duties of officers and men. Most of these books, especially those dealing with the art of war and the basics of drill, would soon seem dated; but the classics (Caesar, Vegetius, Frontinus, and Arrian) and a few of the books dealing with the history and law of war (the life of Turenne and Grotius's *Law of War and Peace*) would remain popular with British officers for at least another century.

[Dalton, *English Army Lists . . .* , 1:92, 190, 226 and 2:4, 120; and Dalton, *George the First's Army,* show only one Winde (Wind or Wynd or Wynde) who attained the rank of captain between 1660 and 1727, William Winde, and only one Winde who had an interest in engineering, the same William Winde. What further links that William Winde with the "Learned Capt. Winde" whose library was sold in 1740 is the close correlation between the dates of publication of the engineering and artillery texts in the "Learned Capt." Winde's library and the years of William Winde's service. And as a guards officer, William Winde would have had the means to own a library of more than fifteen hundred books. *Catalogue of the Library of the Learned Capt. Winde,* BL.]

Wolfe, Major General James (1727–59).

In less than two decades of service James Wolfe became one of the most celebrated soldiers in British history—an assiduous student of warfare, a charismatic leader, and a haunted personality ever identified with the British conquest of Canada. He was born into an army family, attended school with the sons of officers, dreamed of military glory, and at the age of fourteen in 1741 entered his father's regiment as a second lieutenant. While his former schoolmates were studying the classics, he was learning his regimental duty and beginning a rapid rise in the officer corps. He had the advantages of his father's wealth and connections and of the outbreak of the War of the Austrian Succession. In early 1742 he transferred to the 12th

Foot and went with his new regiment to the Continent to serve as an adjutant at the Battle of Dettingen in 1743 and become a captain in the 4th Foot in the following year. When the Jacobite rebellion broke out in 1745, Wolfe returned home to distinguish himself as an aide-de-camp at the battles of Falkirk and Culloden. With the rebellion subdued, he went back to the Low Countries for the final campaigns of the war, commanding a brigade at the Battle of Lauffeldt in 1747, surviving a wound, and emerging from the war a twenty-two-year-old major of the 20th Foot.

His precocious success had served mainly to increase his appetite for fame. He was eager to use the Peace of Aix-la-Chapelle (1748–56) to gain the education he knew essential for higher command and military glory. Promoted to lieutenant colonel in 1750, he welcomed the responsibility of commanding the 20th Foot while it kept the peace in the Highlands of Scotland and the south of England; and he enthusiastically trained his men for war. Yet he chafed at being remote from centers of military learning. He repeatedly sought leave to study on the Continent—to improve his understanding of foreign languages and siegecraft—either in an academy or with the armies of France, Austria, or Prussia. Repeatedly rejected, he struggled to improve himself wherever he was posted. In Glasgow he studied mathematics and Latin; at Inverness, algebra, geometry, and tactics (at nearby Culloden); and at Winchester, the maneuvers of a contingent of visiting Hessians. He gradually developed a reputation as one of the best-informed officers in the army, just the person to help an aspiring subaltern with advice and a reading list on the art of war.

For all of his growing reputation, Wolfe did not win further promotion until well after the Seven Years' War began in 1756. He was too young to become a colonel until that war created additional opportunities for promotion. He tried without success to gain a colonelcy by agreeing to become quartermaster general in Ireland and by seeking a staff appointment with allied forces in Germany. Not until the late summer of 1757 did he find the kind of service that brought preferment, appointment as chief of staff to an expeditionary force sent to raid the French port of Rochefort. Although the raid was a failure, Wolfe managed to create a very favorable impression—exhibiting the energy and aggressive spirit that were all too lacking in his superiors. William Pitt, the prime minister, promoted Wolfe to colonel and made him second in command of an army that was to attack Canada by sea during the summer of 1758. Wolfe made the most of this opportunity, so distinguishing himself during the successful siege of Louisbourg on Cape Breton Island and subsequent raids in the Gulf of St. Lawrence as to gain command of an army for the campaign of 1759.

James Wolfe's letter to Thomas Townshend of July 18, 1756, outlined a course of reading for Townshend's brother Henry, who had recently entered the army as an ensign in the 2nd Foot Guards. In this letter Wolfe, one of the most celebrated soldiers of the century, recommended some thirty books on war—nearly all of which were considered authoritative by his contemporaries.

Wolfe assumed that command at Louisbourg on the last day of April 1759. He was then thirty-two and a major general with orders to sail up the St. Lawrence River, capture Quebec, and cooperate with other British armies advancing overland from New York to conquer Canada. In carrying out these orders—in exercising his first independent command—Wolfe was to be severely tested. He had ever been an impatient subordinate, eager to risk battle and critical of more cautious superiors. On reaching Quebec, he was confronted by an exceptionally skillful enemy, an enemy who persisted in remaining in fortifications around the city that were too extensive to be besieged and too formidable to be assaulted. Wolfe failed to draw the French from their works; he also failed to carry those works by storm. As the summer slipped away, he became frustrated and ill—aware that he might not be able to capture Quebec before the St. Lawrence froze and the campaign ended. In desperation Wolfe decided to embark his army, sail past the city, and attack from the southwest. He did so in a way so daring as to surprise the French and precipitate battle just outside the city walls. Wolfe was killed, but his troops used disciplined fire to defeat the French and capture Quebec. The following summer, other British forces arrived to complete the conquest of Canada. Even so, Wolfe's victory has ever been considered decisive and attributed to his good fortune as well as his skillful, aggressive, and charismatic mastery of the art of war.

Perhaps more than any other officer of his era, Wolfe sought to integrate thought and action, to draw upon his reading not just in preparing men for battle but also in conducting a siege or managing a campaign. Although he left no comprehensive list of his books on war, he regularly mentioned about thirty-five titles that he thought essential reading for an accomplished officer. Those thirty-five included nearly all of the books that contemporary British officers thought most authoritative—indeed, fourteen of the fifteen most popular. And there was scarcely any aspect of war that was not represented among the books that Wolfe bought, recommended, or cited in the 1750s when he was systematically educating himself: from the classics (Caesar, Vegetius, Polybius, and Thucydides) to treatises on engineering (Vauban and Clairac) to reflections on the art of war (Folard, Feuquières, and Puységur) to manuals on drill and discipline (Bland's *Treatise* and *Regulations for Prussian Infantry*) to the campaign histories of Turenne and Marlborough. In such a comprehensive list, the omissions (Saxe's *Reveries* and the engineering texts of Muller and Coehoorn) seem more likely the result of the accidental ways in which his papers were preserved than of Wolfe's efforts to exclude particular authors or titles. He clearly sought to be—and was—familiar with the most authoritative books on war of his era.

[Spiller, *Dictionary of American Military Biography*, 3:1206–9; Willson, *Life of Wolfe*, especially pp. 165–66, 295–96, 298, 380 for books that Wolfe preferred; Stacey, *Quebec, 1759*; GB, WO, *List of the Army*, 1755, 1759.]

Wortley Montagu, Captain Edward (1713–76).

Wortley Montagu's service in the British army was no more than a brief interlude in an otherwise wildly self-indulgent and scholarly life. Sent to Westminster School at five, he eventually rebelled—running away to Oxford, London, and Oporto and marrying "an industrious washerwoman." To nullify his marriage, his parents had him confined in Holland where he became an excellent linguist and a student at Leiden. When the War of the Austrian Succession began, he joined the army as a cornet in the 7th Dragoon Guards (1743) and then a captain lieutenant in the 1st Foot (1745). He fought at Fontenoy, bought a captaincy, and retired from the army in 1748 to become a secretary in the British delegation at the congress of Aix-la-Chapelle. Once the peace had been concluded, he returned home to distinguish himself for his extravagant dress and gambling. His very wealthy father had already taken the precaution of bringing him into Parliament to protect him from his creditors; and young Wortley Montagu now retired to the country to study history and write a polemical book, *Reflections on the Rise and Fall of Antient Republics Adapted to the Present State of Great Britain* (1759). When his father died, leaving him with little to satisfy his creditors, he went into exile: studying briefly at Leiden and then embarking on a succession of Mediterranean travels and exotic liaisons that consumed the rest of his life. He died in Italy in 1776.

Wortley Montagu's library was very much a reflection of his life. Nearly all of his thousand titles dealt with Near Eastern languages, literature, and history—both classical and modern. He had a particularly large collection of dictionaries, grammars, and gazetteers to help him with the texts that he had accumulated. Among all of these works, fewer than twenty-five were on war; and most of those on war were either the classical histories of Caesar, Thucydides, Polybius, and Xenophon—multiple copies in Greek, Latin, and English—or modern histories of Anglo-French struggles on land and sea. He did have four eighteenth-century treatises on engineering, including Vauban's *De l'Attaque et de la Défence des Places*, and several other books including Grotius's *De Jure Belli ac Pacis* and a contemporary manual for young officers. But his was the library of a linguist with much stronger interests in history and literature than in war.

[*DNB*; Namier and Brooke, *House of Commons*, 3:661–62; Sedgwick, *House of Commons*, 2:556–57; *Catalogue of the Library of Edward Wortley Montagu January 1787*; *Catalogue of Books of Edward Wortley Montagu April 1798*, BL.]

PART II

Books Preferred

ritish army officers who served in the age of the American Revolution had literally hundreds of books on war to choose among: histories of campaigns and battles, treatises on engineering and artillery, reflections on the art of war, and works from the ancient world as well as specialized, contemporary works on drill, discipline, law, cartography, defense, and medicine. But which of these books did British officers prefer? We cannot assume that the quality of a book, the frequency with which it was reprinted, or the number of officers who subscribed to its publication are adequate guides to the value that officers placed on a particular work. Such evidence of a book's value is certainly worth considering, but we must also try to find more direct connections between officers and specific books and editions of those books.

This list is intended to establish those more direct connections—specifically between our forty-two officers and the books on war that they preferred. The list is based on our officers' records dated between 1721 and 1799: most often on inventories and catalogues of their libraries but also on records of the books that they bought and sold, recommended for cadets and fellow officers, cited in their own publications, and considered in their notebooks, diaries, and correspondence. Taken together, this evidence gives us a composite list of 650 books on war that our officers preferred in some way, a list that shows which titles those officers valued above others. This list does not include all of the books on war that touched their lives—books that the officers read but did not own or recommend and books, like drill manuals or articles of war, that defined their regimental duties but did not remain in their libraries. Nor does this list contain books that they neglected (see Part III: Books Not Taken).

Because the list has been created to show preferences for particular books and types of books on war, it includes, whenever possible, the exact edition that appears in an officer's records and describes the nature of the connection between each book and officer (or officers), showing how and when an officer expressed a preference for a particular title and what proportion of the officers preferred that title. The 650 books have been arranged alphabetically by author or, where the author is not known, by title. Each entry, following the *Chicago Manual of Style*, includes—when known and appropriate—the author's full name and dates; the title of the work; the translator, editor, or compiler; the edition and number of volumes; the place, printer, and date of publication; and the library where the book may now be found (see Codes Used for Libraries). Each entry also includes a note connecting an officer or officers to the title and calculating the proportion and, in some cases, the percentage of our officers who preferred that title. Those calculations may be used to compare the preferences for books available at different times and to different groups of officers. For example, Julius Caesar's *Commentaries*, like other celebrated works of antiquity, was available to all of our officers; and twenty-eight of forty-two, or 67 percent, showed a preference for Caesar. By contrast, a dozen of our officers had died or recorded their preferences before Saxe's *Reveries* was published in 1753. Thirteen of the remaining thirty, or 43 percent, eventually bought, read, or otherwise recommended Saxe. Caesar and Saxe were both remarkably popular among our officers, but Caesar was clearly more popular than Saxe. A typical entry in Part II would say—after the author, title, details of publication, and current location—"Smith cited, 1779 (1 of 22)," meaning that Smith alone had expressed a preference for this book which had been available to twenty-two of our forty-two officers.

Thus, this list reveals not just that our officers owned, read, and recommended 650 books on war but also that they clearly valued some of those books more than others and that they changed their preferences for particular books and kinds of books over time. To get a sense of which books our officers valued most and how their preferences changed, we must consider 1,265 choices they made among the 650 books they preferred. These 1,265 choices reveal persistent preferences for specific books like Caesar's *Commentaries* and Vauban's *New Method of Fortification* and for particular kinds of books—histories, treatises on engineering and artillery, studies of the art of war, and works of antiquity (see Appendix A4). They also reveal significant shifts in those preferences from one era to another. In the middle of the eighteenth century, for example, our officers, impressed with French victories in the War of the Austrian Succession, became especially interested in books on the art of war and in books by and about French commanders (Appendixes B, B1, B2, B3, and D). These altered preferences would shape the thinking of British officers in both the Seven Years' War and the War for American Independence.

Most important for understanding the eighteenth-century British army and its officer corps are the books that our officers preferred above all others—some 92 of the 650 books in Part II. Those 92 books are clearly marked in Part II and listed separately in Appendix B as "The Authorities." Each of the "authorities" attracted at least 10 percent and no fewer than three of the officers who might have had access to the particular title or cluster of titles (2 or more books by a single author on one topic, books both by and about a single individual, and books about an individual). "The Authorities" of Appendix B, together with Appendixes B1, B3, and D, which show how preferences among the "authorities" changed across time, will be valuable to anyone who is trying to understand the British army and its officer corps during the eighteenth century. They will be indispensible to anyone analyzing such discrete topics as the eighteenth-century military Enlightenment, the origins of the profession of arms, and the art of war in the age of the American Revolution.

Here then are the books that our officers preferred.

Codes Used for Libraries in Parts II and III

AU	University of Alabama, University, Alabama
CaOHM	McMaster University, Hamilton, Ontario, Canada
CLU	University of California, Los Angeles, California
CSmH	Huntington Library, San Marino, California
CSt	Stanford University, Stanford, California
CtY	Yale University, New Haven, Connecticut
DeU	University of Delaware, Newark, Delaware
DLC	United States Library of Congress, Washington, D.C.
DNLM	United States National Library of Medicine, Bethesda, Maryland
DSoC	Society of the Cincinnati, Washington, D.C.
FU	University of Florida, Gainesville, Florida
GyGoN	Niedersächsische Staats-und Universitätsbibliothek, Göttingen, Germany
ICN	Newberry Library, Chicago, Illinois
ICU	University of Chicago, Chicago, Illinois
IEN	Northwestern University, Evanston, Illinois
InU	Indiana University, Bloomington, Indiana
MBAt	Boston Athenaeum, Boston, Massachusetts
MH	Harvard University, Cambridge, Massachusetts

MH-H	Harvard University, Houghton Library, Cambridge, Massachusetts
MHi	Massachusetts Historical Society, Boston, Massachusetts
MiU	University of Michigan, Ann Arbor, Michigan
MnU	University of Minnesota, Minneapolis, Minnesota
NBuU	State University of New York, Buffalo, New York
NcD	Duke University, Durham, North Carolina
NcGU	University of North Carolina, Greensboro, North Carolina
NcU	University of North Carolina, Chapel Hill, North Carolina
NhD	Dartmouth College, Hanover, New Hampshire
NIC	Cornell University, Ithaca, New York
NjP	Princeton University, Princeton, New Jersey
NjR	Rutgers University, New Brunswick, New Jersey
NN	New York Public Library, New York, New York
NNC	Columbia University, New York, New York
NWM	United States Military Academy, West Point, New York
PU	University of Pennsylvania, Philadelphia, Pennsylvania
RNR	Redwood Library and Athenaeum, Newport, Rhode Island
TxHR	Rice University, Houston, Texas
TxU	University of Texas, Austin, Texas
Uk	British Library, London, England
UkCoU	University of Essex, Colchester, Essex, England
UkLG	Guildhall Library, Aldermanbury, London, England
UkOxU	Oxford University, Bodleian Library, Oxford, England
ViU	University of Virginia, Charlottesville, Virginia
WlAbNL	National Library of Wales, Aberystwyth, Dyfed, Wales

Abercromby, Patrick, 1656–1716?.

The Martial Atchievements of the Scots Nation. . . . 2 vols. Edinburgh: Robert Freebairn, 1711–15. DSoC.

    In Maxwell's library, 1769 (1 of 42).

An Abridgment of the English Military Discipline. Printed by Especial Command for the Use of His Majesties Forces. London: Charles Bill, Henry Hills, and Thomas Newcomb, 1686. DSoC.

    Stanhope owned in 1721 (1 of 42).

The Accomplished Officer; a Treatise Containing the Most Essential and Necessary Accomplishments of an Officer. . . . *Written Originally in French by A. R.* . . . London: J. Nutt, 1706. TxU.

In Oglethorpe's library, 1785. Wade (1758) and Tryon (1773) owned unspecified editions of this work (3 of 42).

Aelianus, Tacticus, second century A.D.

The Tactiks of Aelian or Art of Embattailing an Army after ye Grecian Manner. . . . Translated by J[ohn] B[ingham]. London: Laurence Lisle, 1616. DSoC.

> This edition was in Dormer's and in Oglethorpe's libraries in 1741 and 1785, respectively. General Officer owned and Smith purchased an unspecified edition of the *Tacticks* in 1773; and Donkin cited Bingham's translation in 1777 (5 of 42, or 12 percent, and an authority; see Appendix B). See also Frontinus and Vegetius Renatus.

Aeneas, Tacticus.

Commentaires sur la Défense des Places. . . . Translated by Jean Jacques Comte de Beausobre. 2 vols. Amsterdam: and sold in Paris by Pissot, 1757. DSoC.

> Ligonier owned this translation in 1770 (1 of 28).

Agrippa, Camillo, sixteenth century.

Trattato di Scientia d'Arme con un Dialogo di Filosofia. . . . Rome: Antonio Blado, 1553. DSoC.

> In Dormer's library, 1741 (1 of 42).

Albemarle, George Monck, Duke of, 1608–70.

Observations upon Military and Political Affairs. . . . London: Printed by A.C. for Henry Mortlocke and James Collins, 1671. DSoC.

> In General Officer's library, 1773, and Oglethorpe's, 1785; purchased by Smith in 1773 (3 of 42).

Anderson, James.

Essay on the Art of War. New ed. London: A. Millar, 1762. DSoC.

> Smith cited, 1779 (1 of 22).

Anderson, Robert, fl. 1668–96.

The Genuine Use and Effects of the Gunne. . . . London: Printed by J. Darby for William Berry and Robert Morden, 1674. DSoC.

> In General Officer's library, 1773; bought by Smith, 1773 (2 of 42).

Angelo, Domenico, 1717?–1802.

L'École des Armes avec l'Explication Générale des Principales Attitudes et Positions Concernant l'Escrime. London: R. and J. Dodsley, 1763. DSoC.

> In Ligonier's library, 1770 (1 of 21).

Ango, Pierre, 1640–94.
Pratique Generale des Fortifications. . . . Moulins: Claude Vernoy, 1679.
DSoC.
> In General Officer's library, 1773 (1 of 42).

Anno Regni Georgii II Regis . . . *Vicesimo Septimo* [An Act for Punishing Mutiny]. London: T. Baskett, 1751. DSoC.
> In 1758 Wade owned an unspecified edition of the Mutiny Act, which was adopted and published regularly throughout the eighteenth century (1 of 42).

The Answer of the Parliament . . . *also a Narrative of the Late Engagement between the English Fleet under* . . . *Blake; and the Holland Fleet under* . . . *Trump.* . . . London: J. Field, 1652. MH-H.
> In Montresor's library, 1799 (1 of 42).

Appianus of Alexandria, second century A.D.
Historia delle Guerre esterne de Romani di Appiano Alessandrino. Translated by Braccio. 2 vols. Venice: Giol., 1559. Uk.
> In Dormer's library, 1741; and a 1679 edition was in the library of Gentleman in the Army, 1799 (2 of 42).

Appianus of Alexandria, second century A.D.
The History of Appian of Alexandria. . . . Translated by J[ohn] D[avies]. London: J. Amery, 1679. DSoC.
> In Oglethorpe's library, 1785 (1 of 42).
>> Including Donkin, who quoted Appian without specifying an edition (1777), four officers expressed a preference for Appian's history (4 of 42).

Appier Hanzelet, Jean, 1596–1647.
La Pyrotechnie de Hanzelet Lorrain. . . . Pont à Mousson: I. and G. Bernard, 1630. DSoC.
> In Winde's library, 1740, and in Montresor's, 1799 (2 of 42).

Aquino, Carlo d', 1654–1737.
Additiones ad Lexicon Militare. Rome: Bernarbo, 1727. Uk.
> Smith cited, 1779 (1 of 40).

Arçon, Jean Claude Éléonore, Le Michaud d', 1733–1800.
Considerations sur l'Influence du Génie de Vauban dans la Balance des Forces de l'Etat. . . . [Strasbourg?]: n.p., 1786. NcD.
> In Montresor's library, 1799 (1 of 4).

Arcq, Philippe-Auguste de Sainte Foy, Chevalier d', 1721–79.
Histoire Generale des Guerres. . . . 2 vols. Paris: Imprimerie Royale, 1756–58.
ICN.

In Ligonier's library, 1770, and General Officer's library, 1773; Smith recommended, 1779 (3 of 25, or 12 percent, and an authority; see Appendix B).

Ardesoif, J[ohn]. P[lummer]., d. 1790.
An Introduction to Marine Fortification and Gunnery. . . . Gosport: W. Dawkins, 1772. DSoC.
> Smith recommended, 1779 (1 of 19).

Arrian, second century A.D.
Arrianou Nikomedeos Anabaseos Alexandrou . . . Arriani Nicomediensis Expeditionis Alexandri. . . . Translated by Jacob Gronovius. Leiden: Petrus Vander Aa, 1704. DSoC.
> Oglethorpe had this edition in 1785 (1 of 42).

Arrian, second century A.D.
Arrianou Peri Alexandrou Anabaseos Historion Biblia Okto. Arriani De Expeditione . . . Alexandri. . . . Translated into Latin by Bartholomeo Facio. Basel: Roberti Winter, 1539. DSoC.
> Owned by Gentleman in the Army, 1799 (1 of 42).

Arrian, second century A.D.
Arrianou Peri Anabaseos Alexandrou Historion Biblia . . . Arriani De Expedit. Alex. Amsterdam: J. Janssonium, 1668. DSoC.
> Stanhope owned this edition in 1721 (1 of 42).

Arrian, second century A.D.
Arrian's History of Alexander's Expedition. . . . Translated by John Rooke. 2 vols. London: T. Worrall, J. Gray, L. Gilliver, and R. Willock, 1729. DSoC.
> Wade had this edition in 1758, as did Ligonier in 1770 and Oglethorpe in 1785 (3 of 40).

Arrian, second century A.D.
Les Guerres d'Alexandre. Translated by Nicolas Perrot Sieur d'Ablancourt. Paris: L. Billaine, 1664. CSmH
> In Winde's library, 1740, and Dormer's, 1741 (2 of 42). Including Donkin, who repeatedly cited Arrian's history without specifying an edition, 19 percent of the officers (8 of 42) owned, collectively, at least five editions of Arrian. He was clearly considered an authority by our forty-two officers (see Appendix B).

Articles of War. See *Rules and Articles.* . . .

Atlas Militaire: Contenant le Theatre de la Guerre dans les Pays-Bas. Paris and Lille: Gand Anvers, 1746. GyGoN.
> Dury catalogue of 1758 (1 of 33).

Aubert de la Chesnaye-Desbois, François-Alexandre, 1699–1784.
Dictionnaire Militaire, Ou Recueil Alphabetique de Tous les Termes Propres à l'Art de la Guerre. . . . New ed. 2 vols. Dresden: G. C. Walther, 1751. DSoC.
> Ligonier owned in 1770 and General Officer, in 1773 (2 of 31).

An Authentic Account of Our Last Attempt upon the Coast of France. By an Officer. . . . London, 1758. Uk.
> Molyneux cited in 1759 (1 of 25).

Ávila y Zúñiga, Luis de, fl. 1550–64.
Clarissimi Viri D. Ludouici . . . Commentariorum de Bello Germanico. . . . Antwerp: I. Steelsij, 1550. DSoC.
> In Seton's library, 1732 (1 of 42).

Ayscu, Edward, 1549?–1617.
A Historie Contayning the Warres . . . between England and Scotland, from King William the Conqueror, vntill the Happy Union. . . . London: G. Eld, 1607. DSoC.
> In Seton's library, 1732 (1 of 42).

Bardet de Villeneuve, P. P. A.
Cours de la Science Militaire, à l'Usage de l'Infanterie, de la Cavalerie. . . . 11 vols. The Hague: Jean van Duren, 1740–42. DSoC.
> General Officer owned eight of these eleven volumes in 1773 (1 of 35).

Bardet de Villeneuve, P. P. A.
La Tactique ou l'Art de Ranger des Bataillons. . . . The Hague: Jean van Duren, 1740. DSoC.
> Ligonier owned in 1770 (1 of 35). This seems to have been volume 2 of *Cours de la Science Militaire.*

Barre, Joseph, 1692–1764.
Vie de M. le Marquis de Fabert Marechal de France. 2 vols. Paris: Jean-Thomas Herissant, 1752. DSoC.
> Clinton discussed c. 1789 (1 of 31).

Barriffe, William, 1601?–1643.
Militarie Discipline or the Young Artillery-Man. . . . 6th ed. London: Gartrude Dawson, 1661. DSoC.
> In Winde's library, 1740, and Tryon's, 1773 (2 of 42).

Barry, Gerat, fl. 1624–42.
A Discourse of Military Discipline. . . . Brussels: the widow of John Mommart, 1634. DSoC.
> In General Officer's library, 1773; purchased by Smith, 1773 (2 of 42).

Barry, Gerat, fl. 1624–42.
The Siege of Breda. . . . Louvain: ex officina Hastenii, 1627. CSmH.

> In Seton's library in 1732 and Montresor's in 1799 (2 of 42). It seems likely that this book was written by Herman Hugo and translated by Barry. See Hugo, Herman, 1588–1629.

Basnage, Jacques Sieur de Beauval, 1653–1723.
Histoire des Ordres Militaires, ou des Chevaliers des Milices. . . . 4 vols. Amsterdam: P. Brunel, 1721. DSoC.

> In Ligonier's library, 1770 (1 of 41).

Baudier, Michel, 1589?–1645.
Histoire du Mareschal de Toiras. . . . Paris: S. Cramoisy and G. Cramoisy, 1644. DSoC.

> In Dury's library, 1758 (1 of 42).

Bayard, Nicholas, 1644–1707, and Charles Lodowick.
A Journal of the Late Actions of the French at Canada. . . . London: Richard Baldwin, 1693. Uk.

> In Hotham's library, 1738 (1 of 42).

Beaugué, Jean de, sixteenth century A.D.
The History of the Campagnes 1548 and 1549 . . . by the Scots and French on the One Side and by the English and their Foreign Auxiliaries on the Other. . . . [Edinburgh]: n.p., 1707. DSoC.

> Likely in Seton's Library, 1732 (1 of 42).

Beaurain, Jean Chevalier de, 1696–1771.
L'Histoire Militaire du Duc de Luxembourg. . . . 5 vols. The Hague: B. Gibert, 1756–58. DSoC.

> Townshend listed, 1759; Clinton made notes on, 1768–76; and Smith recommended, 1779 (3 of 25).

Beaurain, Jean Chevalier de, 1696–1771.
Histoire Militaire de Flandre, depuis l'Année 1690 jusqu'en 1694 Inclusivement . . . (Ouvrage Fait sur les Mémoires . . . de M. le Maréchal Duc de Luxembourg . . .). 2 vols. Paris: Le Chevalier de Beaurain [and others], 1755. DSoC.

> Owned by Dury in 1758, Ligonier in 1770, and General Officer in 1773; listed by Townshend in 1759 (4 of 30, or 13 percent).
>
> Considered together, Beaurain's histories attracted 20 percent (6 of 30) of the officers who might have expressed a preference for them; he was clearly one of the authors that our officers considered an authority (see Appendix B).

Belidor, M. Bernard Forest de, 1697?–1761.
Le Bombardier François, ou, Nouvelle Methode de Jetter les Bombes. . . . Paris:
Imprimerie Royale, 1731. DSoC.
> Oglethorpe had this edition in 1785. General Officer (1773) had an Amsterdam
> edition of 1734 (DSoC) (2 of 40).

Belidor, M. Bernard Forest de, 1697?–1761.
Dictionnaire Portatif de l'Ingénieur. . . . Paris: Charles-Antoine Jombert,
1755. DSoC.
> Smith cited, 1779 (1 of 30).

Belidor, M. Bernard Forest de, 1697?–1761.
Kurzgefasstes Kriegs-Lexicon. . . . Translated by Fr. W. Kratzenstein. Nuremberg, 1765. DSoC.
> Smith cited, 1779 (1 of 21).

Belidor, M. Bernard Forest de, 1697?–1761.
Nouveau Cours de Mathematique: a l'Usage de l'Artillerie et du Genie. . . .
Paris: Charles-Antoine Jombert, 1725. DSoC.
> In Montresor's library, 1799; in 1779 Smith cited a 1758 edition of this work that
> has not been found (2 of 41).

Belidor, M. Bernard Forest de, 1697?–1761.
La Science des Ingenieurs dans la Conduite des Travaux de Fortification. . . .
Paris: Claude Jombert, 1729. DSoC.
> In the libraries of General Officer (1773), Wortley Montagu (1776), Oglethorpe
> (1785), and Montresor (1799). Montresor had two editions published in Paris,
> 1729—of one and two volumes respectively. Wortley Montagu had another edi-
> tion—The Hague, 1734—in 1776 and Hesse, an unspecified edition in 1758 (5
> of 40, or 13 percent).
>
> Altogether, 15 percent of the officers (6 of 41) expressed a preference for one
> or more of Belidor's works, placing him among the authors that our officers
> considered to be an authority (see Appendix B).

Bell, Thomas, d. 1782.
A Short Essay on Military First Principles. London: T. Becket and P. A. de
Hondt, 1770. DSoC.
> Smith recommended in 1779 (1 of 19).

Belle-Isle, Charles Louis Auguste de Fouquet, Duc de, 1684–1761.
Lettres du Maréchal Duc de Belleisle, au Maréchal de Contades. . . . The
Hague: Pierre de Hondt, 1759. DSoC.
> Hotham Thompson had this correspondence in his library in 1784, perhaps
> this edition (1 of 24).

Bellersheim, P. F. de.

Nouvelle Manière de Defendre et de Fortifier les Places Irregulières. . . . Frankfurt am Main: H. L. Broenner, 1767. DSoC.

> In 1779 Smith recommended a 1765 German edition of this work, *Neue Methode, Irregulare Festungen* . . . , that has not been found (1 of 21).

Bentivoglio, Guido, 1577–1644.

Della Guerra di Fiandra. . . . 3 vols. Colonia: Typographia Erpeniana, 1635–40. MiU.

> Dormer owned in 1741. There was a 1722 edition in Montresor's library in 1799 and an unspecified edition in Hotham Thompson's in 1784 (3 of 42).

Bentivoglio, Guido, 1577–1644.

The History of the Warrs of Flanders. . . . Translated by Henry Earl of Monmouth. London: D. Newman and four others, 1678. DSoC.

> In Seton's library, 1732; Stewart owned a 1685 French edition of this history in 1750 (2 of 42). Altogether, 12 percent of the officers (5 of 42) showed a preference for Bentivoglio's history, placing it among our officers' authorities (Appendix B).

Berkley, George, d. 1747.

The Naval History of Britain from the Earliest Periods . . . to the Conclusion of . . . M.DCC.LVI. Compiled by [John Hill]. London: T. Osborne and J. Shipton, 1756. DSoC.

> In Oglethorpe's library, 1785 (1 of 28).

Bernard, Jean-François.

Nouvelle Maniére de Fortifier les Places: Tirée des Methodes du Chevalier de Ville, du Comte de Pagan, et de Monsieur de Vauban avec des Remarques sur . . . les Desseins du Capitaine Marchi & sur Ceux de M. Blondel. . . . Paris: Estienne Michallet, 1689. DSoC.

> In Winde's library, 1740, and Lord John Murray's, 1762 (2 of 42).

Bernard, Jean-François.

Remarks on the Modern Fortification. To Which Is Added the Easiest and Most Reasonable Manner of Constructing All Sorts of Works. . . . Translated by William Horneck. London: J. and R. Tonson, 1738. DSoC.

> Dury owned in 1758; General Officer owned and Blomefield purchased in 1773; and Smith recommended in 1779, specifying an 1758 edition that has not been found (4 of 36).
>
> Bernard's books on fortification attracted 14 percent (6 of 42) of the officers who might have preferred them. Taken together, those books placed Bernard among our officers' authorities (see Appendix B).

Bernard, Nicholas, d. 1661, and George Walker, d. 1690.
The Whole Proceedings of the Siege of Drogheda. To Which Is Added, A True Account of the Siege of Londonderry. Dublin: R. Reilly for S. Hyde, 1736. DSoC.
>In Dury's library, 1758 (1 of 42).

Berwick, James Fitzjames, 1st Duke of, 1670–1734.
Memoirs of the Marshal Duke of Berwick. Written by himself. Completed by L. J. Hooke. 2 vols. London: T. Cadell, 1779. DSoC.
>In Oglethorpe's library, 1785 (1 of 7). See also La Pause, Guillaume Plantavit de, Abbé de Margon, 1685?–1760.

Béthune, Maximilien de, Duc de Sully, 1560–1641. See Sully.

[Bever, Samuel.]
The Cadet: A Military Treatise, By an Officer. . . . London: W. Johnson, 1756. DSoC.
>In the libraries of Dury (1758), Wade (1758), Ligonier (1770), and General Officer (1773) (4 of 28, or 14 percent). There was a second London edition of this book in 1762 (DSoC). Our forty-two officers clearly held the *Cadet* to be an authority (see Appendix B).

Biggs, William.
The Military History of Europe [1739–48]. . . . Limerick: Andrew Welsh, 1749. Uk.
>In Ligonier's library, 1770 (1 of 33).

Biggs, William.
The Military History of Europe [1739–48]. . . . London: R. Baldwin [and three others], 1755. DSoC.
>Oglethorpe had this edition in 1785. Wade had a 1756 edition (likely that published in London by R. Baldwin, which is also in DSoC) in 1758; Smith recommended what seems to have been the same 1756 edition in 1779; General Officer had and Blomefield purchased another London edition of 1759 in 1773; and Dury had an unspecified edition in 1758 (6 of 30). Altogether, 21 percent of the officers (7 of 33) owned a version of this book, which our officers considered an authority (see Appendix B).

Bigot de Morogues, Sébastien François, 1705–81.
Essay de l'Application des Forces Centrales aux Effets de la Poudre à Canon. Paris: C. A. Jombert, 1737. DSoC.
>In General Officer's library, 1773 (1 of 38).

Billon, Jean de, Sieur de La Prugne.
Les Principes de l'Art Militaire. . . . Rouen: I. Berthelin, 1641. Uk.
    In Winde's library, 1740 (1 of 42).

Binning, Thomas, b. 1620.
A Light to the Art of Gunnery. . . . London: J. D. for W. Fisher and R. Mount, 1689. NN.
    General Officer owned and Smith purchased in 1773 (2 of 42).

Biondi, Giovanni Francesco, 1572–1644.
An History of the Civill Warres of England, betweene the Two Houses of Lancaster and Yorke. . . . Translated by Henry, Earle of Monmouth. 2 vols. London: John Benson, 1641–46. DSoC.
    Oglethorpe owned this book in 1785 (1 of 42).

Birac, le Sieur de.
Les Fonctions de Tous les Officiers de l'Infanterie. . . . The Hague: Henry van Bulderen, 1688. DSoC.
    In General Officer's library, 1773 (1 of 42).

Birac, le Sieur de.
Les Fonctions du Capitaine de Cavalerie & les Principales de ses Officiers Subalternes. . . . The Hague: Henry van Bulderen, 1688. DSoC.
    In General Officer's library, 1773 (1 of 42).

Birnbaum, Johann Moritz.
Unterricht für einen Artilleristen. . . . Dresden, 1752. DSoC.
    Smith recommended in 1779 (1 of 31).

Bisset, Charles, 1717–91.
The Theory and Construction of Fortification. . . . London: Printed for the author and sold by A. Millar, D. Wilson, and R. Dodsley, 1751. DSoC.
    Lord John Murray had this edition in 1762—as did Ligonier in 1770, General Officer and Debbieg in 1773, and Oglethorpe in 1785. Dury had an unspecified edition in 1758 (6 of 31, or 19 percent). Bisset was clearly among our officers' authorities (see Appendix B).

Bland, Humphrey, 1686?–1763.
A Treatise of Military Discipline. . . . London: S. Buckley, 1727. DSoC.
    First published in 1727, Bland's *Treatise* went through nine editions (all DSoC) by the time of his death in 1763. Howe owned a copy in 1732, as did Paget in 1741, Hawley in 1753, Wolfe in 1756, Dury and Wade in 1758, Ligonier in 1770, Tryon and Smith in 1773, Hotham Thompson in 1784, Calderwood in 1787, and Montresor in 1799. Bagshawe in 1751, Lord John Murray in 1762, and General

Officer in 1773 each had two copies. Altogether, 37.5 percent (15 of 40) of all
the officers who might have had the book had one or more copies of Bland's
Treatise. John Houlding seems to have been thoroughly justified in saying that
Bland's was the "best known of all eighteenth-century military treatises in
the English language" (*Fit for Service*, p. 182). Our forty officers certainly preferred Bland to all save eight or nine books on war available in mid-eighteenth-
century Britain (see Appendix B).

Blondel, François, 1618–86.
L'Art de Jetter les Bombes. The Hague: Arnout Leers, 1685. DSoC.
> In Winde's library, 1740, and Hotham Thompson's, 1784 (2 of 42).

Blondel, François, 1618–86.
Nouvelle Manière de Fortifier les Places. . . . The Hague: Arnout Leers, 1686.
   MiU.
> Owned by General Officer and purchased by Smith in 1773. Lord John Murray
> owned an unspecified edition in 1768 (3 of 42).
> Blondel's books attracted 12 percent (5 of 42) of the officers who might have
> shown a preference for them (an authority; see Appendix B).

Bombelles, Henri François, Comte de, 1681–1760.
Nouveaux Memoires sur le Service Journalier de l'Infanterie. . . . 2 vols. Paris:
   La Veuve Delatour, 1746. DSoC.
> Bever referred to in 1756; in General Officer's library, 1773 (2 of 33).

Bombelles, Henri François, Comte de, 1681–1760.
*Traité des Évolutions Militaires les Plus Simples et les Plus Faciles à Exécuter
   par l'Infanterie.* . . . Paris: Jean-Thomas Hérissant, 1754. DSoC.
> Bever referred to in 1756 and General Officer owned in 1773. Dury had an un-
> specified edition in 1758 (3 of 30, or 10 percent, and an authority; see Appen-
> dix B).

Bottée, Claude.
Études Militaires . . . et l'Exercice de l'Infanterie. Paris: C. Jombert, 1731. ICN.
> Oglethorpe owned in 1785 (1 of 40).

Bouhours, Dominique, 1628–1702.
Histoire de Pierre d'Aubusson, Grand-Maistre de Rhodes. Paris: Sebastien
   Mabre-Cramoisy, 1676. DSoC.
> In Dury's library, 1758 (1 of 42).

Bourgelat, Claude, 1712–79.
Le Nouveau Newcastle, ou, Nouveau Traité de Cavalerie. . . . Lausanne and
   Geneva: Marc-Michel Bousquet, 1744. DSoC.
> Calderwood owned Paris edition of 1746 in c. 1787 (1 of 33).

Bourne, William, d. 1583.
Inventions or Devises. Very Nece[ss]ary for all Generalles and Captaines....
  London: Thomas Woodcook, 1578. NN.
    In General Officer's library, 1773 (1 of 42).

Boyer, Abel, 1667–1729.
The Draughts of the Most Remarkable Fortified Towns of Europe.... London:
  Isaac Cleave and John Hartley, 1701. DSoC.
    In the libraries of Seton (1732), Stewart (1750), Dury (1758), Lord John Murray
    (1762), and Oglethorpe (1785) (5 of 42, or 12 percent, and an authority; see
    Appendix B).

Boyer, Abel, 1667–1729, and Martin Bladen, 1680–1746.
An Impartial Enquiry into the Management of the War in Spain.... London:
  John Morphew, 1712. DSoC.
    Stewart owned in 1750 and Wade, in 1758; Molyneux cited in 1759 (3 of 42).

Boyle, Roger. See Orrery.

Brindley, John. See *Theatre of the Present War.*

Briquet, Pierre de, editor.
*Code Militaire, ou Compilation des Ordonnances des Roys de France Con-
  cernant les Gens de Guerre.* 3 vols. Paris: Imprimerie Royale, 1728. DSoC.
    Dury owned in 1758, as did Lord John Murray (an unspecified edition) in 1762
    and Tryon in 1773 (3 of 40). See also Sparre, Lars Magnus, Baron de.

Brodrick, Thomas.
A Compleat History of the Late War in the Netherlands. London: W. Pearson
  for T. Ward, 1713. DSoC.
    In Dury's library, 1758 (1 of 42).

Broglie, Victor François, 1718–1804.
Campagnes du Marechal duc de Broglie . . . en Allemagne 1759-1761 . . .
  (bound with *Instruction pour l'Infanterie; Instruction pour la Cavalerie*).
  Frankfurt am Main and Leipzig, 1761. DSoC.
    In Tryon's library, 1773; Percy made notes on, n.d. (2 of 23).

Brown, Hugh.
*The True Principles of Gunnery Investigated and Explained: Comprehend-
  ing Translations of Professor Euler's Observations upon the New Principles of Gunnery . . . by the Late Mr. Benjamin Robins. . . .* London:
  J. Nourse, 1777. DSoC.
    Recommended by Smith, 1779, and in Montresor's library 1799 (2 of 8).

Bruce, Alexander, d. 1729.
The Institutions of Military Law, Ancient and Modern. Edinburgh: heirs
and successors of Andrew Anderson, 1717. DSoC.

    In Maxwell's library, 1769 (1 of 42).

Brunswick, Friedrich August, Duke of, 1740–1805.
Critical Reflections on the Character and Actions of Alexander the Great.
London: T. Becket and P. A. de Hondt, 1767. CSt.

    In Montresor's library, 1799 (1 of 21).

Bubilan.
*La Science de la Guerre: ou Soit Connoissances Nécessaires pour Tous Ceux
qui Entreprennent la Profession des Armes*. . . . Turin: l'Imprimerie Royale,
1744. DSoC.

    In General Officer's library, 1773 (1 of 33).

Buchner, Johann Siegmund.
Theoria et Praxis Artilleriae. . . . 3 vols. Nuremberg: J. Hoffmanns and C. S.
Froberg, 1682–85. MnU.

    Smith recommended in 1779 (1 of 42).

Buisson, Mr. [pseud. of Courtilz de Sandras, Gatien, 1644–1712].
*The History of the Life and Actions of That Great Captain of His Age the Vis-
count de Turenne*. London: J. B. for Dorman Newman and R. Bentley,
1686. DSoC.

    In Winde's library, 1740 (1 of 42). See also Courtilz de Sandras, Gatien, 1644–
    1712.

Buonamici, Castruccio, 1710–61.
Castruccii Bonamici Commentariorum de Bello Italico. . . . 3 vols. Leiden:
n.p., 1750–51. DSoC.

    Bever referred to in 1756; Dury had in his library in 1758; Townshend included
    in a list in 1759; and a copy was in General Officer's library in 1773 (4 of 31).

Buonamici, Castruccio, 1710–61.
Commentaries of the Late War in Italy. . . . Translated by A. Wishart. London: A. Millar, 1753. DSoC.

    Dury owned in 1758, as did Gentleman in the Army in 1799 (2 of 30). Altogether,
    some 16 percent (5 of 31) of those officers who might have shown a preference
    for Buonamici's *Commentaries* did so; they considered his *Commentaries* one
    of their authorities (see Appendix B).

Burchett, Josiah, 1666?–1746.
A Complete History of the Most Remarkable Transactions at Sea: from the

Earliest Accounts of Time to the Conclusion of the Last War with France. . . .
London: W. B. for J. Walthoe and J. Walthoe, junior, 1720. DSoC.
> Stewart owned in 1750 and Molyneux cited in 1759 (2 of 42).

Burchett, Josiah, 1666?–1746.
Memoirs of Transactions at Sea, during the War with France, Beginning in 1688, and Ending in 1697. London: John Nutt, 1703. DSoC.
> Winde owned in 1740; Molyneux cited in 1759; and Hotham Thompson had in his library in 1784 (3 of 42).

Burnet, Gilbert, 1643–1715.
Bishop Burnet's History of His Own Time. Edited by Thomas Burnet. 2 vols. London: Thomas Ward, 1724–34. DSoC.
> Cited by Molyneux in 1759; in Tryon's library, 1773 (2 of 41).

Busca, Gabriello, fl. 1580.
Della Architettvra Militare. . . . Milan: Girolamo Bordone and Pietro Martire Locarni, 1601. DSoC.
> Winde owned in 1740 (1 of 42).

Byng, John. See Fearne, Charles.

Caesar, Caius Julius, 100–44 B.C.
C. Julii Caesaris de Bellis Gallico et Civili Pompejano. . . . Annotated by Frans van Oudendorp. 2 vols. Leiden: S. Luchtmans; and Rotterdam: J. D. Beman, 1737. DSoC.
> In Calderwood's library, 1787 (1 of 38).

Caesar, Caius Julius, 100–44 B.C.
C. Julii Caesaris et A. Hirtii De rebus a Caesare Gestis Commentarii. . . .
3 vols. Glasgow: Rob. and And. Foulis, 1750. DSoC.
> In Wortley Montagu library, 1776 (1 of 32).

Caesar, Caius Julius, 100–44 B.C.
C. Ivlii Caesaris Quae Extant. . . . Annotated by Ios. Scaligeri. Leiden: Elzevir, 1635. DSoC.
> In Wortley Montagu's library, 1776 (1 of 42).

Caesar, Caius Julius, 100–44 B.C.
C. Julii Caesaris Quae Extant. . . . Interpreted by Joannes Goduinus. London: Abel Swall, 1693. Uk.
> Among Stanhope's books, 1721, and Oglethorpe's, 1785; Lord John Murray had an unspecified edition of this interpretation in 1762 (3 of 42).

Caesar, Caius Julius, 100–44 B.C.
C. Julii Caesaris Quae Extant Omnia. . . . 2 vols. Leiden: C. Boutesteyn and
   S. Luchtmans, 1713. DSoC.
> In Stewart's library (1750) (1 of 42).

Caesar, Caius Julius, 100–44 B.C.
C. Julius Caesar's Commentaries. . . . Translated by Martin Bladen. London:
   Richard Smith, 1705. DSoC.
> Hawley reflected on in 1725; Robert Murray owned Bladen's translation in 1738,
> as did Dury in 1758, Maxwell in 1769, Tryon in 1773, and Hotham Thompson
> in 1784 (6 of 42). This translation was one of the most popular in eighteenth-
> century England; it reached its eighth edition in 1770.

Caesar, Caius Julius, 100–44 B.C.
Les Commentaires de Cesar. Translated by Nicolas Perrot d'Ablancourt.
   2 vols. Lyon: A. and H. Molin, 1689. DSoC.
> In Oglethorpe's library, 1785. In 1770 Ligonier had a 1708 edition of Perrot's
> translation as well as other editions of 1745 (two copies) and 1750 (2 of 42).

Caesar, Caius Julius, 100–44 B.C.
Les Commentaires de Iules Cesar. . . . Translated by Blaise de Vigenere. 2 vols.
   Paris: A. l'Angelier, 1589. Uk.
> In Dormer's library 1741 (1 of 42).

Caesar, Caius Julius, 100–44 B.C.
I Commentari di C. Givlio Cesare. . . . Venice: G. Foglietti, 1618. DSoC.
> In Winde's library, 1740 (1 of 42).

Caesar, Caius Julius, 100–44 B.C.
The Commentaries of C. Julius Caesar. . . . Translated by Clement Edmondes.
   London: R. Daniel [and three others], 1655. DSoC.
> In the libraries of Winde (1740), Ligonier (1770), and Oglethorpe (1785); Clin-
> ton reflected on, 1768–76 (4 of 42).

Caesar, Caius Julius, 100–44 B.C.
The Commentaries of Caesar. . . . Translated by William Duncan. London:
   J. & R. Tonson, 1753. DSoC.
> In the libraries of General Officer (1773), Parker (1773), Wortley Montagu
> (1776), and Oglethorpe (1785: both the 1753 and 1779 editions of Duncan) (4 of
> 30).

Caesar, Caius Julius, 100–44 B.C.
Le Parfait Capitaine, Autrement L'Abbregé des Guerres de Gaule des Com-

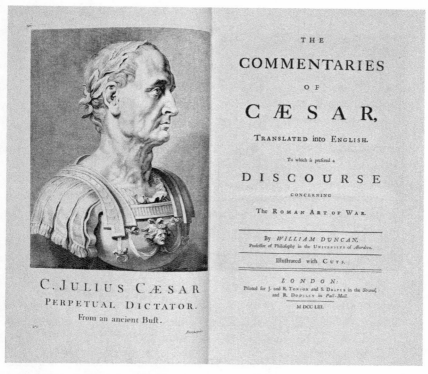

C. JULIUS CÆSAR
PERPETUAL DICTATOR.
From an ancient Buft.

THE
COMMENTARIES
OF
CÆSAR,
TRANSLATED into ENGLISH.

To which is prefixed a
DISCOURSE
CONCERNING
The ROMAN ART of WAR.

By WILLIAM DUNCAN,
Professor of Philosophy in the UNIVERSITY of Aberdeen.

Illustrated with CUTS.

LONDON:
Printed for J. and R. TONSON and S. DRAPER in the Strand,
and R. DODSLEY in Pall-Mall.

M DCC LIII.

As the elegant title page and frontispiece to William Duncan's 1753 folio edition suggest, Caesar's *Commentaries* were very popular in eighteenth-century England. Our forty-two officers clearly preferred Caesar to all other authorities on war and considered Duncan's translation among the best of the twenty-one editions in their hands.

mentaires de Cesar. Abridged by Henri, Duc de Rohan. 3 vols. Paris: Jean Houze, 1640. CSmH.

Dundas considered this edition in 1779; Stewart owned a 1677 edition in 1750; Tryon and General Officer owned and Debbieg purchased a 1744 edition in 1773; Bever (1756) and Dalrymple (1761) both cited the book without specifying an edition (7 of 42).

Many officers recommended, discussed, cited, or listed Caesar's *Commentaries* without specifying a particular edition. Wolfe (1756) and Townshend (1776) included the *Commentaries* in their recommendations for other officers. Hawley discussed (1725); Molyneux and Dalrymple cited (1759 and 1761); and Donkin cited and quoted them repeatedly (1777). Seton (1732), Dormer (1741), Dury (1758), Wade (1758), Lord John Murray (1762), Ligonier (1770), Tryon (1773), and Hotham Thompson (1784) owned copies. Altogether, 67 percent of the officers (28 of 42) showed a preference for Caesar—owning or mentioning among them some sixty copies and twenty-one different editions of his *Commentaries*. Our officers clearly preferred him to any other author on war (see Appendix B, The Authorities).

Caillières, Jacques de, d. 1697.
Histoire du Mareschal de Matignon. . . . Paris: A. Courbé, 1661. Uk.
Oglethorpe owned in 1785 (1 of 42).

Cambray, Chevalier de.
Manière de Fortifier de Mr. de Vauban. . . . Amsterdam: P. Mortier, 1689. DSoC.
In Winde's library in 1740 and Bagshawe's in 1751 (2 of 42). Abel Swall translated and published Cambray's work as *The New Method of Fortification as Practiced by Monsieur de Vauban*, London, 1691, DSoC.

Cambridge, Richard Owen, 1717–1802.
An Account of the War in India between the English and French. . . . London: T. Jefferys, 1761. DSoC.
In General Officer's library, 1773; the 1762 edition was also in Lord John Murray's library in 1762 and in Oglethorpe's in 1785 (3 of 23, or 13 percent, and among our officers' authorities; see Appendix B).

Campagne de Hollande en MDCLXXII sous les Ordres de Mr le Duc de Luxembourg. . . . Edited by [Dumoulin]. The Hague: P. de Hondt, 1759. DSoC.
In the libraries of Ligonier (1770) and General Officer (1773) (2 of 24).

Campagne de Monsieur le Maréchal de Marsin en Allemagne l'An M.DCC. IV. . . . 3 vols. Amsterdam: M. M. Rey, 1762. DSoC.
In General Officer's library, 1773 (1 of 22).

Campagne de Monsieur le Maréchal Duc de Noailles en Allemagne, l'An M.DCC.XLIII. . . . 2 vols. Amsterdam: Marc-Michel Rey, 1760–61. DSoC.
In Ligonier's library, 1770, and General Officer's library, 1773 (2 of 23).

Campbell, John, 1708–75.
Lives of the Admirals, and Other Eminent British Seamen. . . . 4 vols. London: J. Applebee for J. and H. Pemberton and T. Waller, 1742–44. DSoC.
Maxwell owned in 1769, as did Hotham Thompson in 1784 and Oglethorpe, a 1781 edition, in 1785; Molyneux cited an unspecified edition in 1759 (4 of 33, or 12 percent, and one of the authorities; see Appendix B).

Campbell, John, 1708–75.
The Military History of the Late Prince Eugene of Savoy and of the Late John

Duke of Marlborough. . . . 2 vols. London: J. Bettenham for C. Du Bosc, 1736–37. DSoC.

This seems to be the book that Dormer (1741), Ligonier (1770), and Oglethorpe (1785) owned. Dury (1758) also had a two-volume history of Eugene and Marlborough in English and Gentleman in the Army (1799) a 1738 edition of what seems to have been this book; Hotham Thompson owned the first volume of this history in 1784 (6 of 38, or 16 percent). Our officers did consider this book to be one of their authorities (see Appendix B).

According to C. T. Atkinson, *Marlborough and the Rise of the British Army* (New York, 1921), p. xi, Campbell's work "represents a reproduction" of two French histories: J. Dumont, *Batailles Gagnées par le . . . Prince Fr. Eugène* (1725), and J. Rousset de Missy's *Histoire Militaire du Prince Eugene de Savoye, du Prince et Duc de Marlborough . . . .* (1729). See Dumont.

Candid Reflections on the Report . . . of the General-Officers, Appointed to Enquire into the Causes of the Failure of the Late Expedition to the Coasts of France. London: S. Hooper and A. Morley, 1758. DSoC.

Molyneux cited, 1759 (1 of 25).

Capriata, Pietro Giovanni, d. 1660.
The History of the Wars of Italy from the Year MDCXIII to the Year MDCXLIV. Translated by Henry Earl of Monmouth. London: J. Macock to be sold by Tho. Clarke, 1663. DSoC.

In Seton's library, 1732 (1 of 42).

Carloix, Vincent.
Mémoires de la Vie de François de Scepeaux, Sire de Vieilleville. Annotated by Henri Griffet. 5 vols. Paris: H. L. Guerin and L. F. Delatour, 1757. DSoC.

In General Officer's library, 1773 (1 of 28).

Carmarthen, Marquis of. See Osborne, Peregrine Hyde, Marquis of Carmarthen and Duke of Leeds, 1658–1729.

Carr, William, fl. 1676.
A Particular Account of This Last Siege of Mastricht. . . . London: G. Kunholt and Moses Pitt, 1676. DSoC.

In Hotham's library, 1738 (1 of 42).

Cataneo, Girolamo, sixteenth century.
Most Briefe Tables to Knowe Redily Howe Manye Ranckes of Footemen . . . Go to the Making of a Just Battayle. Translated by H. Grantham. London: W. Williamson for John Wight, 1574. DSoC.

In General Officer's library, 1773 (1 of 42).

The "Siege of Lisle" is from Campbell's *Military History . . . of Marlborough* (1736–37), 2:60. Our forty-two officers preferred Campbell to other histories of Marlborough and Marlborough to other English authorities on the art of war. Our officers esteemed Marlborough as much for his successful sieges (Lisle) as for his great battles (Blenheim).

Cautions and Advices to Officers of the Army: Particularly Subalterns.... By
an Old Officer. London: T. Payne, 1760. DSoC.

> In 1785 Cuthbert owned an unspecified edition of this book, which was also
> published in Edinburgh in 1777 (DSoC) (1 of 24).

Cavalier, Jean, 1681–1740.
Memoirs of the Wars of the Cevennes under Col. Cavallier. . . . Dublin:
J. Carson, 1726. CSmH.

> Ligonier owned, 1770 (1 of 41).

Cellarius, Andreas.
Architectura Militaris. . . . Amsterdam: Jodocus Jansson, 1645. MiU.

> In 1779 Smith recommended what seems to have been a 1656 edition of this
> book, no copy of which has been found (1 of 42).

Cerisiers, Réne de, 1609–62.
Le Heros François; ou, l'Idée du Grand Capitaine. Paris: Canusat, 1645. NjP.

> Ligonier owned in 1770 (1 of 42).

Chales, Claude François Milliet de, 1621–78.
L'Art de Fortifier, de Défendre et d'Attaquer les Places. . . . Paris: E. Michallet,
1677. DSoC.

> In Winde's library, 1740 (1 of 42).

Charles V, Duke of Lorraine, 1643–90.
Political and Military Observations, Remarks and Maxims, of Charles, Late
Duke of Lorrain, General of the Emperor's Forces. London: J. Jones and
W. Hawes, 1699. DSoC.

> In Oglethorpe's library, 1785 (1 of 42).

Charles XII, King of Sweden, 1682–1718.

> See Defoe and Voltaire. Including Wolfe, who in 1756 recommended an unspeci-
> fied life, 17 percent of the officers (7 of 42) preferred books about Charles XII.
> Taken together, those books placed Charles XII among our officers' authorities
> (see Appendix B).

Chennevières, François de, 1699–1799.
Détails Militaires, dont la Connoissance Est Nécessaire à Tous les Officiers,
& Principalement aux Commissaires des Guerres. 6 vols. Paris, Versailles:
C.-A. Jombert, J.-H. Fournier, 1750. DSoC.

> In 1776 Wortley Montagu owned a two-volume edition published in Paris in
> 1742 (1 of 32).

Cinuzzi, Imperiale.
La Vera Militar Disciplina Antica e Moderna. 3 vols. Siena: Salvestro Mar-
chetti, 1604. DSoC.
> In Dury's library, 1758 (1 of 42).

Clairac, Louis-André de La Mamie, 1690–1752.
The Field Engineer of M. le Chevalier de Clairac. Translated by Charles Vallancey. Dublin: J. Smith, 1758. NIC.
> In Montresor's library, 1799 (1 of 25).

Clairac, Louis-André de La Mamie, 1690–1752.
The Field Engineer. . . . Translated by John Muller. London: John Millan,
1760. DSoC.
> General Officer owned this book and Blomefield bought it in 1773; Townshend
> recommended it in 1776, as did Smith in 1779 (4 of 24). There was a second
> London edition in 1773 (DSoC).

Clairac, Louis-André de La Mamie, 1690–1752.
L'Ingenieur de Campagne, ou, Traité de la Fortification Passagere. Paris:
C.-A. Jombert, 1749. DSoC.
> Bever cited this book in 1756; Wolfe recommended it in 1756; Townshend listed
> it in 1759; Dury (1758), Hesse (1758), Ligonier (1770), General Officer (1773),
> and Tryon (1773) owned it; Debbieg purchased a copy in 1773; and Dundas
> considered it in 1779 (10 of 33). There was a second edition published in Paris
> in 1757 and another in Philadelphia in 1776 (both in DSoC).
>
> Altogether, 39 percent (13 of 33) of the officers who might have expressed a
> preference for Clairac's *Field Engineer* did so. They clearly preferred that work
> to all except seven or eight of the books on war available in mid-eighteenth-
> century Britain (see Appendix B).

Clarendon, Edward Hyde, Earl of, 1609–74.
*The History of the Rebellion and Civil Wars in England, Begun in the Year
1641*. . . . 3 vols. Oxford: at the Theater, 1702–4. DSoC.
> Oglethorpe owned this edition in 1785; Paget owned a three-volume edition
> in 1741; Ligonier owned a 1707 edition (DSoC) in 1770; Robert Murray had
> another, unspecified six-volume edition among his books in 1738; and Moly-
> neux cited another unspecified edition in 1759 (5 of 42, or 12 percent, and an
> authority; see Appendix B).

Clarendon, Edward Hyde, Earl of, 1609–74.
The Life of Edward Earl of Clarendon. . . . Oxford: Clarendon Printing-
House, 1759. DSoC.
> In Montresor's library, 1799 (1 of 24).

Clermont, Sieur de.

L'Arithmetique Militaire, ou, l'Arithmetique Pratique de l'Ingénieur et de l'Officier. . . . 3rd ed. 2 vols. Paris: Witte, Didot, 1733. DSoC.

> In 1799 Montresor's library contained a Strasburg, 1707, edition of this book— an edition that cannot now be found (1 of 42).

Clinton, Sir Henry, 1730–95.

Narrative of Lieutenant-General Sir Henry Clinton, K.B. Relative to His Conduct . . . in North America . . . in 1781. . . . London: J. Debrett, 1783. DSoC.

> In Oglethorpe's library, 1785, by which time there were seven editions of this pamphlet; Clinton reconsidered, 1791–92 (2 of 7).

Clinton, Sir Henry, 1730–95.

Observations on Some Parts of the Answer of Earl Cornwallis to Sir Henry Clinton's Narrative. . . . London: J. Debrett, 1783. DSoC.

> Clinton reconsidered, 1791–92 (1 of 7).

Code Militaire, ou Compilation des Ordonnances des Roys de France. . . .

> See Briquet, Pierre de, and Sparre, Lars Magnus, Baron de.

Coehoorn, Menno, Baron van, 1641–1704.

The New Method of Fortification. Translated by Thomas Savery. London: Daniel Midwinter, 1705. DSoC.

> Dury owned in 1758, and in 1779 Smith recommended a 1708 edition—no copy of which has been found (2 of 42).

Coehoorn, Menno, Baron van, 1641–1704.

Nieuwe Vestingbouw . . . van de Fransche Royale Seshoek. . . . Leeuwarden: Hendrik Rintjes, 1702. DSoC.

> Oglethorpe owned this edition in 1785. In 1740 Winde had a 1692 Dutch edi- tion—no copy of which has been found—and in 1779 Smith cited and recom- mended an earlier Dutch edition (Leeuwarden: H. Rintjes, 1685, DSoC) (3 of 42).

Coehoorn, Menno, Baron van, 1641–1704.

Nouvelle Fortification, tant pour un Terrain Bas et Humide, que Sec et Élevé. . . . Translated by Hendrik van Bulderen. The Hague: Henry Scheur- leer, 1711. DSoC.

> General Officer owned and Debbieg purchased this translation in 1773; they also owned and purchased in 1773 another edition of the same translation (The Hague, 1741, also DSoC), which was also in Montresor's library in 1799. Ogle- thorpe (1785) and Winde (1740) owned other French editions that were pub- lished at The Hague in 1706 and Wesel in 1706 (DSoC), respectively (5 of 42).

Coehoorn, Menno, Baron van, 1641–1704.
Vesterckinge des Vyf-hoecks. . . . Leeuwarden: H. Rintjes, 1682. DSoC.
> Smith recommended, 1779 (1 of 42).

Coehoorn, Menno, Baron van, 1641–1704.
Wederlegginge des Architectura Militaris. 1683.
> Although no copy of this title has been found, Max Jähns mentioned it in 1891
> in his *Geschichte der Kriegswissenschaften*, 2:1383. Smith recommended, 1779
> (1 of 42).
>
> In addition, five officers showed a preference for Coehoorn's work without
> specifying a particular book or edition. Bland cited Coehoorn in 1727; Towns-
> hend recommended him in 1776; Dundas considered him in 1779; and Winde
> and Hotham Thompson owned one or more of his books in 1740 and 1784, re-
> spectively. Altogether, 26 percent (11 of 42) of those officers who might have ex-
> pressed a preference for Coehoorn, did so, placing his books among the thirty
> that our officers admired most (see Appendix B).

Coigny, François de Franquetot, Duc de, 1670–1759.
*Campagne de Monsieur le Maréchal Duc de Coigny en Allemagne l'An
    M.DCC.XLIV.* . . . 5 vols. Amsterdam: Marc-Michel Rey, 1761. DSoC.
> In General Officer's library, 1773, and purchased by Debbieg in 1773 (2 of 23).

Cole, Benjamin, 1696 or 1697–1783.
*The Soldier's Pocket-Companion or the Manual Exercise of Our British
    Foot.* . . . London: B. Cole, 1746. DSoC.
> Dury owned in 1758 (1 of 33).

Colynet, Antony.
The True History of the Civill Warres of France. London: T. Woodcock, 1591.
    MH-H.
> In Montresor's library, 1799 (1 of 42).

Cope, Sir Anthony, d. 1551.
*The Historie of Two the Moste Noble Capitaines of the Worlde, Anniball and
    Scipio.* . . . London: Thomas Bertheleti, 1568. WlAbNL.
> In Montresor's library, 1799 (1 of 42).

*Copies of All the Minutes and Proceedings Taken at and upon the Several
    Tryals of Captain George Burrish.* . . . [London]: n.p., 1746. DSoC.
> In Lord John Murray's library, 1762 (1 of 33).

Copies of Original Letters from the Army of General Bonaparte in Egypt. . . .
    London: J. Wright, 1798. NN.
> In Montresor's library, 1799 (1 of 2).

Cormontaigne, Louis de.
Architecture Militaire, or l'Arte de Fortifier.... 3 vols. The Hague: J. Neaulme and A. Moetjens, 1741. DSoC.

> Smith recommended, 1779 (1 of 33).

Cornwallis, Charles Earl, 1738–1805.
A Reply to Sir Henry Clinton's Narrative.... London: R. Faulder and J. Debrett, 1783. ICN.

> Clinton reconsidered, 1791–92 (1 of 7). There were two other editions in 1783 (both DSoC).

Courtilz de Sandras, Gatien, 1644–1712.
La Conduite de Mars Necessaire à Tous Ceux Qui Font Profession des Armes.... The Hague: H. van Bulderen, 1685. DSoC.

> In Winde's library, 1740, edition not specified (1 of 42).

Courtilz de Sandras, Gatien, 1644–1712.
La Guerre d'Espagne, de Bavière, et de Flandre.... 2 vols. Cologne: Pierre Marteau, 1707. DSoC.

> Stewart had this largely fictional account in 1750. So too did Maxwell own an unspecified, two-volume edition in 1769 (2 of 42).

Courtilz de Sandras, Gatien, 1644–1712.
Histoire de la Guerre de Hollande ... depuis l'Année 1672 jusques en 1677. The Hague: H. van Bulderen, 1689. DSoC.

> General Officer owned and Debbieg purchased in 1773 (2 of 42).

Courtilz de Sandras, Gatien, 1644–1712.
La Vie du Vicomte de Turenne, Maréchal General des Camps & Armées du Roi.... Cologne: Jean de Clou, 1685. DSoC.

> Hotham Thompson (1784) and Oglethorpe (1785) owned (2 of 42). See also Buisson.
>
> The works of Courtilz de Sandras attracted at least 17 percent (7 of 42) of our officers, which placed him among our officers' authorities (see Appendix B).

Cruso, John, d. 1681.
Militarie Instructions for the Cavallrie.... Cambridge: printers for the Universitie of Cambridge, 1632. DSoC.

> Winde owned in 1740 and General Officer in 1773. Seton (1732) and Oglethorpe (1785) had a 1644 edition (also DSoC) in their libraries (4 of 42).

Curtius Rufus, Quintus, first century A.D.
Quintus Curtius, His History of the Wars of Alexander.... Translated by John Digby. 2 vols. London: Bernard Lintott, 1714. Uk.

> Wade owned in 1758; Townshend recommended in 1776 (2 of 42).

Cuthbertson, Bennett, fl. 1755–68, d. 1789.
A System for the Compleat Interior Management and Oeconomy of a Battalion of Infantry. . . . Dublin: B. Grierson, 1768. DSoC.

> Ligonier owned in 1770, as did Hotham Thompson in 1784 (2 of 21).

Dalrymple, Campbell, fl. 1755–63.
A Military Essay. Containing Reflections on the Raising, Arming, Cloathing, and Discipline of the British Infantry and Cavalry. . . . London: D. Wilson, 1761. DSoC.

> In the libraries of Ligonier (1770), General Officer (1773), Hotham Thompson (1784), and Calderwood (1787); Smith recommended (1779) (5 of 23, or 22 percent). His *Essay* was among the thirty books on war that our officers admired most (see Appendix B).

Danckaertz. See *Historis oft Waerachtich.*

Daniel, Gabriel, 1649–1728.
Histoire de la Milice Françoise. . . . 2 vols. Amsterdam: aux dépens de la compagnie, 1724. DSoC.

> In Dury's library, 1758, and Oglethorpe's, 1785; Smith cited, 1779 (3 of 41).

D'Asti, Charles Theodore.
Remarks on a New System of Fortification Proposed by M. Le Comte De Saxe in His Memoirs on the Art of War. Edinburgh: Apollo Press, 1787. NN.

> What seems to have been an earlier French edition of this book was on Dundas's list in 1779, but only this English translation has been found (1 of 7).

D'Auvergne, Edward, 1660–1737.
A Relation of the Most Remarkable Transactions of the Last Campaigne in the Confederate Army . . . in the Spanish Netherlands . . . 1692. London: Dorman Newman, 1693. DSoC.

> In Oglethorpe's library, 1785 (1 of 42).

Davenant, Charles, 1656–1714.
Essays upon Peace at Home and War Abroad. London: James Knapton, 1704. DSoC.

> In the libraries of Stewart (1750) and Ligonier (1770) (2 of 42).

Davila, Enrico Caterino, 1576–1631.
Historia delle Guerre Civili di Francia. Venice: Paolo Baglioni, 1634. DSoC.

> In Dormer's library, 1741. Calderwood owned another Italian edition of this book (Venice, 1638) in 1787, as did Dury (Rouen, 1646) in 1758 and Wortley Montagu (1751) in 1776; Wolfe recommended an unspecified Italian edition in 1756 (5 of 42).

Davila, Enrico Caterino, 1576–1631.

The Historie of the Civill Warres of France. Translated by [Sir Charles Cotte-
rell and William Aylesbury]. 2 vols. London: R. Raworth, 1647, 1648.
DSoC.

> Oglethorpe owned in 1785 (1 of 42). Oglethorpe also had a four-volume Paris
> edition of 1666 in his library (1785) and Wade owned an unspecified edition in
> 1758. Altogether, 17 percent (7 of 42) of the officers who might have expressed a
> preference had or recommended six different editions of Davila's history, which
> was among our officers' authorities (see Appendix B).

Dazin, d. 1731.

*Nouveau Sisteme sur la Maniere de Defendre les Places par le Moyen des
Contremines. . . .* Paris: Jacques Clouzier, 1731. DSoC.

> General Officer owned and Parker purchased in 1773 (2 of 40).

Defoe, Daniel, 1661?–1731.

The History of the Wars, of . . . Charles XII, King of Sweden . . . . London:
A. Bell [and four others], 1715. DSoC.

> Maxwell owned what seems to have been an edition of this book in 1769 (1 of
> 42).

Deidier, Abbé, 1696–1746.

Le Parfait Ingenieur François ou la Fortification Offensive et Défensive. . . .
New ed. Paris: Charles-Antoine Jombert, 1742. DSoC.

> In General Officer's library, 1773. Wade (1758) and Lord John Murray (1762)
> owned and Smith cited (1779) unspecified editions of this book (4 of 33). Al-
> though Deidier should have been included among the Authorities in Appen-
> dix B, he was not. I did not discover the omission until it was too late to make
> corrections.

De l'Esprit Militaire. London: n.p., 1783. DSoC.

> This work, published anonymously, was attributed to Laissac in the third edi-
> tion of 1789. In Montresor's library, 1799 (1 of 7).

Deschamps, Nicolas, fl. 1670.

*Mémoires des Deux Dernieres Campagnes de Monsieur de Turenne en Alle-
magne. . . .* Revised by C. L. d'Authville des Amourettes. Paris: C.-A. Jombert, 1756. DSoC.

> In Ligonier's library, 1770. Townshend probably referred to this book when list-
> ing the "Memoires de M. Turenne" in 1759 (2 of 28).

A Description of All the Seats of the Present Wars of Europe. . . . London: John
Nicholson and Sam. Ballard, 1704. TxU.

> Seton owned, 1732, as did Tyron, 1773 (2 of 42).

Deville, Antoine, 1596–1656.
De la Charge des Gouverneurs des Places. Paris: M. Guillemot, 1639. UkOxU.

> Molyneux cited an unspecified edition of this work on siege warfare in 1759 (1 of 42).

Deville, Antoine, 1596–1656.
Les Fortifications du Chevalier Antoine de Ville. . . . Lyon: Philippe Borde, 1641. DSoC.

> Oglethorpe had in his library, 1785; Winde owned an earlier edition (Lyon, 1629) in 1740; and Smith recommended a later edition (Paris, 1666, DSoC) in 1779 (3 of 42).

Dictys, Cretensis.
Ditte Candiano della Guerre Trojana. . . . Venice: Vincenzo Vaugris, 1543. DSoC.

> Dormer owned in 1741 (1 of 42).

Digges, Thomas, d. 1595.
An Arithmeticall Militare Treatise, Named Stratioticos. . . . London: Henrie Bynneman, 1579. CSmH.

> Owned by General Officer in 1773; Oglethorpe had a second, revised edition of 1590 (CtY) in 1785 (2 of 42).

Dilich, Wilhelm, d. 1655.
Peribologia, oder Bericht Wilhelmi Dilichij. . . . Frankfurt am Main: by the author, 1640. DSoC.

> In General Officer's library and purchased by Debbieg, 1773; Smith recommended, 1779 (3 of 42).

Dilich, Wilhelm, d. 1655.
Wilhelmi Dilichii . . . Hochvernünfftig Gegründet- und Auffgerichtete . . . Krieges-Schule. Frankfurt am Main: Johann David Zunners, 1689. DSoC.

> In Ligonier's library, 1770 (1 of 42).

Dobson, John, fl. 1760.
Chronological Annals of the War . . . from April 2, 1755 . . . to the . . . Peace. Oxford: Clarendon Press, 1763. DSoC.

> Oglethorpe owned 1761 edition in 1785 (1 of 23).

Dögen, Matthias, 1605– or 1606–1672.
L'Architecture Militaire Moderne, ou, Fortification. . . . Translated by H. Poirier. Amsterdam: Louis Elzevir, 1648. DSoC.

> Winde owned in 1740; and in 1779 Smith recommended a German edition of 1648 that has not been found (2 of 42).

Donkin, Robert, 1727–1821.
Military Collections and Remarks. . . . New York: H. Gaine, 1777. DSoC.
    In Oglethorpe's library, 1785 (1 of 9).

Donneau de Visé, Jean, 1638–1710.
Histoire du Siège de Toulon. . . . Paris: M. Brunet, 1707. NWM.
    In Dury's library, 1758 (1 of 42).

Donneau de Visé, Jean, 1638–1710.
The History of the Siege of Toulon. . . . Translated by Abel Boyer. London:
    A. Collins and J. Morphew, 1708. DLC.
    Also in Dury's library, 1758 (1 of 42).

Douglas, Stuart, d. 1781.
*A Military Dissertation, Containing a Plan for Recruiting the British
    Army.* . . . London: n.p., 1781. DSoC.
    In Hotham Thompson's library, 1784 (1 of 7).

Du Bois, Sieur.
Camps Topographiques de la Campagne de MDCCLVII en Westphalie. The
    Hague: Van Duren, 1760. ICN.
    In Ligonier's library, 1770 (1 of 24).

Du Fay, Abbé.
Maniere de Fortifier selon la Methode de Monsieur de Vauban. . . . Paris: J. B.
    Coignard, 1718. DSoC.
    Hesse owned in 1758, as did General Officer in 1773; Debbieg purchased in
    1773 (3 of 42).

Du Fay, Abbé.
Veritable Maniere de Bien Fortifier de M. de Vauban. Amsterdam: A. Braek-
    man, 1692. DSoC.
    It seems likely that this was the version of Vauban's work that Bagshawe owned
    in 1751; in 1779 Smith recommended a two-volume French edition of 1757 that
    has not been found (2 of 42).
        Du Fay's books on fortification attracted at least 12 percent (5 of 42) of the
    officers who might have preferred them (an authority; see Appendix B).

Dulacq, Joseph, 1706–57.
Theorie Nouvelle sur le Mecanisme de l'Artillerie. Paris: C.-A. Jombert, 1741.
    DSoC.
    In General Officer's library, 1773; in 1779 Smith cited and recommended a 1751
    edition that has not been found (2 of 33).

Dumaine, Louis, Baron de Chabans.
Histoire de la Guerre des Huguenots Faicte en France, sous la Regne du Roy Louys XIII. . . . Paris: T. du Bray, 1634. Uk.

> In Montresor's library, 1799 (1 of 42).

Dumont, Jean, Baron de Carlscroon, 1667–1727.
Batailles Gagnées par le Serenissime Prince Fr. Eugene de Savoye. . . . The Hague: P. Gosse, 1725. DSoC.

> In 1758 Wade owned a French edition of this book—perhaps this edition or another published at The Hague in 1720 (1 of 41).

Dumont, Jean, Baron de Carlscroon, 1667–1727.
Histoire Militaire du Prince Eugene de Savoye, du Prince et Duc de Marlborough, et du Prince de Nassau-Frise. . . . Enlarged by Jean Rousset de Missy. 3 vols. The Hague: n.p., 1729–47. Uk.

> Smith recommended, 1779, and in Montresor's library, 1799 (2 of 33). The DSoC copy of this work has slightly different titles for volumes 1 and 3 and different publishers for volumes 1 and 2 (I. vander Kloot) and 3 (J. Neaulme).

Dumortous, Pierre.
Histoire des Conquêtes de Louis XV . . . 1744 . . . 1748. . . . Paris: De Lormel, 1759. DSoC.

> In Ligonier's library, 1770 (1 of 24).

Dundas, Sir David, 1735–1820.
Principles of Military Movements, Chiefly Applied to Infantry. . . . London: T. Cadell, 1788. DSoC.

> Clinton discussed in 1789; Gentleman in the Army owned 1795 edition in 1799 (2 of 3).
>
> This book became the basis for the drill regulations of 1792—the regulations that would shape British tactics through the wars of the French Revolution and Napoleon (Houlding, *Fit for Service*, pp. 239–40).

Dupleix, Scipion, 1569–1661.
Les Loix Militaires Touchant le Duel. . . . Paris: Dominique Salis, 1602. NN.

> Winde owned in 1740 (1 of 42).

Dupré d'Aulnay, Louis, 1670?–1758.
Traite Général des Subsistances Militaires. . . . 2 vols. Paris: Prault, pere, 1744. DSoC.

> Dury owned in 1758, as did General Officer in 1773; Parker purchased in 1773; and Smith cited and recommended in 1779 (4 of 33, or 12 percent, and an authority; see Appendix B).

[Du Puget, Edme Jean Antoine, 1742–1801.]

Essai sur l'Usage de l'Artillerie. . . . Amsterdam: Arckstée and Merkus, 1771. DSoC.

> Smith cited and recommended, 1779 (1 of 19).

Elton, Richard, fl. 1650.

The Compleat Body of the Art Military. . . . London: for W. L. and sold by H. Brome, 1668. DSoC.

> In General Officer's library, 1773; Lord John Murray also owned an unspecified edition of this book in 1762 (2 of 42).

The English Military Discipline. . . . London: John Overton, 1672. CSmH.

> In Oglethorpe's library, 1785. General Officer owned an unspecified edition in 1773 and Ligonier, an abridgment of 1685 (DSoC) in 1770 (3 of 42).

Entick, John, 1703?–1773.

The General History of the Late War: Containing It's Rise, Progress and Event in Europe, Asia, Africa and America. . . . 3rd ed. rev. 5 vols. London: E. and C. Dilly, 1766. MHi.

> Smith recommended, 1779 (1 of 21).

Entick, John, 1703?–1773.

A New Naval History, or, Compleat View of the British Marine. . . . London: R. Manby [and four others], 1757. DSoC.

> In Wortley Montagu's library, 1776 (1 of 28).

[Espagnac, J. B. J. Damarzit-Sahuguet, Baron d', 1713–83.]

Campagne de l'Armee du Roi en 1747. The Hague: Henry Scheurleer, 1747. Uk [DSoC has but, like MH-H, does not list Espagnac as the author].

> In Lord John Murray's library (1762), Ligonier's (1770), and General Officer's (1773); bought by Smith in 1773 (4 of 33).

[Espagnac, J. B. J. Damarzit-Sahuguet, Baron d', 1713–83.]

Essai sur la Science de la Guerre. . . . 3 vols. The Hague: P. Gosse and J. Neaulme, 1751. DSoC.

> Dury owned in 1758 (1 of 31).

[Espagnac, J. B. J. Damarzit-Sahuguet, Baron d', 1713–83.]

Essai sur la Science de la Guerre. . . . 3 vols. The Hague and in Paris at Ganeau, 1753. DSoC.

> Bever cited in 1756; General Officer owned in 1773 (2 of 30).

Espagnac, J. B. J. Damarzit-Sahuguet, Baron d', 1713–83.

Histoire de Maurice, Comte de Saxe. . . . New ed. 2 vols. Paris: Saillant and Nyon, 1775. DLC.

> In Montresor's library, 1799 (1 of 13).

[Espagnac, J. B. J. Damarzit-Sahuguet, Baron d', 1713–83.]
Journal Historique de la Dernière Campagne de l'Armée du Roi en 1746. . . .
The Hague: H. Scheurleer, 1747. DSoC.
> Ligonier owned in 1770, as did General Officer in 1773 and Oglethorpe in 1785;
> Smith purchased in 1773 (4 of 33).

Espagnac, J. B. J. Damarzit-Sahuguet, Baron d', 1713–83.
*Relation de la Campagne en Brabant et en Flandres, de l'An M.DCC.XLV:
Contenant la Conquête des Païs-Bas Autrichiens & la Prise de Bruxelles en
1746 avec le Plan de la Bataille de Fontenoy.* [The Hague]: Frederic-Henri
Scheurleer, 1748. DSoC.
> In Dury's library in 1758 and General Officer's in 1773 (2 of 33).

Espagnac, J. B. J. Damarzit-Sahuguet, Baron d', 1713–83.
*Relation de la Campagne en Brabant et en Flandres de l'An M.DCC.XLVI:
Ouvrage Enrichi de Plans, & d'Ordres de Batailles.* The Hague: Frederic-
Henri Scheurleer, 1748. DSoC.
> In General Officer's library, 1773 (1 of 33).

Espagnac, J. B. J. Damarzit-Sahuguet, Baron d', 1713–83.
*Relation de la Campagne en Brabant et en Flandres, de l'An M.DCC.XLVII
avec les Plans de la Bataille de Laufeld, & de l'Attaque de la Ville de Bergen-
op-Zoom.* The Hague: Frederic Henri Scheurleer, 1748. DSoC.
> In Ligonier's library, 1770, and General Officer's, 1773 (2 of 33).
>
> In short, 24 percent (8 of 33) of those officers who might have done so owned
> or cited at least one of Espagnac's works; and taken together, his works were
> among the thirty books on war that our officers preferred above all others (see
> Appendix B).

*An Essay on Field Fortification Intended Principally for the Use of Officers of
Infantry. . . .* Translated by J. C. Pleydell. London: J. Nourse, 1768. DSoC.
> Percy made notes on c. 1772, Moyle owned in 1777, Dundas listed and Smith
> cited and recommended in 1779 (4 of 21, or 19 percent).
>
> Houlding (*Fit for Service*, p. 223) says that Pleydell, a lieutenant in the 12th
> Foot, did more than translate this work from that of a Prussian officer—that
> he created the book from the treatises of Clairac and Le Cointe. For his efforts
> Pleydell became one of our officers' authorities (see Appendix B).

Estrades, Godefroi Louis, Comte d', 1607–86.
*Lettres et Negociations de Messieurs le Marechal D'Estrades, Colbert, . . . à la
Paix de Nimegue. . . .* Edited by A. Moetjens. 3 vols. The Hague: A. Moet-
jens, 1710. DSoC.

In Maxwell's library, 1769, and Hotham Thompson's, 1784 (2 of 42). Hotham Thompson also had an unspecified edition of Estrades's memoires.

État Militaire de France, pour l'Année 1758–93. 36 vols. Paris: Guillyn [and others], 1758–93. DSoC.
> Ligonier in 1770 and Tryon in 1773 had copies of this annual. Wade too might have had a copy in 1758 (3 of 25, or 12 percent, and an authority; see Appendix B).

Eugene, Prince of Savoy, 1663–1736.
> See Campbell, Dumont, and Mauvillon. Including Clinton, who reflected on a history of Eugene c. 1775 and 1794, 26 percent of the officers (11 of 42) expressed an interest in books about Eugene, placing him among the thirty authorities that our officers admired most (see Appendix B). See also Marlborough, John Churchill, Duke of, 1650–1722.

Euler, Leonhard, 1707–83?.
Erläuterte Artillerie. 1756.
> Although Smith cited and recommended in 1779, no copy has been found (1 of 28). This might be a subsequent edition of Euler's *Neue Grundsätze der Artillerie....* (Berlin: Aittaude, 1745, MiU). See Hugh Brown for an English translation of Euler.

Exact Account of the Siege of Namur; with a Perfect Diary of the Campagne in Flanders . . . 1695. By a Gentleman attending his Majesty during the whole Campagne. . . . London: T. Goodwin, 1695. Uk.
> In Oglethorpe's library, 1785 (1 of 42).

Exact and Full Account of the Siege of Barcelona . . . 1706. . . . London: Benj. Bragg, 1706. Uk.
> Hotham owned in 1738 (1 of 42).

Exact Diary of the Siege of the City Ments. . . . London: R. Janeway, 1689. CtY.
> In Hotham's library, 1738 (1 of 42).

Exact Journal of the Siege of Namur. . . . London: J. Witlock, 1695. CtY.
> Hotham's library, 1738 (1 of 42).

An Exact Relation of the Several Engagements . . . of His Majesties Fleet, under . . . Prince Rupert . . . 1673. London: J. B., 1673. DSoC.
> In Montresor's library, 1799 (1 of 42).

Exercise for the Horse, Dragoons, and Foot Forces. London: J. Baskett, 1728. DSoC.
> In Wade's library in 1758 and Ligonier's in 1770 (2 of 40).

Exercise of the Foot with the Evolutions, According to the Words of Command. . . . London: Charles Bill and the executrix of Thomas Newcomb, 1696. UkOxU.

> Ligonier owned, 1770 (1 of 42).

Extract of Orders and Regulations for Garrison and Camp Duties from the Year 1743 to . . . 1748. . . . Glasgow: Robert and Andrew Foulis, 1761. Uk.

> General Officer owned and Parker purchased in 1773 (2 of 23).

Fäsch, Georg Rudolph, 1710–87.
Des Grössesten Meisters in der Kriegs-Kunst. . . . Leipzig, 1762. DSoC.

> In 1779 Smith recommended a 1764 edition of this work that has not been found (1 of 22).

Fäsch, Georg Rudolph, 1710–87.
Journaux des Sieges de la Campagne de MDCCXLVI dans les Pais Bas. . . . Amsterdam: P. Mortier, 1750. DSoC.

> Hesse owned in 1758; so too might Tryon in 1773 (1 or 2 of 32).

Faesch, Johann Rudolph.
Kriegs-Ingenieur-Artillerie-und See-Lexicon. . . . Dresden and Leipzig: Friedrich Hekel, 1735. DSoC.

> General Officer owned and Smith bought in 1773; Smith also cited in 1779 (2 of 38).

Fawcett, Sir William, 1728–1804. See *New Regulations for the Prussian Infantry, Regulations for the Prussian Cavalry, Regulations for the Prussian Infantry,* and Maurice de Saxe.

Faulhaber, Johann, 1580–1635.
Ingenieurs Schul. . . . Frankfurt am Main, 1630. Uk.

> General Officer owned and Smith purchased in 1773 (2 of 42).

Fearne, Charles, 1742–94.
The Trial of the Honourable Admiral John Byng, at a Court Martial, as taken by Mr. Charles Fearne. . . . London: R. Manby [and five others], 1757. DSoC.

> Dury and Wade each had in 1758, as did Montresor's library in 1799 (3 of 28, or 11 percent, and an authority; see Appendix B).

Fer, Nicolas de, 1646–1720.
Les Forces de l'Europe, ou Description des Principales Villes avec Leurs Fortifications. . . . Paris: by the author, 1693–96. DsoC.

> In Ligonier's library, 1770, and Oglethorpe's, 1785 (2 of 42).

Fer, Nicolas de, 1646–1720.
Introduction à la Fortification. Paris: by the author, [1705?]. DSoC.
   In Ligonier's library, 1770 (1 of 42).

Fer, Nicolas de, 1646–1720.
*Le Theatre de la Guerre, en Allemagne, ou Representation des Princi-
pales Villes Qui Sont en Allemagne: avec Leurs Fortifications.* . . . Paris:
chez l'auteur, 1697. DSoC.
   Dury might have owned a Paris, 1741 edition of this book in 1773, but no copy
of the 1741 edition has been found (1 of 42).

Feuquières, Antoine de Pas, Marquis de, 1648–1711.
Mémoires de M. le Marquis de Feuquière. . . . New ed. 4 vols. London:
P. Dunoyer; Paris: Rollin fils, 1740. DSoC.
   General Officer owned and Debbieg purchased in 1773; Oglethorpe owned in
1785 (3 of 35).

Feuquières, Antoine de Pas, Marquis de, 1648–1711.
Memoires de M. le Marquis de Feuquière. . . . Amsterdam: F. l'Honore and
sons and Z. Chatelain, 1741. DSoC.
   In Ligonier's library, 1770 (1 of 33).

Feuquières, Antoine de Pas, Marquis de, 1648–1711.
Memoires Historiques et Militaires par Feuquières. . . . 2 vols. Amsterdam:
J. F. Bernard, 1735. DSoC.
   In Dormer's library, 1741 (1 of 38).

Feuquières, Antoine de Pas, Marquis de, 1648–1711.
Memoires sur la Guerre. . . . Amsterdam: J. F. Bernard, 1734. MiU.
   Ligonier owned in 1770; Oglethorpe, in 1785 (2 of 38).

Feuquières, Antoine de Pas, Marquis de, 1648–1711.
Memoirs of the Late Marquis de Feuquières . . . from 1672 to the Year 1710. . . .
2 vols. London: T. Woodward and C. Davis, 1737. DSoC.
   General Officer owned and Blomefield purchased in 1773 (2 of 38).
     In addition, Hawley (c. 1753), Townshend (n.d.), and Clinton (n.d.) noted;
Molyneux (1759), Dalrymple (1761), and Donkin (1777) cited; Wolfe (1756) recommended; Percy ordered (1774); Dundas had on list (1779) and Dury (1758),
Ligonier (1770), and Hotham Thompson (1784) owned unspecified editions
of Feuquières's *Memoires*, which were first published in 1711 [Quimby, *Background*, p. 372]. Altogether, 41 percent of our officers (17 of 42) showed a preference for Feuquières—owning or recommending at least five different editions and twenty copies of his work. Indeed, they preferred his *Memoires* to

all except four or five other books on war available in mid-eighteenth-century Britain (see Appendix B).

Houlding (*Fit for Service*, p. 187) may be right that the British did not profit by the translation of Feuquières's *Memoires*, but they certainly had copies at hand.

Fitzjames, James 1st Duke of Berwick, 1670–1734. See Berwick.

Floriani, Pietro Paolo, 1584–1638.
Difesa et Offesa delle Piazze. Venice: F. Baba, 1654. MH.
     In 1779 Smith recommended what seems to have been this book (1 of 42).

Folard, Jean Charles de, 1669–1752.
L'Esprit du Chevalier Folard, Tiré de Ses Commentaries sur l'Histoire de Polybe. . . . Paris: Jean Marie Bruyzet by La Compagnie des Libraires, 1760. DSoC.
     In General Officer's library, 1773 (1 of 24).

Folard, Jean Charles de, 1669–1752.
Histoire de Polybe, Nouvellement Traduite du Grec Par Dom V. Thuillier. Avec un Commentaire . . . Par M. de Folard. . . . 6 vols. Amsterdam: aux depens de la Compagnie, 1729–30. DSoC.
     Bever cited (1756); Bagshawe, Dury, and Ligonier owned (1751, 1758, 1770); Clinton noted (1768–76); and Smith cited and recommended (1779). Wortley Montagu (1776) owned a seven-volume edition published in Amsterdam in 1751; and Wolfe (1756) recommended an unspecified edition of this title (8 of 40).

Folard, Jean Charles de, 1669–1752.
Nouvelles Découvertes sur la Guerre dans une Dissertation sur Polybe. . . . 2nd ed. Brussels: F. Foppens and N. Tilliard, 1724. DSoC.
     Stewart and Oglethorpe owned in 1750 and 1785, respectively; General Officer had a Paris edition of 1724 in 1773; and three other officers owned (Wade in 1758), noted (Clinton in 1768–76), or considered (Dundas in 1779) unspecified editions of *Nouvelles Découvertes* (6 of 41).

     Four other officers owned or cited Folard without specifying a particular title or edition: Hotham owned one of Folard's works in 1738, as did Hotham Thompson in 1784; Molyneux and Dalrymple both cited Folard—in 1759 and 1761, respectively.

     Altogether, 42 percent (17 of 41) of those officers who might have shown such a preference did prefer one or more of Folard's books. They clearly valued his books above those by or about any other authority on war except Caesar, Vauban, Marlborough, Saxe, or Polybius (see Appendix B). See also Polybius and Savornin.

[Fournier], Georges, 1595–1652.
Traité des Fortifications, ou Architecture Militaire. Paris: Henault, 1648. Uk.
    In Winde's library, 1740 (1 of 42).

Fowler, John, fl. 1635–56.
The History of the Troubles of Suethland and Poland . . . until 1629. . . . London: T. Roycroft for H. Twyford, 1656. Uk.
    In General Officer's library, 1773 (1 of 42).

France, Laws. See Briquet, Pierre de, and Sparre, Lars Magnus, Baron de.

Frederick II, King of Prussia, 1712–86.
Histoire de Mon Temps. 2 vols. Berlin: [Voss and Decker], 1788. WlAbNL.
    Clinton made notes on, 1789, 1790 (1 of 3).

Frederick II, King of Prussia, 1712–86.
Des Königs von Preussen Majestät Unterricht von der Kriegs-Kunst an Seine Generals. Frankfurt am Main: n.p., 1761. DSoC.
    Smith recommended in 1779 (1 of 23).

Frederick II, King of Prussia, 1712–86.
Memoires pour Servir à l'Histoire de la Maison de Brandebourg. . . . 2 parts in 1 vol. [Berlin: J. Neaulme], 1751. DSoC.
    Dury owned in 1758; Townshend listed an unspecified edition in 1759 (2 of 31).
        Percy cited Frederick in 1775 and Donkin quoted him in 1777 without specifying a title. Including those who owned Henry Lloyd's books, 29 percent of the officers (9 of 31) showed an interest in Frederick, making him one of the twenty authorities that our officers admired most (see Appendix B).

Freind, John, 1675–1728.
An Account of the Earl of Peterborough's Conduct in Spain, Chiefly since . . . 1706. . . . 2nd ed. London: W. Wise, 1707. NjR.
    Molyneux cited (probably this printing), 1759, and in Oglethorpe's library, 1785 (2 of 42).

Freind, John, 1675–1728.
An Account of the Earl of Peterborow's Conduct in Spain. 2nd ed., corrected. London: J. Bowyer, 1707. DSoC.
    In Oglethorpe's library, 1785, and Montresor's library, 1799 (2 of 42).

Freitag, Adam.
L'Architecture Militaire . . . par Adam Fritach. Translated by Toussaint Quinet. Leiden: the Elzeviers, 1635. DSoC.
    In Winde's library, 1740, and General Officer's, 1773; purchased by Debbieg in 1773. Seton owned a Paris edition of 1668 (Uk) in 1732; and Smith recom-

mended an Amsterdam edition of 1665 (DSoC) in 1779 (5 of 42, or 12 percent, and an authority; see Appendix B).

Friderici, Christoph Conrad Wilhelm.
Gründliche Einleitung in die Kriegswissenschaft. Breslau and Thorn, 1763.
> Smith recommended in 1779 (1 of 21). Although Jähns included this book in his *Geschichte der Kriegswissenschaften* of 1889–91 (vol. 3, 1909), no copy has now been found.

Friedrich August, Duke of Brunswick, 1740–1805. See Brunswick.

Frontinus, Sextus Julius, A.D. c. 35–c. 103.
S. J. Frontinus . . . de re Militari. Flavius Vegetius de re Militari. Aelianus de Instruendis Aciebus. Modesti Libellus de Vocabulis rei Militaris. Bologna: Ioannes Antonisu de Benedictis, 1505. DSoC.
> In Dormer's library, 1741 (1 of 42).

Frontinus, Sextus Julius, A.D. c. 35–c. 103.
The Stratagems of War, or, A Collection of the Most Celebrated Practices and Wise Sayings of the Great Generals in Former Ages. Translated by M. D. A. London: S. Heyrick, J. Place, and R. Sare, 1686. MH-H.
> Lord John Murray owned in 1762, as did Oglethorpe in 1785 (2 of 42).

Frontinus, Sextus Julius, A.D. c. 35–c. 103.
Veteres de re Militari Scriptores Quotquot Extant. . . . Edited by Pieter Schrijver. Wesel: Andreœ ab Hoogenhuysen, 1670. DSoC.
> In Winde's library, 1740 (1 of 42).
>
> Including Molyneux who in 1759 cited and Harrison who in 1763 owned an unspecified edition of Frontinus, as well as General Officer who in 1773 owned the *Stratagemes* in a compilation of works by Vegetius, Frontinus, Aelianus, and Modestus (1536), 17 percent of the officers (7 of 42) owned at least four different editions of Frontinus's work, which was clearly among our officers' authorities (see Appendix B). See Flavius Vegetius Renatus for the compilation of 1536 that General Officer owned. See also Tacticus Aelianus.

A Full Account of the Situation, Former State, and Late Siege of Stetin [1677]. . . . London: Dan. Brown, 1678. CLU.
> In Dury's library, 1758 (1 of 42).

A Full and Impartial Relation of the Battle Fought on the 13th of August 1704 N.S. In the Plain of Hochstette. . . . London: Ben Bragg, 1704. DSoC.
> Hotham owned in 1738 (1 of 42).

Funck, Jakob, 1715– or 1716–88, and von Illengen.
Plans et Journaux des Siéges de la Dernière Guerre de Flandres. . . . Strasbourg: M. Pauschinger, 1750. DSoC.

Dury owned in 1758, as did Ligonier in 1770 and General Officer in 1773; Smith
purchased in 1773 (4 of 32, or 13 percent, and an authority; see Appendix B).

G., V. D. S., Comte de.
*Abrégé de la Théorie Militaire a l'Usage de Ceux Qui Suivent le Parti des
Armes.* . . . Vienna: Jean-Thomas de Trattnern, 1766. DSoC.
> In Ligonier's library, 1770 (1 of 21).

Galloway, Joseph, 1731–1803.
*The Examination of Joseph Galloway . . . before the House of Commons . . . on
the American Papers.* . . . London: J. Wilkie, 1779. DSoC.
> Clinton reconsidered, 1791–92 (1 of 7).

Galloway, Joseph, 1731–1803.
A Reply to the Observations of Lieut. Gen. Sir William Howe. . . . London:
G. Wilkie, 1780. DSoC.
> In Montresor's library, 1799 (1 of 7).

Gardiner, Richard, 1723–81.
*Account of the Expedition to the West Indies against Martinico, Guadeloupe,
and other the Leeward Islands . . . 1759.* London: Z. Stuart, 1759. NN.
> In Lord John Murray's library, 1762 (1 of 24).

Garimberto, Girolamo, sixteenth century.
Il Capitano Generale di M. Girolamo Garimberto. . . . Venice: Giordano
Ziletti, 1556. DSoC.
> In Oglethorpe's library, 1785 (1 of 42).

Garrard, William, d. 1587.
The Arte of Warre. . . . Corrected and finished by Captain Hichcock. London:
R. Warde, 1591. DSoC.
> In General Officer's library, 1773 (1 of 42).

Gates, Geoffrey.
The Defence of Militarie Profession. . . . London: H. Middleton for Iohn Hari-
son, 1579. CSmH.
> General Officer owned in 1773 (1 of 42).

Gaudi, Friedrich, Wilhelm von, 1725–88.
Instruction Adressée aux Officiers d'Infanterie. . . . The Hague, 1768. Uk.
> In Ligonier's library, 1770 (1 of 21). DSoC has Leipsick edition of the same year.

Gaya, Louis de, and Sébastien le Prestre de Vauban.
*Science Militaire Contenant: L'A.B.C. d'un Soldat. L'Art de la Guerre. Le Di-
recteur General des Fortifications.* . . . The Hague: Adrian Moetjens, 1689.
DSoC.
> Calderwood owned c. 1787 (1 of 42).

*A General History of Sieges and Battles, by Sea and Land . . . such as Relate
to Great Britain and Her Dependencies. . . .* 12 vols. in 6. London: J. Curtis,
1762. NN.
> Maxwell owned in 1769 (1 of 22).

*A Genuine Account of the Late Grand Expedition to the Coast of France under
the Conduct of Admirals Hawke, Knowles, and Broderick and General
Mordaunt. . . .* London: R. Griffiths, 1757. DSoC.
> Molyneux cited in 1759 (1 of 28).

*A Geographical and Historical Description of the Principal Objects of the
Present War in the West-Indies. . . .* London: T. Gardner, 1741. NN.
> In Lord John Murray's library, 1762 (1 of 33).

Gerbier, Sir Balthazar, 1592?–1667.
*The Interpreter of the Academie for Forrain Languages . . . Concerning Mili-
tary Architecture, or Fortification.* [London], 1648. NjR.
> In Winde's library, 1740 (1 of 42).

Girard, Pierre Jacques François.
*Traité des Armes . . . Enseignant la Maniére de Combattre de l'Épée de Point
Seul. . . .* Paris, 1737. Uk.
> In Dury's library, 1758 (1 of 38).

Girard, Pierre Jacques François.
Traité des armes. . . . The Hague: Pierre de Hondt, 1740. DSoC.
> Wortley Montagu owned in 1776 (1 of 35).

Godard d'Aucour, Claude, 1716–95.
L'Académie Militaire, ou, Les Héros Subalternes. . . . Lausanne, 1747. Although no copy of the Lausanne edition of 1747 has been found, DSoC has
a two-volume (Paris?) edition of 1745–46.
> In Ligonier's library, 1770 (1 of 33).

Goldmann, Nicolaus, 1623–65.
La Nouvelle Fortification de Nicolas Goldman. Leiden: Elzeviers, 1645.
DSoC.
> In Winde's library, 1740 (1 of 42).

Goulon, Louis, b. 1640.
Memoires pour l'Attaque et la Defense d'une Place. The Hague: P. Gosse, 1730.
DSoC.
> In General Officer's library, 1773. Wolfe (1756), Dury (1758), Hesse (1758), and
> Tryon (1773) all recommended or owned unspecified editions of Goulon's work
> (5 of 40, or 13 percent, and an authority; see Appendix B).

Gramont, Antoine Charles, Duc de, 1640–1720.
Mémoires du Mareschal de Gramont. . . . 2 vols. Paris: Michel David, 1716. DSoC.

> Owned by General Officer and purchased by Smith in 1773. Lord John Murray (1762) and Hotham Thompson (1784) owned unspecified French editions; and Hotham Thompson also had an English edition (4 of 42).

Grandmaison, Thomas Auguste Le Roy de, 1715–1801.
La Petite Guerre, ou, Traité du Service des Troupes Legeres en Campagne. [Paris?]: n.p., 1756. DSoC.

> In General Officer's library, 1773, and recommended by Smith, 1779 (2 of 28). It is also possible that Wolfe recommended this book c. 1756; see La Croix.

Gray, John, d. 1769.
A Treatise of Gunnery. London: William Innys, 1731. DSoC.

> Dury (1758), Tryon (1773), and Montresor (1799) owned; Smith (1779) cited (4 of 40, or 10 percent, and an authority; see Appendix B).

Graziani, Antonio Maria, 1537–1611.
The History of the War of Cypress. . . . Translated by Robert Midgley. London: J. Rawlins and Randal Taylor, 1687. DSoC.

> In Oglethorpe's library, 1785 (1 of 42).

A Great and Bloody Fight at Sea on Monday 16 August [1652] neere Plimouth: Between Sir George Ayscue and the Holland Fleet. . . . London: Robert Ibbitson, 1652. Uk.

> In Montresor's library, 1799 (1 of 42).

Griendel, Johann Frantz.
Nova Architectura Militaris, das ist: Neuerfundene Fortificationnes, order Festungs-bau. . . . Nuremberg: J. Ziegers and A. Knorzen, 1683, 1677. MiU.

> In 1779 Smith recommended a 1673 edition of this book, no copy of which has been found (1 of 42).

Grose, Francis, 1731?–1791.
Advice to the Officers of the British Army. . . . 7th ed. London: G. Kearsley, 1783. DSoC.

> Cuthbert owned in 1785 (1 of 7). The sixth edition was London, 1782 (Uk); no earlier edition was found, and earlier editions may have had a different title.

Grose, Francis, 1731?–1791.
A Treatise on Ancient Armour and Weapons. . . . London: S. Hooper, 1786. DSoC.

> In Montresor's library, 1799 (1 of 4).

Grotius, Hugo, 1583–1645.
Le Droit de la Guerre et de la Paix. Translated by J. Barbeyrac. 2 vols. Amsterdam: P. de Coup, 1724. DSoC.

> Dormer (1741), Dury (1758), and Wortley Montagu (1776) owned this edition (3 of 41). Lord John Murray (1762) also had a French translation.

Grotius, Hugo, 1583–1645.
H. Grottii de Jure Belli ac Pacis. Paris: W. Buon, 1625. Uk.

> This is the first edition of Grotius's work. Lord John Murray (1762) and Maxwell (1769) owned Latin editions—perhaps this first edition (2 of 42).

Grotius, Hugo, 1583–1645.
The Illustrious Hugo Grotius of the Law of Warre and Peace. Translated by Clement Barksdale. London: T. Warren for William Lee, 1655. DSoC.

> In Oglethorpe's library, 1785. Winde (1740) also owned an English edition—of 1675 (2 of 42).
>
> Including Hotham Thompson, who owned two unspecified editions of Grotius's *Law of War and Peace*, 19 percent of the officers (8 of 42) had among them at least three different editions of this book, which was clearly among the books on war that our officers considered an authority (see Appendix B).

Guérinière. See Robichon de la Guérinière, François.

Guibert, Jacques Antoine Hippolyte, Comte de, 1743–90.
Essai Général de Tactique. . . . 2 vols. in 1. London: Libraires Associés, 1772. DSoC.

> Calderwood and Montresor owned this edition in 1787 and 1799, respectively. In 1779 Smith recommended it as well as a German edition (*Versuch über die Tactik.* 2 vols. Dresden, 1774), which has not been found but which was cited by Max Jähns in 1891 in his *Geschichte der Kriegswissenschaften,* 3:2059. Although Percy and Clinton noted Guibert's *Essai* (after 1772 and 1789) and Dundas considered it (in 1779), none mentioned a particular edition. Altogether, 32 percent (6 of 19) of the officers who might have shown a preference for Guibert's work did so. Noailles sent a copy to Charles Earl Cornwallis after he had surrendered his army to Franco-American forces at Yorktown in 1781 (Ross, *Correspondence,* 1:132). Guibert's *Essai* was clearly among the twenty books on war that our officers admired most (see Appendix B).

Guicciardini, Francesco, 1483–1540.
Histoire des Guerres d'Italie. . . . Translated by H. Chomedey. Paris: M. Sonnius, 1577. Uk.

> In Dormer's library, 1741. Wolfe recommended this history in 1756 without specifying an edition. Hotham Thompson owned what seems to have been another edition of this book in 1784 (3 of 42).

Guignard, Pierre Claude de, 1665–1741.
L'Ecole de Mars ou, Memoires Instructifs sur Toutes les Parties qui Com-
posent le Corps Militaire en France. . . . 2 vols. Paris: Simart, 1725. DSoC.
  Dury (1758) and Ligonier (1770) owned this edition. General Officer had another Paris edition of 1727 (in 1773) and Smith recommended an edition of
  1758 (in 1779)—neither of which has been found (4 of 41).

Guillet de Saint-Georges, Georges, 1625–1705.
Les Arts de l'Homme d'Épée, ou le Dictionnaire du Gentilhomme. . . . 2 vols.
  Paris: Gervais Clouzier, 1678. DSoC.
  Winde owned in 1740 (1 of 42).

Guischardt, Karl Gottlieb, called Quintus Icilius, 1724–75.
Mémoires Militaires sur les Grecs et les Romains. . . . 2 vols. The Hague:
  P. de Hondt, 1758. DSoC.
  Clinton made notes on (c. 1768–76), and Ligonier and General Officer owned
  this edition (in 1770 and 1773, respectively). Ligonier also had a 1760 edition
  published in Lyons by J. M. Bruyset (DSoC). Including Harrison, who owned
  some version of the *Mémoires* in 1763; Townshend, who recommended them
  in 1759 and 1776; and Donkin and Smith, who cited them in 1777 and 1779,
  respectively, 28 percent (7 of 25) of the officers who might have expressed a
  preference for Guischardt's work did so. His *Mémoires* were among the twenty
  books on war that our officers admired most (see Appendix B).

Guise, Henri, Duc de, 1614–64.
Les Memoires de Feu Monsieur le Duc de Guise. 2 vols. Paris: Edme Martin
  and Sebastien Mabre-Cramoisy, 1668. DSoC.
  Dury (1758) and Hotham Thompson (1784) owned unspecified editions of
  Guise's *Memoires* (2 of 42).

Gustavus Adolphus, King of Sweden, 1594–1632. See *Historis oft Waerach-*
tich and Spanheim, Friedrich.
  Including Clinton who reflected on (c. 1775) and Wolfe who recommended
  reading a life of the Swedish king, 12 percent of our officers (5 of 42) expressed
  an interest in books about Gustavus Adolphus.

Hähn, Johann Friedrich, 1710–89.
Anweisung zur Kriegs-bau-kunst. . . . Berlin: Buchhandlung der Real-Schule,
  1767. DSoC.
  In 1779 Smith recommended a 1775 edition that has not been found (1 of 21).

Hamilton, Anthony, Count, c. 1646–1720.
Memoires de Comte de Grammont. . . . New ed. The Hague: P. Gosse and
  J. Neaulme, 1741. CtY.

In General Officer's library, 1773. There was also a London, 1783, edition (DLC) in Montresor's library, 1799 (2 of 33).

Hanger, George, 1751?–1824.
Military Reflections on the Attack and Defence of the City of London. London: J. Debrett, 1795. DSoC.
> In Montresor's library, 1799 (1 of 2).

Hanway, Jonas, 1712–86.
An Account of the Society for the Encouragement of the British Troops in Germany and North America. . . . London: n.p., 1760. DSoC.
> In Ligonier's library, 1770 (1 of 24).

Hanway, Jonas, 1712–86.
The Soldier's Faithful Friend; Being Political, Moral, and Religious Monition to Officers and Private Men in the Army and Militia. . . . 2 vols. London: J. Dodsley, 1766. DSoC.
> Ligonier's library, 1770, and Oglethorpe's, 1785 (2 of 21).

Haversham, John Thompson, Baron, 1647–1710.
An Account of the Late Scotch Invasion. . . . [London]: n.p., 1709. DSoC.
> In Hotham's library, 1732 (1 of 42).

Heath, James, 1629–64, and John Phillips, 1631–1706.
A Chronicle of the Late Intestine War in . . . England, Scotland and Ireland. 2nd ed. London: J. C. for T. Basset, 1676. DSoC.
> Molyneux cited an unspecified edition of Heath's *Chronicle* in 1759 and Montresor's library contained another unspecified edition in 1799 (2 of 42).

Heinsius, Daniel, 1580–1655.
Histoire du Siège de Bolduc, . . . l'An MDCXXIX. Leiden: Elzevir, 1631. DSoC.
> In Dury's library, 1758 (1 of 42).

Hericourt, Nicolas d'.
Elemens de l'Art Militaire. 3 vols. Paris, 1723. Uk has two-volume edition, The Hague, 1748, and DSoC, a five-volume edition, Paris, 1752–56; but no copy of the 1723 edition has been found.
> Bever cited (1756) and General officer owned in 1773; Lord John Murray also seems to have had a 1739 edition, which is also in DSoC (3 of 41).

Herodotus, fifth century B.C.
Herodotou Halikarnasseos Historion Logoi 9. . . . 2nd ed. Geneva: Henricus Stephanus, 1592. MH-H.
> In Oglethorpe's library 1785 (1 of 42).

Herodotus, fifth century B.C.

Les Histoires d'Herodote. Translated by Pierre du Ryer. 2nd ed. Paris: A. Covbre, 1658. DSoC.

> Dury had in 1758; Lord John Murray owned an unspecified edition of Herodotus's history in 1762 (2 of 42).

Herouville de Claye, Antoine de Ricouart, Comte de, c. 1712–82.

Traité des Légions, ou, Mémoires sur l'Infanterie. [The Hague]: aux dépens de la Compagnie, 1753. DSoC.

> General Officer owned and Smith purchased in 1773; Dundas considered a 1757 edition in 1779; and Tryon owned an unspecified edition in 1773 (4 of 30, or 13 percent, and among our officers' authorities; see Appendix B). See also Saxe.

Hexham, Henry, 1585?–1650?.

The Principles of the Art Militarie; Practised in the Warres of the United Netherlands. . . . London: M. P. for Matthew Symmons, 1637–40. DSoC.

> In Seton's library, 1732. General Officer had a 1642 edition of this book in 1773; and Hotham Thompson, an unspecified edition in 1784 (3 of 42). Cockle, *Bibliography*, p. 107, spells the author's name Hexham, citing a 1637 edition of this book in Uk.

Hilliard d'Auberteuil, Michel-René, c. 1740–89.

Histoire de l'Administration de Lord North . . . et de la Guerre de l'Amérique Septentrionale, jusqu'a la Paix. . . . 3 vols. in 2. London and Paris: the author and Couturier, 1784. DSoC.

> In Montresor's library, 1799 (1 of 6).

Hinde, Robert, d. 1786.

The Discipline of the Light-Horse. London: W. Owen, 1778. DSoC.

> Clinton purchased c. 1780; and in Oglethorpe's library, 1785 (2 of 9).

An Historical Description of the Glorious Conquest of the City of Buda . . . by . . . Leopold I. London: for R. Clavell, 1686. Uk.

> In Hotham's library, 1738 (1 of 42).

Historis oft Waerachtich verhael van den Gantschen Toestant van Oorlooge, soo die Ghevoert is in Duytschlandt, door den Grootmachtichsten . . . Koningh. Gustavus Adolphus. Coninck der Sweeden. . . . Amsterdam: Cornelis Danckaertz, 1642. Uk.

> General Officer owned and Smith purchased in 1773 (2 of 42).

The History of the Campaign in Flanders in . . . 1708. . . . London, 1709. Uk.

> In Hotham's library, 1738 (1 of 42).

The History of the Turkish Wars in Hungary . . . from 1432 to . . . 1664. . . .
    London: J. Cottrel for N. Brook, 1664. Uk.
        In Seton's library, 1732 (1 of 42).

Hodges, James, fl. 1697–1706.
War betwixt the Two British Kingdoms Consider'd. . . . London: John Taylor,
    1705. Uk.
        In Seton's library, 1732, and Maxwell's, 1769 (2 of 42).

Holliday, Francis, 1717–87.
An Easy Introduction to Practical Gunnery. . . . London: Innvys, 1756. DSoC.
        In 1779 Smith recommended a 1766 edition of this book—perhaps mistakenly
        because the second edition of *Practical Gunnery* appeared in London in 1774
        (Uk) (1 of 28).

Holtzendorff, Georg Ernst, Freiherr von, 1714–85.
Campagne du Roi de Prusse, de 1778 à 1779. . . . Geneva; and Paris: at Méri-
    got the younger, 1784. DSoC.
        In Calderwood's library, 1787 (1 of 6).

Hondius, Hendrik, 1597–1651.
Description & Breve Declaration des Regles Generales de la Fortification. . . .
    The Hague: n.p., 1625. NN.
        In Oglethorpe's library, 1785 (1 of 42).

Hope, Sir William, fl. 1687–1725.
The Swordsman's Vade Mecum. . . . London: Taylor, 1694. UkLG.
        In Calderwood's library, 1787 (1 of 42).

Horst, Tileman van der.
*Essai sur la Fortification, ou, Éxamen des Causes de la Grande Supériorité de
    l'Attaque sur la Défense. . . .* The Hague: P. Gosse, Jr., 1755. DSoC.
        General Officer owned and Debbieg purchased in 1773; Smith recommended
        in 1779 (3 of 30, or 10 percent, and an authority; see Appendix B).

Hoste, Paul, 1652–1700.
L'Art des Armées Navales. . . . Lyon: Anisson and Posuel, 1697. DSoC.
        Winde had in 1740 (1 of 42).

Hugo, Herman, 1588–1629.
*Obsidio Bredana Armis Philippi IIII Auspiciis Isabellae Ducta Ambr.
    Spinolae Perfecta.* 2nd ed. Antwerp: Ex officina, 1629. DSoC.
        In Oglethorpe's library, 1785 (1 of 42).

Hugo, Herman, 1588–1629.
Le Siège de la Ville de Breda: Conquise par les Armes du Roy Philippe IV. . . .
Translated by Philippe Chifflet. Antwerp: ex officina Platiniana, 1631. DSoC.
In Dury's library, 1758 (1 of 42).

Hugo, Herman, 1588–1629.
The Siege of Breda. . . . Translated by C. H. G. [Henry Gage]. [Ghent]: Iudoci
Dooms, 1627. DSoC.
In Oglethorpe's library, 1785 (1 of 42). See also Barry, Gerat, fl. 1624–42.

Humbert, Abraham von, 1689–1761.
L'Art du Genie pour l'Instruction des Gens de Guerre. Berlin: Haude and
Spener, 1755. TxU.
In 1779 Smith recommended what seems to have been a German edition of this
book (1756)—an edition that has not been found (1 of 30).

Hyde, Edward, 1st Earl of Clarendon, 1609–74. See Clarendon.

*An Impartial Enquiry into the Duke of Ormonde's Conduct in the Campagne
of 1712.* . . . London: J. Roberts, 1715. CtY.
In Hotham's library, 1738 (1 of 42).

Ive, Paul.
The Practise of Fortification. . . . London: Thomas Orwin for Thomas Man
and Toby Cooke, 1589. Uk.
In 1799 there was an unspecified edition of this book in Montresor's library
(1 of 42).

Jacquet de Malzet, Louis Sébastien, 1715–1800.
Le Militaire Citoyen, ou, l'Emploi des Hommes. Amsterdam and Paris: N. B.
Duchesne, 1760. NjP.
In Ligonier's library, 1770 (1 of 24).

Jeney, Capitaine de.
Der Partheyganger oder die Kunst den Kleinen Krieg zu Führen. Stuttgart:
Cotta, 1765. GyGoN.
In 1779 Smith recommended a 1766 edition of this book, no copy of which has
been found (1 of 21).

Jeney, Capitaine de.
Le Partisan, ou l'Art de Faire la Petite-Guerre avec Succès. . . . The Hague:
H. Constapel, 1759. DSoC.
In Ligonier's library, 1770 (1 of 24).

Joly de Maizeroy, Paul Gédéon, 1719–80. See Maizeroy, Paul Gédéon, Joly de.

Jonchère, Étienne Lécuyer de la, 1690–1740.
Nouvelle Methode de Fortifier les Plus Grandes Villes. . . . Paris: Florentin
  Delaulne, 1718. DSoC.
> General Officer owned and Smith purchased in 1773 (2 of 42).

Jones, Robert.
A New Treatise on Artificial Fireworks. . . . London: J. Millan and others,
  1765. CtY.
> In 1779 Smith recommended an edition of 1768 that has not been found. There
> was a second edition in 1766 and a corrected second edition in 1776 (1 of 21).

Josephus, Flavius, A.D. 37–100?
*The Works of Flavius Josephus: Translated into English by Sir Roger
  L'Estrange.* . . . 6th ed. London: R. Ware, 1755. Uk.
> Oglethorpe owned this edition in 1785; Wade owned a three-volume edition
> of L'Estrange's translation in 1758, as did Lord John Murray in 1762 (3 of 30).

Josephus, Flavius, A.D. 37–100?
*The Works of the Learned and Valiant Josephus: Epitomiz'd from the
  Greek.* . . . London: A. Roper and R. Basset, 1699. NcD.
> In Oglethorpe's library, 1785 (1 of 42).
>
> Including Donkin, who cited an unspecified edition of Josephus in 1777, four
> officers expressed a preference for his works(4 of 42).

*Journal du Siège de Maestricht Tiré des Gazettes d'Amsterdam, avec les
  Réflexions du Sieur de Barzel.* [Antwerp?, 1673]. Uk.
> Hesse owned in 1758 (1 of 42).

*A Journal of the Expedition to Carthagena . . . in Answer to a Late Pam-
  phlet, Entitled, An Account of the Expedition to Carthagena.* London:
  J. Roberts, 1744. DSoC.
> Molyneux cited in 1759 (1 of 33).

*A Journal of the Late Motions and Actions of the Confederate Forces against
  the French, in the United Provinces, and the Spanish Netherlands . . . during the Last Campaign.* London: R. Baldwin, 1690. DSoC.
> In Hotham's library, 1738 (1 of 42).

*A Journal of the Siege of Mentz under the Command of . . . the Duke of Lor-
  rain . . . 1689.* . . . London: R. Bentley and R. Baldwin, 1689. Uk.
> Hotham owned in 1738 (1 of 42).

Julien, Roch Joseph.
Atlas Géographique et Militaire de la France. . . . Paris: R. J. Julien, 1751.
  DSoC.

In Dury's library, 1758 (1 of 31).

Justinus, Marcus Junianus, third century A.D.
Justini Historiae Philippicae ... The History of Justin with an English Translation. . . . Translated by John Clarke. 5th ed. London: for W. Clarke and sold by C. Hitch and L. Hawes, 1759. MH-H.

> Molyneux cited (1759) and Townshend recommended (1776) without specifying a particular edition. This is one of many eighteenth-century versions of Justin's work (2 of 42).

Kane, Richard, 1666–1736.
Campaigns of King William and Queen Anne from 1689 to 1712. Also a New System of Military Discipline. . . . London: J. Millan, 1745. Uk.

> Bagshawe (1751), Wade (1758), Lord John Murray (1762), and Tryon (1773) owned either this or the second edition of 1747 of Kane's *Campaigns* (DSoC) (4 of 33).

Kane, Richard, 1666–1736.
A System of Camp-Discipline. . . . To Which Is Added, General Kane's Campaigns of King William and the Duke of Marlborough. 2nd ed. London: J. Millan, 1757. DSoC.

> In General Officer's library, 1773, and Montresor's, 1799 (2 of 28). Including Wolfe who recommended Kane's work in 1752 and Dury who owned it in 1758 (neither specified a title or edition), 24 percent (8 of 33) of the officers who might have shown a preference for Kane did so. He was clearly among the thirty authors that our officers admired most (see Appendix B).

Khevenhüller, Ludwig Andreas, Graf, 1683–1744.
Observations-Puncten. . . . 1. Von Subordination, Gehorsam und Respect. 2. Von Conduite der Herrn Officier. 3. Regiments-Privilegien ... gehandelt wird. 3 vols. in one. Vienna: J. P. Krauss, 1739. DSoC.

> General Officer owned and Smith purchased a 1748 edition of this book in 1773 (2 of 36).

[Kimber, Isaac, 1692–1755].
The Life of Oliver Cromwell. . . . London: J. Brotherton and T. Cox, 1724. DSoC.

> It might well have been this or a subsequent edition of Kimber's Cromwell— DSoC has a second edition of 1725—that Robert Murray owned in 1738 (1 of 41).

Kimber, Isaac, 1692–1755.
La Vie d'Olivier Cromwell. . . . 2 vols. The Hague: Jacob de Jongh, 1725. DSoC.

> Molyneux cited in 1759 and Maxwell owned in 1769 (2 of 41).

Labrune, Jean de.
La Vie de Charles V Duc de Lorraine et de Bar. . . . 3rd ed. Amsterdam:
  J. Garrel, 1691. DSoC.
> Hotham Thompson owned an unspecified edition of this book in 1784 (1 of 42).

La Croix, M. de, d. 1704.
Traité de la Petite Guerre pour les Compagnies Franches. . . . Paris: Antoine
  Boudet, 1759. DSoC.
> In 1756 Wolfe recommended either an earlier edition of this book (none has
> been found) or Grandmaison's *La Petite Guerre*, which was published in 1756.
> (1 of 28).

La Fontaine, Sieur de.
Les Devoirs Militaires des Officiers de l'Infanterie. . . . Paris: Estienne Loyson,
  1675. NWM.
> In Winde's library, 1740 (1 of 42).

La Fontaine, Sieur de.
La Doctrine Militaire, ou de Parfa't General d'Armée. . . . Paris: E. Loyson,
  1671. MiU.
> In General Officer's library, 1773 (1 of 42).

Lajonchère. See Jonchère, Étienne Lécuyer de la.

La M[aire d'Olainville].
*Memoires sur la Guerre Tirés des Originaux de M. de Turenne avec Plusieurs
  Memoires Concernant les Hôpitaux Militaires.* . . . The Hague: Pierre
  Gosse, 1738. DSoC.
> General Officer owned a later edition of this book (The Hague, 1758) in 1773
> (1 of 36).

La Mamie Clairac, Louis-André de, 1690–1752. See Clairac.

Lamoral Le Pippre de Noeufville, Simon.
*Abregé Chronologique et Historique . . . du Progress et de l'Etat Actuel de
  la Maison du Roi et de Toutes les Troupes de France.* . . . 3 vols. Liège:
  E. Kints, 1734–35. MiU.
> In Dury's library, 1758, and General Officer's, 1773 (2 of 38).

Landsberg, Johann Heinrich von [Uk attributes to Johann Heinrick von; the
National Union Catalogue, to Hermann, 1680–1746?].
Maniere de Fortifier les Places. . . . The Hague, 1712 [no copy found].
> Winde owned in 1740; General Officer owned and Debbieg bought in 1773; and
> Dundas considered in 1779 (4 of 42).

Landsberg, Johann Heinrich von [Uk attributes to Johann Heinrick von; the National Union Catalogue, to Hermann, 1680–1746?].
Nouveaux Plans et Projects de Fortifications. . . . The Hague: P. Husson, 1731. Uk.

> Dury owned in 1758 (1 of 40).
>
> Altogether, 12 percent of the officers (5 of 42) indicated a preference for Landsberg's works (an authority; see Appendix B).

La Noue, François de, 1531–91.
Discours Politiques et Militaires du Sieur de La Noue. . . . 2 vols. Lyon: François le Fevre, 1596. DSoC.

> General Officer owned and Smith purchased in 1773 (2 of 42).

La Pause, Guillaume Plantavit de, Abbé de Margon, 1685?–1760.
Memoires du Maréchal de Berwik. 2 vols. The Hague: Pierre Paupie, 1737–38. DSoC.

> Dury owned this and another unspecified edition in 1758; General Officer had a 1757 edition in his library in 1773 (2 of 38). The National Union Catalogue calls this a "spurious compilation" because Berwick's genuine memoirs were not published until 1778 (for the genuine memoirs, see Berwick).

La Pause, Guillaume Plantavit de, Abbé de Margon, 1685?–1760.
Mémoires du Maréchal de Berwik. 2 vols. London: J. Nourse, 1738. Uk.

> Clinton discussed this edition in 1793 (1 of 36).

La Prugne, Jean de Billon, Sieur de. See Billon, Jean de, Sieur de La Prugne.

Laissac. See *De l'Esprit Militaire*.

La Tour d'Auvergne, Henri de, Vicomte de Turenne. See Turenne, Henri de La Tour d'Auvergne, Vicomte de, 1611–75.

La Vardin, Jacques de, sixteenth century.
Histoire de Georges Castriot Surnommé Scanderbeg, Roy d'Albanie: Contenant ses Illustres Faicts d'Armes et Memorables Victoires alencontre des Turcs. . . . La Rochelle: H. Haultin, 1592. Uk.

> Oglethorpe owned a Rochelle, 1593 edition of this book in 1785 (1 of 42).

La Vardin, Jacques de, sixteenth century.
The Historie of George Castriot, Surnamed Scanderbeg, King of Albanie. . . . Translated by Z[achary] J[ones]. London: W. Ponsonby, 1596. Uk.

> Oglethorpe owned in 1785. Wolfe admired Scanderbeg but did not recommend a specific book about him (1 of 42).

Le Blond, Guillaume, 1704–81.
Abregé de l'Arithmetique et de la Géométrie de l'Officier. . . . Paris: Ch. Ant.
Jombert, 1758. DSoC.
> Cited in 1762 edition of Bever (1 of 25).

Le Blond, Guillaume, 1704–81.
Elemens de Fortification. . . . 2nd ed. Paris: Charles-Antoine Jombert, 1742.
DSoC.
> General Officer had a copy in 1773. Unspecified editions of this work were in
> Lord John Murray's library in 1762 and Oglethorpe's in 1785 (3 of 33).

Le Blond, Guillaume, 1704–81.
*Elemens de la Guerre des Sieges ou Traité de l'Artillerie, de l'Attaque et la De-
fence des Places.* . . . 3 vols. Paris, 1743. CSmH.
> General Officer had in library in 1773 (1 of 33).

Le Blond, Guillaume, 1704–81.
Essai sur la Castrametation ou sur la Mesure et le Tracé des Camps. . . . Paris:
Charles-Antoine Jombert, 1748. DSoC.
> General Officer had in 1773 (1 of 33).

Le Blond, Guillaume, 1704–81.
The Military Engineer. . . . 2 vols. London: J. Nourse, 1759. DSoC.
> Smith recommended this book in 1779; Tryon probably owned it in 1773 (2 of
> 24).

Le Blond, Guillaume, 1704–81.
Traité de l'Artillerie, ou des Armes et Machines en Usage a la Guerre. . . . Paris:
Charles-Antoine Jombert, 1743. DSoC.
> In the libraries of Dury (1758), Tryon (1773), and General Officer (1773); bought
> by Debbieg in 1773; and recommended by Smith in 1779 (5 of 33).

Le Blond, Guillaume, 1704–81.
A Treatise of Artillery or of the Arms and Machines Used in War. . . . London:
E. Cave and M. Cooper, 1746. DSoC.
> In General Officer's library, 1773 (1 of 33).
>
> Of the officers who might have shown a preference for Le Blond's books, 24
> percent (8 of 33) did so, placing his works among the thirty that our officers
> admired above all others (see Appendix B).

Le Cointe, Jean Louis, b. 1729.
La Science des Postes Militaires, ou Traité des Fortifications de Campagne. . . .
Paris: Desaint and Saillant, 1759. DSoC.
> In General Officer's library, 1773 (1 of 24).

Le Cointe, Jean Louis, b. 1729.
The Science of Military Posts for the Use of Regimental Officers. . . . Translated
by an Officer. London: T. Payne, 1761. DSoC.

> In Ligonier's library, 1770; Smith recommended, 1779 (2 of 23).
>
> Altogether, 13 percent (3 of 24) of the officers who might have expressed a
> preference for Le Cointe did so (an authority; see Appendix B).

Le Coq Madeleine, fl. 1706–27.
Le Service Ordinaire et Journalier de la Cavalerie. Paris: Louis-Denis Delatour, 1720. DSoC.

> In General Officer's library, 1773 (1 of 42).

Lediard, Thomas, 1685–1743.
The Life of John, Duke of Marlborough. . . . 3 vols. London: J. Wilcox, 1736.
DSoC.

> Paget owned in 1741 as did Maxwell in 1769 (2 of 38). According to Atkinson,
> *Marlborough and the Rise of the British Army*, p. xi, Lediard "appears to have
> been attached to the Duke's staff in a secretarial capacity and was present in
> several of his campaigns."

Lediard, Thomas, 1685–1743.
The Naval History of England. 2 vols. London: John Wilcox and Olive Payne,
1735. DSoC.

> Dury (1758), Tryon (1773 — only one volume), Hotham Thompson (1784), and
> Oglethorpe (1785) owned this history; Molyneux cited it in 1759 (5 of 38, or 13
> percent and among our officers' authorities; see Appendix B).

Leeds, Duke of, 1658–1729. See Osborne, Peregrine Hyde, Duke of Leeds.

Lemau de la Jaisse, Pierre.
Cinquiéme Abregé de la Carte Generale du Militaire de France. . . . Paris:
Gandouin, 1739. DSoC.

> Ligonier had 1735 and 1739 editions of this annual publication in 1770; Dury
> had an unspecified edition in 1758 (2 of 38).

Le Michaud-d'Arcon, Jean Claude Éléonore, 1733–1800. See Arçon.

Leo VI, called the Philosopher, emperor of the Eastern Roman Empire, 866–
912.
*Documenti et Avisi Notabili di Guerra: Ne'quali s'insegna Distintamente
Tutta L'Arte Militare.* . . . Translated by M. F. Pigafetta. Venice: G. A. and
G. de Franceshi, 1602. DSoC.

> In 1777 Donkin cited a Pigafetta translation of Leo's tactics, perhaps this edi-
> tion (1 of 42).

Le Prestre de Vauban, Sébastien, 1633–1707. See Vauban, Sébastien Le Prestre de.

Le Roy de Bosroger.
The Elementary Principles of Tactics. . . . London: Hooper, 1771. DSoC.
> Smith recommended in 1779 (1 of 19).

Lestock, Richard, 1679?–1746.
Vice Admiral Lestock's Defense to the Court-Martial. . . . London: n.p., 1746. NN.
> In Lord John Murray's library, 1762 (1 of 33).

The Life and Glorious Actions of the Right Honourable Sir George Rooke. . . . London: J. Morphew, 1707. CtY.
> Molyneux cited in 1759 (1 of 42).

Ligne, Charles Joseph, Prince de, 1735–1814.
Préjugés Militaires, par un Officier Authrichien. . . . Illustrated by Pierre-Philippe Choffard. 2 vols. Kralovelhota: n.p., 1780. DSoC.
> In Montresor's library, 1799 (1 of 7).

A List of the General and Field-Officers as They Rank in the Army. . . . London: J. Millan, 1754–. Uk.
> Dury (1758), Gentleman in Army (1799), Harrison (1763), Ligonier (1770), Maxwell (1769), Lord John Murray (1762), and Hotham Thompson (1784) owned at least one edition of this annual list of the officers in the British army. Dury and Maxwell—and probably others—had regular runs of the *List*, which was among the thirty books on war that our officers preferred above all others (7 of 30, or 23 percent; see Appendix B).

Lists of the Forces of the Sovereigns of Europe. . . . London: J. Millan, 1761. NN.
> General Officer owned in 1773 (1 of 23).

Lives of Illustrious British Seamen. . . . Edinburgh, 1764. DSoC.
> Maxwell owned in 1769 (1 of 21).

Livy (Titus Livius), 59 B.C.–A.D.17.
Titi Livii Historiarum Quod Exstat. . . . Edited by Jean Le Clerc. 10 vols. Amsterdam: Henricum Wetstenium, 1710. DSoC.
> Stanhope owned (1721), Townshend recommended (1776), and Donkin cited (1777) unspecified Latin editions of Livy—perhaps this one (3 of 42).

Lloyd, Henry, c. 1720?–1783.
Essai sur la Grande Guerre de Main de Maitre, ou Instruction Militaire du

Roi de Prusse pour Ses Generaux. . . . London: Aux Depens de la Compagnie, 1761. DSoC.

> Owned by Ligonier in 1770 and by General Officer in 1773; purchased by Parker in 1773 (3 of 23, or 13 percent). Lloyd's *Essai* was among our officers' authorities (see Appendix B).

Lloyd, Henry, c. 1720?–1783.

The History of the Late War in Germany between the King of Prussia and the Empress of Germany and Her Allies. . . . 2 vols. London: for the author, 1766. DSoC.

> Ligonier owned, 1770; Smith recommended (a 1772 edition), 1779; and Clinton made notes on, 1789–94 (3 of 21, or 14 percent, and among our officers' authorities; see Appendix B).

Lochée, Lewis, d. 1791.

Elements of Fortification. London: the author and sold by T. Cadell and H. Payne, 1780. DSoC.

> In Montresor's library, 1799 (1 of 7).

Lochée, Lewis, d. 1791.

An Essay on Castrametation. London: the author and T. Cadell, 1778. DSoC.

> Smith cited, 1779 (1 of 9).

Lochée, Lewis, d. 1791.

A System of Military Mathematics. 2 vols. London: for the author and T. Cadell, 1776. DSoC.

> Smith cited, 1779, and in Montresor's library, 1799 (2 of 11).

Loen, Johann Michael von, 1694–1776.

Der Soldat oder Der Kriegs Stand. . . . Frankfurt am Main and Leipzig: J. F. Fleischer, 1744. DSoC.

> In 1779 Smith recommended a 1752 edition of this book, an edition that has not been found (1 of 33).

Lorini, Buonaiuto, fl. 1600.

Le Fortificationi di Buonaiuto Lorini. . . . Venice: F. Rampazetto, 1609. DSoC.

> In Winde's library, 1740 (1 of 42).

Luxembourg, François Henri de Montmorency-Bouteville, Duc de, 1628–95.

> See Beaurain, Jean Chevalier de, 1696–1771; and *Campagne de Hollande en MDCLXXII sous . . . Luxembourg.* At least 20 percent (6 of 30) of the officers who might have taken an interest in these books about Luxembourg did so. They clearly considered him among their authorities (see Appendix B).

M., S.

Art of Fortification, or Architecture Militaire as well Offensive as Defensive,
  Compiled . . . by S. M. Augmented and corrected by A. Girard; translated
  by H. Hexham. Amsterdam, 1638. Uk.

>   In Hotham Thompson's library, 1784 (1 of 42).

Maase, J. F. von der.

Manuel Militaire ou Cayers Détachés sur Toutes Différentes Parties de l'Art
  de la Guerre. Copenhagen; and Leiden: at Elie Luzac, 1761. DSoC.

>   In General Officer's library, 1773 (1 of 23).

Machiavelli, Niccolò, 1469–1527.

L'Art de la Guerre. . . . Amsterdam, 1613.

>   In 1750 Stewart owned a French edition of the *Art of War*, published in Amster-
>   dam in 1613. No copy of this edition has been found (1 of 42).

Machiavelli, Niccolò, 1469–1527.

The Arte of Warre. . . . Translated by Peter Withorne. London: W. Williamson
  for John Wight, 1573. Uk.

>   In General Officer's library, 1773. Seton owned another edition of Withorne's
>   translation (London: Thomas East for John Wight, 1588; DSoC) in 1732 (2 of 42).

Machiavelli, Niccolò, 1469–1527.

Libro della Arte della Guerra. . . . Florence, 1521. Uk.

>   In 1758 Dury owned an unspecified Italian edition of *The Art of War*—most
>   likely one of the many editions published in Florence, Venice, and Palermo in
>   the sixteenth century (1 of 42).

Machiavelli, Niccolò, 1469–1527.

Opere di Nic. Machiavelli. The Hague: n.p., 1726. DSoC.

>   In 1762 Lord John Murray owned an unspecified Italian edition of Machia-
>   velli's works, probably this edition of 1726 (1 of 41).

Machiavelli, Niccolò, 1469–1527.

The Works of Nicholas Machiavel. . . . Translated by Ellis Farneworth. 2 vols.
  London: T. Davies, 1762. DSoC.

>   In Ligonier's library, 1770. Hotham Thompson also owned an English transla-
>   tion of Machiavelli's works—probably Farneworth's—in 1784 (2 of 22).

Machiavelli, Niccolò, 1469–1527.

The Works of the Famous Nicholas Machiavel. . . . Translated by Henry
  Neville. London: John Starkey, Charles Harper, John Amery, 1680. DSoC.

>   Oglethorpe owned this edition; Gentleman in the Army owned the third edi-
>   tion (London, 1720; NN) in 1799 (2 of 42).

Altogether, 21 percent (9 of 42) of those officers who might have owned either Machiavelli's *Art of War* or his complete works did so. His writings were clearly among the thirty that our officers admired most (see Appendix B).

Maffei, Alessandro, Marchese, 1662–1730.
Mémoires du Marquis Maffei. 2 vols. The Hague: Jean Neaulme, 1740. DSoC.
General Officer owned this edition in 1773; Dury had an unspecified edition in 1758 (2 of 35).

Maggi, Girolamo, d. 1572.
Della Fortificatione delle Citta. . . . Venice: C. Borgominiero, 1564. CtY.
In 1779 Smith recommended a 1559 edition of this book; and in 1785 Oglethorpe's library contained an edition of 1538 — neither of which has been found (2 of 42).

Maigret.
Treatise on the Safety and Maintenance of States by the Means of Fortresses. Translated by [J. Heath]. London, 1747. Uk.
In Ligonier's library, 1770, in General Officer's and Tryon's, 1773, and in Montresor's, 1799 (4 of 33, or 12 percent, and an authority; see Appendix B).

Maizeroy, Paul Gédéon, Joly de, 1719–80.
Mémoire sur les Opinions Qui Partagent les Militaires: Suivi du Traité des Armes Défensives. . . . Paris: C. A. Jombert, 1773. DSoC.
Hotham Thompson owned in 1784. In 1779 Dundas was considering and Smith cited collections of Maizeroy's works (but no *Oeuvres* has been found) (3 of 14). Maizeroy was among those officers that our officers considered an authority (see Appendix B).

Mallet, Allain Manesson, 1630?–1706?. See Manesson-Mallet, Allain.

Malzet, Louis Sébastien, Jacquet de, 1715–1800. See Jacquet de Malzet, Louis Sébastien, 1715–1800.

Manesson-Mallet, Allain, 1630?–1706?.
Les Travaux de Mars, ou l'Art de la Guerre. . . . 3 vols. Paris: Denys Thierry, 1684–85. DSoC.
In Winde's, Stewart's, and Oglethorpe's libraries, 1740, 1750, and 1785 respectively. General Officer owned and Smith purchased a later, revised edition (The Hague: Adrian Moetjens, 1696) in 1773; and Hotham Thompson had an unspecified edition in 1784 (6 of 42, or 14 percent). Manesson-Mallet's *Travaux* was among our officers' authorities (see Appendix B).

Manley, Sir Roger, 1626?–1688.
The History of the Late Warres in Denmark . . . 1657, 1658, 1659, 1660. . . . London: Thomas Basset, 1670. DSoC.

In 1740 Winde's library contained a 1683 edition of this history—no copy of which has been found (1 of 42).

Manningham, Henry. See Saint-Rémy, Pierre Surirey de.

Manstein, Cristof Hermann, 1711–57.
Memoirs of Russia, from the Year 1727, to the Year 1744. 2nd ed. London: T. Becket and P. A. De Hondt, 1773. DSoC.
> Percy ordered in 1774 (1 of 14).

Mante, Thomas, fl. 1772.
The History of the Late War in North-America, and the Islands of the West-Indies. . . . London: W. Strahan and T. Cadell, 1772. DSoC.
> Percy ordered in 1774 (1 of 19).

Marchi, Francesco de, b. 1506.
Della Architettura Militare. . . . Brescia: C. Presegni, 1599. CLU.
> In 1779 Smith cited and recommended what seems to have been a three-volume edition of this book, an edition of 1546 that has not been found (1 of 42).

Markham, Francis, 1565–1627.
Five Decades of Epistles of Warre. London: A. Matthewes, 1622. DSoC.
> General Officer owned and Smith purchased in 1773 (2 of 42).

Marlborough, John Churchill, Duke of, 1650–1722.
> See books by Campbell, Dumont, Kane, Lediard, and Millner as well as *Full and Impartial Relation . . . of Hochstette* and *History of the Campaign in Flanders in . . . 1708.* In addition to the officers who showed a preference for one or more of those books, Clinton and Donkin (1777) reflected on Marlborough's campaigns, and Wade had a book about his battles. Altogether, 48 percent of our officers (20 of 42) expressed an interest in Marlborough. They clearly preferred him to all other authorities on war except Caesar and Vauban (see Appendix B). See also Eugene, Prince of Savoy, 1663–1736.

Marsigli, Luigi Ferdinando, Count, 1658–1730.
État Militaire de l'Empire Ottoman. The Hague: P. Gosse, 1732. Uk.
> In Wortley Montagu's library, 1776. Dury owned an unspecified edition in French in 1758 (2 of 38).

Marsollier, Jacques, 1647–1724.
Histoire de Henry de la Tour d'Auvergne, Duc de Bouillon. . . . 3 vols. Paris: François Barois, 1719. DSoC.
> In Dury's library, 1758 (1 of 42).

Martin, Samuel of Antigua.
A Plan for Establishing and Disciplining a National Militia. London:
A. Millar and sold by M. Cooper, 1745. DSoC.
> In Dury's library, 1758 (1 of 33).

Martini, Francesco di Giorgio da Siena, 1439–1502.
Trattato di Architettura Civile e Militare. N.p., n.d.
> This was probably the book that Smith recommended in 1779 as Francisco
> Jeorg Senensis, *Fortificazione* (n.p., n.d.). See Mariano d'Ayala, *Bibliografia
> Militare Italiana* (Turin: Stamperia reale, 1854), pp. 107–8 (1 of 42).

Massuet, Pierre, 1698–1776.
*Histoire de la Guerre Présente . . . en Italie, sur le Rhin, en Pologne et dans la
Plupart des Cours de l'Europe. . . .* Amsterdam: F. L'Honoré, 1735. DSoC.
> In Dury's library, 1758 (1 of 38).

Maubert de Gouvest, Jean Henri, 1721–67.
Mémoires Militaires sur les Anciens. . . . 2 vols. Brussels: n.p., 1762. DSoC.
> There was a Paris edition of 1762 in Montresor's library, 1799 (1 of 22).

Mauvillon, Eléazar de, 1712–79.
Histoire du Prince François Eugene de Savoie. . . . 5 vols. Amsterdam: Arkstée
and Merkus, 1740. DSoC.
> In General Officer's library, 1773. Dury had another, two-volume edition of this
> work in 1758 (2 of 35).

McArthur, John, fl. 1780.
*The Army and Navy Gentleman's Companion or, a New and Complete Trea-
tise on the Theory and Practice of Fencing. . . .* London: J. Lavers, 1780.
DSoC.
> There was an unspecified edition of this book in Montresor's library, 1799 (1 of
> 7).

Meadows, Sir Philip, 1626–1718.
*A Narrative of the Principal Actions Occurring in the Wars betwixt Sueden
and Denmark.* London: A. C. and H. Brome, 1677. CtY.
> In Seton's library, 1732 (1 of 42).

Melville, Sir James of Hal-Hill, 1535–1617.
Mémoires de J. Melvil. . . . Translated by G. D. S. 2 vols. The Hague: A. Moetjens, 1694. Uk.
> Dury owned in 1758 (1 of 42).

Melzo, Lodovico, 1567–1617.
*Regole Militari del Cavalier Melzo sopra il Governo e Servitio della Caval-
leria.* Antwerp: Gioachimo Trognaesio, 1611. DSoC.
> In Oglethorpe's library, 1785 (1 of 42).

Mervault, Pierre, b. 1608.
*Le Journal des Choses les Plus Memorables Qui Se Sont Passées au Dernier
Siege de la Rochelle.* 2 vols. Rouen: I. Lucas, 1671. NN.
> In Oglethorpe's library, 1785 (1 of 42).

Mervault, Pierre, b. 1608.
The Last Famous Siege of the City of Rochel.... London: John Wickins, 1680.
DLC.
> In Winde's library, 1740, and Dury's 1758 (2 of 42).

Mésnil-Durand, François Jean de Graindorge d'Orgeville, Baron de, 1729–
99.
Observations sur le Canon.... Amsterdam and Paris: C. A. Jombert, 1772.
DSoC.
> In 1779 Smith recommended a 1771 edition of this book that has not been
> found (1 of 19).

Mésnil-Durand, François Jean de Graindorge d'Orgeville, Baron de, 1729–
99.
Projet d'un Ordre François en Tactique.... Paris: Antoine Boudet, 1755.
DSoC.
> In General Officer's library, 1773. In 1756 Wolfe recommended and in 1768–76
> Clinton made notes on this book (3 of 30, or 10 percent, and an authority; see
> Appendix B).

Mey, Sieur de, fl. 1708.
An Exact Journal of the Siege of Lisle.... 2nd ed. London: B. Bragg, 1709.
TxU.
> Hotham owned in 1738 (1 of 42).

Meynier, Honorat de, c. 1570–1638?
Les Nouvelles Inventions de Fortifier les Places.... Illustrated by Crispijn van
de Passe. Paris, 1626. UkCoU.
> Winde owned 1740 (1 of 42).

*Military and Sea Dictionary: Explaining All Difficult Terms in Martial
Discipline....* 4th ed. London: J. Morphew, 1711. DSoC.
> In Seton's library, 1732 (1 of 42).

Milliet de Chales, Claude François. See Chales, Claude François Milliet de,
1621–78.

Millner, John, fl. 1712.
A Compendious Journal of All the Marches, Famous Battles, Sieges . . . under the Conduct and Command of . . . Marlborough. London: n.p., 1733. DSoC.
> Dury owned in 1758 as did Lord John Murray in 1762 and General Officer in 1773; Blomefield purchased in 1773; and Hotham Thompson owned an unspecified edition in 1784. It also seems likely that in 1758 Wade owned this book, which was preferred by 16 percent (6 of 38) of the officers and was among their authorities (see Appendix B). The catalogue of General Officer's books shows that Millner's book was published in 1712; that date seems to have been taken by mistake from the full title of the book.

Millot, Claude François Xavier, 1726–85.
Memoires Politiques et Militaires: pour Servir à l'Histoire de Louis XIV & de Louis XV, Composé sur les Pièces Originales Recueillies par Adrien-Maurice Duc de Noailles. 6 vols. Paris: Moutard, 1777. DSoC.
> Hotham Thompson owned, 1784, and Clinton made notes on, c. 1793 (2 of 9).

Mirabeau, Honoré-Gabriel de Riquetti, Comte de, 1749–91.
Système Militaire de la Prusse. . . . London: n.p., 1788. DSoC.
> Clinton made notes on c. 1791–92 (1 of 3).

Mitchell, John, 1711–68.
The Contest in America between Great Britain and France. . . . London: A. Millar, 1757. DSoC.
> Dury owned in 1758 as did Wortley Montagu in 1776 (2 of 28).

Modestus. See Vegetius Renatus, *Flaue Vegece Rene . . . du Fait de Guerre. . . .* (Paris, 1536), as well as Frontinus and Aelianus.

Molesworth, Richard Viscount, 1680–1758.
A Short Course of Standing Rules for the Government and Conduct of an Army. . . . Dublin: Charles Leslie, 1745. Uk.
> In 1752 Wolfe recommended and in 1758 Dury owned, but neither specified an edition (2 of 33). DSoC has a London edition of 1744.

Moll, Herman, d. 1732.
A History of the English Wars in France, Spain, Portugal, Netherlands, Germany, &c., . . . from William the Conqueror to the Present Time. . . . London: for T. Newborough and J. Senex, 1705. Uk.
> Seton owned in 1732 (1 of 42).

Molyneux, Thomas More, 1724– or 1725–76.
Conjunct Expeditions: or Expeditions That Have Been Carried on Jointly by the Fleet and Army. . . . London: R. and J. Dodsley, 1759. DSoC.
> General Officer owned 1773 (1 of 24).

Molyneux, Thomas More, 1724– or 1725–76.
The Target: or, a Treatise upon a Branch of Art Military. . . . London: R. and
   J. Dodsley, 1756. DSoC.

> Molyneux cited this, his own work, in 1759 (1 of 28). See Molyneux, *Conjunct*
> *Expeditions* . . . , part II, p. 186, and Powers, "Authorship."

Monro or Munro, Robert, d. 1680?.
Monro, His Expedition with the Worthy Scots Regiment. . . . London:
   W. Jones, 1637. DSoC.

> Lord John Murray owned in 1762 as did General Officer in 1773 and Ogle-
> thorpe in 1785; there was a copy in Montresor's library in 1799 (4 of 42).

Monson, William, 1569–1643.
Sir William Monson's Naval Tracts in Six Books. . . . London: A. and J. Churchill, 1703. DSoC.

> Molyneux cited in 1759 (1 of 42).

Montecuccoli, Raimondo, Prince, 1609–80.
Memoires de Montecuculi, Generalissime des Troupes de l'Empereur, ou,
   Principes de l'Art Militaire en Général. Paris: Jean Geoffroy Nyon, 1712.
   DSoC.

> In Oglethorpe's library, 1785 (1 of 42).

Montecuccoli, Raimondo, Prince, 1609–80.
Memoires de Montecuculi Generalissime des Troupes de l'Empereur. 2 vols.
   Amsterdam: Wetstein, 1746. AU.

> In General Officer's library, 1773 (1 of 33).
>
> In addition to Oglethorpe and General Officer, Smith recommended (1779)
> a 1758 edition of Montecuccoli's *Memoires* that has not been found. Nine other
> officers showed a preference for Montecuccoli's *Memoires* without specifying
> an edition: Wolfe recommended and Bever cited in 1756; Dury owned in 1758;
> Molyneux cited in 1759; Clinton made notes on c. 1768–76; Maxwell owned
> in 1769 as did Tryon in 1773; Donkin quoted in 1777; and Dundas considered
> in 1779. Altogether, 29 percent (12 of 42) of the officers who might have ex-
> pressed a preference for Montecuccoli did so in one way or another. Those offi-
> cers clearly placed Montecuccoli among their twenty most influential writers
> on war (see Appendix B).

Montgon, [Charles Alexandre] de, 1690–1770.
Mémoires de Monsieur l'Abbé de Montgon. 8 vols. Lausanne: M. M. Bousquet, 1748, 1753. MiU.

> Dury owned in 1758 (1 of 30).

Moody, James, 1744–1809.

Lieut. James Moody's Narrative of His Exertions and Sufferings. . . . 2nd ed. London: Richardson and Urquhart, 1783. NcGU.

> There seems to have been a first edition of this book in Montresor's library in 1799 (1 of 7).

Moore, Sir Jonas, 1617–79.

Modern Fortification: or, Elements of Military Architecture. . . . London: W. Godbid, 1673. CSmH.

> In Winde's library in 1740 and General Officer's in 1773. Oglethorpe had editions of 1684 and 1689 in 1785 (3 of 42).

Morogues, S. F. Bigot de. See Bigot de Morogues, Sébastien François, 1705–81.

Muller, John, 1699–1784.

Appendix, or, Supplement to the Treatise of Artillery. . . . London: J. Millan, 1768. DSoC.

> Smith recommended, 1779 (1 of 21).

Muller, John, 1699–1784.

The Attack and Defence of Fortify'd Places. . . . London: J. Millan, 1747. DSoC.

> In General Officer's library, 1773. Tryon (in 1773) and Moyle (in 1777) owned this or a later edition of *Attack and Defence*; Townshend recommended it in 1776, as did Smith in 1779 (a 1759 edition that has not been found) (5 of 33).

Muller, John, 1699–1784.

A Treatise Containing the Elementary Part of Fortification. . . . London: J. Nourse, 1746. DSoC.

> In General Officer's library, 1773. Townshend recommended this book in 1776 and Moyle owned it in 1777 (neither specifying a particular edition) (3 of 33).

Muller, John, 1699–1784.

A Treatise Containing the Practical Part of Fortification. . . . London: A. Millar, 1755. DSoC.

> In Ligonier's library, 1770. Moyle owned an unspecified edition of this book in 1777; and Smith recommended what seems to have been the 1764 edition (DSoC) in 1779 (3 of 30).

Muller, John, 1699–1784.

A Treatise of Artillery. . . . London: John Millan, 1757. DSoC.

> General Officer owned and Smith purchased this book in 1773; Townshend recommended it—without specifying an edition—in 1776; and Smith recommended the 1768 edition (NWM) in 1779 (3 of 28).

Dury (1758), Hesse (1758), and Tryon (1773) owned either Muller's *Elementary Part of Fortification* or his *Practical Part of Fortification*; and Dundas considered all of Muller's works in 1779. Indeed, 27 percent (9 of 33) of the officers who might have expressed a preference for Muller's books did so. At least five of those officers owned two or more of his books; and taken together, his books were among the twenty that our officers admired most (see Appendix B). See also Clairac.

Mutiny Act. See *Anno Regni Georgii*. . . .

Nannini, Remigio, 1521?–1581?.
Orationi Militari. Venice: Gabriel Giolito de Ferrari, 1560. NcD.
> In Stanhope's library, 1721 (1 of 42).

Naudin, ingenieur ordinaire du Roy.
L'Ingenieur François Contenant la Géometrie Pratique. . . . Avec la Methode de Monsieur de Vauban et l'Explication de Son Nouveau Systeme. . . . Amsterdam: George Gallet, 1697. DSoC.
> Winde owned a 1697 Paris edition of this work in 1740 (DSoC) and Wortley Montagu a 1734 Amsterdam edition in 1776 (DSoC) (2 of 42).

Néel, Louis-Balthazar, c. 1695–1754.
The History of Maurice Count Saxe. . . . 2 vols. London: T. Osborne, 1753. DSoC.
> In Ligonier's library, 1770 (1 of 30).

Nemours, Marie d'Orléans, Duchess of, 1625–1707.
Memoires de Madame la Duchesse de Nemours: . . . Pendant la Guerre de Paris, Jusqu'a . . . 1652. . . . Amsterdam: J. F. Bernard, 1718. DSoC.
> In Wade's library, 1758 (1 of 42).

The New Art of War. London: E. Midwinter, 1726. Uk.
> This second edition of *The Art of War* of 1707 is a compilation and translation of four works by French authors. Pagett owned *The New Art of War* in 1741, as did Harrison in 1763. Tryon owned this or a later edition in 1773 (3 of 41).

A New Military Dictionary: or, the Field of War. . . . London: J. Cooke, 1760. DSoC.
> Ligonier owned in 1770; so too, probably, did Oglethorpe in 1785 (2 of 24). Smith considered it to be "extremely imperfect" (*Universal Military Dictionary* [1779], vii).

New Regulations for the Prussian Infantry. . . . [Translated by William Fawcett]. London: J. Rivington and J. Fletcher [and two others], 1757. DSoC.

Hotham Thompson owned in 1784 (1 of 28). See also *Regulations for the Prussian Infantry.*

The News-Readers Pocket-Book, or, a Military Dictionary. . . . London: J. Newbery, 1759. DSoC.

> In Montresor's library, 1799 (1 of 24).

Noble, Mark, 1754–1827.
Memoirs of the Protectorate-House of Cromwell. . . . 2 vols. Birmingham: Pearson and Rollason for R. Baldwin [and three others], 1784. DSoC.

> Hotham Thompson owned, 1784 (1 of 6).

Nodot, François, seventeenth century.
Le Munitionaire des Armées de France. . . . Paris: Cusson and Wit, 1697. FU.

> In Dury's library, 1758 (1 of 42).

Nolin, Jean Baptiste, 1657–1725 [National Union Catalogue, but 1648–1708 in Uk, DLC].
Nouvelle Edition du Théâtre de la Guerre en Italie Contenant les Cartes Particulières de Tous les Estats. . . . Paris: J. B. Nolin, 1717. DLC.

> Oglethorpe (1785) and Lord John Murray (1762) owned what seem to have been 1701 and 1704 editions of this work—editions that have not been found. Dury (1758) also had what seems to have been an earlier, unspecified edition of this work (3 of 42).

Nye, Nathaniel, b. 1624.
The Art of Gunnery. . . . London: William Leak, 1670. CtY.

> Winde (1740) and Oglethorpe (1785) had this edition; that of 1647 is in DSoC (2 of 42).

Oldmixon, John, 1673–1742.
The British Empire in America. 2nd ed. 2 vols. London: J. Brotherton and J. Clarke, 1741. DSoC.

> Probably the edition that Molyneux cited in 1759 (1 of 33).

[Oldmixon, John, 1673–1742.]
The History and Life of Robert Blake . . . General and Admiral of the Fleets and Naval Forces of England. . . . London: J. Millan and R. Davis, [1740?]. DSoC.

> Molyneux cited in 1759 (1 of 35).

Old Officer. See *Cautions and Advices to Officers of the Army.*

Ordonnance du Roy. . . . Uk.

> The British Library and the Society of the Cincinnati have about three hundred ordonnances issued by kings of France on military and naval topics throughout

the eighteenth century. Hesse and Wade in 1758, Lord John Murray in 1762, and Tryon in 1773 had copies of one or more of these ordonnances (4 of 42).

Ordonnances du Roy, Concernant l'Infanterie Françoise Ordinaire. . . . 2 vols. Lausanne: Bousquet, 1744. CLU.
> In General Officer's library, 1773 (1 of 33).

Orlers, Jan Janszn, 1570–1646, and Henrick van Haestens.
Description & Representation de Toutes les Victoires . . . souz . . . Maurice de Nassau. Leiden: J. J. Orlers and H. de Haestens, 1612. DSoC.
> In Oglethorpe's library, 1785 (1 of 42).

Ormonde, James Butler, Duke of, 1665–1745.
An Impartial Account of All the Material Transactions of the Grand Fleet and Land Forces . . . June the 29 till . . . November the 7th 1702. . . . London: R. Gibson and sold by J. Nutt, 1703. DSoC.
> In Hotham's library, 1738 (1 of 42).

O'Rourke, John, Count.
A Treatise on the Art of War. . . . London: T. Spilsbury and sold by J. Dodsley [and five others], 1778. DSoC.
> In Oglethorpe's library, 1785; Lord John Murray made notes on, n.d. (2 of 9).

Orrery, Roger Boyle, Earl of, 1621–79.
A Treatise of the Art of War. . . . [London]: T. N. for Henry Herringman, 1677. DSoC.
> Winde owned in 1740 as did General Officer in 1773 and Oglethorpe in 1785. Dalrymple cited in 1761 and Hotham Thompson owned in 1784 without specifying a particular edition (5 of 42, or 12 percent, and an authority; see Appendix B).

Osborne, Peregrine Hyde, Duke of Leeds, 1658–1729.
A Journal of the Brest-Expedition. London: Randal Taylor, 1694. DSoC.
> Hotham owned in 1738 and Molyneux cited in 1759 (2 of 42).

Ottieri, Francesco Maria, Marchese, d. 1742?.
Istoria delle Guerre Avvenute in Europa e Particolarmente in Italia . . . 1696 all'Anno 1725. . . . 8 vols. Rome: R. Bernabó, 1728–57. ICU.
> Hotham Thompson owned an unspecified edition of this book in 1784 (1 of 28).

Ozanam, Jacques, 1640–1717.
Traité de Fortification: Contenant les Methodes Anciennes et Modernes. . . . Paris: J. Jombert, 1694. DSoC.
> Winde owned in 1740. Dury also had an unspecified edition of this book in 1758 (2 of 42).

Pagan, Blaise François de, Comte de Merveilles, 1604–65.
Les Fortifications du Comte de Pagan. Paris: Cardin Besogne, 1645. DSoC.

> In Winde's library, 1740. In 1773 General Officer owned and Smith purchased
> a new edition of this book that had been published in Brussels by F. Foppens
> in 1668 (MiU); Smith also recommended the 1668 edition in 1779 (3 of 42).

Papacino d'Antoni, Alessandro Vittorio, 1714–86, and Gasparo Tignola.
Dell'Artiglieria Practica. . . . 2 vols. Turin: n.p., 1774–75. CtY.

> Smith cited in 1779 (1 of 13).

Papacino d'Antoni, Alessandro Vittorio, 1714–86, and Jean Baptiste Gratien.
Examen de la Poudre. Translated by G. J. B. L., Vicomte de Flavigny. Amsterdam: M.-M. Rey, 1773. MBAt.

> Smith cited and recommended in 1779 (1 of 14).

Park, Robert.
The Art of Sea-Fighting. . . . London: Rich. Mount and Tho. Page, 1706. NN.

> In Lord John Murray's library, 1762 (1 of 42).

Parker, Robert, fl. 1668–1718.
*Memoirs of the Most Remarkable Military Transactions from the Year 1683
to 1718.* . . . London: S. Austen and W. Frederick, 1747. DSoC.

> General Officer owned and Blomefield purchased this book in 1773; Dury
> owned an unspecified edition in 1758 (3 of 33).

Pechel, Samuel.
*An Historical Account of the Settlement and Possession of Bombay . . . and
. . . of the War with the Mahratta Nation.* London: W. Richardson for
J. Robson, 1781. DSoC.

> In Montresor's library, 1799 (1 of 7).

The Perfection of Military Discipline after the Newest Method. . . . London:
Nicholas Boddington, 1690. CLU.

> In Montresor's library, 1799 (1 of 42).

Pétis de la Croix, François the Elder, 1622–95.
The History of Genghizcan the Great. . . . Edited by [F. Pétis de la Croix,
1653–1713]. Translated by [P. Aubin]. London: J. Darby [and five others],
1722. DSoC.

> In General Officer's library 1773 (1 of 41).

Pictet, Gabriel.
Essai sur la Tactique de l'Infanterie. . . . 2 vols. Geneva: Em. Du Villard, 1761.
DSoC.

In Ligonier's library in 1770, and General Officer's in 1773; Tryon probably owned this book as well (the "Tactique de l'Infantry" in the inventory of his books of 1773) (3 of 23, or 13 percent, and an authority; see Appendix B).

Plantavit de la Pause de Margon, Guillaume, 1685?–1760. See La Pause, Guillaume Plantavit de, Abbé de Margon.

Pleydell, J. C. See *An Essay on Field Fortification*.

Plutarch, c. A.D. 46 to after 119.
Plutarch's Lives. . . . Translated by many linguists and edited by John Dryden. 5 vols. London: Jacob Tonson, 1693. DSoC.

> Molyneux cited an unspecified English edition of Plutarch in 1759, likely one of those edited by Dryden; so too did Wade in 1758 and Hotham Thompson in 1784 have unspecified editions of Plutarch. Townshend recommended a French edition in 1776; and Donkin quoted a Latin edition in 1777 (5 of 42, or 12 percent, and an authority; see Appendix B).

Polyaenus, second century A.D.
Polyainou Strategematon Bibloi Okto. Polyaeni Strategematum Libri Octo. Translated by Pancratius Maasvicius. Leiden: Jordanum Luchtmans and Johannem Du Vivié, 1691. DSoC.

> In Stanhope's library in 1721 and Wortley Montagu's in 1776 (2 of 42).

Polyaenus, second century A.D.
Les Ruses de Guerre de Polyen. . . . 2 vols. Paris: Ganeau, 1739. NWM.

> Dury and General Officer owned in 1758 and 1773 respectively, and Smith purchased in 1773 (3 of 36). Both the sale catalogue of 1773 and the notes to WorldCat entry say that this edition also contained *Les Stratagèmes de Frontin*. Clinton reflected on a French translation, probably this one, c. 1768–76, and Molyneux cited an unspecified edition of Polyaenus in 1759. Altogether, 17 percent of our officers (7 of 42) showed a preference for Polyaenus's compilation, which was among the officers' authorities (see Appendix B). See also Frontinus, Sextus Julius, c. A.D. 35–c. 103.

Polybius, c. 200–c. 118 B.C.
The General History of Polybius. Translated by Mr. Hampton. 2 vols. London: J. Hughs for R. and J. Dodsley, 1756–72. DSoC.

> Oglethorpe owned in 1785 (1 of 19).

Polybius, c. 200–c. 118 B.C.
The History of Polybius the Megalopolitan. Translated by Edward Grimeston. London: N. Okes for Cornelius Bee, 1634. DSoC.

> Oglethorpe owned in 1785 (1 of 42).

Polybius, c. 200–c. 118 B.C.

The History of Polybius the Megalopolitan. . . . Translated by Henry Sheeres. 2 vols. London: S. Briscoe, 1693. DSoC.

> In Gentleman in the Army's library in 1799; General Officer owned the second edition of 1698 (also DSoC) in 1773 (2 of 42).

Polybius, c. 200–c. 118 B.C.

Polybii Lycortae F. Megalopolitani Historiarum Libri qui Supersunt. Translated by Jacobus Gronovius. 3 vols. Amsterdam: Johannis Janssonii à Waesberge and Johannis van Someren, 1670. DSoC.

> Wortley Montagu owned in 1776 (1 of 42).

Polybius, c. 200– c.118 B.C.

Polybii Megalopolitani Historiarum. Translated by W. Musculo. 2 vols. Lyon: S. Gryphium, 1554. DSoC.

> In Wortley Montagu's library, 1776 (1 of 42).
>
> In addition, eight other officers showed a preference for Polybius without specifying a particular edition or translation: Stanhope (1721), Wade (1758), Tryon (1773), and Hotham Thompson (1784) all owned copies of his history while Wolfe (1756) and Townshend (1776) recommended and Dalrymple (1761) and Donkin (1777) cited it. Altogether—and including six officers who had a translation of Polybius with Folard's commentary—43 percent (18 of 42) of the officers who might have shown a preference for Polybius did so. They clearly valued his history above all save four or five other books on war available in mid-eighteenth-century Britain (see Appendix B). See also Folard, Jean Charles de, 1669–1752.

Pringle, John, 1707–82.

Observations on the Diseases of the Army. . . . London: A. Millar, 1752. DSoC.

> In Ligonier's library, 1770. Dury (1758) and Oglethorpe (1785) also owned unspecified editions (3 of 31). DSoC has five other English editions—all by Millar—of 1753, 1761, 1764, 1765, and 1768.

Proctor, Thomas, fl. 1578.

Of the Knowledge and Conducte of Warres. . . . Amsterdam: Theatrum Orbis Terrarum, 1578. CSmH.

> In General Officer's library, 1773 (1 of 42).

Pufendorf, Samuel, Freiherr von, 1632–94.

Histoire du Regne de Charles Gustave, Roy de Suède. . . . Nuremberg: Christophle Riegel, 1697. DSoC.

> Wade had an unspecified edition of this work in 1758 (1 of 42).

Puységur, Jacques François de Chastenet, Marquis de, 1656–1743.
Art de la Guerre, par Principes et par Règles. 2 vols. Paris: C.-A. Jombert,
1748. DSoC.

> Dury (1758), Ligonier (1770), and General Officer (1773) owned this edition
> of Puységur. Wolfe recommended Puységur in 1756 and gave a copy of the
> Paris edition of 1749 (DSoC) to Lord Fitzmaurice; Smith also recommended
> the Paris edition of 1749 (in 1779). Bever (1756), Molyneux (1759), Dalrymple
> (1761), and Donkin (1777) cited *Art de la Guerre*; Tryon (1773) owned a copy;
> and Townshend (1759) and Clinton (1768–76) made notes on it—all without
> specifying a particular edition. Indeed, 36 percent (12 of 33) of the officers who
> might have expressed a preference for Puységur did so. His was among the
> twenty books that our officers preferred to all others (see Appendix B).

Quincy, Charles Sévin, Marquis de, 1666–1736.
L'Art de la Guerre, ou, Maximes et Instructions sur l'Art Militaire.... 2 vols.
Paris: Pierre-Jean Mariette, 1740. DSoC.

> In 1758 Dury had a two-volume edition of this work published at The Hague
> in 1741. In 1773 General Officer owned and Debbieg purchased another two-
> volume edition published at The Hague in 1745. Bever cited Quincy's *L'Art de
> la Guerre* without specifying an edition in 1756 (4 of 35, or 11 percent, and an
> authority; see Appendix B).
>
> *L'Art de la Guerre* was first published as the second part of volume 7 of
> Quincy's *Histoire Militaire du Règne de Louis le Grand*; thus, 12 percent (5 of
> 42) of the officers who might have preferred *L'Art de la Guerre* did so.

Quincy, Charles Sévin, Marquis de, 1666–1736.
Histoire Militaire du Regne de Louis le Grand.... 7 vols. Paris: D. Mariette,
1726. NN.

> Molyneux cited in 1759, calling Quincy "the most exact and most moderate of
> all the French Writers" (*Conjunct Expeditions*, 1:83) (1 of 41).

R., Mr.
Mémoires d'un Militaire: Depuis l'Année 1735 jusqu'au ... 1758. Wesel: Chez
les Libraires, 1759. DSoC.

> In General Officer's library, 1773 (1 of 24).

Raguenet, François, 1660?–1722.
Histoire du Vicomte de Turenne. 2 vols. The Hague: Jean Neaulme, 1738.
DSoC.

> In General Officer's library, 1773 (1 of 36).

Railton, John.
The Army's Regulator, or, The British Monitor. Discovering, I. The Fre-

quent Infringements upon His Majesty's Articles of War, and Military Acts of Parliament. . . . London: W. Smith, 1738. DSoC.

> In Wade's library, 1758 (1 of 36).

Ramsay, Chevalier [Andrew Michael], 1686–1743, and others.
Histoire du Vicomte de Turenne Maréchal Général des Armées du Roi. 2 vols. Paris: La Veuve Mazieres and J. B. Garnier, 1735. DSoC.

> In General Officer's library, 1773. Wortley Montagu likely owned Ramsey's 1735 edition in 1776 (2 of 38).

Ramsay, Chevalier [Andrew Michael], 1686–1743, and others.
The History of Henri de la Tour d'Auvergne, Viscount de Turenne, Marshal-General of France. 2 vols. London: James Bettenham and [sold by three others], 1735. DSoC.

> Molyneux cited an English translation in 1759, probably this one (1 of 38).

Ranby, John, 1703–73.
The Method of Treating Gun-Shot Wounds. 2nd ed. London: R. Horsfield, 1760. DSoC.

> General Officer owned and Parker purchased in 1773. In 1758 Dury had an earlier edition — possibly that published in London in 1744 [DSoC] (3 of 33).

Ray de Saint-Geniès, J. M., 1712–77.
L'Art de la Guerre Pratique. 2 vols. Paris: A. Jombert, 1754. DSoC.

> Dury owned a 1755 edition of this book in 1758 as did General Officer in 1773; and in 1779 Smith recommended a German edition of 1760 (DSoC). Wolfe also recommended Ray de Saint-Geniès in 1756 (4 of 30, or 13 percent, and among our officers' authorities; see Appendix B).

Recherches sur l'Art Militaire, ou, Essai d'Application de la Fortification à la Tactique. Paris: Desaint, 1766. DSoC.

> In Ligonier's library, 1770. DSoC attributes this and a subsequent edition (The Hague, 1767) to Robert de Lo-Looz, 1730–86 (1 of 21).

Regulations for the Prussian Cavalry. Translated by William Fawcett. London: J. Haberkorn, 1757. DSoC.

> Dury had this edition in 1758 as did Ligonier in 1770, Calderwood c. 1787, and Montresor's library in 1799. In 1773 General Officer owned and Smith purchased an edition of 1758 (no copy of which has been found). Wolfe (1756) recommended and Dury (1758), Tryon (1773), and Hotham Thompson (1784) owned unspecified editions (9 of 28, or 32 percent). This translation was among the twenty books on war that our officers admired most (see Appendix B).

Regulations for the Prussian Infantry. Translated by William Fawcett. London: Paul Vaillant, 1754. DSoC.

> Wolfe recommended in 1756; Ligonier owned in 1770; and there was a copy in Montresor's library in 1799. Tryon (1773), Cuthbert (1785), and Hotham Thompson (1784) owned and Clinton (c. 1789) reflected on *Regulations for the Prussian Infantry.* General Officer also owned and Smith purchased in 1773 (9 of 30, or 30 percent). See also *New Regulations.*
>
> The regulations for cavalry and for infantry, each of which appealed to at least 30 percent of our officers, were among the twenty books on war that those officers preferred above all others (see Appendix B).

Relation de la Nouvelle Descente des Anglois à Saint Malo. [1758 or 1759].

> No copy has been found of this book or pamphlet, which Molyneux cited in 1759 (1 of 25).

Relation de la Victoire Remportée sur les Anglois le 11 Sept 1758 près St. Cast à Saint Malo. . . . [1758 or 1759].

> No copy has been found of this book or pamphlet, which Molyneux cited in 1759 (1 of 25).

A Relation of the Siege of Candia . . . to Its Surrender, the 27th of September, 1669. London: T. Williams and I. Starkey, 1670. MH.

> In Winde's library in 1740, and Dury's in 1758 (2 of 42).

Renaldo, Giovanni.
An Exact Journal of the Siege of Coni in Piemont . . . 1691. . . . London: Tho. Basset, 1691. CSmH.

> Hotham owned in 1738 (1 of 42).

A Representation of the Cloathing of His Majesty's Household, and of All the Forces upon the Establishments of Great Britain and Ireland . . . to the Year 1742. [London], 1742. Uk.

> General Officer owned and Smith purchased in 1773 (2 of 33).

Retz, Jean François Paul de Gondi de, 1613–79.
Mémoires du Cardinal de Retz . . . Pendant les Premières Années du Regne de Louis XIV. New, enlarged ed. 4 vols. Amsterdam: J. Frédéric Bernard, 1731. DSoC.

> In Wade's library, 1758 (1 of 40).

Rich, Barnabe, 1540?–1617.
A Path-Way to Military Practise. Containinge Offices, Lawes, Disciplines and Orders to Be Observed in an Army. . . . London: John Charlewood for Robert Walley, 1587. CSmH.

> In General Officer's library, 1773 (1 of 42).

Richter, Christoph Gottlieb, 1717–74.
Die Historie des Kriegs zwischen den Prussen . . . und den Oesterreichern. . . .
  6 vols. N.p., 1758–63. MiU.
    In 1779 Smith recommended this and what might have been a French transla-
    tion of the same, six-volume work—no copy of which has been found (1 of 21).

Riou, Stephen, editor.
*The Elements of Fortification . . . . Translated and Collected from the Works of
  the Most Celebrated Authors. . . .* 2 vols. London, 1746. DSoC.
    Smith cited and recommended, 1779 (1 of 33).

Roberts, John of Weston.
The Compleat Cannoniere: Or, The Gunners Guide. . . . London: J. Okes for
  George Hurlock, 1639. Uk.
    Winde had a 1652 edition of this book in 1740 (1 of 42).

Robichon de la Guérinière, François, d. 1751.
*École de Cavalerie, Contenant la Connaissance, l'Instruction, et la Conserva-
  tion du Cheval. . . .* Paris: Jacques Collombat, 1733. DSoC.
    Ligonier owned in 1770. Dury (1758) owned a two-volume, French edition pub-
    lished in Paris in 1736 (2 of 38).

Robins, [Benjamin, 1707–51].
New Principles of Gunnery. . . . London: J. Nourse, 1742. DSoC.
    Smith cited and recommended in 1779, conflating the title of this book with
    the number of volumes and date of publication of *Mathematical Tracts of the
    Late Benjamin Robins. . . .* 2 vols. in 1. (London: J. Nourse, 1761; NN) (1 of 33).

Rogers, Robert, 1731–95.
*Journals of Major Robert Rogers . . . upon the Continent of North America
  during the Late War. . . .* London: for the author and sold by J. Millan,
  1765. DSoC.
    In Ogelthorpe's library, 1785, and Montresor's, 1799 (2 of 21).

Rohan, Henri, Duke de, 1579–1638.
The Memoires of the Duke of Rohan. Translated by G. Bridges. London: E. M.
  for G. Bedell and T. Collins, 1660. DSoC.
    In Oglethorpe's library, 1785. Molyneux cited in 1759 and Hotham Thompson
    had in 1784 unspecified editions of the *Memoires* (3 of 42). See also C. J. Caesar,
    Le Parfait Capitaine (Paris, 1640).

Rolt, Richard, 1724– or 1725–70.
*An Impartial Representation of the Conduct of the Several Powers of Europe,
  Engaged in the Late General War . . . 1739 . . . 1748.* 4 vols. London: S. Birt
  [and four others], 1749–50. DSoC.

In Oglethorpe's library, 1785. Lord John Murray (1762) and Maxwell (1769) had unspecified editions (3 of 32).

Rolt, Richard, 1724– or 1725–70.
Memoirs of the Life of the Late Right Honourable John Lindesay, Earl of Craufurd and Lindesay. . . . London: H. Köpp and sold by Newbery, 1753. DSoC.
> In Oglethorpe's library, 1785 (1 of 30).

Rosemond, Jean Baptiste de.
Histoire des Guerres Civiles d'Angleterre. . . . Amsterdam: H. Désbordes, 1690. Uk.
> Seton owned in 1732 (1 of 42).

R[otberg], F. D., Baron de.
L'Ingenieur Moderne, ou Essai de Fortification. . . . The Hague: Frederic-Henri Scheurleer, 1744. DeU.
> General Officer owned and Smith purchased in 1773; and a new edition of 1756 (DLC) was on Dundas's list in 1779 (3 of 33).

Rousset de Missy, Jean, 1686–1762.
Exposition des Motifs Apparens et Réels qui Ont Causé & Perpétué la Guerre Présente. Amsterdam: aux depens de la Compagnie, 1746. DSoC.
> Lord John Murray owned, 1762 (1 of 33).

Rousset de Missy, Jean, 1686–1762.
Histoire Mémorable des Guerres entre les Maisons de France et d'Autriche. . . . 6 vols. Amsterdam, 1748. Uk.
> In General Officer's library, 1773 (1 of 33).

Roy, William, 1726–90.
The Military Antiquities of the Romans in Britain. London: W. Bulmer, 1793. DSoC.
> In Montresor's library, 1799 (1 of 3).

Rules and Articles for the Better Government of His Majesty's Horse and Foot Guards: and All Other His Land Forces in Great Britain and Ireland and Dominions Beyond the Seas. London: J. Baskett, 1734. IEN.
> Howe owned, in 1732, an earlier edition of this book; so too in 1758 did Wade have an unspecified edition of this book, which was called informally—and in its running title—the Articles of War (2 of 38).

Ruse, Hendrik 1624–79.
The Strengthening of Strong-Holds. . . . [London] the Savoy: John Bill and Christopher Barker, 1668. Uk.
> In Winde's library, 1740 (1 of 42).

Ruse, Hendrik 1624–79.
Versterckte Vesting Uytgevonden in Velerley Voorvallen en Geobserveert in dese Laeste Oorloogen. . . . Amsterdam: Joan Blaeu, 1654. DSoC.
> In Winde's library, 1740 (1 of 42).

S., J.
The Souldiers Companion, or, Military Glory Display'd in a True and Impartial Description of All the Memorable Battels and Fights by Land and Sea . . . to Which Is Added Seasonable Advice to Young Souldiers and Officers. . . . London: Nath. Ponder, 1688. CtY.
> In Winde's library, 1740 (1 of 42).

Sackville, George Germain, Viscount, 1716–85.
The Trial of the Right Honourable Lord George Sackville at a Court-Martial . . . February 29, 1760. . . . London: W. Owen, [1760]. DSoC.
> In Hotham Thompson's library, 1784 (1 of 24).

Saint-Geniès, J. M., Ray de. See Ray de Saint-Geniès, J. M. 1712–77.

Saint-Germain, Claude-Louis, Comte de, 1707–78.
Commentaires des Mémoires de Monsieur le Comte de Saint-Germain. . . . London: n.p., 1780. DSoC.
> Hotham Thompson owned in 1784 (1 of 7).

Saint-Rémy, Pierre Surirey de, c. 1650–1716.
A Compleat Treatise of Mines. . . . Translated by Henry Manningham. London: Charles Say for J. Nourse [and two others], 1752. DSoC.
> Dury owned this and a 1756 edition (also DSoC) in 1758; General Officer owned the 1752 edition in 1773 (2 of 31).

Saint-Rémy, Pierre Surirey de, c. 1650–1716.
Memoires d'Artillerie. 2 vols. Paris: J. Anisson, 1697. DSoC.
> In Winde's library, 1740 (1 of 42).

Saint-Rémy, Pierre Surirey de, c. 1650–1716.
Memoires d'Artillerie: où Il Est Traité des Mortiers, Petards, Arquebuses. . . . 2 vols. Amsterdam: Pierre Mortier, 1702. DSoC.
> Dury (1758), Ligonier (1770), and Oglethorpe (1785) owned this edition. In 1773 General Officer owned and Debbieg purchased an edition published at The Hague in 1741 (DSoC); and in 1779 Smith cited and recommended a three-volume, Paris edition of 1745 (also DSoC). In 1756 Wolfe recommended and in 1758 Wade had an unspecified edition. Altogether, 21 percent (9 of 42) of the officers who might have shown a preference for *Memoires d'Artillerie* did so. Our forty-two officers clearly considered him an authority (see Appendix B).

Sallustius Crispus, Gaius, 86–34 B.C.
*C. Sallustius Crispus, Primus in Historia, Sui Bellum Catilinarium, et
Jugurthinum.* . . . Rotterdam: Regneri Leers, 1695. Uk.

> Hotham Thompson made notes on *Bellum Catilinarium* and *Bellum Jugur-
> thinum*—perhaps this edition—about 1744; and Molyneux cited an unspeci-
> fied edition of *Bellum Jugurthinum* in 1759 (2 of 42).

Sallustius Crispus, Gaius, 86–34 B.C.
The Works of Sallust Translated into English with Political Discourses . . . *[by
T. Gordon].* London: for T. Woodward and J. Peele and sold by J. Osborne,
1744. DSoC.

> In Lord John Murray's library, 1762 (1 of 33). Harrison (1763), Tryon (1773),
> and Hotham Thompson (1784) owned unspecified editions of Sallust's works.
> Altogether, 12 percent (5 of 42) of the officers showed some preference for Sal-
> lust (an authority; see Appendix B).

Sandoval, Prudencio de c. 1560–1620.
The Civil Wars of Spain in the Beginning of the Reign of Charls the 5t. . . . .
Translated by J[ames] W[adsworth]. London: W. Dugard, 1652. MH-H.

> In Oglethorpe's library, 1785 (1 of 42).

San Felipe, Vicente Bacallar y Sanna, Marqués de, 1669–1726, and Matheo
Garviza.
*Comentarios de la Guerra de Espana e Historia de Su Rey Phelipe V. el Ani-
moso.* . . . 2 vols. Genoa: Matheo Garviza, 1725. DSoC.

> In Montresor's library, 1799 (1 of 41).

Santa Cruz de Marcenado, Alvaro Navia Osorio, Marqués de, 1684–1732.
Reflections, Military and Political. London, 1737–. DLC.

> Molyneux cited an English translation in 1759—perhaps this one (1 of 38).

Santa Cruz de Marcenado, Alvaro Navia Osorio, Marqués de, 1684–1732.
Reflexions Militaires et Politiques. . . . . Translated by M. de Vergy. 11 vols.
Paris: Jacques Guerin, 1735–38. RNR.

> Dury owned in 1758 (1 of 36). In 1773 General Officer owned and Parker pur-
> chased two earlier French translations (10 vols., Turin, 1724; and 12 vols., Paris,
> 1725) that cannot now be found (3 of 41).
>
> In addition, Wolfe (1756) and Townshend (1776) recommended; Dundas
> (1779) considered; and Bever (1756) cited Santa Cruz de Marcenado's *Reflec-
> tions* without specifying a particular translation or edition. All considered, 20
> percent (8 of 41) of the officers who might have shown some preference for this
> work did so; he was clearly among our officers' authorities (see Appendix B).

Sardi, Pietro, b. 1559.

Corona Imperiale dell'Architettura Militare. Venice: the author, 1618. CtY.

> In 1779 Smith recommended a 1677 edition that has not been found (1 of 42).

Sarpi, Paolo, 1552–1623.

The Free Schoole of Warre, or, a Treatise Whether It Be Lawfull To Beare Armes for the Service of a Prince That Is of a Divers Religion. Translated by William Bedell. London: Bill, 1625. MiU.

> In Winde's library, 1740 (1 of 42).

Savornin, de.

Sentimens d'un Homme de Guerre sur le Nouveau Systême du Chevalier de Folard. . . . Paris: Briasson, 1733. DSoC.

> In Bagshawe's library, 1751. General Officer owned and Debbieg purchased in 1773 (3 of 38).

Sawle, William, fl. 1691.

An Impartial Relation of All the Transactions between the Army of the Confederates and That of the French King, in Their Last Summers Campaign in Flanders. . . . London: Randal Taylor, 1691. Uk.

> In Hotham's library, 1738 (1 of 42).

Saxe, Maurice, Comte de, 1696–1750.

Edition Portative des Reveries, ou Mémoires sur l'Art de la Guerre. Edited by Viols. Dresden: the Editor, 1757. DSoC.

> Calderwood owned c. 1787 (1 of 28).

Saxe, Maurice, Comte de, 1696–1750.

Mes Rêveries Ouvrage Posthume de Maurice Comte de Saxe. . . . Edited by Gabriel-Louis-Calabre, Abbé Pérau. 2 vols. Amsterdam and Leipzig: Arkstée and Merkus, 1757. DSoC.

> In General Officer's library, 1773 (1 of 28).

Saxe, Maurice, Comte de, 1696–1750.

Reveries; or, Memoirs upon the Art of War. . . . Translated by Sir William Fawcett. London: J. Nourse, 1757. DSoC.

> In Maxwell's library in 1769, General Officer's in 1773, and Montresor's in 1799 (3 of 28).

Saxe, Maurice, Comte de, 1696–1750.

Les Reveries, ou, Memoires sur l'Art de la Guerre de Maurice Comte de Saxe. . . . Edited by Zacharie de Pazzi de Bonneville. 2 vols. The Hague: Pierre Gosse, Junior, 1756. DSoC.

> In Ligonier's library, 1770 (1 of 28).

LES REVERIES

O U

MEMOIRES

SUR L'ART DE LA GUERRE

D E

MAURICE COMTE DE SAXE,

DUC DE COURLANDE ET DE SEMIGALLE,

MARECHAL-GENERAL DES ARME'ES DE S. M. T. C. &c. &c. &c.

DEDIÉS A MESSIEURS LES OFFICIERS GENERAUX

PAR MR. DE BONNEVILLE *Capitaine Ingenieur de Campagne de Sa Majesté le Roi de Prusse.*

A LA HAYE,

CHEZ PIERRE GOSSE Junior, *Libr. de S. A. R.*

M. D. C C. L V I.

Title page for one of the eight French editions of Saxe's *Reveries* (this of 1756) that our forty-two officers preferred. Impressed with his success in the War of the Austrian Succession, our officers considered Saxe among the most important authorities on the mid-eighteenth-century art of war. They particularly admired his prudential approach to warfare—his ability to win battles and gain territory while minimizing the risks of war.

Saxe, Maurice, Comte de, 1696–1750.

Traité des Légions; ou Mémoires sur l'Infanterie. The Hague: Aux depens de
la Compagnie, 1753. DSoC.

> Bever cited in 1756 (1 of 30). This work has also been attributed to Antoine de
> Ricouart, Comte Herouville de Claye, c. 1712–82.
>
> In addition, Hawley (c. 1753) made notes on Saxe; Dury (1758) owned two
> copies of his *Reveries*; Townshend (1776) recommended and Dundas (1779)
> considered the *Reveries*; and Dalrymple (1761), Percy (1775), and Donkin
> (1777) cited them—all without specifying a particular edition.
>
> Altogether at least 43 percent of the officers (13 of 30) showed a preference
> for Saxe. They considered his *Reveries* among the five most influential books
> on war available in mid-eighteenth-century Britain (see Appendix B). See also
> D'Asti, Espagnac, Herouville de Claye, and Néel.

Scheffer, Johannes, 1621–79.

Joannis Schefferi . . . De Militia Navali Veterum Libri Quatuor. . . . Uppsala:
Johannes Janssonius, 1654. DSoC.

> Seton owned in 1732 (1 of 42).

Scheither, Johann Bernhard, fl. 1644–78.

*Novissima Praxis Militaris oder Neu-Vermehrte und Verstärdte Festungs-
Bau und Krieges Schule. . . .* Brunswick, 1672.

> Although no copy of this edition has been found, Max Jähns cited it in his 1891
> *Geschichte der Kriegswissenschaften*, 2:1348. Smith recommended in 1779 (1 of
> 42).

Segar, Sir William, d. 1633.

Honor Military, and Civill Contained in Foure Bookes. . . . London: Robert
Barker, 1602. DSoC.

> Seton owned in 1732 (1 of 42).

Seran de la Tour, Abbé, c. 1700–c. 1770.

*Histoire d'Épaminondas . . . avec . . . les Observations de M. le Chevalier de
Folard. . . .* Leiden: Boudouin Vander Aa, 1741. CaOHM.

> General Officer owned in 1773. In 1777 Donkin referred to Epaminondas but
> without specifying a source (2 of 33).

*A Short but Impartial Account of the Most Remarkable Occurrences . . . of
the Two Last Campaigns in the Netherlands.* London: n.p., 1704. CSmH.

> Hotham's library, 1738 (1 of 42).

Siemienowicz, Kazimierz, d. 1651?.

Grand Art d'Artillerie. Translated by Pierre Noizet. Amsterdam: Joannem
Janssonium, 1651. DSoC.

> Winde owned in 1740 as did Dury in 1758 (2 of 42).

Siemienowicz, Kazimierz, d. 1651?.
The Great Art of Artillery of Casimir Simienowicz. Translated by George
  Shelvocke. London: J. Tonson, 1729. DSoC.
  > General Officer owned in 1773 (1 of 40).

Simcoe, John Graves, 1752–1806.
*A Journal of the Operations of the Queen's Rangers from . . . 1777, to the Con-
  clusion of the Late American War.* Exeter: for the author, 1787. CtY.
  > Clinton reflected on, after 1787 (1 of 3).

Simes, Thomas, fl. 1757–80.
The Military Guide for Young Officers. London: for the author and sold by
  J. Millan, 1772. DSoC.
  > Smith cited and recommended this and perhaps Simes's *The Military Medley*
  > in 1779. Dundas considered *The Military Guide* in 1779, referring either to the
  > first edition of 1772 or to the second of 1776, which is also in DSoC (2 of 19).

Simes, Thomas, fl. 1757–80.
*The Military Medley: Containing the Most Necessary Rules and Directions
  for Attaining a Competent Knowledge of the Art. . . .* 2nd ed. London: n.p.,
  1768. DSoC.
  > Oglethorpe had a copy of this second edition in 1785 (1 of 21). The first edition
  > of *Military Medley* had been printed by S. Powell in Dublin in 1767 (DSoC).
  >
  > Together, Simes's works attracted 14 percent (3 of 21) of the officers who
  > might have preferred them and were among their authorities (see Appendix B).

Simpson, Thomas, 1710–61.
Theory of Gunnery. 1758.
  > Smith recommended in 1779 (1 of 25). Although no copy of this book has been
  > found, the University of Virginia has among its "Natural History Manuscripts
  > Collected by Cromwell Mortimer, 1746–1749," a manuscript by Thomas Simp-
  > son describing "the motion of projectiles" for "gentlemen employed in the prac-
  > tice of gunnery" (ViU). Simpson's and Charles Hutton's *Select Exercises for
  > Young Proficients in the Mathematicks . . .* (London: F. Wingrave, 1792) also
  > contains a section entitled "Theory of Gunnery." MiU.

Skinner, Thomas, 1629?–1679, and W. Webster, 1689–1758.
The Life of General Monk: Duke of Albemarle. . . . 2nd ed. London: J. Graves,
  J. Isted and J. Hooke, 1724. DSoC.
  > In Wade's library, 1758, General Officer's, 1773, and Oglethorpe's, 1785 (3 of 41).

Smith, George, Captain.
An Universal Military Dictionary. . . . London: J. Millan, 1779. DSoC.
  > Dundas considered, 1779 (1 of 7).

Solaro della Margarita, Giuseppe Maria Maurizio, Conte, 1644–1719.
Journal Historique du Siège de la Ville ... de Turin, l'Année 1706. ... Amsterdam: Pierre Mortier, 1708. MiU.
> In Wade's library, 1758 (1 of 42).

Solleysel, Jacques de, 1617–80.
Le Parfait Mareschal: Qui Enseigne a Connoistre la Beauté, la Bonté, & les Defauts des Chevaux. New ed. 2 vols. Paris: Pierre Emery, 1723. MH.
> Dury owned in 1758 (1 of 41).

Solis y Ribadeneyra, Antonio, 1610–86.
The History of the Conquest of Mexico by the Spaniards. Translated by T. Townsend. London, 1724. DSoC.
> Molyneux cited an unspecified English translation of this history in 1759—perhaps this one (1 of 41).

Spanheim, Friedrich, 1600–49.
Le Soldat Suédois, ou Histoire Veritable de Ce Qui s'Est Passé depuis l'Auenuë du Roy de Suède en Allemagne jusques à Sa Mort. Rouen: Jean Berthelin, 1633. DSoC.
> Dury owned in 1758 (1 of 42).

Spar, Joseph I. M., Comte de.
Instructions Militaires. Paris: Briasson, 1753. DSoC.
> Bever cited in 1756; Dury owned in 1758 as did General Officer and Tryon in 1773 (4 of 30, or 13 percent, and among our officers' authorities; see Appendix B).

Sparre, Lars Magnus, Baron de.
Code Militaire, ou, Compilation des Reglemens et Ordonnances de Louis XIV. ... Paris: D. Mariette, 1708. DSoC.
> Stanhope had in 1721 (1 of 42).

Speckle, Daniel.
Architectura von Vestungen. ... 2nd ed. Strasbourg: Zetzner, 1608. GyGoN.
> In 1779 Smith cited and recommended this and the first edition of 1592—no copy of which has been found (1 of 42).

Stedman, Charles, 1753–1812.
The History of the Origin, Progress, and Termination of the American War. 2 vols. London: for the author and sold by J. Murray, 1794. DSoC.
> Clinton made notes on, c. 1794, and his annotated copy is in DSoC (1 of 3).

Steed, John, Capt.
Fortification and Military Discipline in Two Parts. ... London: Robert Morden, 1688. DSoC.
> In Oglethorpe's library, 1785 (1 of 42).

Stevenson, Roger.

Military Instructions for Officers Detached in the Field: Containing a Scheme for Forming a Corps of a Partisan. . . . London: D. Wilson and three others, 1770. DSoC.

> In 1779 Smith cited and recommended this book, which was reprinted in Philadelphia in 1775 and in London in 1779 (1 of 19).

Stone, Nicholas, 1586–1647.

Enchiridion of Fortification, or a Handfull of Knowledge in Martiall Affaires. . . . London: M. F. for Richard Royston, 1645. Uk.

> In Winde's library, 1740, and Lord John Murray's, 1762 (2 of 42).

Story, George Warter, d. 1721.

An Impartial History of the Wars of Ireland [1689–92]. . . . London: R. Chiswell, 1693. Uk.

> Seton owned in 1732 (1 of 42).

Strada, Famianus, 1572–1649.

De Bello Belgico. The History of the Low-Countrey Warres. Translated by Sir R. Stapylton. London: H. Mosley, 1650. DSoC.

> In Oglethorpe's library, 1785 (1 of 42).

Strada, Famianus, 1572–1649.

Famiani Stradae . . . De Bello Belgico Decas Prima. 6th ed. 2 vols. Rome: Sumptibus Hermanni Scheus, 1640, 1647. DSoC.

> In Dormer's library, 1741 (1 of 42).

Strada, Famianus, 1572–1649.

Famiani Stradae . . . De Bello Belgico Decas Prima (Secunda). 2 vols. [Lyon]: Juxta exemplar Romae impressum, 1653. Uk.

> In Oglethorpe's library, 1785 (1 of 42).

Strada, Famianus, 1572–1649.

Histoire de la Guerre de Flandre. Translated by Pierre Du Ryer. 2 vols. "Suivant la Copie imprimé a Paris," 1665. DSoC.

> In Montresor's library, 1799; Dormer (1741) and Dury (1758) owned a four-volume Paris edition of 1675 (3 of 42).

Strada, Famianus, 1572–1649.

Histoire de la Guerre des Pays Bas. Translated by Pierre Du Ryer. New ed. 4 vols. Brussels: G. Fricx, the younger, 1739. DSoC.

> Ligonier owned, 1770 (1 of 36).
>
> General Officer (1773) owned another edition of Du Ryer's translation (6 vols., Brussels, 1727), which has not been found; and Wolfe (1756) recom-

mended an unspecified French edition. Altogether, 17 percent of the officers (7 of 42) had at least seven different editions of Strada's history—which was one of our officers' authorities (see Appendix B).

Struensee, Karl August von, 1735–1804.
Anfangsgründe der Artillerie. Leipzig and Liegnitz: D. Siegertischen, 1769. DSoC.

> Smith recommended, 1779 (1 of 20).

Stubbe, Henry, 1632–76.
A Justification of the Present War against the United Netherlands. . . . London: H. Hills and J. Starkey, 1673. DSoC.

> In Seton's library, 1732 (1 of 42).

Sturm, Leonhard Christoph, 1669–1719.
Architectura Militaris Hypothetico-Eclectica, oder, Gründliche Anleitung zu der Kriegs-Baukunst. . . . Vienna: P. C. Monath, 1755. DSoC.

> Smith cited and recommended, 1779 (1 of 30).

Sturm, Leonhard Christoph, 1669–1719.
Le Veritable Vauban Se Montrant au Lieu du Faux Vauban. . . . 2nd ed. rev. The Hague: Nicolas Wilt, 1710. DSoC.

> In Bagshawe library, 1751; General Officer owned and Debbieg purchased in 1773 (3 of 42).

Suckow, Lorenz Johann Daniel, 1722–1801.
Erste Gründe der Kriegs Baukunst. Frankfurt am Main: T. Goebhardt, 1769. MiU.

> Smith recommended, 1779 (1 of 20).

Suetonius, A.D. c. 69–c. 122.
Caius Suetonius Tranquillus. . . . Strasbourg: Johannes Philippus Mülbius, 1647. DSoC.

> Stanhope owned in 1721. Otherwise, Wolfe recommended (1756), Molyneux cited (1759), and Lord John Murray owned (1762)—all without specifying an edition of Suetonius (4 of 42).

Suite de la Relation et de la Victoire Remportée par le Duc d'Aiguilon, 1758, Suivant une Lettre Ecrite de St. Malo le 13 Suivant [1758 or 1759].

> No copy has been found of this pamphlet, which Molyneux cited in 1759 (1 of 25).

Sully, Maximilien de Béthune, Duc de, 1559–1641.
Memoires de Maximilien de Bethune, Duc de Sully. . . . Adapted by P. M. de l'Écluse des Loges. Revised ed. 3 vols. London: n.p., 1747. DSoC.

In Dury's library in 1758 and in Tryon's in 1773 (without specifying an edition); moreover, Wolfe (1756) recommended, Townshend (1759) listed, and Donkin (1777) quoted these memoirs without specifying an edition (5 of 42, or 12 percent, and an authority; see Appendix B).

Sully, Maximilien de Béthune, Duc de, 1559–1641.
Memoires ou Oeconomies Royales d'Estat. . . . 4 vols. Paris: L. Billaine, 1664. Uk.
> In Dury's library, 1758 (1 of 42).

Sutcliffe, Matthew, 1550?–1629.
The Practice, Proceedings, and Lawes of Armes. . . . London: Christopher Barker, 1593. DSoC.
> Seton owned in 1732 (1 of 42).

Tacitus, Publius Cornelius, A.D. c. 56–c. 120.
Les Oeuvres de Tacite. Translated by N. Perrot, Sieur d'Ablancourt. New ed. Paris: T. Jolly, 1665. Uk.
> In Winde's library, 1740. Wade owned (1758) and Donkin cited (1777) unspecified editions of Tacitus's works; and Hotham Thompson had an undated Justus Lipsius edition in 1784 (4 of 42).

Tarleton, Banastre, 1754–1833.
A History of the Campaigns of 1780 and 1781, in the Southern Provinces of North America. London: T. Cadell, 1787. DSoC.
> There were Dublin and London editions of this book in 1787 and 1796 (DSoC), respectively. In late 1787 Clinton read with notes (1 of 3).

Tartaglia, Niccolò, d. 1557.
Three Bookes of Colloquies Concerning the Arte of Shooting in Great and Small Peeces of Artillerie. . . . Translated by Cyprian Lucar. London: Thomas Dawson for John Harrison, 1588. TxU.
> In Montresor's library, 1799 (1 of 42).

Taylor, James, 1706– or 1707–53.
Remarks on the German Empire . . . and the Operations of the Campaign 1743. London: J. Watts and B. Dod, 1745. ICU.
> In Ligonier's library, 1770 (1 of 33).

Teyler, Johannes, b. 1648.
Architectura Militaris. Rotterdam: Petrum vander Slaart, 1697. MnU.
> General Officer owned and Smith purchased in 1773 (2 of 42).

The Theatre of the Present War in the Netherlands and upon the Rhine. . . . London: J. Brindley, 1745. DSoC.
> Oglethorpe owned in 1785; so too probably did Cuthbert in 1785 (2 of 33).

Theti, Carlo, 1529–89.
Discorsi delle Fortificationi. . . . Venice: Francesco de Franceschi Senese,
1589. DSoC.
> In Winde's library, 1740 (1 of 42).

Thucydides, d. c. 401 B.C.
Eight bookes of the Peloponnesian Warre. . . . Translated by Thomas Hobbes.
London: Hen. Seile, 1629. DSoC.
> In Dormer's library, 1741 (1 of 42).

Thucydides, d. c. 401 B.C.
Eight Bookes of the Peloponnesian Warre. . . . Translated by T[homas] Hobbes.
London: H. Mynne, 1634. DSoC.
> In Wortley Montagu's library, 1776 (1 of 42).

Thucydides, d. c. 401 B.C.
The History of the Grecian War. . . . Translated by Thomas Hobbes. 2nd ed.
London: A. Clark for C. Harper, 1676. DSoC.
> Oglethorpe owned in 1785 (1 of 42).

Thucydides, d. c. 401 B.C.
The History of the Peloponnesian War. Translated by William Smith. 2 vols.
London: John Watts, 1753. DSoC.
> Hotham Thompson owned in 1784; and Oglethorpe had a later edition of this
> translation in 1785 (2 of 30).

Thucydides, d. c. 401 B.C.
*The Hystory Writtone by Thucidides the Athenyan of the Warre, which Was
betwene the Peloponesians and the Athenyans.* Translated by Thomas
Nicolls. [London,] 1550. MH-H.
> Gentleman in the Army owned in 1799 (1 of 42).

Thucydides, d. c. 401 B.C.
*Thoukudidou peri tou Peloponnesiakou Polemou Biblia Okto. Thucydidis de
Bello Peloponnesiaco Libri Octo.* Edited by J. Hudson. Oxford: E Theatro
Sheldoniano, impensis T. Bennet, 1696. DSoC.
> In Oglethorpe's library, 1785 (1 of 42).

Thucydides, d. c. 401 B.C.
*Thoukudidou tou Olorou peri tou Peloponnesiakou Polemou Biblia Okto.
Thucydidis Olori de Bello Peloponnesiaco Libri Octo.* Geneva: H. Stepha-
nus, 1564. DSoC.
> In Wortley Montagu's library, 1776 (1 of 42). Wortley Montagu owned an earlier
> Greek edition (Florence, 1506)—no copy of which has been found.

Thucydides, d. c. 401 B.C.

Thucydidis . . . De Bello Peloponnesiaco Libri Octo. . . . Frankfurt am Main: Andreae Wecheli, 1594. DSoC.

> In Dormer's library, 1741 (1 of 42).

> In addition, Seton (1732) owned an edition of 1694 that cannot now be found; and nine other officers owned or referred to Thucydides without specifying an edition. Stanhope had two copies in 1721; Dury, a French translation in 1758; and Tryon and Hotham Thompson, Hobbes's translations in 1773 and 1784, respectively. Molyneux cited Thucydides in 1759 as did Dalrymple in 1761; Donkin quoted him in 1777; and both Wolfe and Townshend recommended him in 1756 and 1776 respectively. In short, 33 percent of the officers (14 of 42) expressed a preference for Thucydides and had among them at least eleven different editions of his history; he was clearly among the twenty authors that our officers admired most (see Appendix B).

Tielke, Johann Gottleib, 1731–87.

Beyträge zur Kriegs-Kunst. . . . 4 vols. Freiburg: Gedruckt mit Barthelischen Schriften, 1776–86. DSoC.

> Smith recommended, 1779 (1 of 11).

> C. and R. Craufurd translated what seems to have been a portion of this work as *An Account of Some of the Most Remarkable Events of the War between the Prussians, Austrians, and Russians from 1756 to 1763. And a Treatise on . . . the Military Art . . . .* 2 vols. London: for the translators and sold by J. Walter, 1777–78 (also DSoC).

Tielke, Johann Gottleib, 1731–87.

Unterricht für die Officiers, die sich zu Feld-Ingenieurs Bilden. . . . Dresden and Leipzig: J. N. Gerlachs, 1774. DSoC.

> Smith recommended, 1779 (1 of 13).

Töllner.

Die Bildung eines Zukunstigen Vollkommenen Offiziers. Frankfurt am Main: n.p., 1755.

> Smith recommended, 1779 (1 of 30). Although no copy of this book has been found, Max Jähns cited it in 1891 in his *Geschichte der Kriegswissenschaften,* 3:2439.

Trenchard, John, 1662–1723.

A Short History of Standing Armies in England. 3rd ed. London: A. Baldwin, 1698. DSoC.

> In Montresor's library, 1799 (1 of 42).

Tronchin du Breuil, Jean, 1641–1721.
Relation de la Campagne de Flandre et du Siège de Namur en l'Année 1695. . . .
2nd ed. The Hague: H. v. Bulderen, 1696. DSoC.

> Wade owned an unspecified edition in 1758 (1 of 42).

A True and Exact Relation of the Imperial Expedition in Hungaria in the Year 1684. Wherein Is Contained an Impartial and Full Account of the Siege and Defence of the City of Buda. . . . London: R. Taylor, 1685. DLC.

> In Winde's library in 1740 and Montresor's in 1799 (2 of 42).

A True Narrative of the Late Mutiny Made by Several Troopers of Captain Savage's Troop in Col. Whaley's Regiment. . . . London: John Field, 1649. Uk.

> In Montresor's library, 1799 (1 of 42).

A True Relation or Journal of the Siege . . . of Belgrade . . . September, 1688. London: Richard Baldwin, 1688. UkOxU.

> In Hotham's library, 1738 (1 of 42).

Tucker, Josiah.
Dispassionate Thoughts on the American War. London: J. Wilkie, 1780. MH-H.

> In Montresor's library, 1799 (1 of 7). Thomas R. Adams, ed., *The American Controversy*, 2:739, attributes this book to Tucker.

Turenne, Henri de La Tour d'Auvergne, Vicomte de, 1611–1675.
Military Memoirs and Maxims of Marshal Turenne. . . . Remarks by A. Williamson. London: J. and P. Knapton, 1740. DSoC.

> In Dury's library, 1758, and in General Officer's, 1773, which copy Smith purchased in 1773. Wade owned (1758), Molyneux cited (1759), and Tryon owned (1773) unspecified editions of Turenne's *Memoirs* (6 of 35).

Turenne, Henri de La Tour d'Auvergne, Vicomte de, 1611–75.
Military Memoirs and Maxims of Marshal Turenne. . . . Remarks by A. Williamson. 2nd ed. London: J. and P. Knapton, 1744. DSoC.

> Wade owned in 1758 (1 of 33).
>
> Six officers showed a preference for Turenne's *Memoirs* (6 of 35, or 17 percent). Another six officers owned or cited one of his biographies (those of Buisson/Courtilz de Sandras, Deschamps, Raguenet, and Ramsay). Bever (1756), Donkin (1777), and Clinton (post-1781 and 1792–95) repeatedly referred to Turenne without citing a particular book. Altogether, 36 percent of the officers (15 of 42) expressed an interest in Turenne, making him one of the twenty authorities that our officers admired most (see Appendix B). See also La M[aire d'Olainville].

Turner, James, 1615–1686?.
Pallas Armata. Military Essayes of the Ancient Grecian, Roman, and Modern Art of War. . . . London: M. W. for R. Chiswell, 1683. DSoC.

> General Officer (1773), Hotham Thompson (1784), and Oglethorpe (1785) owned this book; so too, probably, did Seton (1732) (4 of 42).

Turpin de Crissé, Lancelot, Comte, 1709–99.
Commentaires sur les Mémoires de Montecuculi . . . par Monsieur le Comte Turpin de Crissé. 3 vols. Paris: Lacombe, 1769. DSoC.

> Dundas considered in 1779 (1 of 20).

Turpin de Crissé, Lancelot, Comte, 1709–99.
Essai sur l'Art de la Guerre. 2 vols. Paris: Prault fils l'aîne, 1754. DSoC.

> Dury owned in 1758 as did Ligonier in 1770 and General Officer in 1773; and Dundas considered it in 1779. It is also very likely that Wolfe (c. 1756) and Townshend (1759) recommended Turpin's *Essai* of 1754 and that Lord John Murray (1762) owned it (7 of 30, or 23 percent).

Turpin de Crissé, Lancelot, Comte, 1709–99.
An Essay on the Art of War. Translated by Joseph Otway. 2 vols. London: A. Hamilton for W. Johnston, 1761. DSoC.

> In Ligonier's library, 1770, and cited and recommended by Smith, 1779 (2 of 23). Altogether, 27 percent (8 of 30) expressed a preference for Turpin's *Essay*, which was clearly among the twenty books on war that the officers valued most (see Appendix B).

Tutchin, John, 1661?–1707.
The Present Condition of the English Navy. . . . London: E. Mallet, 1702. DLC.

> Molyneux cited in 1759 (1 of 42).

Ufano, Diego.
Artillerie, C'Est à Dire, Vraye Instruction de l'Artillerie et de Toutes Ses Appartenances. . . . Translated by J. T. de Bry. Frankfurt am Main: Egenole Emmel, 1614. Uk.

> In Winde's library, 1740 (1 of 42).

Ufano, Diego.
Tratado de la Artilleria y Uso della Platicado por el Capitán Diego Ufano en las Guerras de Flandres. Brussels: Ivan Momarte, 1613. DSoC.

> In Winde's library, 1740 (1 of 42).

V., J. B.
État Général des Troupes de France, sur Pied en Mai 1748. . . . Paris: n.p., 1748. Uk has 1901 reprint of 1748 edition.

> In Dury's library in 1758 and Ligonier's in 1770 (2 of 33).

Valcaren or Vaelckern, Johann Peter von.
A Relation or Diary of the Siege of Vienna [1683]. London: W. Nott, 1684.
NN.

> Hotham owned in 1738 as did Oglethorpe in 1785; it also seems likely that this
> was the "Siege of Vienna" in Dury's library, 1758 (3 of 42).

Vattel, Emer de, 1714–67.
The Law of Nations. . . . 2 vols. London: J. Coote, 1759. NNC.

> In Tryon's library, 1773 (1 of 24).

Vauban, Sébastien Le Prestre de, 1633–1707.
*De l'Attaque et de la Defense des Places (Traité Pratique des Mines; et un
Autre de la Guerre en Général par un Officier de Distinction).* 2 vols. The
Hague: P. de Hondt, 1737–42. DSoC.

> Bever (1756) cited this edition; Dury (1758), Ligonier (1770), General Officer
> (1773), and Oglethorpe (1785) owned it; and Smith (1773, 1779, 1779) pur-
> chased, cited, and recommended it. In 1776 Wortley Montagu had a Leiden,
> 1740, printing; and Wolfe (c. 1756) recommended and Hesse (1758) owned an
> unspecified edition of this title (9 of 38).

Vauban, Sébastien Le Prestre de, 1633–1707.
The New Method of Fortification, as Practised by Monsieur de Vauban . . . *To
Which Is Now Added a Treatise of Military Orders, and the Art of Gun-
nery.* By W. Allingham. 4th ed. London: A. Bettesworth, J. Batley, and
S. Ballard, 1722. DSoC.

> In Oglethorpe's library, 1785 (1 of 41).
>
> Another seven officers expressed a general preference for Vauban's works.
> Bland (1727) cited them; Wade (1758), Lord John Murray (1762), Tryon (1773),
> and Hotham Thompson (1784) owned at least one of them; and Townshend
> (1776) recommended and Dundas (1779) considered them. And an additional
> five officers—Winde (1740), Bagshawe (1751), Debbieg (1773), Calderwood
> (1787), and Montresor (1799)—preferred Vauban through the compilations re-
> spectively of Bernard, Cambray, Du Fay, Gaya, and Le Michaud-d'Arcon.
>
> Altogether, 50 percent of the officers (21 of 42) cited, purchased, owned, or
> recommended some version of Vauban's work. Those officers clearly held him,
> after Caesar, as the most important authority on war in their era (see Appen-
> dix B). See as well Bernard, Cambray, Du Fay, Gaya, Le Michaud-d'Arcon,
> Naudin, and Sturm for commentaries on and compilations of his works.

Vaultier, Commissaire d'Artillerie.
*Journal des Marches, Campemens, Batailles, Sieges et Mouvemens des Armées
du Roy en Flandres* . . . *depuis l'Année 1690 jusqu'en 1694.* . . . 3rd ed. Paris,
1740. Uk.

> General Officer owned and Smith purchased in 1773 (2 of 35).

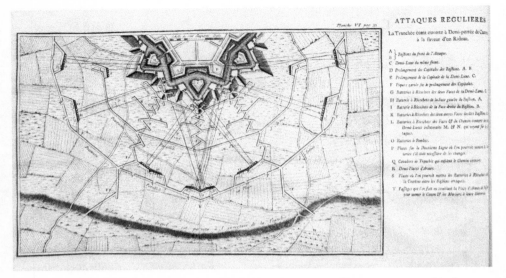

"Attaques Regulieres" was one of the many engravings used in Vauban's *De l'Attaque et de la Defense des Places* (1737–42), 1:35, to explain how the French engineer captured a fortress with a minimum loss of life. Our forty-two officers considered Vauban not just the preeminent engineer of the age but also, after Caesar, the principal authority on warfare. They preferred *De l'Attaque et de la Defense des Places* to all books describing his methods.

Vaultier, Commissaire d'Artillerie.
Observations sur l'Art de Faire la Guerre, Suivant les Maximes les Plus Grands Generaux. . . . Paris: Delaulne, 1740. NN.
> General Officer owned in 1773 (1 of 35).

Vegetius Renatus, Flavius, fourth century A.D.
Fl Vegetti Renati . . . De re Militari Libri Quatuor. . . . Paris: C. Wecheli, 1535. DSoC.
> In Winde's library, 1740 (1 of 42).

Vegetius Renatus, Flavius, fourth century A.D.
Flaue Vegece Rene . . . du Fait de Guerre. . . . Sexte Jule Frontin . . . des Strata-gemes. . . . Aelian de l'Ordre et Instruction des Batailles. . . . Modeste des Vocables du Fait de Guerre. . . . Paris: Chrestian Wechel, 1536. DSoC.
> In General Officer's library, 1773 (1 of 42). See also Frontinus, Sextus Julius, and Tacticus Aelianus.

Vegetius Renatus, Flavius, fourth century A.D.
Institutions Militaires. Amsterdam: J. Wetstein, 1744. DSoC.

In 1773 General Officer owned and Parker purchased this book; Clinton reflected on an unspecified French translation c. 1775 (3 of 33).

Vegetius Renatus, Flavius, fourth century A.D.
Military Institutions of Vegetius in Five Books. Translated by John Clarke.
   London: for the author [i.e., translator] and sold by W. Griffin, 1767. DSoC.
   Ligonier and Oglethorpe owned in 1770 and 1785, respectively (2 of 21).

Vegetius Renatus, Flavius, fourth century A.D.
*Sextus Julius Fro[n]tinus . . . De re Militari. Flavius Vegetius de re Militari.
   Aelianus de Instruendis Aciebus. Modesti Libellus de Vocabulis rei Mili-
   taris.* Bologna: Ioannes Antonius de Benedictus, 1505. DSoC.
   In Dormer's library, 1741 (1 of 42).

Vegetius Renatus, Flavius, fourth century A.D.
Veteres de re Militari Scriptores Quotquot Extant. . . . Edited by Pieter Schrijver. Wesel: Andreœ ab Hoogenhuysen, 1670. DSoC.
   Stanhope owned in 1721, as did Winde in 1740 and Oglethorpe in 1785 (3 of 42).
      In addition another eight officers owned, recommended, cited, or quoted
   Vegetius without specifying an identifiable edition: Seton (1732) and Dury
   (1758) owned; Wolfe (1756) and Townshend (1776) recommended; Bever
   (1756), Molyneux (1759), and Dalrymple (1761) cited; and Donkin (1777)
   quoted his writings. Altogether, 38 percent of the officers (16 of 42) demonstrated some preference for Vegetius—placing him among the ten authorities
   on war that they valued above all others (see Appendix B).

Vendôme, Louis Joseph, Duc de, 1654–1712, and others.
Histoire des Campagnes de Monseigneur le Duc de Vendosme. Paris: Saugrain
   l'aîné, 1715. DSoC.
   General Officer owned and Smith purchased in 1773 (2 of 42).

Vere, Sir Francis, 1560–1609.
The Commentaries of Sr. Francis Vere, Being Diverse Pieces of Service. . . .
   Cambridge: J. Field, 1657. DSoC.
   General Officer and Oglethorpe owned in 1773 and 1785, respectively (2 of 42).

Vere, Sir Francis, 1560–1609.
*The Commentaries of Sr Francis Vere Giving an Account of Divers Remark-
   able Sieges, Fights, and Other Eminent Services . . . in the Low Countrys.*
   London: Peter Parker, 1672. DSoC.
   Oglethorpe owned in 1785 (1 of 42).

Villars, Claude Louis Hector, Duke of, 1653–1734.

Memoires du Duc de Villars, Pair de France. . . . 3 vols. The Hague: Pierre
Gosse, 1734–36. DSoC.

> In Dury's library, 1758. Volumes 2 and 3 of this edition were completed by Guil-
> laume Plantavit de la Pause, Abbé de Margon (see La Pause). Hotham Thomp-
> son also owned a French edition of Villars's *Memoires* in 1784 (2 of 38).

Villars, Claude Louis Hector, Duke of, 1653–1734.
Memoirs of the Duke de Villars, Marshal-General. . . . London: T. Woodward,
1735. DSoC.

> In Oglethorpe's library, 1785 (1 of 38).
>
> Including Donkin, who drew an illustration from Villars without citing a par-
> ticular edition in 1777, 11 percent of the officers (4 of 38) expressed a preference
> for his memoirs (an authority; see Appendix B).

Voltaire, François Marie Arouet de, 1694–1778.
The Age of Lewis XIV. 2 vols. London: R. Dodsley, 1752. DSoC.

> Molyneux cited in 1759 (1 of 31).

Voltaire, François Marie Arouet de, 1694–1778.
Histoire de Charles XII Roi de Suéde. . . . 2 vols. Basel: Christopher Revis,
1731. Uk.

> Wade (1758), Hotham Thompson (1784), and Montresor (1799) each owned
> and Molyneux (1759) cited an unspecified French edition of this history, per-
> haps that of 1732 (DSoC) (4 of 40, or 10 percent, and an authority; see Appen-
> dix B).

Voltaire, François Marie Arouet de, 1694–1778.
Histoire de la Guerre de Mil Sept Cent Quarante & Un. London: Jean Nourse,
1756. DSoC.

> In Dury's library, 1758; General Officer owned and Smith purchased in 1773;
> Hotham Thompson had an unspecified edition in 1784 (4 of 28, or 14 percent,
> and among our officers' authorities; see Appendix B).

Voltaire, François Marie Arouet de, 1694–1778.
The History of Charles XII, King of Sweden. . . . London: C. Davis and A. Lyon,
1732. DSoC.

> Gentleman in the Army owned in 1799 (1 of 38).
>
> French and English editions considered, 13 percent (5 of 40) of the officers
> who might have preferred this work did so.

Walker, George, 1645?–1690.
A True Account of the Siege of London-Derry. 3rd ed. London: R. Clavel and
R. Simpson, 1689. DSoC.

> In Hotham's library, 1738 (1 of 42).

Walker, George, 1645?–1690.

A Vindication of the True Account of the Siege of Derry in Ireland. London: Rob. Clavel, 1689. MiU.

> In Hotham's library, 1738 (1 of 42). See Bernard, Nicholas.

Walker, Sir Hovenden, 1656?–1728.

A Full Account of the Late Expedition to Canada. . . . London: G. Strahan, [1720?]. Uk.

> Molyneux cited in 1759 (1 of 42).

Walker, Sir Hovenden, 1656?–1728.

A Journal . . . of the Late Expedition to Canada. . . . London: D. Browne, 1720. DSoC.

> Likely the book that Dury owned in 1758 (1 of 42).

Wallhausen, Johann Jacobi von, seventeenth century.

Art Militaire a Cheval. Instruction des Principes et Fondements de la Cavallerie. . . . Frankfurt am Main: P. Jacques, 1616. DSoC.

> General Officer owned, 1773 (1 of 42).

Wallhausen, Johann Jacobi von, seventeenth century.

L'Art Militaire pour l'Infanterie. . . . Franeker: Uldrick Balck, 1638?. DSoC.

> In General Officer's library, 1773 (1 of 42).

Ward, Robert.

Anima'dversions of Warre; or, . . . Ablest Instructions for the Managing of Warre. . . . 2 vols. London: John Dawson, 1639. DSoC.

> In General Officer's library, 1773 (1 of 42).

Watson, J.

A Military Dictionary: Explaining All Difficult Terms in Martial Discipline. . . . 5th ed. London: T. Read, 1758. DSoC.

> In 1799 Montresor's library contained an unspecified edition of this dictionary, which had been published at least as early as 1708 (DSoC) and which Smith disparaged in his *Universal Military Dictionary* (1779), p. vii (1 of 42).

Watts, William, 1590?–1649.

The Principall Passages of Germany, Italy, France, and Other Places for These Last Sixe Moneths. . . . London: Nath. Butler and Nicholas Bourne, 1636. NN.

> In Montresor's library, 1799 (1 of 42).

Whithorne, Peter, fl. 1550–63.

Certain Waies for the Orderyng of Souldiers in Battelray. . . . 2nd ed. London: W. Williamson for John Wight, 1573. DSoC.

> General Officer owned in 1773 (1 of 42).

Whittel, John.
An Exact Diary of the Late Expedition of His Illustrious Highness the Prince of Orange. . . . London: R. Baldwin, 1689. DSoC.

> In Montresor's library, 1799 (1 of 42).

Wicquefort, Abraham de.
Advis Fidelle aux Veritables Hollandois . . . Avec un Memoire de la Derniere Marche de l'Armée du Roy de France en Brabant & en Flandre. Illustrated by Romein de Hooge. The Hague: Johannes and Daniel Steucker, 1673. DSoC.

> In Montresor's library, 1799 (1 of 42).

Williamson, Adam. See Turenne, *Military Memoirs and Maxims.*

Willyams, Cooper, 1762–1816.
An Account of the Campaign in the West Indies, in the Year 1794. . . . London: T. Bensley for G. Nicol, B. and J. White, and J. Robson, 1796. DSoC.

> In Montresor's library, 1799 (1 of 2).

Windham, William, 1717–61.
A Plan of Discipline, Composed for the Use of the Militia of the County of Norfolk. London: J. Shuckburg, 1759. DSoC.

> Ligonier owned in 1770 as did General Officer in 1773; Smith purchased in 1773 (3 of 24, or 13 percent, and an authority; see Appendix B).

Winstanley, William, 1628?–1698.
The Honour of the Taylors, or, the Famous and Renowned History of Sir John Hawkwood. . . . 2nd ed. London: Alexander Milbourn for William Whitwood, 1687. TxU.

> In Montresor's library, 1799 (1 of 42).

Wishart, George, 1599–1671.
A Complete History of the Wars in Scotland: Under the Conduct of the Illustrious James Marquis of Montrose. [London?], 1720. DSoC.

> In Seton's library, 1732 (1 of 42). Although the British Library conjectures that this book was published in London, the cataloguer of Seton's library recorded Amsterdam as the place of publication.

Xenophon, c. 431–c. 352 B.C.
Cyropaedie; ou l'Histoire de Cyrus. . . . Translated by Charpentier. 2 vols. The Hague: P. Gosse and J. Neaulme, 1732. NBuU.

> In 1773 General Officer had an earlier edition of this translation (The Hague, 1718) and in 1777 Donkin referred to a translation by Maurice Ashley, neither of which has been found (2 of 38). Wolfe also recommended Xenophon's "Life of Cyrus."

Xenophon, c. 431–c. 352 B.C.

The Expedition of Cyrus. Translated by Edward Spelman. 2nd ed. 2 vols. London, 1742. Uk.

> Oglethorpe owned in 1785; and Wortley Montagu had a 1749 printing of this Spelman translation in 1776 (2 of 33).

Xenophon, c. 431–c. 352 B.C.

Le Guerre de Greci. . . . Translated by Francesco Strozzi. Venice: Gabriel Giolito de Ferrari, 1562. MiU.

> Dormer owned in 1741 (1 of 42).

Xenophon, c. 431–c. 352 B.C.

Kurou Paideia . . . : or, the Institution and Life of Cyrus the Great. The first four books translated by Francis Digby and John Norris. London: Matthew Gilliflower and James Norris, 1685. DSoC.

> Gentleman in the Army owned in 1799 (1 of 42).

Xenophon, c. 431–c. 352 B.C.

La Retraite des Dix Mille de Xenophon. Translated by Nicolas Perrot, Sieur d'Ablancourt, 1644–1718. Paris: Augustin Courbé, 1658. DSoC.

> Oglethorpe had what seems to have been a 1648 edition of this book in 1785; Wolfe (c. 1756) recommended and Dury (1758) owned unspecified editions of Xenophon's *Retreat* (3 of 42).

Xenophon, c. 431–c. 352 B.C.

Trois Ouvrages. . . . New ed. 2 vols. Amsterdam: F. L'Honore, 1744, 1745. DSoC.

> In General Officer's library, 1773 (1 of 33).

Xenophon, c. 431–c. 352 B.C.

Xenophon's History of the Affairs of Greece. Translated by John Newman. London: R. H. for William Freeman, 1685. DSoC.

> Hotham Thompson owned Newman's translation, perhaps this edition, in 1784 (1 of 42).
>
> Including Stanhope (1721), who had other books by Xenophon, it seems likely that ten officers owned or recommended his books on war (10 of 42, or 24 percent). Xenophon's works, taken together, were among the thirty that our officers admired most (see Appendix B).

PART III

Books Not Taken

here were many books on war available in eighteenth-century Britain that did not appear in our officers' records. Our officers very likely relied on some of the books that escaped their lists, inventories, and catalogues. We cannot be sure which titles they deliberately ignored and which titles simply did not survive in their lists. We can try to create a checklist of books on war that our officers were most likely to have known about and that are not among the books that they preferred. This is such a checklist—243 books on war that were either advertised or published in eighteenth-century Britain but that were not included in our officers' lists and inventories. It gives us an idea of the books and kinds of books on war that did not retain a conspicuous place in the memories or on the shelves of forty-two unusually wealthy, experienced, and well-informed officers.

Should we be interested in knowing which books our officers neglected or, perhaps, deliberately rejected? Yes, and for several reasons. To know that our officers preferred some books and kinds of books to others is to get a much sharper understanding of their preferences. If, for example, we know that our officers admired the Duke of Marlborough, that they bought and read books about him and his campaigns, and that they also neglected other well-known books about him, we can better appreciate not just how Marlborough was understood across time but especially how eighteenth-century British officers chose to see themselves and the art of war. Similarly, to know that our officers preferred and neglected books quite out of proportion to what was available—to know, for example, that their preference for the art of war and neglect of drill in the mid-eighteenth century was not just a result of what was in print—is to increase our appreciation for what mattered most to them and to make us wary of thinking drill books and manuals "made up most eighteenth-century military literature" (Brewer, *Sinews of Power*, 57). Indeed, to know which books our officers preferred and which they neglected should help us in understanding the eighteenth-century

176 LE PARTISAN.

la Plaie eſt profonde, vous ferez de vo-
tre Baume des Pilulles longues que vous
fourrerez dans les cavités.

Pour la Morve & le Tic.

L'on a imaginé & pratiqué pluſieurs Ré-
mèdes contre ces deux Accidens, mais
j'en ai vu ſi peu de ſuccès que le meilleur
& le plus ſûr à mon avis, eſt de faire
tuer le premier & de ſe défaire au plutôt
du Second.

F I N.

CATALOGUE

CATALOGUE
D E S
LIVRES NOUVEAUX,
ET AUTRES QU'ON TROUVE

Chez H. CONSTAPEL,
Libraire à la Haye 1759.

A.

Abrégé de la Republique de Bodin, 12°.
2 vol. *Londres* (Paris) 1755.
Annales Romaines par Mr. Macquer, 8vo.
Haye 1757.
Attaques & Defences des Places, par Vauban 4to. 2 vol. avec fig. *Haye* 1737.
Art de la guerre par Mr. Ray de Saint Ge-
nies, 12°. 2 vol. *Paris* 1754.
Abrégé de l'Hiſtoire de l'Empire depuis l'an
1273. par l'Abbé L**. 12°. *Bruſſ.* 1757.
———— de l'Hiſtoire Univerſelle, par Mr.
de la Croſe, Continué par Mr. Formey
8vo. *Gotha* 1755.
Art (l') de Deſoppiler la Rate, *ſive de modo*
C. . . . *prudenter*, entre - mêlé de pluſieurs bonne Choſes 12°. 2 vol. *Gallipo-
ly*, l'an de la folie 1757.
Art de la Peinture par Alph: du Frenoy, tra-
duit & augmenté de Remarques par Mr.
Piles avec un Dictionnaire des Termes de
l'art. 12°. *Paris* 1751.
M   Ami

"Catalogue des Livres Nouveaux," which accompanied Constapel's edition of
Jeney, *Le Partisan* (1759), 176–77, included many titles of books on war. Among
the books that Constapel advertised were some, such as Vauban's *Attaques &
Defences des Places*, that our forty-two officers preferred as well as three that they
did not—three that are now listed in Part III (Books Not Taken).

British army and in choosing sources for the history of that army. Without
such a perspective on sources, we are all too likely to prefer books that appeal to our sensibilities or sustain our prejudices. This checklist gives us a
rare opportunity to know more about our subjects and our sources.

The list has been assembled from advertisements in books that our officers did prefer and from references in later, scholarly works dealing with the
British army in the age of the American Revolution. Finding advertisements
of books on war that our officers could have seen—advertisements included
in books that they did own, read, or recommend—has been difficult but rewarding. The Society of the Cincinnati has roughly two-thirds of the 650

titles that our officers preferred; and it has been possible to inspect some 390 of those books. But only 72 of the 390 books in the Society's collections contain advertisements; and of those 72 advertisements, only 21 contain notices of books on war that were not in our officers' libraries or reading lists (the other advertisements contain either no books on war or books on war that are among the 650 that our officers did prefer).

If few in number, the twenty-one advertisements have proved to be diverse and rich sources. They represent the offerings of twenty-one publishers: nine British, six Dutch, five French, and one Belgian, including some of the most prominent military publishers of the century (John Millan and T. & J. Egerton of London, Charles-Antoine Jombert—father—of Paris, and Pierre De Hondt of The Hague). These advertisements have yielded some 120 titles of books on war that were available in the era of the American Revolution, that would very likely have come to the notice of our officers, but that do not appear in their lists and inventories.

However diverse and rich these advertisements, they do not contain a full representation of the books on war that our officers neglected. Standard bibliographies and histories of the eighteenth-century British army make clear that there are many other books on war—books that have survived more than two centuries of scholarly sifting and appraisal to remain among the sources that historians continue to value—that are not among our officers' records. A survey of recent scholarship dealing with the eighteenth-century army—with training and administration; with wars, campaigns, and battles; and with kings, ministers, and generals—has supplied another 123 books on war, available in eighteenth-century Britain, that continue to attract historians but that did not appear in the lists or inventories of our officers or, for that matter, in advertisements in the collections of the Society of the Cincinnati. These 123 titles do not include books on war published in the British colonies of North America. Although thirteen of our forty-two officers served in North America, and although many officers subscribed to books published there (see Robert Donkin's *Military Collections* [New York, 1777]), our officers did not regularly include colonial books in their libraries and lists. Only 1 of the 650 books on war that our officers owned, read, and recommended was published in America. Our officers turned almost exclusively to books printed and sold in the British Isles or on the Continent; and standard histories and bibliographies of the eighteenth-century British army can help to identify some of those books that do not appear in our officers' catalogues and lists, particularly books published in the British Isles.

Taken together, eighteenth-century advertisements and recent scholarly studies of the British army have provided 243 titles of books on war that were not included in our officers' records: 120 titles from advertisements and 123 titles from standard histories. The full citations for the advertisements are in the composite list of the 650 books that our officers preferred and, for the recent scholarly studies of the British army, in the bibliography of manuscripts, catalogues, and scholarly works at the conclusion of this book.

An Account of the Surrending [sic] of the Castle of Namur to the Confederates. . . . London: R. Baldwin, A. Roper, and E. Wilkingson, 1695. Uk.
　　Cited in Childs, *Nine Years' War*, 1991.

Adlerfeld, Gustavus, 1671–1709.
Histoire Militaire de Charles XII, Roi de Suede: Depuis l'An 1700, jusqu'a . . . 1709. Translated by Carl Maximilian Emanuel Adlerfeld. 4 vols. Amsterdam: J. Wetstein & G. Smith, 1740. ICU.
　　Advertised in *État Militaire*, 1780.

Advice from a Father to a Son Just Entered into the Army and about to Go Abroad into Action. . . . London: J. Johnson, 1776. DSoC.
　　Cited in Guy, *Oeconomy*, 1985.

Adye, Stephen Payne, d. 1794.
A Treatise on Courts Martial . . . an Essay on Military Punishments and Rewards. London: J. Murray, 1769. Uk.
　　There were at least five London editions of this work in the eighteenth century (the second and third by J. Murray in 1778 and 1786 are in DSoC). Included in Aimone, "Genesis," 1999.

Anburey, Thomas.
Travels through the Interior Parts of America. 2 vols. London: William Lane, 1789. DSoC.
　　There were another five editions of Anburey's *Travels* in the 1790s, including one by William Lane in 1791 (DSoC). Included in Pargellis and Medley, *Bibliography*, 1951.

An Authentic Journal of the Remarkable and Bloody Siege of Bergen-op-Zoom. . . . London: R. Griffiths, 1747. DSoC.
　　Cited in Duffy, *Fortress in Age of Vauban*, 1985.

An Authentic Narrative of the Russian Expedition against the Turks by Sea and Land. . . . London: S. Hooper, 1772. DLC.
　　Cited in Duffy, *Fortress in Age of Vauban*, 1985.

An Authentic Register of the British Successes . . . from the Taking of Louis-bourgh, July 26, 1758. . . . London: G. Kearsly, 1760. NN.
> Cited in Frégault, *War of Conquest*, 1969.

Authville des Amourettes, Charles Louis d', b. 1716.
Essai sur la Cavalerie, tant Ancienne que Moderne. . . . Paris: Charles-Antoine Jombert, 1756. DSoC.
> Advertised in *État Militaire*, 1780.

Bancks, John, 1709–51.
The History of Francis-Eugene Prince of Savoy . . . Containing the Military Transactions of Above Thirty Campaigns. . . . London: James Hodges, 1741. DSoC.
> Cited in Taylor, *Wars of Marlborough*, 1921.

Bancks, John, 1709–51.
The History of John, Duke of Marlborough . . . of the Late War upon the Danube, the Rhine, and in the Netherlands. . . . London: J. Hodges, 1741. NNC.
> Included in Higham, *Guide*, 1971.

Bassompierre, [François] de, 1579–1646.
Memoires du Mareschal de Bassompierre. . . . 2 vols. Cologne: Pierre du Marteau, 1665. NjP.
> Advertised in Estrades, *Lettres*, 1710.

Baudartius, Willem, 1565–1640.
Les Guerres de Nassau. 2 vols. Amsterdam: Michel Colin, 1616. CtY.
> Advertised in Ray de Saint-Geniès, 1754.

Beaurain, Jean, Chevalier de.
Histoire de la Campagne de M. le Prince de Condé, en Flandre en 1674. . . . Paris: L'auteur and Ch. Ant. Jombert pere, 1774. DSoC.
> Advertised in *État Militaire*, 1780.

Beaurain, Jean, Chevalier de.
Histoire des Quatre Dernieres Campagnes du Maréchal de Turenne en 1672, 1673, 1674, & 1675. . . . Paris: Le Chevalier de Beaurain, 1782. DSoC.
> Advertised in *État Militaire*, 1780.

Belle-Isle, Charles Louis Auguste Fouquet, Duc de, 1684–1761.
Lettres de Mr. le Maréchal duc de Belle-Isle, a Mr. le Maréchal de Contades. Frankfurt am Main: Les freres Van Duren, 1761. CLU.
> Advertised in *État Militaire*, 1780.

Beneton de Morange de Peyrins, Étienne Claude.
Histoire de la Guerre. GyGoN.
> Advertised in Ray de Saint-Geniès, 1754.

Bishop, Matthew.
Life and Adventures of Matthew Bishop . . . from 1701–1711. . . . London:
J. Brindley, 1744. DSoC.
> Cited in Chandler, *Marlborough as Military Commander*, 1973.

Blackwell, John, d. 1739.
*A Compendium of Military Discipline as It Is Practised by the Honourable
the Artillery Company of the City of London*. . . . London: For the author,
1726. DSoC.
> Included in Greer, "Books," 2000.

Bligh, Thomas, 1685–1775.
A Letter from the Honourable L—t G—n B—gh to the Rt. Hon. W—m P—t. . . .
London: T. Payne, 1758. CtY.
> Cited in Cormack and Jones, *Todd*, 2001.

Bonneval, Claude Alexander, Comte de, 1675–1747.
A Complete History of the Wars in Italy. Translated by John Sparrow. London: W. Mears and Olive Payne, 1734. DSoC.
> Advertised in Lediard, *Naval History*, 1735.

Bonneville, Zacharie de Pazzi de, c. 1710–80.
*An Essay on Fortification . . . with a Supplement Containing Marshal Saxe's
New System of Fortification and Construction of Wooden Forts*. Translated
by Charles Vallancey. Dublin, 1757. Uk.
> Included in Higham, *Guide*, 1971.

Boyer, Abel, 1667–1729.
The History of King William the Third. 3 vols. London: A. Roper, 1702–1703.
CtY.
> Cited in Taylor, *Wars of Marlborough*, 1921.

Boyer, Abel, 1667–1729.
The History of the Reign of Queen Anne, Digested into Annals. . . . 11 vols.
London: A. Roper and F. Coggan, 1703–13. DSoC.
> Cited in Taylor, *Wars of Marlborough*, 1921.

Boyse, Samuel.
An Impartial History of the Late Rebellion in 1745. . . . Dublin: Edward and
John Exshaw, 1748. Uk.
> Cited in Prebble, *Culloden*, 1979.

Brandt, Geeraert, 1626–85.
La Vie de Michel de Ruiter. . . . Translated by Aubin. Amsterdam: Waesberge, Boom, for Someren & Goethals, 1698. CtY.
> Advertised in Estrades, *Lettres*, 1710.

Brantôme, Pierre de Bourdeille, Seigneur de, 1540–1614.
Oeuvres du Seigneur de Brantome. New ed. 15 vols. The Hague: Aux depens du librarie, 1740. CtY.
> Advertised in Ray de Saint-Geniès, 1754.

Breton, William.
Militia Discipline: The Words of Command and Directions for Exercising. . . . 2nd ed. London: J. Morphew, 1717. Uk.
> Cited in Houlding, *Fit for Service*, 1981.

Brézé, [Argentero], Marquis de.
Réflexions sur les Préjugés Militaires. Turin: Les freres Reycends, 1779. DSoC.
> Advertised in *État Militaire*, 1780.

Brocklesby, Richard.
Oeconomical and Medical Observations . . . Tending to the Improvement of Military Hospitals, and to the Cure of Camp Diseases. . . . London: T. Becket and P. A. De Hondt, 1764. CtY.
> Included in Pargellis and Medley, *Bibliography*, 1951.

Bruslé de Montpleinchamp, Jean Chrysostôme, 1641–1724.
L'Histoire d'Alexandre Farneze, duc de Parme. . . . Amsterdam: Michils, 1692. NjP.
> Advertised in Estrades, *Lettres*, 1710.

Buchotte, M.
Les Régles du Dessein, et du Lavis, pour les Plans Particuliers des Ouvrages & des Bâtimens. New ed. Paris: Ch. Ant. Jombert, 1743. DSoC.
> Advertised in Le Blond, *Essai sur Castrametation*, 1748.

Burgoyne, John, 1722–92.
A State of the Expedition from Canada as Laid before the House of Commons. . . . London: J. Almon, 1780. DSoC.
> Cited in Frey, *British Soldier*, 1981.

Burgoyne, John, 1722–92.
The Substance of General Burgoyne's Speeches . . . 26th of May . . . 28th of May, 1778. London: J. Almon, 1778. DSoC.
> Cited in Frey, *British Soldier*, 1981.

*By His Majesty's Command . . . General Regulations and Orders for His Maj-
esty's Forces.* London: War Office, J. Walter, 1786. Uk.
> Cited in Houlding, *Fit for Service*, 1981.

Callender, James.
Military Maxims: Illustrated by Examples. London: T. Cadell, 1782. DSoC.
> Included in Greer, "Books," 2000.

Campbell, Robert.
The Life of the Most Illustrious Prince John, Duke of Argyle. . . . London:
Charles Corbett, 1745. Uk.
> Cited in Whitworth, *Ligonier*, 1958.

*The Case of the Hon. Brig. Genl. Ingoldsby in Relation to His Conduct in the
Late Action at Fontenoy.* London, 1745. Uk.
> Cited in Whitworth, *Ligonier*, 1958.

Caton de Court, Charles.
*La Campagne de L'Ille, Contenant un Journal Fidèle de Ce Qui s'Est Passé
au Siège de Cette Importante Place. . . .* The Hague: Pittusson, 1709. NhD.
> Advertised in Estrades, *Lettres*, 1710.

Centorio degli Hortensi, Ascanio.
*Memoires de la Guerre de Transilvanie & de Hongrie: entre l'Empereur Leo-
pold I & le Grand Seigneur Mehemet IV, Georges Ragetski & les Autres
Successeurs Princes de Transilvanie.* 2 vols. Amsterdam: Daniel Elsevier,
1680. MH-H.
> Advertised in Estrades, *Lettres*, 1710.

Chappuys, Gabriel.
*Histoire Generale de la Guerre de Flandre . . . depuis l'An M.D.LIX. jusques à
Present.* New ed. rev. Paris: Robert Foüet, 1633. UkOxU.
> Advertised in Strada, *Histoire Pays Bas*, 1739.

Cholmley, Hugh, 1632–89.
An Account of Tangier. . . . [N.p., 1787]. IEN.
> Cited in Taylor, *Wars of Marlborough*, 1921.

Clinton, Sir Henry, 1730–95.
*A Narrative of Sir Henry Clinton's Co-operations with Sir Peter Parker, on
the Attack of Sullivan's Island . . . in the Year 1776 and with Vice-Admiral
Arbuthnot . . . at Rhode Island, in 1780.* London, 1781 [no copy in Uk or
WorldCat].
> Cited in Willcox, *Clinton*, 1964.

Commynes, Philippe de, c. 1447–1511.
Les Memoires de Messire Philippe de Commines, Seigneur d'Argenton. Leiden: Elzeviers, 1648. MH-H.
Advertised in Ray de Saint-Geniès, 1754.

The Compleat Gentleman Soldier; or, a Treatise of Military Discipline, Fortifications and Gunnery. London: T. Ballard, 1702. TxHR.
Included in Higham, *Guide,* 1971.

The Complete Militia-Man, or a Compendium of Military Knowledge . . . By an Officer of the British Forces. London: R. Griffiths, 1760. Uk.
Cited in Houlding, *Fit for Service,* 1981.

The Conduct of a Noble Commander in America, Impartially Reviewed. . . . London: R. Baldwin, 1758. DSoC.
Cited in Frégault, *War of Conquest,* 1969.

Considerations on the Establishment of the British Engineers. London: T. Cadell, 1768. MH-H.
Included in Pargellis and Medley, *Bibliography,* 1951.

Cornwallis, Charles Earl, 1738–1805.
An Answer to That Part of the Narrative of Lieutenant-General Sir Henry Clinton, K. B. Which Relates to the Conduct of Lieutenant-General Earl Cornwallis . . . in the Year 1781. London: J. Debrett, 1783. DSoC.
Cited in Frey, *British Soldier,* 1981.

Cumberland, Richard, 1732–1811.
Character of the Late Lord Viscount Sackville. London: C. Dilly, 1785. CtY.
Cited in Mackesy, *War for America,* 1964.

Cunningham, James.
Strictures on Military Discipline: In a Series of Letters. . . . London: John Donaldson, 1774. DSoC.
Included in Greer, "Books," 2000.

Dalrymple, John.
Considerations upon the Different Modes of Finding Recruits for the Army. London: T. Cadell, 1775. NN.
Included in Pargellis and Medley, *Bibliography,* 1951.

Dalrymple, John, 1726–1810.
Memoirs of Great Britain and Ireland. . . . 2 vols. London: W. Strahan, T. Cadell, [and three others], 1771–73. CtY.
Cited in Chandler, *Marlborough as Military Commander,* 1973.

Dalrymple, William.
Tacticks. London: W. Faden, 1781. DSoC.
> Cited in Houlding, *Fit for Service*, 1981.

Danet, Guillaume.
L'Art des Armes, ou, la Maniere la Plus Certaine de se Servir Utilement de l'Épée. . . . 2 vols. Paris: Jombert, Herissant, fils, Lacombe, 1766–67. DSoC.
> Advertised in *État Militaire*, 1780.

D'Auvergne, Edward, 1660–1737.
The History of the Campagne in Flanders, for the Year 1691. . . . London: J. Roberts, 1735. DSoC.
> D'Auvergne wrote similar histories for each of the campaigns in Flanders from 1693 to 1697 (all published initially in the 1690s and all in Uk; DSoC has those for 1694–97). Cited in Taylor, *Wars of Marlborough*, 1921.

Davelourt, Daniel.
Briefue Instruction sur le Faict de l'Artillerie de France. Paris: Frederic Morel, 1617. Uk.
> Advertised in Saint-Rémy, *Memoires*, 1702.

Defoe, Daniel, 1661?–1731.
An Impartial Account of the Late Famous Siege of Gibraltar. . . . London: T. Warner, 1728. CtY.
> Included in Pargellis and Medley, *Bibliography*, 1951.

Deidier, Abbé, 1696–1746.
Elemens Généraux des Principales Parties des Mathématiques, Necessaires à l'Artillerie et au Génie. 2 vols. Paris: Charles Antoine Jombert, 1745. DSoC.
> Advertised in Le Blond, *Traité Artillerie*, 1743.

The Detail and Conduct of the American War. . . . 3rd ed. London: Richardson and Urquhart, 1780. DSoC.
> This is an expanded version of a *View of the Evidence Relative to the Conduct of the American War*, London: Richardson and Urquhart, 1779 (also DSoC) Cited in Frey, *British Soldier*, 1981.

Diodorus Siculus.
Histoire Universelle de Diodore de Sicile. Translated by l'Abbe Terrasson. New ed. 7 vols. Paris, 1737–44. Uk.
> Advertised in Ray de Saint-Geniès, 1754.

Dionysius of Halicarnassus.
Les Antiquités Romaines de Denys d'Halicarnasse. Translated by François
  Bellenger. 2 vols. Paris: P. N. Lottin, 1723. DLC.
    Advertised in Ray de Saint-Geniès, 1754.

Dirom, Alexander, d. 1830.
A Narrative of the Campaign in India Which Terminated the War with Tip-
  poo Sultan, in 1792.... London: W. Bulmer and W. Faden, 1793. MH-H.
    Included in Higham, *Guide,* 1971.

Doddridge, Philip, 1702–51.
Some Remarkable Passages in the Life of the Honourable Col. James
  Gardiner.... London: J. Buckland and J. Waugh, 1747. DSoC.
    Cited in Guy, *Oeconomy,* 1985.

Dorset, Michael, fl. 1775–82.
An Essay on Defensive War, and a Constitutional Militia. . . . London:
  T. Evans, J. Robson, and J. Sewell, 1782. DSoC.
    Included in Pargellis and Medley, *Bibliography,* 1951.

Drinkwater, John, 1762–1844.
A History of the Late Siege of Gibraltar.... London: T. Spilsbury, 1785. DSoC.
    Included in Higham, *Guide,* 1971. There were many other eighteenth- and
    nineteenth-century editions of this book.

Du Chastelet, Paul Hay, Marquis, b. c. 1630.
Traité de la Guerre, ou Politique Militaire. Amsterdam: Abraham Wolf-
  ganck, [c. 1675]. DSoC.
    Advertised in *État Militaire,* 1780. NjP has a Paris edition of 1668.

Du Moulin, Pierre François, ed.
[Recueil des Campagnes de Divers Marechaux de France]. 27 vols. Amsterdam, 1760–73. Uk.
    Advertised in *État Militaire,* 1780.

Dundas, Sir David, 1735–1820. See *Instructions and Regulations for the For-*
mations and Movements of the Cavalry.

Dupain de Montesson, c. 1720–90.
L'Art de Lever les Plans de Tout Ce Qui a Rapport à la Guerre.... 2nd ed. rev.
  Paris: Ch. Ant. Jombert, pere, 1775. DSoC.
    Advertised in *État Militaire,* 1780.

Dupain de Montesson, c. 1720–90.
Les Connoissances Géométriques à l'Usage des Officers ... des Armées. Paris:
  Charles-Antoine Jombert, 1774. DSoC.
    Advertised in *État Militaire,* 1780.

Dupain de Montesson, c. 1720–90.
La Science des Ombres par Rapport au Dessin Ouvrage Nécessaire à Ceux Qui Veulent Dessiner l'Architecture Civile & Militaire.... Paris: Charles-Antoine Jombert, 1760. DSoC.
> Advertised in *État Militaire*, 1780.

Du Villars, François de Boyvin.
Memoires sur les Guerres du Piemont.... London, 1787. GyGoN.
> Advertised in Ray de Saint-Geniès, 1754.

Emmerich, Andreas, 1739?–1810?.
The Partisan in War; or the Use of a Corps of Light Troops to an Army. London, 1789.
> Although no English edition of this work has been found, Duke University has a 1791 German translation of the English text. Included in Higham, *Guide*, 1971.

Erskine, Thomas, Baron, 1750–1823.
Observations on the Prevailing Abuses in the British Army.... London: T. Davies, J. Bews, 1775. DSoC.
> Cited in Hayter, *Barrington*, 1988.

An Essay on the Command of Small Detachments.... London: J. Millan, 1766. DSoC.
> Advertised in *List of Army*, 1767. DSoC attributes this to Sir William Young, 1725?–1788. Millan sold it as one part of Young's *Manoeuvres, or, Practical Observations on the Art of War*, [1771].

The Exercise of the Foot . . . to Which Is Added, the Exercise of the Horse, Grenadiers of Horse, and Dragoons. Dublin: R. Thornton and M. Gunne, 1701. Uk.
> Cited in Houlding, *Fit for Service*, 1981.

Fage, Edward, d. 1809.
A Regular Form of Discipline for the Militia, as It Is Perform'd by the West-Kent Regiment.... London, 1759. CtY.
> Cited in Houlding, *Fit for Service*, 1981.

Fallois, Joseph de.
L'École de la Fortification, ou les Élémens de la Fortification Permanente, Réguliere et Irréguliere.... Dresden: George Conrad Walther, 1768. DSoC.
> Advertised in *État Militaire*, 1780.

Fawcett, Sir William, 1728–1804. See *Rules and Regulations for the Formations, Field-Exercise, and Movements, of His Majesty's Forces.*

Fleurance, David Rivault, Sieur de.
Les Elemens de l'Artillerie.... Paris: Adrian Beys, 1605. Uk.
> Advertised in Saint-Rémy, *Memoires,* 1702.

Fortune, T.
The Artillerist's Companion: Containing the Discipline, Returns ... of That Corps.... London: J. Millan, 1778. DSoC.
> Included in Greer, "Books," 2000.

Frederick II, King of Prussia, 1712–86.
Lettres du Roi de Prusse à Mr. le Baron de la Motte Fousquet, Son Lt. Général. 1767. Uk.
> Advertised in *État Militaire,* 1780.

Frederick II, King of Prussia, 1712–86.
Military Instructions Written by the King of Prussia, for the Generals of His Army.... Translated by an Officer. London: T. Becket and P. A. De Hondt, 1762. DSoC.
> Advertised in Dalrymple, *Essay,* 1761 [repr. c. 1796]. Although none of our officers showed a preference for this English translation, three of them did purchase Henry Lloyd's French edition of 1761.

A Full and Impartial History of the Expedition into Spain; in the Year 1702.... London: Will Davis, 1704. Uk.
> Cited in Francis, *Peninsular War,* 1975.

Galloway, Joseph, 1731–1803.
Letters to a Nobleman on the Conduct of the War in the Middle Colonies. London: J. Wilkie, 1779. MH-H.
> Advertised in Galloway, *Reply,* 1780.

Galloway, Joseph, 1731–1803.
Plain Truth: or, a Letter to the Author of Dispassionate Thoughts on the American War.... London: G. Wilkie and R. Faulder, 1780. CtY.
> Advertised in Galloway, *Reply,* 1780.

The General Review Manoeuvres: or, the Whole Evolutions of a Battalion of Foot ... to Which Is Annexed, the Manual Exercise. 1779 [no copy found].
> Cited in Houlding, *Fit for Service,* 1981.

German Officer.
Manoeuvres for a Battalion of Infantry, upon Fixed Principles.... London: J. Millan, 1766. DSoC.
> Advertised in *List of Army,* 1766.

Gibson, James, c. 1690–1752.
A Journal of the Late Siege . . . of Louisbourg. . . . London: J. Newbery, 1745. DSoC.
> Cited in Skrine, *Fontenoy*, 1906.

Glenie, James, 1750–1817.
A Reply to the Answer to a Short Essay on the Modes of Defence . . . of This Island &c: in a Letter to . . . the Duke of Richmond. London: G. and T. Wilkie, 1785. DSoC.
> Included in Pargellis and Medley, *Bibliography*, 1951.

Glenie, James, 1750–1817.
A Short Essay on the Modes of Defence Best Adapted to the Situation and Circumstances of This Island. . . . London: G. and T. Wilkie, 1785. DSoC.
> Included in Pargellis and Medley, *Bibliography*, 1951.

Godfrey, John.
A Treatise upon the Useful Science of Defence: Connecting the Small and Back-Sword . . . with Some Observations upon Boxing. . . . 2nd ed. London: T. Osborne, 1747. DSoC.
> Included in Greer, "Books," 2000.

Grandchamp, Comte de, d. 1702.
La Guerre d'Italie, ou Memoires du Comte D*** [i.e., de Grandchamp]. . . . Cologne: Pierre Marteau, 1703. Uk.
> Advertised in Estrades, *Lettres*, 1710.

Grant. See *The Rudiments of War. . . .*

Grant, George.
The New Highland Military Discipline, or a Short Manual Exercise Explained. . . . London: George Bickham, 1757. Lake St. Louis Historical Society.
> Cited in Houlding, *Fit for Service*, 1981.

Grimarest, Jean Léonor le Gallois de, 1659–1713.
Les Campagnes de Charles XII, Roi du Suède. 3 vols. The Hague: Guillaume de Voys, 1705–8. InU.
> Advertised in Estrades, *Lettres*, 1710.

Grose, Francis, 1731?–1791.
Military Antiquities Respecting a History of the English Army. . . . 2 vols. London: S. Hooper, 1786–88. CtY.
> Cited in Houlding, *Fit for Service*, 1981.

Guibert, Jacques Antoine Hippolyte, Comte de, 1743–90.
Défense du Système de Guerre Moderne, ou Réfutation Complette du Système de M. de M . . . D. . . . 2 vols. Neuchâtel, 1779. DSoC.
> Advertised in *État Militaire*, 1780.

Guibert, Jacques Antoine Hippolyte, Comte de, 1743–90.
A General Essay on Tactics. . . . Translated by Lieut. Douglas. London: J. Millan, 1781. DSoC.
> Although six of nineteen officers expressed a preference for Guibert's work (which first appeared in 1772), none seems to have had this English translation, which is cited in Houlding, *Fit for Service*, 1981.

Guibert, Jacques Antoine Hippolyte, Comte de, 1743–90.
Observations sur la Constitution Militaire et Politique des Armées de Sa Majesté Prussienne. . . . Amsterdam: n.p., 1778. DSoC.
> Advertised in *État Militaire*, 1780.

Hamilton, Robert, 1749–1830.
The Duties of a Regimental Surgeon Considered. . . . 2 vols. London: J. Johnson, 1787. DNLM.
> Cited in Frey, *British Soldier*, 1981.

Hamilton, Robert, 1749–1830.
Thoughts Submitted to the Consideration of the Officers in the Army Respecting the . . . Relief of the Sick . . . Wives of the Private Soldiers. Lincoln, 1783. Uk.
> Cited in Frey, *British Soldier*, 1981.

Hanger, George, 1751–1824.
An Address to the Army; in Reply to Strictures by Roderick M'Kenzie . . . on Tarleton's History of the Campaigns of 1780 and 1781. London: James Ridgeway, 1789. Uk.
> Cited in Wickwire and Wickwire, *Cornwallis*, 1970.

Henderson, Andrew.
The History of the Rebellion, 1745 and 1746. . . . London, 1748. Uk.
> By 1753 this history, which is cited in Prebble, *Culloden*, 1979, had reached a fifth edition.

Henderson, Andrew.
The Life of William Augustus, Duke of Cumberland. . . . London: J. Ridley, 1766. Uk.
> Cited in Prebble, *Culloden*, 1979.

Heriot, John, 1760–1833.
A Historical Sketch of Gibraltar, with an Account of the Siege Which That Fortress Stood against the Combined Forces of France and Spain. . . . London: B. Millan and J. Edward, 1792. NN.

> Included in Higham, *Guide*, 1971.

Historical Memoirs of His Late Royal Highness William Augustus Duke of Cumberland. . . . London: T. Waller, 1767. CtY.

> Cited in Skrine, *Fontenoy*, 1906. Skrine attributes the book to Richard Rolt, 1724 or 1725–70.

The History of the Mediterranean Fleet from 1741 to 1744, with the Original Letters that Passed between the Admirals Mathews and Lestock. 2nd ed. London: J. Millan, 1745. DSoC.

> Advertised in *List of Army*, 1759.

The History of the Venetian Conquests, from the Year 1684 to This Present Year 1688. Translated by J. M. London, 1689. Uk.

> Estrades, *Lettres*, 1710, advertised a French edition of this book that cannot now be found.

Howe, Sir William, 1729–1814.
The Narrative of Lieut. Gen. Sir William Howe in . . . the House of Commons . . . Relative to His Conduct . . . in North America. . . . 2nd ed. London: H. Baldwin [and four others], 1780. DSoC.

> Cited in Gruber, *Howe Brothers*, 1972. There was a first London edition in 1780 as well as a third London edition and a French translation in 1781.

Hutton, Charles, 1737–1823.
The Force of Fired Gun-Powder, and the Initial Velocities of Cannon Balls, Determined by Experiments. . . . London: J. Nichols, 1778. DSoC.

> Cited in Langins, *Conserving the Enlightenment*, 2004.

An Impartial History of the Late Glorious War. . . . Manchester: R. Whitworth, 1764. Uk.

> Cited in Willcox, *Clinton*, 1964.

Instructions and Regulations for the Formations and Movements of the Cavalry. London, 1796. Uk.

> Cited in Houlding, *Fit for Service*, 1981. DSoC attributes to Sir David Dundas, 1735–1820, and has a printing dated 1797.

Jeney.
The Partisan; or, the Art of Making War in Detachment. . . . Translated by Thomas Ellis. London: R. Griffiths, 1760. NWM.

Although Ligonier owned a French edition of this book in 1770, neither he nor any of the twenty-three other officers who might have preferred this English translation (cited in Frey, *British Soldier*, 1981) did so.

A Journal of the Campaign on the Coast of France, 1758. London: J. Townsend, 1758. DSoC.
> Cited in Cormack and Jones, *Todd*, 2001.

A Journal of the Several Sieges of Keiserswaert, Landau and Venlo. . . . London: Daniel Brown and J. Nutt, 1702. DSoC.
> Cited in Duffy, *Fortress in Age of Vauban*, 1985.

A Journal of the Siege of San Matheo. . . . London, 1707. Uk.
> Cited in Duffy, *Fortress in Age of Vauban*, 1985.

A Journal of the Venetian Campaigne, A.D. 1687. London, 1688. Uk.
> Cited in Duffy, *Fortress in Age of Vauban*, 1985.

La Croix, M. de, d. 1704.
Guerres des Turcs avec la Pologne, Moscovie et la Hongrie. The Hague: J. Garrel, 1689. CtY.
> Advertised in Estrades, *Lettres*, 1710.

La Noue du Vair, Stanislas Louis, Comte, 1729–61.
Nouvelles Constitutions Militaires avec une Tactique. . . . Frankfurt am Main: Knoch & Eslinger, 1760. DSoC.
> Advertised in *État Militaire*, 1782.

La Rochefoucauld, François, Duc de, 1613–80.
Memoires de M. D. L. R. sur les Brigues à la Mort de Louys XIII: les Guerres de Paris & de Guyenne. . . . 2nd ed. Cologne: Pierre van Dyck, 1669. CtY.
> Advertised in Estrades, *Lettres*, 1710.

La Roche-Guilhen, Mlle de, 1644–1707.
Histoire des Guerres Civiles de Grenade. . . . Paris: C. Barbin, 1688. InU.
> Advertised in Estrades, *Lettres*, 1710.

Laveaux, Jean Charles, 1749–1827.
The Life of Frederick the Second, King of Prussia. . . . 2 vols. London: J. Debrett, 1789. DSoC.
> Included in Aimone, "Genesis," 1999.

Le Blond, Guillaume, 1704–81.
Abregé de Geometrie à l'Usage des Pages de la Grande Ecurie du Roy où l'On Donne Ce Qui Est le Plus Nécessaire pour Entrer dans l'Etude des Fortifications. Paris: Joseph Bellot, Jombert, 1737. DSoC.
> Advertised in Le Blond, *Traité Artillerie*, 1743.

Le Blond, Guillaume, 1704–81.
L'Arithmétique et la Geometrie de l'Officer. . . . 2 vols. Paris: Charles-Antoine Jombert, 1748. DSoC.
> Advertised in Le Blond, *Essai sur Castrametation*, 1748. A 1758 abridgment of this book (DSoC) is cited in the second edition of Bever, *The Cadet*, 1762.

Le Blond, Guillaume, 1704–81.
L'Artillerie Raisonnée. New ed. Paris: Cellot and Jombert, 1776. DSoC.
> Advertised in *État Militaire*, 1780.

Le Blond, Guillaume, 1704–81.
Elemens d'Algebra ou du Calcul Littéral. Paris: A. Jombert, 1768. NN.
> Advertised in *État Militaire*, 1780.

Le Blond, Guillaume, 1704–81.
Élémens de Tactique. . . . Paris: Charles-Antoine Jombert, 1758. DSoC.
> Advertised in *État Militaire*, 1780. General Henry Lloyd also recommended this book to Sir Henry Clinton, but there is no evidence that Clinton took any notice of *Élémens de Tactique* ("List of books from G. Loyd," n.d., in unmarked box at the end of the Clinton Papers, William L. Clements Library, MiU).

Le Blond, Guillaume, 1704–81.
Traité de l'Attaque des Places. Paris: Charles-Antoine Jombert, 1743. DSoC.
> There were second and third revised Paris editions in 1762 (DSoC) and 1780 (MBAt). It is not clear which of these editions was advertised in *État Militaire*, 1780.

Le Blond, Guillaume, 1704–81.
Traité de la Defense des Places avec . . . un Petit Dictionnaire des Termes . . . de la Guerre des Sièges. Paris: Charles-Antoine Jombert, 1743. TxHR.
> DSoC has another Paris edition of 1769. Advertised in *État Militaire*, 1780.

Le Cointe, Jean Louis, b. 1729.
Commentaires sur la Retraite des Dix-Mille de Xénophon. . . . 2 vols. Paris: Nyon [and two others], 1766. DSoC.
> Advertised in *État Militaire*, 1780.

Le Laboureur, Jean, 1623–75.
Histoire du Mareschal de Guebriant. . . . Paris: Robert de Nain, 1656. ICU.
> Advertised in Gaya, *Science*, 1689.

Lens, Bernard the Younger.
The Granadiers Exercise of the Granado, in His Majesty's First Regiment of Foot-Guards. . . . London, 1744. Uk.
> Cited in Houlding, *Fit for Service*. 1981.

Le Roy de Bosroger.
Principes de l'Art de la Guerre. . . . Paris: Cellot and Jombert fils jeune, 1779. DSoC.
> Advertised in *État Militaire*, 1780.

Leti, Gregorio, 1630–1701.
La Vie d'Olivier Cromwel. New ed. 2 vols. Amsterdam: H. Schelte, 1703. NjP.
> Advertised in Estrades, *Lettres*, 1710.

A Letter to the Gentlemen of the Army. London: R. Griffiths, 1757. Uk.
> Cited in Guy, *Oeconomy*, 1985.

Ligonier, Sir John, 1680–1770.
The Exercise for the Foot: With the Differences to Be Observed in the Dragoon Exercise for 1757. [London]: n.p., 1757. DSoC.
> Included in Greer, "Books," 2000.

Lindsay, Colin, 1755–95.
Extracts from Colonel Tempelhoffe's History of the Seven Years War. . . . 2 vols. London: T. Cadell, 1793. DSoC.
> Cited in Speelman, *Lloyd*, 2002.

Littleton, Edward, b. 1626.
Observations upon the Warre of Hungary. London: Randall Taylor, 1689. CSmH.
> Cited in Duffy, *Fortress in the Age of Vauban*, 1985.

The Lives of the Two Illustrious Generals, John Duke of Marlborough and Francis Eugène Prince of Savoy. London: Andrew Bell [and two others], 1713. DSoC.
> DSoC and Uk attribute this work to Arthur Maynwaring, 1668–1712. Cited in Taylor, *Wars of Marlborough*, 1921.

Lloyd, Henry, c. 1720–83.
A Political and Military Rhapsody on the Invasion and Defence of Great Britain and Ireland. . . . 4th ed. London: Debrett and Egerton, 1795. DSoC.
> Advertised in Dalrymple, *Essay*, 1761 [c. 1796]. This book, first published in 1779 (Uk), was frequently reprinted during the Wars of the French Revolution and Napoleon.

Lochée, Lewis, d. 1791.
Elements of Field Fortification. London: the author and T. Cadell, 1783. DSoC.
> Mentioned in Screen, "Royal Military Academy of Lewis Lochée," 1992.

Lochée, Lewis, d. 1791.
An Essay on Military Education. London: J. Nourse, B. White, and G. Riley, 1773. DSoC.
>   Advertised in Lochée, *Elements Fortification*, 1780.

Lo-Looz, Robert de, 1730–86.
Recherches d'Antiquités Militaires avec la Défense du Chevalier Folard. . . . Paris: Charles-Antoine Jombert pere, 1770. DSoC.
>   Advertised in *État Militaire*, 1780.

McAlpine, John.
Genuine Narratives and Concise Memoirs of J. McAlpine. . . . Greenock: W. McAlpine, 1780. NN.
>   Cited in Conway, "To Subdue America," 1986.

Mac Intire, John.
A Military Treatise on the Discipline of the Marine Forces, When at Sea. Together with Short Instructions for Detachments Sent to Attack on Shore. London: T. Davies [and three others], 1763. DSoC.
>   Included in Greer, "Books," 2000.

Mackenzie, Roderick.
Strictures on Lt.-Col. Tarleton's History of the Campaigns of 1780 and 1781. . . . London: the author, and sold by R. Faulder [and three others], 1787. DSoC.
>   Cited in Wickwire and Wickwire, *Cornwallis*, 1970.

Maizeroy, Paul Gédéon, Joly de, 1719–80.
A System of Tactics, Practical, Theoretical, and Historical. Translated by Thomas Mante. 2 vols. London, 1781. Uk.
>   Cited in Houlding, *Fit for Service*, 1981. Nor did any of our forty-two officers prefer the original French version of this book, *La Tactique Discutée*, which was published in Paris in 1773 (DSoC).

Malthus, Francis.
Pratique de la Guerre Contenant l'Usage de l'Artillerie. . . . Paris: La veuve Gervais Clousier, 1681. DSoC.
>   Advertised in Saint-Rémy, *Memoires*, 1702.

The Manual Exercise, with Explanations: As Ordered by His Majesty. London: J. Millan, 1770. DSoC.
>   Advertised in *List of Army*, 1770.

The Manual and Platoon Exercise. [London, 1792]. Uk.
>   Cited in Houlding, *Fit for Service*, 1981.

Marchant, John.
The History of the Present Rebellion.... London: R. Walker, 1746. Uk.
> Cited in Charteris, *Cumberland*, 1913–23.

Mauduit, Israel, 1708–87.
Considerations on the Present German War. London: John Wilkie, 1760.
DSoC.
> Cited in Whitworth, *Ligonier*, 1958. There were six editions of this pamphlet
> by the end of 1761.

Mauvillon, Eléazer de, 1712–79.
Histoire de la Derniere Guerre de Boheme. 3 vols. Frankfurt am Main: P. Len-
clume, 1745–47. DLC.
> Advertised in Jeney, *Partisan*, 1759. DSoC has Lenclume edition of 1745 in two
> volumes.

Mauvillon, Eléazer de, 1712–79.
Histoire de Gustave-Adolphe, Roi de Suede.... 4 vols. Amsterdam: Z. Chatelain et fils, 1764. DSoC.
> Advertised in *État Militaire*, 1780.

Maynwaring, Arthur, 1668–1712. See *The Lives of the Two Illustrious Generals, John Duke of Marlborough and Francis Eugène Prince of Savoy.*

Memoirs of the Life and Actions of ... General W[illiam] Blakeney.... London: the author, 1756. NN.
> Cited in Houlding, *Fit for Service*, 1981.

Mésnil-Durand, François Jean de Graindorge d'Orgeville, Baron de, 1729–99.
Fragments de Tactique, ou, Six Memoires.... Paris: Ch. Ant. Jombert pere,
1774. DSoC.
> Advertised in *État Militaire*, 1780.

Mésnil-Durand, François Jean de Graindorge d'Orgeville, Baron de, 1729–
99.
*Réflexions sur l'Ordre et les Manoeuvres de l'Infanterie Extraites d'un Mé-
moire Écrit en 1776.* Bayeux: Antoine-J. Nicolle, 1778. DSoC.
> Advertised in *État Militaire*, 1780.

Mésnil-Durand, François Jean de Graindorge d'Orgeville, Baron de, 1729–
99.
*Réponse a la Brochure Intitulée: l'Ordre Profond et l'Ordre Mince, Considé-
rés par Rapport aux Effets de l'Artillerie.* Amsterdam; and sold at Paris:
L. Cellot and Jombert fils jeune, 1776. DSoC.
> Advertised in *État Militaire*, 1780.

Mestre, Alain Claude de.
Annibal et Scipion: ou les Grands Capitaines. . . . The Hague, 1675. GyGoN.
    Advertised in *État Militaire*, 1780.

Mézeray, François Eudes de, 1610–83.
Histoire de France, depuis Faramond jusqu'a Maintenant. 3 vols. Paris:
    M. Mathieu Guillemot, 1643–51. InU.
    Advertised in Ray de Saint-Geniès, 1754.

The Military History of Great Britain, for 1756, 1757. . . . London: J. Millan,
    1757. DLC.
    Advertised in Jeney, *Partisan*, 1759.

The Militia-Man, Containing Necessary Rules for Both Officer and Soldier. . . .
    London: n.p., 1740. Uk.
    Cited in Houlding, *Fit for Service*, 1981.

Monro, Donald.
*An Account of the Diseases Which Were Most Frequent in the British Military
    Hospitals in Germany . . . 1761 to . . . 1763*. . . . London: A. Millar, D. Wil-
    son, T. Durham, and T. Payne, 1764. DSoC.
    Cited in Frey, *British Soldier*, 1981.

Montalembert, Marc-René, Marquis de, 1714–1800.
*Correspondance de Monsieur le Marquis de Montalembert . . . pendant les
    Campagnes de 1757, 58, 59, 60 & 61*. . . . 2 vols. London: n.p., 1777. DSoC.
    Cited in Langins, *Conserving the Enlightenment*, 2004.

Moodie, John.
*Remarks on the Most Important Military Operations of the English Forces,
    on the Western Side of the Peninsula of Hindoostan in 1783, and in 1784*. . . .
    London: Robson and Clarke, J. Sewell, 1788. CLU.
    Included in Higham, *Guide*, 1971.

Mottin de la Balme, Auguste, 1736–80.
Elemens de Tactique pour la Cavalerie. Paris: Jombert, fils aîné, [and]
    Ruault, 1776. DSoC.
    Advertised in *État Militaire*, 1780.

Muller, John, 1699–1784.
*Elements of Mathematics . . . for the Use of the Royal Academy of Artillery at
    Woolwich*. . . . 3rd ed. rev. 2 vols. London: J. Millan, 1765. DSoC.
    Included in Higham, *Guide*, 1971.

Nevers, Louis de Gonzague, Duc de 1539–95.
Les Memoires de Monsieur le Duc de Nevers . . . Lieutenant General pour les

Rois Charles IX, Henri III, et Henri IV.. . . 2 vols. Paris: L. Billaine, 1665.
CtY.
> Advertised in Estrades, *Lettres*, 1710.

New Manual Exercise, as Performed by His Majesty's Dragoons, Foot-Guards, Foot, Artillery, Marines, and by the Militia. 2nd ed. rev. London: J. Millan, 1758. DSoC.
> Advertised in *List of Army*, 1759.

A New Manual and Platoon Exercise with an Explanation.. . . Dublin: B. Grierson, 1764. Uk.
> This is the earliest known version of the 1764 manual and platoon regulations that would govern British practice for the ensuing thirty years; these regulations would be reprinted many times in Britain and British North America in the 1760s and 1770s. See Houlding, *Fit for Service*, 1981, pp. 209–14.

New Military Instructions for the Militia.. . . London: J. Fuller, 1760. Uk.
> Cited in Houlding, *Fit for Service*, 1981.

The New Platoon-Exercise as Practiced in 1756. Edinburgh: Sands, Donaldson, Murray, and Cochran, 1756. NWM.
> This seems to be the exercise that Houlding referred to in *Fit for Service*, 1981, p. 199.

Newcastle, William Cavendish, Duke of, 1592–1676.
A General System of Horsemanship in All Its Branches.. . . Translated by Gaspar de Saunier. 2 vols. London: J. Brindley, 1743. Uk.
> Advertised in *Theatre of the Present War*, 1745.

Nordberg, Jöran Andersson, 1677–1744.
Histoire de Charles XII, Roi de Suéde.. . . 4 vols. The Hague: P. Dettondt, 1748. NN.
> Advertised in Guischardt, *Mémoires*, 1758.

Norwood, Richard, 1590?–1675.
Fortification or Architecture Military.. . . London: Thomas Cotes for Andrew Crooks, 1639. PU.
> Amsterdam edition of 1639 cited in Langins, *Conserving the Enlightenment*, 2004.

Officer, An.
A Genuine and Particular Account of the Late Enterprise on the Coast of France, 1758. London: R. Griffiths, 1758. CtY.
> Cited in Cormack and Jones, *Todd*, 2001.

The Operations of the Allied Army under Ferdinand Duke of Brunswic, . . .
    1757–1762. London, 1764. Uk.
    Cited in Savory, *Army in Germany,* 1966.

The Operations of the British and the Allied Arms, during the Campaigns of
    1743 and 1744. . . . London: M. Cooper, 1744. DSoC.
    Included in Pargellis and Medley, *Bibliography,* 1951.

[Orme, Robert].
A History of the Military Transactions of the British Nation in Indostan,
    from the Year MDCCXLV. . . . 2 vols. London: John Nourse, 1763, 1778. Uk.
    Cited in Guy, *Bagshawe,* 1991. There were at least three London editions as well
    as a German translation of this book before 1788.

Osorio, Antonio.
Histoire de Ferdinand-Alvarez de Tolede, . . . *Duc d'Albe.* 2 vols. Paris:
    J. Guignard, 1699. MiU.
    Advertised in Estrades, *Lettres,* 1710.

Papacino d'Antoni, Alessandro Vittorio, 1714–86.
Principes Fondamentaux de la Construction des Places . . . *un Nouveau*
    Systême de Fortification. . . . Translated by Louis Flavigny. London, Paris:
    Ruault, Jombert le fils, L'Esprit, 1775. DSoC.
    Advertised in *État Militaire,* 1780.

Papacino d'Antoni, Alessandro Vittorio, 1714–86.
A Treatise on Gun-Powder: a Treatise on Fire-Arms: and a Treatise on the
    Service of Artillery in Time of War. Translated by Captain [Henry T.]
    Thomson. London: T. and J. Egerton, 1789. DSoC.
    Advertised in Dalrymple, *Essay,* 1761 [repr. c. 1796].

Pembroke, Henry Herbert, Earl of, 1734–94.
A Method of Breaking Horses, and Teaching Soldiers to Ride. . . . London:
    J. Hughs, 1761. DSoC.
    Cited in Guy, *Oeconomy,* 1985. Although a 1778 edition of this book was in the
    catalogue of Ligonier's library (1783), that edition was clearly added after his
    death in 1770; and the book has not been included among those that our forty-
    two officers preferred.

Pezay, Alexandre Frédéric Jacques de Masson, Marquis de, 1741–77.
Histoire des Campagnes de M. le Mal de Maillebois en Italie, pendant les An-
    nées 1745 et 1746. . . . 2 vols. Paris: Imprimerie Royale, 1775. UkOxU.
    Advertised in *État Militaire,* 1780.

Phipps, Joseph, 1708–87.
A System of Military Discipline for His Majesty's Army. London: J. Millan,
1777. DSoC.
> Advertised in Dalrymple, *Essay,* 1761 [repr. c. 1796].

Pilham, de.
Histoire du Marêchal de Boucicaut . . . depuis l'An 1378, jusqu'a 1415. Paris:
Charles Coignard, 1697. DLC.
> Advertised in Estrades, *Lettres,* 1710.

Plans et Journaux des Sieges de la Derniere Guerre en Flandre. Strasbourg:
Pauschniger, 1750. DSoC.
> Advertised in *État Militaire,* 1780.

Porzio, Luca Antonio, 1637–1715, and Friedrich Hoffmann, 1660–1742.
*The Soldier's Vade Mecum: or, the Method of Curing the Diseases and Preserv-
ing the Health of Soldiers. . . .* London: R. Dodsley, 1747. DSoC.
> Advertised in Voltaire, *Age Louis XIV,* 1752.

*The Proceedings of a General Court Martial . . . upon the Trial of Lord George
Sackville. . . .* London: A. Millar, 1760. DSoC.
> Cited in Mackesy, *Coward of Minden,* 1979.

Prudhomme, ancien officer.
Nouveau Traité des Mines et des Contre-Mines. Paris: C.-A. Jombert père,
1770. DSoC.
> Advertised in *État Militaire,* 1780.

Pure, Michel de, 1620–80.
*Histoire du Marêchal de Gassion . . . soûs le Ministére des Cardinaux de
Richelieu, & de Mazarin. . . .* 4 vols. Amsterdam: J. Louis de Lorme &
Estienne Roger, 1696. MH-H.
> Advertised in Estrades, *Lettres,* 1710.

Puységur, Jacques de Chastenet, Seigneur de, 1601–82.
*Les Memoires de Messire Jacques de Chastenet, Chevalier, Seigneur de Puyse-
gur . . . Lieutenant General des Armées du Roy: sous les Regnes de Louis XIII
et de Louis XIV.* 2 vols. Paris: Charles-Ant. Jombert, 1747. DSoC.
> Advertised in Le Blond, *Essai sur Castrametation,* 1748.

Ramsay, David, 1749–1815.
Military Memoirs of Great Britain: or, a History of the War 1755–1763. Edinburgh: the author, 1779. DSoC.
> Included in Higham, *Guide,* 1971.

Ray, James.
A Compleat History of the Rebellion from . . . 1745 to . . . April 1746. Manchester: the author and R. Whitworth, [1747?]. DSoC.
> Cited in Skrine, *Fontenoy*, 1906. This book was reprinted at least nine times
> in the 1750s.

A Relation of the Battle of Landen. London: Edward Jones, 1693. CtY.
> Cited in Childs, *Nine Years' War*, 1991.

*Relation de Ce Qui s'Est Passé en Portugal par Rapport aux Opérations de la
Campagne de 1705.* . . . N.p., 1708. NNC.
> Advertised in Estrades, *Lettres*, 1710.

Relation du Siege de Grave, en 1674, et de Celui de Mayence, en 1689. . . .
Paris: C. A. Jombert, 1756. DSoC.
> Advertised in *État Militaire*, 1780.

*Remarks on the Military Operations of the English and French Armies
. . . during the Campaign of 1747, by an Officer.* London: T. Becket, 1760.
DSoC.
> Cited in Whitworth, *Ligonier*, 1958.

*Report from the Committee Appointed to Consider the State of His Majesty's
Land Forces and Marines.* . . . [London], 1746. DSoC.
> Included in Pargellis and Medley, *Bibliography*, 1951.

*The Report of the . . . Board of General Officers on Their Examination into
the Conduct . . . of Sir John Cope, Peregrine Lascelles, and Thomas Fowke
. . . in North-Britain in the Year 1745.* . . . London: W. Webb, 1749. DSoC.
> Included in Pargellis and Medley, *Bibliography*, 1951.

*The Report of the General Officers, Appointed . . . to Inquire into the Causes of
the Failure of the Late Expedition to the Coasts of France.* London: A. Millar, 1758. DSoC.
> Cited in Cormack and Jones, *Todd*, 2001.

Richmond, Charles Lennox, Duke of, 1735–1806.
*An Answer to "A Short Essay on the Modes of Defence Best Adapted to . . . this
Island."* London: J. Almon, 1785. DSoC.
> Included in Pargellis and Medley, *Bibliography*, 1951. See Glenie, *A Short
> Essay.* . . .

Robson, Joseph.
*The British Mars, Containing Several Schemes and Inventions . . . Shewing
More Plainly, the Great Advantage Britain Has Over Other Nations by*

Being Masters at Sea. . . . London: for the author and sold by William
Flaxney, 1763. DSoC.

> Cited in Houlding, *Fit for Service*, 1981.

Rolt, Richard, 1724– or 1725–70. See *Historical Memoirs of His Late Royal
Highness William Augustus Duke of Cumberland.*

*The Rudiments of War: Comprising the Principles of Military Duty in a
Series of Orders Issued by Commanders in the English Army.* . . . London:
N. Conant, 1777. DSoC.

> According to Houlding, *Fit for Service*, 1981, p. 225, this was taken from a
> manuscript prepared by John La Faussille, an officer in the British army. Wolfe
> knew of La Faussille's work as early as 1752 (Willson, *The Life and Letters of
> James Wolfe*, p. 166). Advertised in Dalrymple, *Essay*, 1761 [repr. c. 1796].

*Rules and Regulations for the Formations, Field-Exercise, and Movements,
of His Majesty's Forces.* [London, 1792]. Uk.

> Based on David Dundas's *Principles of Military Movements* (1788), these rules
> were issued to the whole British army in 1792 — to accompany the new manual
> and platoon exercises of that year. Houlding, *Fit for Service*, 1981, p. 245. DSoC
> attributes the rules to Sir William Fawcett, who signed the preface in 1792 in
> his official capacity as adjutant general.

Sackville, Charles, Duke of Dorset, 1711–69.
A Treatise Concerning the Militia in Four Sections. . . . London: J. Millan,
1752. DSoC.

> Advertised in *List of Army*, 1774.

Saint Julien, Antoine, Chevalier de and Mr. Grimaret.
Fonctions des Généraux, ou, l'Art de Conduire une Armée. . . . The Hague:
Pierre Husson, 1710. DSoC.

> Advertised in *État Militaire*, 1780.

Saint Julien, Antoine, Chevalier de.
La Forge de Vulcain: ou l'Appareil des Machines de Guerre. . . . The Hague:
Guillaume De Voys, 1710. DSoC.

> Advertised in *État Militaire*, 1780.

Saldern, Friedrich Christoph von, 1719–85.
*Elements of Tacticks, and Introduction to Military Evolutions for the Infan-
try.* . . . Translated by Isaac Landmann. London: the author by P. Elmsley
and T. and J. Egerton, 1787. DSoC.

> Advertised in Dalrymple, *Essay*, 1761 [repr. c. 1796].

Saxe, Maurice, Comte de, 1696–1750.
Esprit des Loix de la Tactique, et de Différentes Institutions Militaires . . .
   Commentées par M de Bonneville. . . . 2 vols. The Hague: Pierre Gosse,
   1762. DSoC.
   Advertised in *État Militaire*, 1780.

Sharaf al-Din 'Ali Yazdi.
The History of Timur-Bec Known by the Name of Tamerlain the Great. . . .
   Translated by J. Darby. 2 vols. London: J. Darby, 1723. CtY.
   Advertised in Pétis de la Croix, *History Genghizcan*, 1722.

Silva, Marquis de.
Pensées sur la Tactique et sur Quelques Autres Parties de la Guerre. Paris:
   Charles-Antoine Jombert, 1768. DSoC.
   Advertised in *État Militaire*, 1780. DSoC has what seems to have been a later
   edition of this book (*Pensées sur la Tactique, et la Stratégique . . .*), which was
   published in Turin in 1778 and which included Silva's *Considérations sur la
   Guerre de 1769 entre les Russes et les Turcs*, also Turin, 1778.

Silva, Marquis de.
Remarques sur Quelques Articles de l'Essai Général de Tactique. Turin: les
   freres Reycends, 1773. DSoC.
   Advertised in *État Militaire*, 1780.

Simes, Thomas, fl. 1757–80.
*A Military Course for the Government and Conduct of a Battalion . . . with
   . . . Instructions for Their Manner of Attack and Defence.* London: for the
   author and sold by Almon [and eight others], 1777. DSoC.
   Advertised in Dalrymple, *Essay*, 1761 [repr. c. 1796].

Simes, Thomas, fl. 1757–80.
*The Military Instructor: For the Non-Commissioned Officers and Private
   Men of the Infantry.* London: for the author by H. Reynell; and sold by
   Millan [and eight others], 1778. DSoC.
   Advertised in Dalrymple, *Essay*, 1761 [repr. c. 1796].

Simes, Thomas, fl. 1757–80.
*The Regulator: or, Instructions to Form the Officer, and Complete the Sol-
   dier. . . .* London: W. Richardson, 1780. DSoC.
   Advertised in Dalrymple, *Essay*, 1761 [repr. c. 1796].

Simes, Thomas, fl. 1757–80.
A Treatise on the Military Science, Which Comprehends the Grand Opera-

tions of War, and General Rules for Conducting an Army in the Field. . . .
London: H. Reynell, 1780. DSoC.

> Advertised in Dalrymple, *Essay*, 1761 [repr. c. 1796].

Smirke, Robert, 1752–1845.
Review of a Battalion of Infantry Including the Eighteen Manoeuvres. . . .
London: T. Bensley for R. Bowyer [and four others], 1799. DSoC.

> Cited in Houlding, *Fit for Service*, 1981.

Smith, William.
An Authentic Journal of the Expedition to Belleisle. . . . London, 1761. DSoC.

> Cited in Whitworth, *Ligonier*, 1958.

Smith, William, 1727–1803.
*An Historical Account of the Expedition against the Ohio Indians in the Year
1764.* . . . Philadelphia: [W. Bradford, 1765]; reprinted London: T. Jef-
feries, 1766. DSoC.

> Cited in Houlding, *Fit for Service*, 1981. This book was also reprinted in Dublin
> and Amsterdam in 1769.

Starrat, William.
The Doctrine of Projectiles, Demonstrated and Apply'd. . . . Dublin: S. Powell,
1733. DSoC.

> Advertised in Smith, *Dictionary*, 1779.

Stille, Christoph Ludwig von, 1696–1752.
*The King of Prussia's Campaigns in 1742 and 1745: With Remarks on the
Causes of the Several Events.* London: T. Becket and P. A. De Hondt, 1763.
DSoC.

> Advertised in Dalrymple, *Essay*, 1761 [repr. c. 1796].

Stuart, James.
*Correspondence during the Indisposition of the Commander in Chief in Sep-
tember 1782.* [London, 1783]. Uk.

> Included in Higham, *Guide*, 1971.

*The Succession of Colonels to All His Majesties Land Forces, from Their Rise
to 1742.* . . . London: J. Millan, 1742. DSoC.

> Advertised in *List of Army*, 1759.

Sulivan, Richard Joseph, Sir, 1752–1806.
*Thoughts on Martial Law, with a Mode Recommended for Conducting the
Proceedings of General Courts Martial.* . . . 2nd ed. rev. London: T. Becket,
1784. DSoC.

> Included in Higham, *Guide*, 1971.

Swieten, Gerard, Baron van, 1700–1772.
A Short Account of the Most Common Diseases Incident to Armies. . . . 2 vols.
London: T. Beckett and P. A. de Hondt, 1762. Uk.
> Cited in Frey, *British Soldier*, 1981. This book was reprinted in London, Dublin,
> Philadelphia, and Boston in the ensuing fifteen years.

Temple, William, Sir, 1628–99.
*Memoires de Ce Qui s'Est Passé dans la Chrétienté: Depuis le Commencement
de la Guerre en 1672 Jusqu'à la Paix Concluë en 1679.* The Hague: Adrian
Moetjens, 1693. MH-H.
> Advertised in Estrades, *Lettres*, 1710.

Tencin, Claudine Alexandrine Guérin de and Pont-de-Veyle.
Le Siège de Calais: Nouvelle Historique. 2nd ed. 2 vols. The Hague: Jean
Neaume, 1739. ViU.
> Advertised in Vauban, *Attaque Defense*, 1737.

Thompson, George.
*An Abstract of General Bland's Treatise of Military Discipline, Revised by
Mr. Faucett for the Use of the Militia of the County of York.* . . . York:
A. Ward, 1760. Uk.
> Cited in Houlding, *Fit for Service*, 1981.

Townshend, George, Marquis, 1724–1807.
A Brief Narrative of the Late Campaigns in Germany and Flanders. . . . London: J. Lion, 1751. CtY.
> Cited in Skrine, *Fontenoy*, 1906.

Tronson du Coudray, Charles, 1738–77.
*L'Artillerie Nouvelle, ou, Examen des Changements Faits dans l'Artillerie
Française depuis 1765.* Amsterdam: n.p., 1773. DSoC.
> Advertised in *État Militaire*, 1780.

Tyndale, W.
Instructions for Young Dragoon Officers. London: T. Egerton, 1796. NWM.
> Advertised in Dalrymple, *Essay*, 1761 [repr. c. 1796].

Vallière, Jean Florent de, 1667–1759.
*Traité de la Défense des Places par les Contre-Mines, avec les Réflexions sur
les Principes de l'Artillerie.* Paris: Charles-Antoine Jombert, 1768. DSoC.
> Advertised in *État Militaire*, 1780.

Varennes, Pierre Augustine de, fl. 1779.
Réflexions Morales, Relatives au Militaire François. Paris: Cellot & Jombert,
1779. DSoC.
> Advertised in *État Militaire*, 1780.

Vattel, Emer de, 1714–67.

Le Droit de la Guerre, ou, Principes de la Loi Naturelle. . . . Amsterdam and Leiden: Aux depens de la compagnie, 1757. NcU.

> Advertised in Jeney, *Partisan*, 1759.

Vauban, Sébastien le Prestre de, 1633–1707.

Mémoire pour Servir d'Instruction dans la Conduite des Siéges et dans la Défense des Places. Leiden: Jean & Herman Verbeek, 1740. DSoC.

> Advertised in Dulacq, *Theorie*, 1741.

Vega, Garcilaso de la.

Histoire des Guerres Civiles des Espagnols dans les Indes. . . . 2 vols. Amsterdam: G. Kuyper, 1706. ICU.

> Advertised in Strada, *Histoire Pays Bas*, 1739.

La Vie du Prince Eugène de Savoie, Maréchal de Camp Général des Armées de l'Empereur, en Italie. The Hague: Adrian Moetjens, 1702. InU.

> Advertised in Estrades, *Lettres*, 1710.

Warnery, Charles Emmanuel de, 1719– or 1720–86.

Remarks on Cavalry. Translated by G. K. Koehler. London: J. Barfield for the translator and sold by T. Egerton, 1798. DSoC.

> Included in Aimone, "Genesis," 1999. In 1792 Sir Henry Clinton reflected on one of Warnery's many earlier books, none of which was translated into English before his *Remarques sur la Cavaliere* (1781).

Williamson, John, 1751?–1801.

The Elements of Military Arrangement . . . and Discipline of the British Infantry. . . . 2nd ed. London: Thomas Egerton, 1782. DSoC (copy owned by Bennet Cuthbertson, author of *A System for the Compleat Interior Management and Oeconomy of a Battalion of Infantry.* . . . Dublin: Boulter Grierson, 1768).

> Advertised in Dalrymple, *Essay*, 1761 [repr. c. 1796]. There were at least three other editions of this book between 1785 and 1800.

Williamson, John, 1751?–1801.

A Treatise on Military Finance. . . . London: T. Egerton, 1795. DSoC.

> Reprinted at least three times between 1787 and 1798. Advertised in Dalrymple, *Essay*, 1761 [repr. c. 1796].

Withall, Benjamin.

A Detection of the Exhorbitant Oppressions, Publick Frauds, and Mismanagements . . . in His Majesty's Victualling and Ordnance Offices. . . . London: J. Roberts, 1717. CtY.

> Included in Pargellis and Medley, *Bibliography*, 1951.

Wolfe, James, 1727–59.

General Wolfe's Instructions to Young Officers: Also His Orders for a Battalion and an Army. . . . London: J. Millan, 1768. DSoC [also has 1778 and 1780 editions].

> Advertised in Dalrymple, *Essay*, 1761 [repr. c. 1796].

Young, Sir William, 1725?–1788.

Manoeuvres, or Practical Observations on the Art of War. . . . London: J. Millan, [1771]. DSoC.

> See as well *An Essay on the Command of Small Detachments . . .* , which Millan sold as part of Young's *Manoeuvres*. Advertised in *List of Army*, 1773.

APPENDIXES

Appendix A. Books Preferred: Subject and Date of Publication

Subject	16th century	1600–1624	1625–1649	1650–1674	1675–1699	1700–1709	1710–1719
History, biography	9 (23%)	3 (17%)	17 (35%)	16 (35%)	36 (41%)	17 (52%)	10 (46%)
Engineering, artillery	6 (15%)	6 (33%)	17 (35%)	9 (20%)	18 (21%)	4 (12%)	5 (23%)
Drill, discipline	5 (13%)	2 (11%)	3 (6%)	1 (2%)	8 (9%)		
Advice				1 (2%)	1 (1%)	1 (3%)	
Laws, regulations		2 (11%)	2 (4%)	1 (2%)		1 (3%)	1 (5%)
Art of war	7 (18%)	3 (17%)	4 (8%)	5 (11%)	8 (9%)		1 (5%)
Classics	13 (33%)	2 (11%)	6 (12%)	9 (20%)	13 (15%)	2 (6%)	3 (14%)
Maps, plans, lists, dictionaries					2 (2%)	2 (6%)	2 (9%)
Defense				1 (2%)		1 (3%)	
Medicine							
Naval				3 (7%)	1 (1%)	5 (15%)	
Total	40	18	49	46	87	33	22

1720–1729	1730–1739	1740–1749	1750–1759	1760–1769	1770–1779	1780–1789	1790–1799	No Date	Total
16 (44%)	15 (33%)	21 (30%)	28 (30%)	12 (23%)	6 (23%)	15 (60%)	4 (80%)		225 (35%)
4 (11%)	9 (20%)	15 (21%)	16 (17%)	8 (15%)	9 (35%)	3 (12%)		1	130 (20%)
4 (11%)	4 (9%)	6 (9%)	7 (8%)	7 (13%)	1 (4%)	2 (8%)			50 (8%)
			1 (1%)	2 (4%)	1 (4%)	1 (4%)			8 (1%)
2 (6%)	2 (4%)	2 (3%)	2 (2%)					1	16 (2%)
7 (20%)	9 (20%)	14 (20%)	21 (23%)	16 (30%)	8 (31%)	3 (12%)			106 (16%)
1 (3%)	3 (7%)	4 (6%)	6 (7%)	1 (2%)					63 (10%)
1 (3%)	3 (7%)	4 (6%)	8 (9%)	4 (8%)	1 (4%)				27 (4%)
		1 (1%)		1 (2%)		1 (4%)	1 (20%)		6 (1%)
			1 (1%)	1 (2%)					2 (0%)
1 (3%)	1 (2%)	3 (4%)	2 (3%)	1 (2%)					17 (3%)
36	46	70	92	53	26	25	5	2	650 (100%)

Appendix A1. Books Preferred: Language and Date of Publication

Language	16th century	1600– 1624	1625– 1649	1650– 1674	1675– 1699	1700– 1709	1710– 1719	1720– 1729
Dutch			1 (2%)	1 (2%)	2 (2%)	1 (3%)		
English	16 (40%)	4 (22%)	19 (39%)	24 (52%)	47 (54%)	25 (76%)	8 (36%)	16 (44%)
French	7 (18%)	5 (28%)	19 (39%)	13 (28%)	30 (36%)	6 (18%)	12 (55%)	16 (44%)
German		1 (6%)	2 (4%)	1 (2%)	2 (2%)			
Greek	2 (5%)				2 (2%)			
Italian	8 (20%)	8 (44%)	3 (6%)	2 (4%)				1 (3%)
Latin	7 (18%)		5 (10%)	5 (11%)	4 (5%)	1 (3%)	2 (9%)	2 (6%)
Spanish								1 (3%)
Total	40	18	49	46	87	33	22	36

Appendix A2. Books Preferred: Cities and Dates of Publication

Place of Publication	16th century	1600– 1624	1625– 1649	1650– 1674	1675– 1699	1700– 1709	1710– 1719	1720– 1729
Amsterdam	1	1	4	4	5	2	2	4
Antwerp	1	1	2	1				
Basel	1							
Berlin								
Birmingham								
Bologna	2							
Brescia	1							
Breslau								
Brunswick					1			
Brussels			1	1				1
Cambridge			1	1				
Cologne						1	1	
Colonia				1				
Copenhagen								
Dresden								
Dublin								1

1730–1739	1740–1749	1750–1759	1760–1769	1770–1779	1780–1789	1790–1799	No Date	Total
								5 (.8%)
14 (30%)	27 (39%)	42 (46%)	29 (55%)	16 (62%)	17 (68%)	5 (100%)		309 (48%)
29 (63%)	42 (60%)	43 (48%)	16 (30%)	7 (27%)	8 (32%)		1	254 (39%)
2 (4%)	1 (1%)	5 (5%)	8 (15%)	2 (8%)				24 (4%)
								4 (.6%)
				1 (4%)			1	24 (4%)
1 (2%)		2 (2%)						29 (5%)
								1 (.2%)
46	70	92	53	26	25	5	2	650 (100%)

1730–1739	1740–1749	1750–1759	1760–1769	1770–1779	1780–1789	1790–1799	No Date	Total
4	7	3	4	3				44
								5
1								2
		2	1		1			4
					1			1
								2
								1
			1					1
								1
1			1					5
								2
								2
								1
			1					1
1		3		1				5
1	1	1	1					5

Appendix A2 (*continued*)

Place of Publication	16th century	1600–1624	1625–1649	1650–1674	1675–1699	1700–1709	1710–1719	1720–1729
Edinburgh						1	2	
Exeter								
Florence	1							
Franeker			1					
Frankfurt am Main	1	2	2		1			
Freiburg								
Geneva	2							
Genoa								1
Ghent			1					
Glasgow								
Gosport								
The Hague			1	1	9		4	4
Kralovethota								
La Rochelle	1							
Lausanne								
Leeuwarden					1	1		
Leiden		1	4		1	1	1	
Leipzig								
Liège								
Limerick								
London	15	4	14	23	48	23	6	15
Louvain			1					
Lyon	2		1	1	2			
Milan		1						
Moulins					1			
New York								
Nuremberg					3			
Oxford					1	1		
Paris	4	1	9	8	11	3	7	8
Pont à Mousson			1					
Rome	1		1					2
Rotterdam					2			
Rouen			2	1				
Siena			1					
Strasbourg			1	1				
Stuttgart								
Turin								
Uppsala				1				
Venice	7	4	1	1				
Vienna								
Wesel				2				
Place not given				1	1			
Total	40	18	49	46	87	33	22	36

1730–1739	1740–1749	1750–1759	1760–1769	1770–1779	1780–1789	1790–1799	No Date	Total
			1		1			5
					1			1
								1
								1
	1	1	4					12
				1				1
			1		1			4
								1
								1
		1	1					2
				1				1
9	12	11	2					53
					1			1
								1
	4							4
								2
1	1	1						11
			2					2
1								1
	1							1
14	26	40	26	15	18	5		292
								1
								6
								1
								1
				1				1
			1					4
		1	1					4
12	16	19	3	3				104
								1
								4
								2
								3
								1
		1			1			4
			1					1
	1			1				2
								1
								13
1			1					3
		1						3
		6					2	10
46	70	92	53	26	25	5	2	650

Appendix A3. Books Preferred: Countries and Dates of Publication

Country of Publication	16th century	1600– 1624	1625– 1649	1650– 1674	1675– 1699	1700– 1709	1710– 1719
Austria							
Austrian Netherlands	1 (3%)	2 (11%)	5 (10%)	1 (2%)			
British North America							
Denmark							
England	15 (38%)	4 (22%)	15 (31%)	24 (52%)	49 (56%)	24 (73%)	6 (27%)
France	7 (18%)	2 (11%)	14 (29%)	10 (22%)	14 (16%)	3 (9%)	7 (32%)
Germany/Prussia	1 (3%)	2 (1%)	3 (6%)	3 (7%)	5 (6%)	1 (3%)	
Ireland							
Italy	12 (30%)	6 (33%)	2 (4%)	1 (2%)			
United Netherlands	1 (3%)	2 (11%)	10 (20%)	5 (11%)	18 (21%)	4 (12%)	7 (32%)
Scotland						1 (3%)	2 (9%)
Sweden				1 (2%)			
Switzerland	3 (8%)						
Place not given				1 (2%)	1 (1%)		
Total	40	18	49	46	87	33	22

1720–1729	1730–1739	1740–1749	1750–1759	1760–1769	1770–1779	1780–1789	1790–1799	No Date	Total
	1 (2%)		1 (1%)	1 (2%)					3 (1%)
1 (3%)	2 (4%)			1 (2%)					13 (2%)
					1 (4%)				1 (0%)
				1 (2%)					1 (0%)
15 (42%)	14 (30%)	26 (37%)	41 (45%)	27 (51%)	16 (62%)	20 (80%)	5 (100%)		301 (46%)
8 (22%)	12 (26%)	16 (23%)	20 (22%)	3 (6%)	3 (12%)	1 (4%)			120 (19%)
	1 (2%)	1 (1%)	7 (8%)	10 (19%)	2 (8%)	1 (4%)			37 (6%)
1 (3%)	1 (2%)	2 (3%)	1 (1%)	1 (2%)					6 (1%)
3 (8%)		1 (1%)			1 (4%)				26 (4%)
8 (22%)	14 (30%)	20 (29%)	15 (16%)	6 (11%)	3 (12%)				113 (17%)
			1 (1%)	2 (4%)		1 (4%)			7 (1%)
									1 (0%)
	1 (2%)	4 (6%)		1 (2%)		1 (4%)			10 (2%)
			6 (7%)			1 (4%)		2 (100%)	11 (2%)
36	46	70	92	53	26	25	5	2	650 (101%)

Appendix A4. Officers' Preferences among Books Preferred
(by subject and date of preference)

Subject	1710–1719	1720–1729	1730–1739	1740–1749	1750–1759	1760–1769	1770–1779
History, biography	44 (36%)	2 (13%)	5 (31%)	37 (34%)	87 (32%)	29 (30%)	90 (17%)
Engineering, artillery	32 (26%)	2 (13%)		20 (19%)	36 (13%)	5 (5%)	162 (31%)
Drill, discipline	5 (4%)	1 (7%)	1 (6%)	6 (6%)	19 (7%)	8 (8%)	53 (10%)
Advice	1 (1%)			1 (1%)	1 (0%)	2 (2%)	4 (1%)
Laws, regulations	5 (4%)	1 (7%)	1 (6%)	4 (4%)	9 (3%)	3 (3%)	5 (1%)
Art of war	11 (9%)		4 (25%)	14 (13%)	63 (23%)	22 (23%)	126 (24%)
Classics	17 (14%)	9 (60%)	2 (13%)	15 (14%)	35 (13%)	17 (18%)	47 (9%)
Maps, plans, lists, dictionaries	3 (3%)		1 (6%)	6 (6%)	11 (4%)	5 (5%)	25 (5%)
Defense			1 (6%)	1 (1%)	1 (0%)		4 (1%)
Medicine					3 (1%)		3 (1%)
Naval	3 (3%)		1 (6%)	4 (4%)	9 (3%)	5 (5%)	2 (0%)
Total	121	15	16	108	274	96	521

Note: Our forty-two officers owned, read, or recommended 650 books on war in the age of the American Revolution. But they clearly preferred some of those books to others. It was not just that two-thirds of the officers had Caesar's *Commentaries* on their shelves or that half admired Vauban: three or more of them shared an interest in more than 100 of the 650 titles on their list. This appendix attempts, then, to show how shared interests in particular titles shaped collective preferences for books on war during the eighteenth century. The appendix reflects the 1,265 choices that our officers made among the 650 books on their list—choices expressed in inventories, catalogues, lists, sales, notes, and correspondence. Although an officer sometimes had more than one edition or copy of a book, his preference has been recorded only once for each title; and that preference has been dated in all except nine cases from an inventory, catalogue, list, or correspondence. In nine cases—Cuthbert, Dormer, Hotham, Hotham Thompson, Lord John Murray, Oglethorpe, Seton, Stewart, and Winde—the date of preference has been adjusted to reflect the officer's active service and collecting of books (see Appendix E for the specific adjustments). Thus, Oglethorpe's preferences have been recorded for 1746, when his active service ended, rather than for 1785, when his library was catalogued.

The evidence of our officers' preferences for books on war—to say nothing of the preferences themselves—is certainly not symmetrical. Inventories, catalogues, citations, lists of purchases, reading notes, military notebooks, and recommendations provide very different kinds of evidence of what an officer valued—both quantitatively and qualitatively. Four of our forty-two officers

1780–1789	1790–1799	No Date	Total
11 (41%)	40 (48%)	1 (25%)	346 (27%)
	14 (17%)		271 (21%)
7 (26%)	7 (8%)		107 (9%)
1 (4%)	1 (1%)		11 (1%)
			28 (2%)
5 (19%)	10 (12%)	3 (75%)	258 (20%)
1 (4%)	5 (6%)		148 (12%)
	3 (4%)		54 (4%)
1 (4%)	1 (1%)		9 (1%)
			6 (1%)
1 (4%)	2 (2%)		27 (2%)
27	83	4	1,265 (100%)

cited or owned only 2 or 3 books on war; four owned, cited, or recommended between 120 and 220; and the remaining thirty-four officers, between 5 and 91. The average number of books on war that our forty-two preferred was 35; the median, 24 (see Appendix E). Some of our officers exerted far more influence than others on our understanding of what eighteenth-century officers preferred. An officer who owned 220 books on war did much more to shape lists of 650 titles or of 1,265 choices than an officer who cited only 2 — however well or ill informed the particular officers might have been. Indeed, the officers who assembled the six largest collections of books on war contributed, among them, half of the 1,265 choices expressed by our forty-two officers in this appendix. Yet because the officers with the six largest collections were men of discriminating tastes and wide experience, and because they expressed themselves from the 1740s to the 1790s, their choices were — on the whole — comprehensive and authoritative for the era of the American Revolution. General Officer had a diverse collection of books emphasizing the Continental art of war, military history, and engineering (some 220 books sold in 1773); Smith, the latest and most authoritative books on artillery, engineering, and the art of war (127 books of 1773 and 1779); Oglethorpe, the classics, military history, and engineering (125 books of 1746); Dury, the classics, the Continental art of war, and military history (120 books of 1758); Ligonier, military history, the art of war, engineering, and the classics (91 books of 1770); and Montresor, military history, engineering, and the art of war (67 books in 1799). See Part I and Appendix E.

Appendix B. Books Preferred: The Authorities

This appendix lists the books on war most often preferred by our forty-two officers. It has been arranged to show the importance of particular authors and titles or clusters of titles. Seventy-two of the ninety-two entries contain an author and a title (including variations on that title) or merely a title: Caesar's *Commentaries*, Saxe's *Reveries*, or *Regulations for the Prussian Cavalry*. Thirteen contain an author and two or more of his works on closely related topics: Coehoorn's, Muller's, and Le Blond's on military engineering; Espagnac's on the War of the Austrian Succession; and Xenophon's on ancient Greece. Three entries have works both by and about a famous commander—Vauban, Turenne, and Frederick the Great. And the remaining four, clusters of books about Marlborough, Eugene, Luxembourg, and Charles XII of Sweden, celebrated generals who did not publish their memoirs. Each of the ninety-two titles or clusters of titles in this appendix was preferred by at least 10 percent of our officers and by no fewer than three of them.

The appendix has been designed to reflect, in descending order, the books on war that our officers preferred above all others. It begins with Caesar's *Commentaries*, which appealed to two-thirds of the officers, and proceeds through Vauban and other authoritative authors and titles to those books that attracted at least 10 percent (and three officers) of the forty-two officers. In each of the ninety-two entries, summaries of the officers' preferences have been grouped sequentially to reveal the shifting popularity of authors and titles across time; and each entry includes all the editions that the officers owned, read, or recommended—altogether some 268 editions in seven languages.

Those 268 editions—and the choices that our officers made among them—reveal a midcentury surge of interest in Continental treatises on the art of war. Of the 268 editions, 65 percent were in European languages other than English, and more than half appeared between 1730 and 1770 (Appendix B2). Although the 268 editions were quite evenly divided among military history (24 percent of the whole), the art of war (24 percent), engineering and artillery (24 percent), and the classics (21 percent), the officers' preferences among those editions showed a much clearer interest in the art of war (30 percent), particularly in the second half of the century (Appendixes B1, B3). Although British officers valued their own military history and texts, they remained dependent until the American Revolution on Continental books on war—the campaign histories of Saxe and Frederick the Great, the engineering manuals of Vauban and Clairac, and, above all, the treatises on the art of war of Saxe, Feuquières, Turenne, Guibert, and Turpin de Crissé (Appendix B). This persistent British dependence on Continental authorities is apparent in the books listed in this appendix and in the choices that our officers made among those books (Appendixes B1–B3).

The dates of officers' preferences for authors and titles have been adjusted in nine cases to reflect the dates on which officers expressed themselves rather than the dates on which their preferences were eventually recorded (see Appendix E). Thus, four of the forty-two officers' preferences have been reported for periods earlier than those in which their preferences were recorded. Lord John Murray's and James Oglethorpe's selections are reported for the period 1710–54—when they were actively serving and collecting military books—even though their libraries were not inventoried until 1762 and 1785, respectively. Similarly, Thomas Cuthbert's and Sir Charles Hotham Thompson's preferences have been included in the period 1756–63 (their period of active service and collecting), although their books were not catalogued until the 1780s. Here then are the books on war that our officers preferred above all others.

Author	Title, with language[a] and dates of publication	Officers' Preferences			Summary of Preferences (max N = 42)
		1710–54 (max N = 14)	1756–63 (max N = 10)	1768–99 (max N = 18)	
Caesar	*Commentaries*, F1589, L1618, L1635, F1640, E1655, F1689, L1693, E1705, L1713, L1737, L1750, E1753	9 of 14	7 of 10	12 of 18	28 of 42 (67%)
Vauban	*New Method of Fortification*, E1722; *De L'Attaque et de la Defense des Places*, F1737–42. See as well the commentaries and compilations of Bernard, F1689; Cambray, F1689; Du Fay, F1692, F1718; Gaya, F1689; Arçon, F1786; Naudin, F1697; Sturm, F1710.	5 of 14	6 of 10	10 of 18	21 of 42 (50%)
[Marlborough]	See the biographies and memoirs of Campbell, E1736–37; Dumont, F1725, F1729; Kane E1745, E1747, E1757; Lediard E1736; Millner E1733. See as well *Full and Impartial Relation of Hochstette*, E1704; *History Campaign in Flanders*, E1709.	6 of 14	4 of 10	10 of 18	20 of 42 (48%)
Saxe	*Reveries*, F1753, F1756, E1757, F1757, F1757	1 of 2	3 of 10	9 of 18	13 of 30 (43%)
Polybius	*History*, L1554, E1634, L1670, E1693, E1756–72	3 of 14	6 of 10	9 of 18	18 of 42 (43%)
Folard	*Histoire de Polybe ... avec un Commentaire*, F1729–30, F1751; *L'Esprit du Chevalier Folard*, F 1760; *Nouvelles Descouvertes*, F1724	4 of 13	7 of 10	6 of 18	17 of 41 (42%)
Feuquières	*Memoires*, F1734, F1735, E1737, F1740, F1741	3 of 14	5 of 10	9 of 18	17 of 42 (41%)
Clairac	*Ingenieur de Campagne*, F1749, E1758, E1760	0 of 5	4 of 10	9 of 18	13 of 33 (39%)
Vegetius	*De re Militari*, L1505, L1535, F1536, L1670, E1744, E1767	5 of 14	5 of 10	6 of 18	16 of 42 (38%)

Author	Title, with language[a] and dates of publication	Officers' Preferences			Summary of Preferences (max N = 42)
		1710–54 (max N = 14)	1756–63 (max N = 10)	1768–99 (max N = 18)	
Bland	*Treatise*, E1727, E1734, E1753, E1759	5 of 12	4 of 10	6 of 18	15 of 40 (38%)
Puységur	*Art de la Guerre*, F1748, F1749	0 of 5	5 of 10	7 of 18	12 of 33 (36%)
Turenne	*Military Memoirs and Maxims*, E1740, E1744. See as well the biographies by Buisson/ Courtilz de Sandras, E1686; Deschamps, F1756, Raguenet, F1738; Ramsay, F1735.	2 of 14	5 of 10	8 of 18	15 of 42 (36%)
Thucydides	*Peloponnesian War*, E1550, G1564, L1594, E1629, E1634, E1676, G1696, E1753	4 of 14	5 of 10	5 of 18	14 of 42 (33%)
	Regulations for the Prussian Cavalry, E1757		3 of 10	6 of 18	9 of 28 (32%)
Guibert	*Essai Général de Tactique*, F1772, Ger1774		0 of 1	6 of 18	6 of 19 (32%)
	Regulations for the Prussian Infantry, E1754	0 of 2	3 of 10	6 of 18	9 of 30 (30%)
Montecuccoli	*Memoires*, F1712, F1746, F1758	1 of 14	4 of 10	7 of 18	12 of 42 (29%)
Frederick the Great	*Historie de Mon Temps*, F1788; *Kriegs-Kunst*, Ger1761; *Mémoires*, F1751; Lloyd, *Essai*, F1761	0 of 3	2 of 10	7 of 18	9 of 31 (29%)
Guischardt	*Mémoires Militaires sur les Grecs et les Romains*, F1758, F1760		2 of 7	5 of 18	7 of 25 (28%)
Muller	*Attack and Defence*, E1747; *Treatise of Artillery*, E1757; *Elementary Part of Fortification*, E1746; *Practical Part of Fortification*, E1755	0 of 5	2 of 10	7 of 18	9 of 33 (27%)
Turpin de Crissé	*Essai sur l'Art de la Guerre*, F1754, E1761	0 of 2	4 of 10	4 of 18	8 of 30 (27%)

Author	Title, with language[a] and dates of publication	Officers' Preferences			Summary of Preferences (max N = 42)
		1710–54 (max N = 14)	1756–63 (max N = 10)	1768–99 (max N = 18)	
Coehoorn	*Nieuwe Vestingbouw,* D1685, D1692, D1702; *New Method of Fortification,* E1705, E1708; *Nouvelle Fortification,* F1706, F1711, F1741; *Vesterckinge des Vyfhoecks,* D1682	3 of 14	2 of 10	6 of 18	11 of 42 (26%)
[Eugene]	See the biographies and histories of Campbell, E1736–37; Dumont F1725, F1729; Mauvillon F1773.	2 of 14	3 of 10	6 of 18	11 of 42 (26%)
Espagnac	*Campagne en 1747,* F1747; *Essai sur la Guerre,* F1751, F1753; *Histoire de Saxe,* F1775; *Journal Historique,* F1747; *Relation de la Campagne en Brabant . . . M.DCC.XLV,* F1748; *Relation de la Campagne en Brabant . . . M.DCC. XLVI,* F1748; *Relation de la Campagne en Brabant . . . M.DCC.XLVII,* F1748	2 of 5	2 of 10	4 of 18	8 of 33 (24%)
Kane	*Campaigns of King William and Queen Anne,* E1745, E1747; *System of Camp-Discipline,* E1757	2 of 5	3 of 10	3 of 18	8 of 33 (24%)
Le Blond	*Abregé de l'Arithmetique,* F1758; *Elemens de la Guerre des Sieges,* F1743; *Elemens de Fortification,* F1742; *Essai sur la Castrametation,* F1748; *Military Engineer,* E1759; *Traité de l'Artillerie,* F1743, E1746	2 of 5	2 of 10	4 of 18	8 of 33 (24%)

Author	Title, with language[a] and dates of publication	Officers' Preferences			Summary of Preferences (max N = 42)
		1710–54 (max N = 14)	1756–63 (max N = 10)	1768–99 (max N = 18)	
Xenophon	Cyropaedie, F1718, F1732, E1685; Expedition of Cyrus, E1742, E1749; Le Guerre de Greci, I1562; La Retraite des Dix Mille, F1648, F1658; Trois Ouvrages, F1744; Xenophon's History of ... Greece, E1685	3 of 14	3 of 10	4 of 18	10 of 42 (24%)
	List of the General and Field-Officers ... in the Army, E1754 and annual editions thereafter	1 of 2	3 of 10	3 of 18	7 of 30 (23%)
Dalrymple	Military Essay, E1761		1 of 5	4 of 18	5 of 23 (22%)
Machiavelli	L'Art de la Guerre, F1613; Arte of Warre, E1573, E1588; Libro della Arte della Guerra, I1521; Opere di Nic. Machiavelli, I1726; Works, E1680, E1720, E1762	4 of 14	2 of 10	3 of 18	9 of 42 (21%)
Saint-Rémy	Memoires d'Artillerie, F1697, F1702, F1741, F1745	2 of 14	3 of 10	4 of 18	9 of 42 (21%)
Maizeroy	Mémoire, F1773			3 of 14	3 of 14 (21%)
Biggs	Military History of Europe, E1749, E1755, E1756, E1759	1 of 5	2 of 10	4 of 18	7 of 33 (21%)
Beaurain	Histoire Militaire de Flandre, F1755; Histoire Militaire du Duc de Luxembourg, F1756–58	0 of 2	2 of 10	4 of 18	6 of 30 (20%)
[Luxembourg]	See Beaurain, F1755, F1756–58; Campagne de Hollande en MDCLXXII sous ... Luxembourg, F1759.	0 of 2	2 of 10	4 of 18	6 of 30 (20%)
Santa Cruz de Marcenado	Reflexions Militaires et Politiques, F1724, F1725, F1735–38, E1737	0 of 13	4 of 10	4 of 18	8 of 41 (20%)

Author	Title, with language[a] and dates of publication	Officers' Preferences			Summary of Preferences (max N = 42)
		1710–54 (max N = 14)	1756–63 (max N = 10)	1768–99 (max N = 18)	
Bisset	*Theory and Construction of Fortification*, E1751	2 of 3	1 of 10	3 of 18	6 of 31 (19%)
Grotius	*De Jure Belli ac Pacis*, L1625, E1655, F1724	4 of 14	2 of 10	2 of 18	8 of 42 (19%)
Arrian	*Anabaseos Alexandrou*, L1539, F1664, L1668, L1704, E1729	4 of 14	1 of 10	3 of 18	8 of 42 (19%)
	Essay on Field Fortification [Pleydell], E 1768		0 of 3	4 of 18	4 of 21 (19%)
[Charles XII]	See Defoe, E1715; Voltaire, F1731, E1732.	0 of 14	3 of 10	4 of 18	7 of 42 (17%)
Courtilz de Sandras	*Conduite de Mars*, F1685; *Guerre d'Espagne*, F 1707; *Histoire Guerre de Hollande*, F 1689; *Vie de Turenne*, F1685, E1686	3 of 14	1 of 10	3 of 18	7 of 42 (17%)
Davila	*Historia delle Guerre Civili di Francia*, I1634, I1638, I1646, E1647–48	2 of 14	3 of 10	2 of 18	7 of 42 (17%)
Frontinus	*Stratagemes*, L1505, F1536, L1670, E,1686	4 of 14	2 of 10	1 of 18	7 of 42 (17%)
Polyaenus	*Strategematon*, L1691, F1739	1 of 14	2 of 10	4 of 18	7 of 42 (17%)
Strada	*De Bello Belgico*, L1640–47, L1653, E1650, F1665, F1675, F1727–39	2 of 14	2 of 10	3 of 18	7 of 42 (17%)
Buonamici	*Commentariorum de Bello Italico*, L1750–51, E1753	0 of 3	3 of 10	2 of 18	5 of 31 (16%)
Campbell	*Military History of ... Eugene ... [and] Marlborough*, E1736–37	2 of 10	2 of 10	2 of 18	6 of 38 (16%)
Millner	*Compendious Journal*, E1733	1 of 10	3 of 10	2 of 18	6 of 38 (16%)
Belidor	*Bombardier*, F1731, F1734; *Dictionnaire Portatif*, F1755; *Kriegs-Lexicon*, Ger1765; *Mathematique*, F1725, F1758; *Science des Ingenieurs*, F1729, F1734	1 of 12	1 of 10	4 of 18	6 of 41 (15%)

Author	Title, with language[a] and dates of publication	Officers' Preferences			Summary of Preferences (max N = 42)
		1710–54 (max N = 14)	1756–63 (max N = 10)	1768–99 (max N = 18)	
Bernard	*Nouvelle Maniére de Fortifier*, F1689; *Modern Fortification*, E1738	2 of 14	1 of 10	3 of 18	6 of 42 (14%)
Bever	*Cadet*, E1756, E1762		2 of 10	2 of 18	4 of 28 (14%)
Lloyd	*History of the Late War*, E1766		0 of 3	3 of 18	3 of 21 (14%)
Manesson-Mallet	*Travaux de Mars*, F1684–85, F1696	3 of 14	1 of 10	2 of 18	6 of 42 (14%)
Simes	*Military Guide*, E1772; *Military Medley*, E1768		1 of 3	2 of 18	3 of 21 (14%)
Voltaire	*Histoire de la Guerre de 1741*, F1756		2 of 10	2 of 18	4 of 28 (14%)
Herouville de Claye	*Traité des Légions*, F1753	0 of 2	0 of 10	4 of 18	4 of 30 (13%)
Spar	*Instructions Militaires*, F1753	0 of 2	2 of 10	2 of 18	4 of 30 (13%)
Ray de Saint-Geniès	*L'Art de la Guerre Pratique*, F1754, F1755, Ger1760	0 of 2	2 of 10	2 of 18	4 of 30 (13%)
Lediard	*Naval History of England*, E1735	1 of 10	3 of 10	1 of 18	5 of 38 (13%)
Cambridge	*Account of the War in India*, E1761, E1762		1 of 5	2 of 18	3 of 23 (13%)
Lloyd	*Essai sur la Grande Guerre*, F1761		0 of 5	3 of 18	3 of 23 (13%)
Pictet	*Essai sur la Tactique*, F1761		0 of 5	3 of 18	3 of 23 (13%)
Funck	*Plans et Journaux des Siéges*, F1750	0 of 4	1 of 10	3 of 18	4 of 32 (13%)
Goulon	*Memoires pour l'Attaque et la Defense d'une Place*, F1730	0 of 12	3 of 10	2 of 18	5 of 40 (13%)
Le Cointe	*Postes Militaires*, F1759, E1761		0 of 6	3 of 18	3 of 24 (13%)
Voltaire	*Histoire de Charles XII*, F1731, E1732	0 of 12	3 of 10	2 of 18	5 of 40 (13%)
Windham	*Plan of Discipline*, E1759		0 of 6	3 of 18	3 of 24 (13%)
Quincy	*L'Art de la Guerre*, F1726, F1740, F1741	0 of 13	3 of 10	2 of 18	5 of 41 (12%)
Campbell	*Lives of the Admirals*, E1742–44	1 of 5	2 of 10	1 of 18	4 of 33 (12%)

Author	Title, with language[a] and dates of publication	Officers' Preferences			Summary of Preferences (max N = 42)
		1710–54 (max N = 14)	1756–63 (max N = 10)	1768–99 (max N = 18)	
Dupré d'Aulnay	*Subsistances Militaires*, F1744	0 of 5	1 of 10	3 of 18	4 of 33 (12%)
Maigret	*Treatise on the Safety and Maintenance of States by . . . Fortresses*, E1747	0 of 5	0 of 10	4 of 18	4 of 33 (12%)
Arcq	*Histoire des Guerres*, F1756–58		0 of 7	3 of 18	3 of 25 (12%)
	État Militaire de France, F1758–93		1 of 7	2 of 18	3 of 25 (12%)
Aelianus	*Tactiks*, E1616	2 of 14	0 of 10	3 of 18	5 of 42 (12%)
Bentivoglio	*Della Guerra di Fiandra*, I1635–40, E1678, F1685, I1722	3 of 14	1 of 10	1 of 18	5 of 42 (12%)
Blondel	*Jetter les Bombes*, F1685; *Fortifier les Places*, F1686	2 of 14	1 of 10	2 of 18	5 of 42 (12%)
Boyer	*Draughts of . . . Fortified Towns of Europe*, E1701	4 of 14	1 of 10	0 of 18	5 of 42 (12%)
Clarendon	*History of the Rebellion*, E1702–4	3 of 14	1 of 10	1 of 18	5 of 42 (12%)
Du Fay	*Véritable Maniere*, F1692; *Maniere de Fortifier*, F1718, F1757	0 of 14	1 of 10	4 of 18	5 of 42 (12%)
Freitag	*Architecture Militaire*, F1635, F1665, F1668	2 of 14	0 of 10	3 of 18	5 of 42 (12%)
Landsberg	*Maniere de Fortifier*, F1712; *Nouveaux Plans et Projects de Fortifications*, F1731	1 of 14	1 of 10	3 of 18	5 of 42 (12%)
Orrery	*Treatise of the Art of War*, E1677	2 of 14	2 of 10	1 of 18	5 of 42 (12%)
Plutarch	*Lives*, E1683–93	0 of 14	3 of 10	2 of 18	5 of 42 (12%)
Sallustius	*Bellum Catilinarium et Jugurthinum*, L1695; *Works*, E1744	1 of 14	3 of 10	1 of 18	5 of 42 (12%)
Sully	*Memoires*, F1747	0 of 14	3 of 10	2 of 18	5 of 42 (12%)
Fearne	*Trial of . . . Byng*, E1757		2 of 10	1 of 18	3 of 28 (11%)
Villars	*Memoires*, F1734–36, E1735	1 of 10	2 of 10	1 of 18	4 of 38 (11%)

Author	Title, with language[a] and dates of publication	Officers' Preferences			Summary of Preferences (max N = 42)
		1710–54 (max N = 14)	1756–63 (max N = 10)	1768–99 (max N = 18)	
Bombelles	*Traité des Évolutions Militaires*, F1754	0 of 2	2 of 10	1 of 18	3 of 30 (10%)
Gray	*Treatise of Gunnery*, E1731	0 of 12	1 of 10	3 of 18	4 of 40 (10%)
Horst	*Fortification*, F1755	0 of 2	0 of 10	3 of 18	3 of 30 (10%)
Mésnil-Durand	*Projet d'un Ordre François en Tactique*, F1755	0 of 2	1 of 10	2 of 18	3 of 30 (10%)

Note: The fourteen officers whose preferences are listed for the period from 1710 to 1754 are: Bagshawe (1751), Bland (1727), Dormer (1741 [c. 1715]), Hawley (1725, 1753), Hotham (1738 [c. 1715]), Howe (1732), Lord John Murray (1762 [c. 1748]), Robert Murray (1738), Oglethorpe (1785 [c. 1746]), Paget (1741), Seton (1732 [c. 1710]), Stanhope (1721), Stewart (1750 [c. 1730]), and Winde (1740 [c. 1715]). Those for 1756 to 1763 are: Bever (1756), Cuthbert (1785 [c. 1763]), Dalrymple (1761), Dury (1758), Harrison (1763), Hesse (1758), Hotham Thompson (1784 [c. 1763]), Molyneux (1759), Wade (1758), and Wolfe (1756). And those for 1768 to 1799: Blomefield (1773), Calderwood (1787), Clinton (c. 1768–76, 1789–94), Debbieg (1773), Donkin (1777), Dundas (1779), General Officer (1773), Gentleman in the Army (1799), Ligonier (1770), Maxwell (1769), Montresor (1799), Moyle (1777), Parker (1773), Percy (1772, 1774, 1775), Smith (1773), Townshend (1759, 1776), Tryon (1773), and Wortley Montagu (1776). (The dates in parenthesis are the dates of record for the officers' preferences; the dates in brackets are the dates on which officers expressed preferences—that is, where dates of expression are significantly different from the dates of record.)

a. Language key: D = Dutch, E = English, F = French, G = Greek, Ger = German, I = Italian, L = Latin.

Appendix B1. Subject and Date of Publication of All Editions of Books in Appendix B

Subject	16th century	1600–1624	1625–1649	1650–1674	1675–1699	1700–1709	1710–1719
History, biography			6 (43%)	3 (23%)	7 (19%)	4 (33%)	1 (11%)
Engineering, artillery			1 (7%)	2 (15%)	13 (36%)	6 (50%)	5 (56%)
Drill, discipline							
Laws, regulations			1 (7%)	1 (8%)			
Art of war	3 (20%)	1 (33%)			5 (14%)		1 (11%)
Classics	12 (80%)	2 (67%)	6 (43%)	7 (54%)	11 (31%)	2 (17%)	2 (22%)
Maps, plans, lists, dictionaries							
Naval							
Total	15	3	14	13	36	12	9

1720–1729	1730–1739	1740–1749	1750–1759	1760–1769	1770–1779	1780–1789	1790–1799	Total
6 (32%)	8 (29%)	8 (22%)	14 (25%)	4 (21%)	2 (33%)	1 (50%)		64 (24%)
3 (16%)	8 (29%)	12 (32%)	11 (20%)	3 (16%)		1 (50%)		65 (24%)
1 (5%)	1 (4%)		6 (11%)	2 (11%)	1 (17%)			11 (4%)
1 (5%)			2 (4%)					5 (2%)
7 (37%)	7 (25%)	11 (30%)	17 (31%)	9 (47%)	3 (50%)			64 (24%)
1 (5%)	3 (11%)	5 (14%)	4 (7%)	1 (5%)				56 (21%)
			1 (2%)					1 (0%)
	1 (4%)	1 (3%)						2 (1%)
19	28	37	55	19	6	2		268 (100%)

Appendix B2. Language and Date of Publication of All Editions of Books in Appendix B

Language	16th century	1600–1624	1625–1649	1650–1674	1675–1699	1700–1709	1710–1719	1720–1729
Dutch					3 (8%)	1 (8%)		
English	3 (20%)	1 (33%)	4 (29%)	3 (23%)	11 (31%)	7 (58%)	1 (11%)	4 (21%)
French	3 (20%)	1 (33%)	3 (21%)	5 (39%)	18 (50%)	3 (25%)	7 (78%)	13 (68%)
German								
Greek	1 (7%)				1 (3%)			
Italian	2 (13%)		4 (29%)					2 (11%)
Latin	6 (40%)	1 (33%)	3 (21%)	5 (39%)	3 (8%)	1 (8%)	1 (11%)	
Spanish								
Total	15	3	14	13	36	12	9	19

1730–1739	1740–1749	1750–1759	1760–1769	1770–1779	1780–1789	1790–1799	Total
							4 (1%)
13 (46%)	14 (38%)	21 (38%)	12 (63%)	1 (17%)			95 (35%)
14 (50%)	23 (62%)	32 (58%)	4 (21%)	4 (67%)	2 (100%)		132 (49%)
			3 (16%)	1 (17%)			4 (1%)
							2 (1%)
							8 (3%)
1 (4%)		2 (4%)					23 (9%)
28	37	55	19	6	2		268 (99%)

Appendix B3. Officers' Preferences among the Authorities (by subject and date of preference)

Subject	1710–1719	1720–1729	1730–1739	1740–1749	1750–1759	1760–1769	1770–1779
History, biography	6 (16%)		4 (36%)	11 (24%)	25 (16%)	12 (18%)	35 (13%)
Engineering, artillery	8 (21%)	2 (20%)		9 (20%)	28 (18%)	5 (7%)	73 (28%)
Drill, discipline			1 (9%)	2 (4%)	12 (8%)	5 (7%)	24 (9%)
Advice							
Laws, regulations	2 (5%)			2 (4%)	1 (1%)	2 (3%)	1 (0%)
Art of war	7 (18%)		3 (27%)	9 (20%)	55 (36%)	20 (29%)	84 (32%)
Classics	14 (37%)	8 (80%)	2 (18%)	10 (22%)	26 (17%)	17 (25%)	41 (15%)
Maps, plans, lists, dictionaries	1 (3%)		1 (9%)	2 (4%)	4 (3%)	4 (6%)	6 (2%)
Defense							
Medicine							
Naval				1 (2%)	3 (2%)	3 (4%)	1 (0%)
Total	38	10	11	46	154	68	265

Note: Our forty-two officers clearly preferred some books on war to others—the books listed in Appendix B as their authorities. But even among their authorities they had preferences; and this appendix is intended to show how those preferences for particular authors and titles shaped their collective appreciation for books on war during the eighteenth century. This appendix reflects, then, the 636 choices that our forty-two officers made among ninety-two entries in Appendix B. Although an officer sometimes had more than one edition or copy of a book, his preference has been recorded only once for each entry; similarly, although eight books appear twice in Appendix B (e.g., Kane's under both Marlborough and Kane), none of those books is counted more than once in Appendixes B1, B2, and B3. The date of an officer's preference has been fixed by the date of an inventory, catalogue, list, or correspondence in all save nine cases. In those nine cases—Cuthbert, Dormer, Hotham, Hotham Thompson, Lord John Murray, Oglethorpe, Seton, Stewart, and Winde—the date of preference has been adjusted to reflect the officer's active service and collecting of books on war (see Appendix E for the specific adjustments) rather than the date on which his books were inventoried or listed. Thus Dormer's preferences were recorded under 1715 to reflect his active service rather than the date of his death (1741) or the date on which his library was eventually inventoried and sold (1764).

1780–1789	1790–1799	No Date	Total
3 (21%)	10 (36%)		106 (17%)
1 (7%)	6 (21%)		132 (21%)
4 (29%)	3 (11%)		51 (8%)
			8 (1%)
4 (29%)	4 (14%)	2 (100%)	188 (30%)
1 (7%)	4 (14%)		123 (19%)
	1 (4%)		19 (3%)
1 (7%)			9 (1%)
14	28	2	636 (100%)

Appendix B4. Officers' Preferences among the Authorities Compared
(by subject and period in Appendixes B, B1, and B3)

Subject	Books Preferred among Authorities (App. B1)	Preferences among Authorities				
		1710–54 (App. B)	1756–63 (App. B)	1768–99 (App. B)	1756–99 (App. B)	1710–99 (App. B3)
History, biography	64 (24%)	23 (19%)	30 (16%)	53 (16%)	83 (16%)	106 (17%)
Engineering, artillery	65 (24%)	22 (18%)	29 (15%)	81 (25%)	110 (21%)	132 (21%)
Drill, discipline	11 (4%)	5 (4%)	16 (9%)	30 (9%)	46 (9%)	51 (8%)
Advice						
Laws, regulations	5 (2%)	4 (3%)	2 (1%)	2 (1%)	4 (1%)	8 (1%)
Art of war	64 (24%)	22 (18%)	63 (34%)	103 (31%)	166 (32%)	188 (30%)
Classics	56 (21%)	36 (30%)	37 (20%)	50 (15%)	87 (17%)	123 (19%)
Maps, plans, lists, dictionaries	1 (0%)	5 (4%)	6 (3%)	8 (2%)	14 (3%)	19 (3%)
Defense						
Medicine						
Naval	2 (1%)	2 (2%)	5 (3%)	2 (1%)	7 (1%)	9 (1%)
Total	268 (100%)	119 (98%)	188 (101%)	329 (100%)	517 (100%)	636 (100%)

Appendix B5. Popularity of Top Thirty Authorities Considered across Time (from Appendix B)

| | Officers' Preferences | | | | Rank | | |
Authority	1710–54 (N = 14)	1756–63 (N = 10)	1768–99 (N = 18)	1710–99 (N = 42)	1710–99 (N = 42)	Origin	Language[a]
Increasing							
Marlborough	43%	40%	56%	48%	3	English	E, F
Saxe	50%[2]	30%	50%	43%	4	Continental	F, E
Feuquières	21%	50%	50%	41%	7	Continental	F, E
Clairac	0%[5]	40%	50%	39%	8	Continental	F, E
Regulations for the Prussian Cavalry		30%	33%	32%	14	Continental	E
Guibert		0%[1]	33%	32%	15	Continental	F, Ger
Regulations for the Prussian Infantry	0%[2]	30%	33%	30%	16	Continental	E
Montecuccoli	7%	40%	39%	29%	17	Continental	F
Frederick	0%[3]	20%	39%	29%	18	Continental	F, Ger
Muller	0%[5]	20%	39%	27%	20	English	E
Coehoorn	21%	20%	33%	26%	22	Continental	D, E, F
Eugene	14%	30%	33%	26%	23	Continental	F, E
Cresting (1756–63)							
Caesar	64%	70%	67%	67%	1	Classical	E, L, F
Vauban	36%	60%	56%	50%	2	Continental	F, E
Polybius	21%	60%	50%	43%	5	Classical	E, L
Folard	31%	70%	33%	42%	6	Continental	F
Vegetius	36%	50%	33%	38%	9	Classical	E, L, F
Puységur	0%[5]	50%	39%	36%	11	Continental	F
Turenne	14%	50%	44%	36%	12	Continental	F, E
Thucydides	29%	50%	28%	33%	13	Classical	E, G, L
Turpin de Crissé	0%[2]	40%	22%	27%	21	Continental	F, E
Xenophon	21%	30%	22%	24%	26	Classical	F, E, I
Saint-Rémy	14%	30%	22%	21%	30	Continental	F
Level							
Guischardt		29%[7]	28%	28%	19	Continental	F
Espagnac	40%[5]	20%	22%	24%	24	Continental	F
Le Blond	40%[5]	20%	22%	24%	25	Continental	F, E
Dalrymple		20%[5]	22%	22%	28	English	E
Declining							
Bland	42%	40%	33%	38%	10	English	E
List of Army	50%[2]	30%	17%	23%	27	English	E
Machiavelli	29%	20%	17%	21%	29	Continental	E, I, F

a. Language key: D = Dutch, E = English, F = French, G = Greek, Ger = German, I = Italian, L = Latin.

Appendix C. Books Not Taken: Subject and Date of Publication

Subject	16th century	1600–1624	1625–1649	1650–1674	1675–1699	1700–1709	1710–1719
History, biography		1 (33%)	3 (75%)	4 (100%)	15 (88%)	12 (86%)	1 (20%)
Engineering, artillery		2 (67%)	1 (25%)		1 (6%)		1 (20%)
Drill, discipline						2 (14%)	1 (20%)
Advice							
Laws, regulations							
Art of war					1 (6%)		1 (20%)
Classics							
Maps, plans, lists, dictionaries							
Defense							1 (20%)
Medicine							
Naval							
Total		3	4	4	17	14	5

1720–1729	1730–1739	1740–1749	1750–1759	1760–1769	1770–1779	1780–1789	1790–1799	No Date	Total
3 (75%)	4 (67%)	20 (61%)	10 (48%)	17 (40%)	8 (21%)	19 (50%)	3 (27%)	1	121 (50%)
	2 (33%)	6 (18%)	1 (5%)	6 (14%)	7 (18%)	2 (5%)			29 (12%)
1 (25%)		4 (12%)	5 (24%)	9 (21%)	7 (18%)	3 (8%)	4 (36%)		36 (15%)
					1 (3%)				1 (0%)
			1 (5%)	1 (2%)	1 (3%)	1 (3%)	2 (18%)		6 (3%)
			2 (10%)	6 (14%)	11 (28%)	7 (18%)			28 (12%)
		1 (3%)							1 (0%)
		1 (3%)	2 (10%)	1 (2%)	4 (10%)	4 (11%)	2 (18%)		15 (6%)
		1 (3%)		3 (7%)		2 (5%)			6 (3%)
4	6	33	21	43	39	38	11	1	243 (100%)

Appendix C1. Books Not Taken: Language and Date of Publication

Language	16th century	1600–1624	1625–1649	1650–1674	1675–1699	1700–1709	1710–1719	1720–1729
Dutch								
English			1 (25%)		5 (29%)	7 (50%)	3 (60%)	3 (75%)
French		3 (100%)	3 (75%)	4 (100%)	12 (71%)	7 (50%)	2 (40%)	1 (25%)
German								
Greek								
Italian								
Latin								
Spanish								
Total		3	4	4	17	14	5	4

Note: Nearly half of the books "not taken" were published between 1760 and 1789; and, three-quarters, between 1740 and 1789.

1730–1739	1740–1749	1750–1759	1760–1769	1770–1779	1780–1789	1790–1799	No Date	Total
3 (50%)	22 (67%)	16 (76%)	30 (70%)	19 (49%)	36 (95%)	11 (100%)		156 (64%)
3 (50%)	11 (33%)	5 (24%)	13 (30%)	20 (51%)	2 (25%)		1	87 (36%)
6	33	21	43	39	38	11	1	243 (100%)

Appendix C2. Books Not Taken: Countries and Dates of Publication

Country of Publication	16th century	1600– 1624	1625– 1649	1650– 1674	1675– 1699	1700– 1709	1710– 1719
Austria							
Austrian Netherlands							
Denmark							
England			1 (25%)		5 (29%)	6 (43%)	3 (60%)
France		2 (67%)	2 (50%)	2 (50%)	4 (24%)		
Germany/Prussia				2 (50%)		1 (7%)	
Ireland						1 (7%)	
Italy							
United Netherlands		1 (33%)	1 (25%)		8 (47%)	5 (36%)	2 (40%)
Scotland							
Sweden							
Switzerland							
Place not given						1 (7%)	
Total		3	4	4	17	14	5

1720–1729	1730–1739	1740–1749	1750–1759	1760–1769	1770–1779	1780–1789	1790–1799	No Date	Total
3 (75%)	2 (33%)	21 (64%)	14 (67%)	29 (67%)	19 (49%)	35 (92%)	11 (100%)		149 (61%)
1 (25%)	2 (33%)	6 (18%)	4 (19%)	6 (14%)	14 (36%)	1 (3%)			44 (18%)
		1 (3%)		3 (7%)					7 (3%)
	1 (17%)	1 (3%)	1 (5%)	1 (2%)					5 (2%)
					2 (5%)				2 (1%)
	1 (17%)	4 (12%)	1 (5%)	3 (7%)	2 (5%)				28 (12%)
			1 (5%)		1 (3%)	1 (3%)			3 (1%)
					1 (3%)				1 (0%)
				1 (2%)		1 (3%)		1	4 (2%)
4	6	33	21	43	39	38	11	1	243 (100%)

Appendix D. Preferences Compared (Appendixes A, B, and C)

Subject	Books			Officers'	
	Preferred (App. A)	Authorities (App. B1)	Not Taken (App. C)	Books Preferred (App. A4)	Authorities 1710–54 (App. B3)
History, biography	225 (35%)	64 (24%)	121 (50%)	346 (27%)	23 (19%)
Engineering, artillery	130 (20%)	65 (24%)	29 (12%)	271 (21%)	22 (18%)
Drill, discipline	50 (8%)	11 (4%)	36 (15%)	107 (9%)	5 (4%)
Advice	8 (1%)		1 (0%)	11 (1%)	
Laws, regulations	16 (2%)	5 (2%)	6 (3%)	28 (2%)	4 (3%)
Art of war	106 (16%)	64 (24%)	28 (12%)	258 (20%)	22 (18%)
Classics	63 (10%)	56 (21%)		148 (12%)	36 (30%)
Maps, plans, lists, dictionaries	27 (4%)	1 (0%)	1 (0%)	54 (4%)	5 (4%)
Defense	6 (1%)		15 (6%)	9 (1%)	
Medicine	2 (0%)		6 (3%)	6 (1%)	
Naval	17 (3%)	2 (1%)		27 (2%)	2 (2%)
Total	650 (100%)	268 (100%)	243 (100%)	1265 (100%)	119 (98%)

Preferences		
Authorities 1756–63 (App. B3)	Authorities 1768–99 (App. B3)	Authorities 1710–99 (App. B3)
30 (16%)	53 (16%)	106 (17%)
29 (15%)	81 (25%)	132 (21%)
16 (9%)	30 (9%)	51 (8%)
2 (1%)	2 (1%)	8 (1%)
63 (34%)	103 (31%)	188 (30%)
37 (20%)	50 (15%)	123 (19%)
6 (3%)	8 (2%)	19 (3%)
5 (3%)	2 (1%)	9 (1%)
188 (101%)	329 (100%)	636 (100%)

Appendix E. Officers, Service, and Books (by earliest active service)

Name, with highest rank and dates of birth and death	Service: Branch (G = Guards), Years Active, Wars,[a] [Years Inactive]	Books in Library	Books on War	Date of Records for Books[b]	Adjusted Date for Books[c]
Capt. William Winde, c. 1660–1740	Cavalry (G) & engineer, 1667–88	1,561	57	1740	c. 1715
LTG James Earl Stanhope, 1673–1721	Infantry (G), 1691–1711, WLA, WSS, [1711–15]	928	27	1721	
LTG Henry Hawley, 1684–1759	Cavalry, 1696–1759, WSS, WAS		6/7	c. 1725, 1753	
LTG James Dormer, 1679–1741	Infantry (G), 1700–14, WSS, Scot '15, [1715–40]	3,082	30	1741	c. 1715
FM John Earl Ligonier, 1680–1770	Cavalry (G), 1702–70, WSS, WAS, SYW	1,441	91	1770	
Capt. Robert Seton, c. 1685–c. 1732	Infantry (G), 1702–15, WSS	1,600	29	1732	c. 1710
LTG Humphrey Bland, c. 1686–1763	Cavalry (G), 1704–63, WSS, Scot '15, WAS, Scot '45, SYW		2	1727	
BG Robert Murray, 1689–1738	Infantry (G), 1705–38, WSS	77	3	1738	
Col. Charles Hotham, 1693–1738	Infantry & cavalry (G), 1706–38, WSS		22	1738	c. 1715
BG Thomas Paget, c. 1685–1741	Infantry (G), 1707–41, WSS	143	5	1741	
Gen. James Oglethorpe, 1696–1785	Infantry (G), c. 1708–15, 1737–45, WSS, Scot '45, [1745–85]	2,000	125	1785	c. 1746
Maj. William Howe, d. c. 1732/1733	Infantry, 1711–c. 32/33, Scot '19	49	2	c. 1732	
LTC William Wade, d. 1758	Infantry & cavalry (G), 1715–58, Scot '45, SYW	354	46	1758	
General Officer, d. before 1773		550	220	1773	
MG Alexander Dury, d. 1758	Infantry (G), 1721–58, WAS, SYW	523	120	1758	
Gen. Lord John Murray, 1711–87	Infantry (G), 1727–47, WAS, [1747–87]	456	48	1762	c. 1748

Appendix E (*continued*)

Name, with highest rank and dates of birth and death	Service: Branch (G = Guards), Years Active, Wars,[a] [Years Inactive]	Books in Library	Books on War	Date of Records for Books[b]	Adjusted Date for Books[c]
Sir William Maxwell, c. 1715–71	Infantry, 1734–?	1,281	17	1769	
Capt. Thomas Cuthbert, d. c. 1784	Infantry, 1737– c. 1770, WAS, SYW	77	3	1785	c. 1763
Col. Samuel Bagshawe, 1713–62	Infantry, 1738–62, WAS		7	1751	
LTC John Stewart, d. 1750	Infantry, c. 1739– 50, WAS?	350	12	1750	c. 1730
Col. Campbell Dalrymple, fl. 1740–63	Cavalry, 1740–67, WAS		11	1761	
LTC Samuel Bever, d. 1758	Infantry, c. 1740– 58, FIW		18	1756	
MG James Wolfe, 1727–59	Infantry, 1741–59, WAS, SYW, FIW		34	1752, 1756	
Capt. Edward Wortley Montagu, 1713–76	Cavalry (G) & infantry, 1743–48, WAS	1,000	23	1776	
FM George Marquis Townshend, 1724–1807	Infantry & cavalry (G), 1743–50, 1758–63, WAS, Scot '45, FIW, SYW, [1763–1807]		25	1759, 1776	
Gen. Sir Henry Clinton, 1730–95	Infantry (G), 1745– 95, WAS, SYW, WAI		29	c.1768–76, 1789–94	
Gen. Hugh Debbieg, 1731–1810	Engineer, 1746–83, WAS, FIW, [1783– 1810]		18	1773	
MG Sir Charles Hotham Thompson, 1729–94	Infantry (G), 1746– 76, WAS, SYW	824	58	1784	1763
Gen. Robert Donkin, 1727–1821	Infantry, 1746–63, 1770–83, SYW, WAI, [1783–1821]		24	1777	
Col. James Dundas, 1721–80	Infantry, 1747–48, 1780, WAS, WAI		24	1779	
Col. Thomas More Molyneux, c. 1725–76	Infantry (G), 1747– 76, WAS?		46	1759	

Appendix E (*continued*)

Name, with highest rank and dates of birth and death	Service: Branch (G = Guards), Years Active, Wars,[a] [Years Inactive]	Books in Library	Books on War	Date of Records for Books[b]	Adjusted Date for Books[c]
LTG George Lane Parker, 1724–91	Infantry (G), 1749–83, WAS?, [1783–91]		9	1773	
LTG William Tryon, 1729–88	Infantry (G), 1751–83, SYW, WAI, [1783–88]	255	40	1773	
Capt. Thomas Harrison, d. 1763	Infantry, 1751–63, SYW	37	6	1763	
Capt. John Montresor, 1736–99	Engineer, 1754–79, FIW, WAI	808	67	1799	
Lt. Emanuel Hesse, d. 1759	Infantry, 1756–59, FIW	29	16	1758	
Gen. Sir Thomas Blomefield, 1744–1822	Artillery, 1759–1822, SYW, WAI, WN		6	1773	
Gen. Hugh Lord Percy, Duke of Northumberland, 1742–1817	Infantry (G), 1759–77, SYW, WAI, [1777–1817]		8	1772, 1774, 1775	
Capt. George Smith, fl. 1772–83			127	1773, 1779	
LTC William Calderwood, d. 1787	Cavalry (G), 1761–87, WAS?	431	11	1787	
LTC Thomas Coppinger Moyle, d. 1787	Infantry, 1766–87, WAI	40	5	1777	
Gentleman in the Army		235	11	1799	
Summaries	Average length of active service: 27 years; average length of total service: 35 years; median date of middle year of active service: 1750 (N = 38)	Average size of library: 725 (N = 25)	Average number of books on war: 35 (N = 42); median: 24 (N = 42)	Median date: 1766 (N = 42)	

Appendix E (*continued*)

a. Key to wars: FIW = French and Indian War, 1754–63; Scot '15, Scot '19, Scot '45 = Scottish Rebellions of 1715, 1719, 1745; SYW = Seven Years' War, 1756–63; WAI = War for American Independence, 1775–83; WAS = War of the Austrian Succession, 1740–48; WLA = War of the League of Augsburg, 1688–97; WN = Wars of Napoleon, 1802–15; WSS = War of the Spanish Succession, 1701–13.

b. The "date of records" for each posthumous inventory or catalogue has been adjusted to coincide with the date of an officer's death. Thus although Dormer's books were not catalogued and sold until 1764, he died in 1741; and 1741 has been used as the date of the records for his books. So too have death dates been used as dates of records for Calderwood, Hesse, Howe, Ligonier, Montresor, Oglethorpe, Stewart, and Wortley Montagu.

c. The "adjusted date for books" represents those nine cases in which an officer's active service and collecting of books on war was significantly different from the date on which his books were inventoried or listed. Thus Winde's preferences were recorded under 1715 to reflect his active service rather than the date of his death and the date on which his books were inventoried (1740).

BIBLIOGRAPHY OF MANUSCRIPTS,
CATALOGUES, AND SCHOLARLY WORKS

MANUSCRIPTS

Alnwick Castle, Northumberland, England
  Percy Papers, L, LI Syon Miscellany, F 3/5
British Library, London, England
  Additions to the Manuscripts, 34,413 [Auckland]
  Additions to the Manuscripts, 50,012.A and 50,012.B [Townshend]
  Additions to the Manuscripts, 51,378 [Oglethorpe]
Chatsworth House, Derbyshire, England
  Chatsworth Manuscripts, 416.51 [H. S. Conway]
William L. Clements Library, University of Michigan, Ann Arbor, Michigan
  Clinton Papers
East Suffolk Record Office, Ipswich, Suffolk, England
  Barrington Papers
      HA 174/1026/3b [letters of recommendation for commissions]
      HA 174/1026/6a/1 [correspondence with officers re appointments and promotions]
      HA 174/1026/6a/2 [letters of recommendation and correspondence with Thomas Gage]
      HA 174/1026/6a/3 [correspondence re War for American Independence]
      HA 174/1026/111 [correspondence with King George III]
Brynmore Jones Library, Hull University, Yorkshire, England
  Hotham Papers
      DDHO 20/154, 155 [Sir Charles Hotham]
      DDHO 4/1 [Beaumont Hotham]
      DDHO 4/283, 284, 287, 293 [Sir Charles Hotham Thompson]
      DDHO 20/120, 159 [Sir Charles Hotham Thompson]
Kent County Archives, Maidstone, Kent, England
  Amherst Manuscripts
      U1350 C6/4 [Sir Jeffery Amherst]
      U1350 F26 [William Wade]
  Stanhope Manuscripts
      U1590 C11
National Army Museum, Chelsea, London, England
  Hawley Papers, 7411–24
  Townshend Papers, 6806-41-4-2-3 and 6806-41-4-2-4

National Library of Scotland, Edinburgh, Scotland
    Dundas of Dundas Papers, Adv. MS, 80.7.2
Public Record Office, Kew, London, England
    Probate Records
        3 37/69 [Robert Murray]
        3 41/22 [Thomas Paget]
        3 60/32 [Thomas Harrison]
    War Office Papers
        4/52, 92, 93, 94 [Barrington correspondence with officers]
        25/3191 [Warrants for leaves of absence]
        27/30, 35, 36 [Reviews of Regiments]
        30/120 [Townshend's *Rules and Orders for . . . Woolwich*, 1776]
        64/9 [List of the Army, 1736]
        71/10 [Boards of General Officers]
        71/18, 19, 21, 22, 28, 54, 58 [courts-martial, c. 1740–82]
John Rylands University Library of Manchester, Manchester, England
    Bagshawe Papers, 2/2/1-59
    Clinton Papers
    Lord John Murray Papers, 5/1/1-110, 5/2/16, 5/3/7, and 17/1/7
Scottish Record Office, Edinburgh, Scotland
    CC 8/12/8(2) [Robert Seton]
    CC 8/12/8/1 [William Howe]
    CC 8/12/10 [John Stewart]
    CC 8/12/12 [Sir William Maxwell]
    CC 8/12/13 [Thomas Cuthbert]
    Cunninghame of Thorntoun Papers
        GD 21/492, 3 [Thomas Coppinger Moyle]

PRINTED CATALOGUES

[Calderwood, William]. [Sotheby and Company catalogue for the sale of Calder-
    wood's library, April 10, 1788, is in the British Library, London, England—title
    page missing.]
[Dormer, James]. *A Catalogue of the Genuine and Elegant Library of the Late Sir
    Clement Cottrell Dormer, Collected by Lieutenant-General James Dormer Which
    Will Be Sold . . . February the 20th, 1764. . . .* London, 1764.
[Dury, Alexander]. *A Catalogue of the Neat and Elegant Library of Books of the Hon-
    ourable Gen. Alexander Dury Deceas'd . . . Which Will Be Sold by AUCTION By
    Mr. Prestage . . . 6th of December 1758 at His Great Room . . . Hanover Square.*
    London, 1758.
[General Officer]. *A Catalogue of the Library of a General Officer, Lately Deceas'd . . .
    Which Will Be Sold by Auction, by S. Baker and G. Leigh . . . 3d and 4th of June
    1773.* London, 1773.
[Gentleman in the Army]. *A Catalogue of a Valuable and Elegant Collection of Books,*

the Property of a Gentleman in the Army (Going Abroad.) . . . Which Will Be Sold at Auction by Leigh and Sotheby, Booksellers . . . Covent-Garden on Tuesday, June 25, 1799. London, 1799.

[Ligonier, John, Earl]. *A Catalogue of the Library of His Excellency John Earl Ligonier. . . .* London, 1783.

[Montresor, John]. *The First Part of W. Collins's Catalogue for 1800. A Catalogue of Part of the Library of John Montresor, Esq. Formerly Chief Engineer in America. . . .* London, 1800.

[————]. *W. Lowe's Catalogue for 1800. Containing a Valuable Collection of Books . . . also a Large Collection of upwards of Two Thousand Drawings of Plans and Fortifications . . . Late the Property of John Montressor Esq. of Belmont-Hall, Kent Most of Them Taken by Him on the Spot. . . .* London, 1800.

[Oglethorpe, James Edward]. *A Catalogue of the Entire and Valuable Library of General Oglethorpe Lately Deceased to Which Is Added the Library of Another Gentleman Which Will Be Sold by Auction by Leigh and Sotheby . . . May 5, 1788 and the Nine Following Days Sunday Excepted.* London, 1788.

[Winde, William]. *A Catalogue of the Entire and Valuable Library of the Learned Capt. Winde, Late of Bolton-Street, Piccadilly (Deceased) . . . Which Will Be Sold by Auction . . . 31st of the Instant October 1740 and the Ten Following Evenings. . . .* London, 1740.

[Wortley Montagu, Edward]. *A Catalogue of the Library and Oriental Manuscripts of the Late Edward Wortley Montagu . . . Which Will Be Sold by Auction, By Leigh and Sotheby, Booksellers . . . January the 22d, 1787. . . .* London, 1787.

[————]. *A Catalogue of a Valuable Collection of Books, Being Part of the Library of the Late Edward Wortley Montagu . . . Which Will Be Sold by Auction by Leigh and Sotheby, Booksellers . . . April 23, 1798. . . .* London, 1798.

BOOKS AND ARTICLES

Adams, Thomas R. *The American Controversy: A Bibliographical Study of the British Pamphlets . . . 1764–1783.* 2 vols. Providence, R.I., 1980.

Aimone, Alan C. "Genesis of the First American Technical and Military Science Library." Unpublished essay. West Point, N.Y., May 1999.

Alden, John R. *General Gage in America.* Baton Rouge, 1948.

American National Biography. See Garraty, John.

Anderson, Fred. *Crucible of War: The Seven Years' War and the Fate of Empire in British North America, 1754–1766.* New York, 2000.

Atkinson, C. T. *Marlborough and the Rise of the British Army.* New York, 1921.

Austen-Leigh, Richard Arthur. *Eton College Lists, 1678–1790.* Eton, 1907.

Ayala, Mariano d'. *Bibliografia Militare Italiana.* Turin, 1854.

Bargar, B. D. "Governor Tryon's House in Fort George." *New York History* 35 (1954): 297–309.

Barker, G. F. Russell. *Record of Old Westminsters.* London, 1928.

Bever, Samuel. *The Cadet: A Military Treatise By an Officer.* 2nd ed. London, 1762.

Billias, George A., ed. *George Washington's Opponents: British Generals and Admirals in the American Revolution.* New York, 1969.

Black, Jeremy. *A Military Revolution? Military Change and European Society, 1550–1800.* London, 1991.

———. *War for America: The Fight for Independence, 1775-1783.* New York, 1991.

Bland, Humphrey. *A Treatise of Military Discipline.* . . . 8th ed. London, 1759.

Bolitho, Hector. *The Galloping Third: The Story of the 3rd, the King's Own Hussars.* London, 1963.

Bolton, C. K., ed. *Letters of Hugh, Earl Percy from Boston and New York, 1774-1776.* Boston, 1902.

Bowler, Arthur R. *Logistics and the Failure of the British Army in America, 1775–1783.* Princeton, 1975.

Braddick, M. J. "An English Military Revolution." *Historical Journal* 36 (1993): 965–75.

Brewer, John. *The Sinews of Power: War, Money and the English State, 1688-1783.* London, 1989.

Browning, Reed. *The War of the Austrian Succession.* New York, 1993.

Bruce, Anthony. *The Purchase System in the British Army, 1660-1871.* London, 1980.

Burke, Bernard. *Burke's Genealogical and Heraldic History of the Peerage, Baronetage, and Knightage.* . . . 102d ed. London, 1959.

Burke, John. *A Genealogical and Heraldic History of the Commoners of Great Britain and Ireland.* . . . 4 vols. London, 1836.

Caesar, Caius Julius. *C. Julius Caesar's Commentaries of His Wars in Gaul, and Civil War with Pompey.* . . . Translated by Martin Bladen. 8th ed. London, 1770.

Campbell, John. *The Military History of the Late Prince Eugene of Savoy and of the Late John Duke of Marlborough.* . . . 2 vols. London, 1736–37.

Chandler, David. *Marlborough as Military Commander.* New York, 1973.

Channing, Edward, et al., eds. *The Barrington-Bernard Correspondence* . . . *1760–1770.* Cambridge, Mass., 1912.

Charteris, Evan. *William Augustus, Duke of Cumberland.* 2 vols. London, 1913–23.

Childs, John. *Armies and Warfare in Europe, 1648-1789.* New York, 1982.

———. *The Nine Years' War and the British Army, 1688-1697.* . . . Manchester and New York, 1991.

Churchill, Winston. *Marlborough: His Life and Times.* 6 vols. London, 1933–38.

Cipolla, Carlo M. "The Professions: The Long View." *Journal of European Economic History* 2 (1973): 37–52.

Clairac, Louis-André de La Mamie. *The Field Engineer.* . . . Translated by John Muller. London, 1760.

———. *L'Ingenieur de Campagne.* Translated by Lewis Nicola. Philadelphia, 1776.

Cockle, Maurice J. D. *A Bibliography of Military Books Up to 1642.* 2nd ed. London, 1957.

Cockayne, George Edward. *The Complete Baronetage.* 5 vols. Exeter, 1900, 1906.

———. *The Complete Peerage.* . . . New ed., rev. 13 vols. London, 1910–59.

Conway, Stephen. "British Army Officers and the American War for Independence." *William and Mary Quarterly* 41 (1984): 265–76.

―――. "'The Great Mischief Complained of': Reflections on the Misconduct of British Soldiers in the Revolutionary War." *William and Mary Quarterly* 47 (1990): 370–90.

―――. "To Subdue America: British Army Officers and the Conduct of the Revolutionary War." *William and Mary Quarterly* 43 (1986): 381–407.

―――. *The War of American Independence, 1775–1783.* London, 1995.

Cormack, Andrew, and Alan Jones, eds. *The Journal of Corporal Todd, 1745–1762.* Stroud, Gloucestershire, 2001.

Craig, Gordon A. *The Politics of the Prussian Army.* London, 1955.

Curtis, Edward E. *The Organization of the British Army in the American Revolution.* New Haven, 1926.

Cuthbertson, Bennett. *A System for the Compleat Interior Management and Oeconomy of a Battalion of Infantry.* . . . Dublin, 1768.

Dalrymple, Campbell. *A Military Essay. Containing Reflections on the Raising, Arming, Clothing, and Discipline of the British Infantry and Cavalry.* . . . London, 1761.

Dalton, Charles. *English Army Lists and Commission Registers, 1660–1714.* 6 vols. London, 1960.

―――. *George the First's Army, 1714–1727.* 2 vols. London, 1910–12.

Danley, Mark H. "Military Writings and the Theory and Practice of Strategy in the Eighteenth-Century British Army." Ph.D. diss., Kansas State University, 2001.

De Fonblanque, Edward B. *Political and Military Episodes . . . from the Life and Correspondence of John Burgoyne, General.* . . . London, 1876.

Dictionary of American Biography. See Johnson, Allen.

Dictionary of National Biography. See Stephen, Leslie.

Donkin, Robert. *Military Collections and Remarks.* . . . New York, 1777.

Doughty, Robert A., and Ira D. Gruber, et al. *Warfare in the Western World.* 2 vols. Lexington, 1996.

Duffy, Christopher. *The Fortress in the Age of Vauban and Frederick the Great, 1660–1789.* London, 1985.

―――. *Frederick the Great: A Military Life.* London, 1985.

―――. *The Military Experience in the Age of Reason.* New York, 1988.

Duffy, Michael, ed. *The Military Revolution and the State, 1500–1800.* Exeter, 1980.

Estrades, Godefroi Louis, Comte d'. *Lettres et Negociations de Messieurs le Marechal D'Estrades, Colbert.* . . . 3 vols. The Hague, 1710.

État Militaire de France pour l'Annee 1780. Paris, 1780.

Everett, Henry. *The History of the Somerset Light Infantry . . . , 1685–1914.* London, 1934.

Ferrar, M. L. *A History of the Services of the 19th Regiment . . . 1688 to 1911.* London, [1911].

Feuquières, Antoine de Pas, Marquis de. *Memoirs Historical and Military . . . 1672 to the Year 1710.* . . . 2 vols. Westport, Conn., 1968.

Forbes, Archibald. *The Black Watch*. . . . New York, 1897.

Ford, W. C., comp. *British Officers Serving in America, 1754–1774*. Boston, 1894.

———, comp. *British Officers Serving in the American Revolution, 1774–1783*. Brooklyn, 1897.

Fortescue, J. W. *A History of the British Army*. . . . 13 vols. London, 1899–1930.

———, ed. *The Correspondence of King George the Third from 1760 to December 1783*. 6 vols. London, 1927–28.

Foster, Joseph. *Alumni Oxonienses . . . 1500–1714*. . . . 4 vols. Oxford and London, 1891–92.

———. *Alumni Oxonienses . . . , 1715–1886*. 6 vols. London, 1887–88.

Francis, David. *The First Peninsular War, 1702–1713*. New York, 1975.

Frégault, Guy. *Canada: The War of the Conquest*. Translated by Margaret M. Cameron. Toronto, 1969.

Frey, Sylvia R. *The British Soldier in America: A Social History of Military Life in the Revolutionary Period*. Austin, Tex., 1981.

Fryer, Mary Beacock, and Christopher Dracott. *John Graves Simcoe, 1752–1806: A Biography*. Toronto, 1998.

Garraty, John Arthur, and Marc C. Carnes, eds. *American National Biography*. 24 vols. New York, 1999.

Gat, Azar. *A History of Military Thought from the Enlightenment to the Cold War*. Oxford, 2001.

———. *The Origins of Military Thought from the Enlightenment to Clausewitz*. New York, 1989.

Gentleman's Magazine. 302 vols. London, 1731–1907.

Gipson, Lawrence H. *The British Empire before the American Revolution*. 15 vols. New York, 1936–70.

Grässe, Johann G. T. *Orbis Latinus: Lexikon Lateinischer Geographischer Namen des Mitlelalters und der Newzeit*. . . . 3 vols. Braunschweig, 1972.

Great Britain, War Office. *A List of His Majesty's Land-Forces in North America*. New York, 1761.

———. *A List of the General and Field-Officers, as they Rank in the Army*. . . . London, 1754–.

———. *A List of the General and Field Officers . . . in North America*. New York, 1778.

Greer, William. "Books on War in English in the Society of the Cincinnati." Manuscript list prepared for Ira Gruber. Washington, D.C., March 2000.

Gruber, Ira D. "The Anglo-American Military Tradition and the War for American Independence." In Kenneth J. Hagan and William R. Roberts, eds., *Against All Enemies: Interpretations of American Military History from Colonial Times to the Present*, 21–47. Westport, Conn., 1986.

———. "British Strategy: The Theory and Practice of Eighteenth-Century Warfare." In Don Higginbotham, ed., *Reconsiderations on the Revolutionary War*, 14–31, 166–70. Westport, Conn., 1978.

———. "Classical Influences on British Strategy in the War for American Independence." In John W. Eadie, ed., *Classical Traditions in Early America*, 175–90. Ann Arbor, Mich., 1976.

———. "The Education of Sir Henry Clinton." *Bulletin of the John Rylands University Library of Manchester* 72 (1990): 131–53.

———. "For King and Country: The Limits of Loyalty of British Officers in the War for American Independence." In Edgar Denton III, ed., *Limits of Loyalty*, 23–40. Waterloo, Ontario, 1980.

———. "George III Chooses a Commander in Chief." In Ronald Hoffman and Peter J. Albert, eds., *Arms and Independence: The Military Character of the American Revolution*, 166–90. Charlottesville, 1984.

———. *The Howe Brothers and the American Revolution*. Chapel Hill, 1972.

———. "Sir Henry Clinton." In Colin Matthew and Brian Harrison, eds., *Oxford Dictionary of National Biography*, 12:140–43. Oxford, 2004.

———, ed. *John Peebles' American War: The Diary of a Scottish Grenadier, 1776–1782*. Stroud, Gloucestershire, 1997.

Guggisberg, F. G. *"The Shop": The Story of the Royal Military Academy*. 2nd ed. London, 1902.

Guilmartin, John F. *Gunpowder and Galleys: Changing Technology and Mediterranean Warfare at Sea in the 16th Century*. Rev. ed. London, 2003.

Guy, Alan J. *Oeconomy and Discipline: Officership and Administration in the British Army, 1714–63*. Manchester, 1985.

———, ed. *Colonel Samuel Bagshawe and the Army of George II, 1731–1762*. London, 1990.

Hayes, J. W. "Lieutenant Colonel and Major Commandants of the Seven Years' War." *Journal of the Society for Army Historical Research* 36 (1958): 3–13, 38–39.

———. "The Royal House of Hanover and the British Army, 1714–1760." *Bulletin of the John Rylands Library* 40 (1957–58): 328–57.

———. "Scottish Officers in the British Army, 1714–63." *Scottish Historical Review* 37 (1958): 23–33.

———. "The Social and Professional Background of the Officers of the British Army, 1714–1763." M.A. thesis, University of London, 1956.

Hayter, Tony, ed. *An Eighteenth-Century Secretary at War: The Papers of William, Viscount Barrington*. London, 1988.

Higginbotham, Don. *The War of American Independence*. New York, 1971.

———. "Military Education before West Point." In Robert M. S. McDonald, ed., *Thomas Jefferson's Military Academy: Founding West Point*, 23–53. Charlottesville, 2004.

Higham, Robin. "The Selection, Education, and Training of British Officers, 1740–1920." In Bela A. Kiraly and Walter Scott Dillard, eds., *The East Central European Officer Corps, 1740–1920: Social Origins, Selection, Education, and Training*, 39–56. Highland Lakes, N.J., 1988.

———, ed. *A Guide to the Sources of British Military History*. Berkeley and Los Angeles, 1971.

Holmes, Geoffrey S. *Augustan England: Professions, State, and Society, 1680–1730*. London, 1982.

Houlding, J. A. *Fit for Service: The Training of the British Army, 1715–1795*. New York, 1981.

Howard-Vyse, Edward. "A British Cavalry Officer's Report on the Army Manoeuvres of Frederick the Great, 1773." *Journal of the Society for Army Historical Research* 60 (1982): 66–70.

Huntington, Samuel P. *The Soldier and the State: The Theory and Politics of Civil-Military Relations.* Cambridge, 1957.

Jähns, Max. *Geschichte der Kriegswissenschaften vornehmlich in Deutschland.* 3 vols. 1889–91. Reprint, New York and Hildesheim, 1966.

Jeney, Capitaine de. *Le Partisan, ou l'Art de Faire la Petite-Guerre avec Succès. . . .* The Hague, 1759.

Johnson, Allen, et al., eds. *Dictionary of American Biography.* 20 vols. New York, 1928–36.

Kamen, Henry. *The War of Succession in Spain, 1700–15.* Bloomington, Ind., 1969.

Kane, John. *List of Officers of the Royal Regiment of Artillery from the Year 1716 to the Present Date.* Woolwich, 1869.

Kane, Richard. *A System of Camp-Discipline . . . To Which Is Added General Kane's Campaigns of King William and the Duke of Marlborough . . . 1689 to 1712. . . .* 2nd ed. London, 1757.

Kehoe, Vincent J.-R. "The Works of Captain Thomas Simes." *Journal of the Society for Army Historical Research* 78 (2000): 214–17.

Kennedy, Paul M. *The Rise and Fall of British Naval Mastery.* London, 1976.

Kohn, Richard H. *Eagle and Sword: The Beginnings of the Military Establishment in America.* New York, 1965.

Langins, Janis. *Conserving the Enlightenment: French Military Engineering from Vauban to the Revolution.* Cambridge, Mass., 2004.

Le Blond, Guillaume. *Essai sur la Castrametation. . . .* Paris, 1748.

———. *Traité de l'Artillerie. . . .* 2 vols. Paris, 1743.

Leslie, N. B. *The Succession of Colonels of the British Army from 1660 to the Present Day.* London and Aldershot, 1974.

Long, J. C. *Lord Jeffrey Amherst: A Soldier of the King.* New York, 1933.

Luvaas, Jay. *The Education of an Army: British Military Thought, 1815–1940.* Chicago, 1964.

Lynn, John. *Giant of the Grand Siècle: The French Army, 1610–1715.* Cambridge, 1997.

———. *The Wars of Louis XIV, 1667–1714.* New York, 1999.

Mackesy, Piers. *The Coward of Minden: The Affair of Lord George Sackville.* London, 1979.

———. *The War for America, 1775–1783.* Cambridge, Mass., 1964.

Mackey, Albert Gallatin, et al. *An Encyclopaedia of Freemasonry and Its Kindred Sciences. . . .* 2 vols. Chicago, 1927.

Matthew, Colin, and Brian Harrison, eds. *Oxford Dictionary of National Biography.* 60 vols. Oxford, 2004.

Millner, John. *A Compendious Journal of All the Marches, Famous Battles . . . 1701 . . . 1712.* London, 1733.

Molyneux, Thomas More. *Conjunct Expeditions: Expeditions . . . by the Fleet and Army. . . .* London, 1759.

Musgrave, William, comp. *Obituary Prior to 1800 (. . . England, Scotland, and Ireland)*. London, 1899–1901.

Namier, Lewis, and John Brooke. *The House of Commons, 1754–1790*. 3 vols. New York, 1964.

Nelson, Paul David. *William Tryon and the Course of Empire: A Life in British Imperial Service*. Chapel Hill, 1990.

Nickerson, Hoffman. *The Turning Point of the Revolution or Burgoyne in America*. Boston, 1928.

Nicolas, Armand. *Histoire de la Martinique*. Paris, 1996.

Nosworthy, Brent. *The Anatomy of Victory: Battle Tactics, 1689–1763*. New York, 1990.

O'Day, Rosemary. "The Anatomy of a Profession: the Clergy of the Church of England." In Wilfrid Prest, ed., *The Professions in Early Modern England*, 25–63. London, 1987.

Oxford Dictionary of National Biography. See Matthew, Colin, and Brian Harrison.

Paret, Peter. *Yorck and the Era of the Prussian Reform, 1807–1815*. Princeton, 1966.

———, ed. *Makers of Modern Strategy: From Machiavelli to the Nuclear Age*. Princeton, 1986.

Pargellis, Stanley. *Lord Loudoun in North America*. New Haven, 1933.

———, ed. *Military Affairs in North America, 1748–1765: Selected Documents from the Cumberland Papers in Windsor Castle*. New York, 1969.

Pargellis, Stanley, and D. J. Medley, comps. *Bibliography of British History: The Eighteenth Century, 1714–1789*. Oxford, 1951.

Parker, Geoffrey. *The Military Revolution: Military Innovation and the Rise of the West, 1500–1800*. Cambridge, 1988.

———. *The Thirty Years' War*. London, 1984.

Paul, James Balfour. *The Scots Peerage. . . .* 9 vols. Edinburgh, 1904–14.

Peddie, R. A. *Place Names in Imprints. . . .* London, 1968.

Pollak, Martha D. *Military Architecture, Cartography and the Representation of the Early Modern European City: A Checklist of Treatises on Fortification in the Newberry Library*. Chicago, 1991.

Polybius. *The General History of Polybius*. Translated by Mr. Hampton. 2nd ed. 2 vols. London, 1761.

———. *Histoire de Polybe*. Translated by Vincent Thuillier. Commentary by Jean Charles de Folard. Rev. ed. 7 vols. Amsterdam, 1774.

———. *The History of Polybius the Megalopolitan*. Translated by Edward Grimeston. London, 1634.

Powers, Sandra. "Authorship of Military Tract." *Journal of the Society for Army Historical Research* 70 (Winter 1992): 273–74.

Prebble, John. *Culloden*. Harmondsworth, Middlesex, 1979.

Prest, Wilfrid. *The Professions in Early Modern England*. London, 1987.

Quimby, Robert S. *The Background of Napoleonic Warfare: The Theory of Military Tactics in Eighteenth-Century France*. New York, 1957.

Records of the Royal Military Academy: 1741–1892. Woolwich, 1892.

Ritter, Gerhard. *Frederick the Great: A Historical Profile.* Berkeley, 1964.

Roberts, Michael. *Gustavus Adolphus: A History of Sweden, 1611–1632.* 2 vols. London, 1953–58.

Robson, Eric. "The Armed Forces and the Art of War." In J. O. Lindsay, ed., *The New Cambridge Modern History*, vol. 8, *The Old Regime, 1713–1763*, 163–89. Cambridge, 1957.

Rogers, Clifford J., ed. *The Military Revolution Debate: Readings on the Military Transformation of Early Modern Europe.* Boulder, 1995.

Ross, Charles, ed. *Correspondence of Charles, First Marquis Cornwallis.* 2nd ed. rev. 4 vols. London, 1859.

Roy, Ian. "The Profession of Arms." In Wilfrid Prest, ed., *The Professions in Early Modern England*, 181–219. London, 1987.

Savory, Reginald. *His Britannic Majesty's Army in Germany during the Seven Years' War.* Oxford, 1966.

Saxe, Maurice Comte de. *Reveries, or Memoirs upon the Art of War.* . . . Translated by William Fawcett. Westport, Conn., 1971.

Screen, J. E. O. "The Royal Military Academy of Louis Lochee." *Journal of the Society for Army Historical Research* 70 (1992): 143–56.

Sedgwick, Romney. *The House of Commons, 1715–1754.* 2 vols. New York, 1970.

Shy, John. *A People Numerous and Armed: Reflections on the Military Struggle for American Independence.* New York, 1976.

———. *Toward Lexington: The Role of the British Army in the Coming of the American Revolution.* Princeton, 1965.

———. "Thomas Gage: Weak Link of Empire." In George A. Billias, ed., *George Washington's Opponents: British Generals and Admirals in the American Revolution*, 3–38. New York, 1969.

Simes, Thomas. *The Military Guide for Young Officers.* Philadelphia, 1776.

Skelton, William B. *An American Profession of Arms.* Lawrence, 1992.

Skrine, Francis Henry. *Fontenoy and Great Britain's Share in the War of the Austrian Succession, 1741–48.* Edinburgh and London, 1906.

Smith, George. *An Universal Military Dictionary.* London, 1779.

———. *The Use and Abuse of Free-Masonry.* . . . London, 1783.

Smyth, John George. *Sandhurst . . . Woolwich . . . 1741–1961.* London, 1961.

Society for Army Historical Research. *The Army List of 1740.* . . . Sheffield, 1931.

Speelman, Patrick J. *Henry Lloyd and the Military Enlightenment of Eighteenth-Century Europe.* Westport, Conn., 2002.

———, ed. *War, Society and Enlightenment: The Works of General Lloyd.* Leiden, 2005.

Spiller, Roger, ed. *The Dictionary of American Military Biography.* 3 vols. Westport, Conn., 1984.

Stacey, C. P. *Quebec, 1759: The Siege and the Battle.* New York, 1959.

Starkey, Armstrong. *European and Native American Warfare, 1675–1815.* London, 1998.

———. *War in the Age of the Enlightenment, 1700–1789.* Westport, Conn., 2003.

Stedman, Charles. *The History of the Origin, Progress, and Termination of the American War*. London, 1794.

Stephen, Leslie, and Sidney Lee, eds. *The Dictionary of National Biography from the Earliest Times to 1900*. 22 vols. London, 1921–22.

Stewart, Charles H., comp. *The Service of British Regiments in Canada and North America*. Ottawa, 1964.

Stirling, A. M. W. *The Hothams*. 2 vols. London, 1918.

Sturgill, Claude C. *Marshall Villars and the War of the Spanish Succession*. Lexington, Ky., 1965.

Taylor, Frank. *Wars of Marlborough, 1702–9*. 2 vols. Oxford, 1921.

Teitler, Gerke. *The Genesis of the Professional Officer Corps*. Beverly Hills, Calif., 1977.

Thorne, R. G. *The House of Commons, 1790–1820*. 5 vols. London, 1986.

Townshend, C. V. F. *The Military Life of Field-Marshal George First Marquess Townshend, 1724–1807*. . . . London, 1901.

Townshend, George Lord Viscount. *Rules and Orders for the Royal Military Academy at Woolwich*. London, 1776.

Trim, D. J. B., ed. *The Chivalric Ethos and the Development of Military Professionalism*. Leiden, 2003.

Turenne, Henri de La Tour d'Auvergne, Vicomte de. *Military Memoirs and Maxims of Marshal Turenne*. . . . Remarks by A. Williamson. London, 1740.

Vauban, Sébastien Le Prestre de. *De L'Attaque et de la Defense des Places*. . . . 2 vols. The Hague, 1737–42.

Vegetius Renatus, Flavius. *The Military Institutions of the Romans*. Edited by Thomas R. Phillips. Translated by John Clarke. Harrisburg, Pa., 1952.

Venn, J. A. *Alumni Cantabrigienses . . . to 1900*. 10 vols. Cambridge, 1922–54.

Waddell, Louis M., ed. *The Papers of Henry Bouquet, September 1, 1759–August 31, 1760*. Vol. 4 of *The Papers of Henry Bouquet, 1719–1765*. Harrisburg, Pa., 1978.

Ward, Christopher. *The War of the Revolution*. 2 vols. New York, 1952.

Watson, Samuel J. "Professionalism, Social Attitudes, and Civil Military Accountability in the United States Army Officer Corps, 1815–1846." Ph.D. diss., Rice University, 1996.

Weigley, Russell F. *The Age of Battles: The Quest for Decisive Warfare from Breitenfeld to Waterloo*. Bloomington, 1991.

Wheeler, James Scott. *The Making of a World Power: War and the Military Revolution in Seventeenth Century England*. Stroud, 1999.

White, Jon Manchip. *Marshal of France: The Life and Times of Maurice, Comte de Saxe*. Chicago, 1962.

Whitworth, Rex. *Field Marshal Lord Ligonier: A Story of the British Army, 1702–1770*. Oxford, 1958.

———. "Major General Alexander Dury." *Journal of the Society for Army Historical Research* 71 (1993): 146–53.

Wickwire, Franklin, and Mary Wickwire. *Cornwallis: The American Adventure*. Boston, 1970.

Willcox, William B. *Portrait of a General, Sir Henry Clinton in the War of Independence.* New York, 1964.

——, ed. *The American Rebellion: Sir Henry Clinton's Narrative of His Campaigns, 1775-1782.* . . . New Haven, 1954.

Willson, Beckles. *The Life and Letters of James Wolfe.* New York and London, 1909.